ABOUT ISLAND PRESS

Island Press, a nonprofit organization, publishes, markets, and distributes the most advanced thinking on the conservation of our natural resources—books about soil, land, water, forests, wildlife, and hazardous and toxic wastes. These books are practical tools used by public officials, business and industry leaders, natural resource managers, and concerned citizens working to solve both local and global resource problems.

Founded in 1978, Island Press reorganized in 1984 to meet the increasing demand for substantive books on all resource-related issues. Island Press publishes and distributes under its own imprint and offers these services to other nonprofit organizations.

Support for Island Press is provided by The Geraldine R. Dodge Foundation, The Energy Foundation, The Charles Engelhard Foundation, The Ford Foundation, Glen Eagles Foundation, The George Gund Foundation, William and Flora Hewlett Foundation, The John D. and Catherine T. MacArthur Foundation, The Andrew W. Mellon Foundation, The Joyce Mertz-Gilmore Foundation, The New-Land Foundation, The J. N. Pew, Jr. Charitable Trust, Alida Rockefeller, The Rockefeller Brothers Fund, The Rockefeller Foundation, The Tides Foundation, and individual donors.

Crossing the Next Meridian

CROSSING THE NEXT MERIDIAN

Land, Water, and the Future of the West

Charles F. Wilkinson

ISLAND PRESS

Washington, D.C. ❑ *Covelo, California*

Maps by Karen Lewotsky
Text design by David Bullen

The author is grateful for permission to use excerpts from the following previously copyrighted material. From "Scientists Try to Find Out What Is Wiping Out Life at Carson Sink" by Tom Harris, *Fresno Bee*, February 15, 1987, p. A1. From "The Public Range Begins to Green Up" by Ed Marston, *High Country News*, May 7, 1990, p. 1. From "Forest Service Out on a Limb on Timber Sales," *Denver Post*, September 23, 1984, p. 2C. From "Boldt's Good Deeds Will Live After Him" by John de Yonge, *Seattle Post-Intelligencer*, March 21, 1984, p. A11. Reprinted courtesy of *Seattle Post-Intelligencer*. From "Quality Water for the Future," *Idaho Statesman*, January 4, 1987, p. 2F. From "Water in the West: Growing Beyond Nature's Limits" by Wallace Stegner, *Los Angeles Times*, December 29, 1985, Opinion p. 3. From *Boundaries Carved in Water: An Analysis of River and Water Management in the Upper Missouri Basin* by Mark D. O'Keefe et al. Northern Lights Institute, Missoula, Montana, 1986. From *Beyond the Hundredth Meridian: John Wesley Powell and the Second Opening of the West* by Wallace Stegner. Copyright © 1954. Reprinted by permission of Brandt & Brandt Literary Agents, Inc. From *Coming into the Country* by John McPhee. Copyright © 1976, 1977 by John McPhee. Reprinted by permission of Farrar, Straus & Giroux, Inc.

LIBRARY OF CONGRESS CATALOGING-IN-PUBLICATION DATA

Wilkinson, Charles F., 1941–
   Crossing the next meridian : land, water, and the
future of the West / Charles F. Wilkinson.
     p.   cm.
   Includes bibliographical references and index.
   ISBN 1-55963-150-3.—ISBN 1-55963-149-x (pbk.)
     1. Natural resources—Law and legislation—
West (U.S.) 2. Land use—Law and legislation—
West (U.S.) 3. Water—Law and legislation—
West (U.S.) I. Title.
KF5505.W55 1992
346.7804'4—dc20
[347.80644]   92-16869
                        CIP

I dedicate this to my sons and my nieces and nephews in the hope that theirs will be the generation finally to unite progress and wisdom in the American West.

Contents

Preface

My first deep contact with the American West was in Arizona in 1965, a time and place when you could see historical eras laid out in front of your eyes, almost like a highway cut through a hillside, exposing the geologic layers of soil and rock. You could still see an occasional rider on horseback in downtown Phoenix, loping near the aluminum and glass towers that were fast on their way up. The stockyards were operating with a full head of steam, and the trick was to schedule your day to stay upwind. Carl Hayden was United States senator; he had served Arizona continuously in Congress since statehood, in 1912. The leading lawyers in Phoenix were mostly native Arizonans, people with close-to-the-ground childhoods on the ranches or farms or in the mines.

History also was palpable in the outlying towns. I felt it with my own hands on an investigatory trip to Prescott, once the state capital, where the litigation pleadings filed in the old courthouse were folded twice and neatly tied up with ribbons. I was disbelieving, during a trial in Holbrook, as I watched a senior lawyer peel off layer after layer of a convoluted 1950s land fraud that would have done a nineteenth-century Old West land ring proud. This went far beyond any kind of romanticism. This was factual: the Old West, the nineteenth century—today, right in front of my own eyes.

Arizona's backcountry drew me in, too. I eventually learned how to drop a fly on a bathtub-sized hole in a trickle of a trout stream that slipped down through a miscellaneous, hot, rocky draw. I went down into proud, red-rock Havasupai Canyon, riding on horseback past a stolid Indian village that I could not begin to comprehend. A friend and I backpacked through the pine stands of the White Mountains almost in New Mexico, camping in a *ciénaga* (Spanish for marshy meadow). We talked at night about heading over the ridge to Pea Soup Creek, but a storm came up the next day. A few years later, my friend hiked over to Pea Soup, but I have yet to get there.

Ever since those first days, my work has focused on the American West and the juxtaposition of its past, present, and future. After practicing law with private firms in Phoenix and San Francisco, I served as a staff attorney from 1971 through 1975 with the Native American Rights Fund in Boulder, Colorado, where I was blessed to be able to work on a number of major Indian land, water, education, and sovereignty matters. In 1975, I joined the faculty at the University of Oregon law school. Over the years, I visited at the Michigan and Minnesota law schools and, in 1987, finally settled in at the University of Colorado School of Law.

Chapin Clark, my dean at Oregon when I entered teaching, helped set my course from the beginning by detecting my thirst to learn about distinctively western issues. In addition to assigning me Indian law, he urged me toward federal public land law, water law, and natural resources issues in general, including timber harvesting, mining, wilderness, and the management of Pacific salmon and steelhead.

Most of these fields were new to law school curricula, and I was fortunate to be a working scholar in them as interest began to burgeon. During this time, I was lucky in another, even better, way: through speaking engagements, field trips with my seminar students, and other travels, I was able to see a great amount of the West and to talk with all manner of westerners.

Gradually, I began to see that many critical issues in the West are dominated by the thinking of another century. I came to realize, for example, although I did not understand it then, that when I was in Arizona, distinctively western laws and policies set in place half a century before statehood were at work in all corners of the state, playing central roles in shaping Arizona society in a different age. The same dynamic still holds in Arizona and every other western state.

In the case of Indians, there is a uniquely compelling case for honoring the old laws. The key provisions derive from promises made in treaties with a small minority group that ceded away vast areas of land in reliance on those guarantees. The majority society rightly holds a profound commitment to honor those promises.

The context, I found, was very different with respect to the nineteenth-century laws and policies that govern the West's rivers, mountains, forests, rangeland, minerals, and federal public lands (50 percent of all land in the region). Natural resources are far more than amenities in the West. They drive the region economically. They also drive the society intellectually and emotionally, for the American West is a place where its people are fixed to their natural settings.

These natural resources are governed by what I have come to think of as the "lords of yesterday," which are laws, policies, and ideas, not people. In field after field, the controlling legal rules, usually coupled with extravagant subsidies, simply do not square with the economic trends, scientific knowledge, and social values in the modern West. This is not to say that these rules were irrational when originally adopted: much to the contrary, they arose for good reason in a particular historical and societal context, the westward expansion of the nineteenth century, a fascinating and colorful era that I explore in this book. Nevertheless, whatever may have been the original rationale for these old laws, I have been able to find few principled reasons that justify their continuation in the late-twentieth-century West.

The lords of yesterday wield extraordinary influence. These outmoded ideas pervade land and resource decision making in the West, far more so than in almost any other area of American public policy. This is the dead hand of the law at its most stultifying.

Critical though these issues may be to the West and its future, public awareness of them is astonishingly low. The lords of yesterday have been walled off from public scrutiny by a shield of perceived complexity. But although there is surely intricacy here, the general public, by directly juxtaposing the historical and contemporary settings, can grasp these problems and the various alternative solutions with some ease. It is important that this be so, because law, after all, tends to be derivative and instrumental. Law grows up from the people it serves by codifying the values of nonlawyers, of the citizenry at large. Viewed in this light, law must be accessible to the public, for it is—or ought to be—the manifestation of the public will.

This book, then, is my attempt to set out for a general audience some of the core problems facing the American West now and in the years to come. My hope, of course, is that my analysis and approaches for reform will be of use to those great many people who love the American West. It is as glorious as any place in the world, and it deserves, and needs, our vigilance in charting the best path.

CROSSING THE NEXT MERIDIAN

Chapter One

The Lords of Yesterday

In 1960, Harold Thomas founded the Trus Joist Corporation. The Idaho company was based on the invention of a unique structural truss that joins together two-by-fours or two-by-sixes with steel tubing and a patented pin connection. These open-web trusses, used to support roofs and floors in commercial buildings, combine the lightweight, nailable qualities of wood with the strength of steel. Over the years, Trus Joist has expanded its operations to produce several other product lines, including an all-wood laminated truss used in residential construction. Today, corporate headquarters remain in Boise, but the company, now called TJ International and generating annual sales of $327 million, also operates manufacturing facilities in California, Oregon, Colorado, Ohio, Louisiana, Georgia, and Alberta, Canada. Thomas, who graduated from the University of Idaho with a degree in forestry, continues as chairman of the board of the highly successful firm. A native Idahoan and a lifelong outdoorsman, he has parlayed his accomplishments in the wood products industry into ownership of Allison Ranch, a fly-in guest ranch on the main branch of the Salmon River, far back in central Idaho's vast knot of mountain ranges and deep canyons, which holds more wild land than any other place in the lower 48 states.

For years, the Forest Service has had plans for a logging and roading complex in an area locals call "Jersey-Jack," not far from the Allison Ranch. The Jersey-Jack project, which will open up a 41,000-acre area to allow the Forest Service to harvest 76 million board feet of timber, will cut through a roadless area but will not intrude on any congressionally declared wilderness area, neither the Gospel Hump directly to the west nor

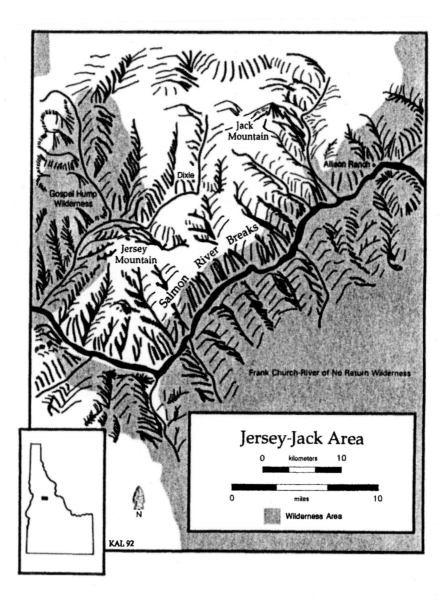

Jack
Mountain

Allison Ranch

Dixie

Gospel Hump
Wilderness

Jersey
Mountain

Salmon River Breaks

Frank Church-River of No Return Wilderness

KAL 92

Jersey-Jack Area

0   kilometers   10

0   miles   10

Wilderness Area

N

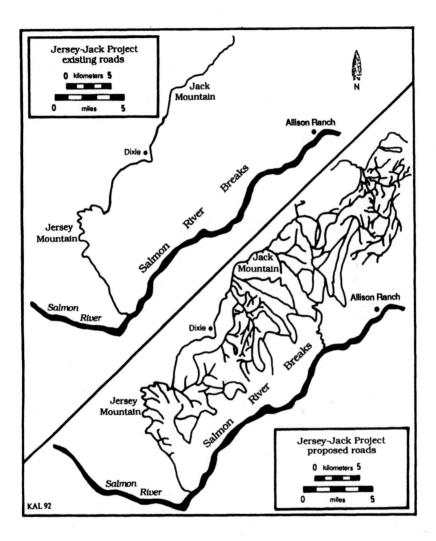

Jersey-Jack Project
existing roads

0 kilometers 5

0 miles 5

N

Jack
Mountain

Allison Ranch

Dixie

Jersey
Mountain

Salmon River Breaks

Salmon
River

Jack
Mountain

Allison Ranch

Dixie

Jersey
Mountain

Salmon River Breaks

Salmon
River

Jersey-Jack Project
proposed roads

0 kilometers 5

0 miles 5

KAL 92

the Frank Church–River of No Return just to the south. There will be considerable construction work. A network of 150 miles of logging roads, nearly 2½ miles of road for every square mile of land within the project, will be built to allow access to the area's stands of lodgepole pine. And let there be no doubt that these roads will get plenty of use: since it takes about 200 fully loaded logging trucks to carry out 1 million board feet, this logging operation—not a large one by Forest Service standards—will require about 15,000 truckloads to haul out the downed timber.[1]

Most of the residents of Elk City, in another drainage about 45 miles north of the Jersey-Jack area, support this roading and logging. Although the newly minted civic sign at the city limits styles Elk City as the "Year Round Recreation Land," the town is still dominated by the Bennett Lumber Mill, owned by Dick Bennett of Potlatch, Idaho. Most of the logging contracts at Jersey-Jack will go to the Bennett Mill, and people in Elk City favor the jobs and revenue that will result. This is not easy country to make a living in, and 76 million board feet of timber provides a measure of security.

But Harold Thomas, with his square, chiseled features and red hair now leavened by gray, begins to smolder when he talks about roadless area logging that makes what he thinks is bad economic policy. The problem for Thomas is that timber sales in the Jersey-Jack region, like many Forest Service timber sales in the Rocky Mountains, will result in a net loss to the government—up to $4.5 million in the case of Jersey-Jack alone. Thomas goes at these issues in a measured way, deliberately stacking up the glory values in this deep backcountry and gauging them against the economic facts. "These lodgepole stands are low-value land. There's no demand for these trees. So of course you end up with subsidies. Wilderness in these areas benefits Idaho, because of the tourism, more than logging ever will. What the Forest Service is doing just doesn't make any economic sense."

Most people in Dixie, the town nearest the Jersey-Jack project, agree with Thomas. Dixie sits where Fourth of July Creek, Boulder Creek, and Crooked Creek meet and the canyon spreads out to form a meadow just flat and wide enough to allow the early morning sun to flow in. The small dirt-road, log-cabin settlement was founded in 1862 during the Idaho gold rush and once boomed to a population of nearly 5000, but it is now dependent on recreation, especially hunting. The area south of Dixie, of which the Jersey-Jack region is a part, is home to some of the finest elk herds in the world. The lodgepole forests, 6000 to 7000 feet in elevation, provide excellent summer range. For winter range, the herds move down to the Salmon River Breaks, where the high country breaks sharply down to the free-flowing river, at about 2000 feet. These steep, sunny slopes and bottomland offer warmth and nutritious tallgrasses for the grazing ungulates during the hard winter months.

Emmett and Zona Smith own Dixie Outfitters. Zona, lightheartedly efficient, handles the business side—the mailings, replies to inquiries, grocery purchases, bookkeeping, and tax returns. She also looks after the hunters, making sure they pack all of their gear, and cooks up hearty country breakfasts before they set out for their week-long hunts. Emmett handles the pack animals and equipment and guides the hunting parties. He knows this wild country cold.

Emmett and Zona explain that their customers, who come from all over the nation, want two things. One is trophy elk. The hunters also invariably want to take their pack trips into pristine country. The Smiths will show you numerous letters in their files to that effect, such as an inquiry from Texas asking whether Dixie Outfitters can assure their customers of "a remote wilderness area." The Texan was "not looking for a country club party type of hunt. . . . What it amounts to, is that we are tired of hunting in overcrowded areas with little game."

The Jersey-Jack road complex will transform all of this. Although most of the roads will be closed after logging, enforcement in large backcountry areas is difficult. Pickup-truck and trail-bike hunters will surely move in, and the herds will be depleted; these effects are already evident north of Dixie, where Burpee Road was cut into previously roadless country for logging. And Emmett Smith, backed up by the Idaho Department of Fish and Game, knows that an increase in numbers of hunters will be coupled with the aversion of elk for roads. Elk seldom roam within half a mile of a road, so the Forest Service's transportation system will create mile-wide swaths through this prime elk habitat. Elk cows bear their calves in the spring, when, as Smith puts it, "they want complete solitude and silence. The cows won't drop their calves where there's a ruckus." Road graders to punch in logging roads, chain saws to fell the timber, and Caterpillar tractors and logging trucks to haul out the trees easily amount to a continuing series of ruckuses.

The animals will thus be pushed elsewhere, but the Smiths may not be able to follow. The Idaho state outfitters' board awards each licensed outfitter a territory—the idea is to ensure limited pressure from commercial parties (although private parties are free to hunt in any territory) and to guarantee party hunters an outfitter who knows the area. The Jersey-Jack area is in the heart of Smith's territory. Smith fully supports the state's system but, in the slow and easy drawl of his native Montana, explains in his precise way the effects of the roads on Dixie Outfitters. "Those roads would wipe us out. We'd just become a roadside lodge. We'd have no outfitting. That's what I enjoy. I'm no environmentalist, but I love this backcountry."

Harold Thomas, Emmett and Zona Smith, and other people who use the Jersey-Jack area, including hikers from Boise and Portland and owners and guests of the several nearby guest ranches, worry about things in addition to the elk. Northern Rocky Mountain gray wolves, killed off south of the Canadian border decades ago, have returned. Expert outdoorsmen in Dixie have seen the wolves' paw prints and heard their piercing, one-of-a-kind, shiver-up-the-backbone howl. Wolves, even more than the elk, do not like human contact. Already on the endangered species list, they will be forced out if the Jersey-Jack road system goes ahead.

Further, these tendrils of roads will be constructed in the Idaho Batholith, an enormous pile of extraordinarily unstable granitic soils. Over the eons, granitic rock has been broken down and decomposed into powder by the grinding of the earth's crust and by the relentless freezes and thaws in this climate of violent annual temperature swings. In an undisturbed condition, these fine sandy loams are held in place by the root systems of the ground cover. But when the grasses and shrubs are torn off—as they repeatedly will be when logging roads are cut into the slopes—there will be a great deal of erosion. The research arm of the Forest Service (not the Nez Perce National Forest, which is planning the logging and roading) has found that "[b]atholith soils tend to be highly erodible and prone to mass soil movement particularly when disturbed by road construction and timber harvesting."[2]

Even a layperson can appreciate these conclusions by expert soil scientists. When you dig your fingers into this gray dust-dirt and grab a handful, it seeps out or swirls away. It will not stay put in your hand. You can easily imagine that if strips of this land were raked open where there are slopes, the rain and snowmelt would cut gullies in the sugary stuff, the gullies would deepen and widen, and support for the rocks and trees on the canyon sides would be gouged out.

The landslides and slumps that the Jersey-Jack project will probably cause—the "mass soil movement" referred to by the Forest Service researchers—will end up in tributary streams like Mallard Creek and Jersey Creek and in the Salmon River itself, one of the world's great Pacific salmon and steelhead rivers. The ocean is more than 700 river miles from this stretch of the Salmon, but the fish nevertheless find their way as young smolt down to the Snake and Columbia rivers, then navigate as many as 2000 more miles out into the Pacific Ocean. They mature in the Gulf of Alaska and other rich ocean feeding grounds. Then, as adults, obeying some inner compass that scientists understand only vaguely, they fight their way back up the Columbia River system to the very spawning beds where they were hatched. The Salmon River chinook salmon, which grow to be as large as 40 pounds, are a prized commercial catch for the nation's dinner tables and are the quarry of offshore sport trolling rigs running out of coastal ports in Alaska, Washington, and Oregon. The chinook are also the mainstay of the Indian treaty fishery on the main stem of the Columbia. The smaller steelhead—still a bruising fish that can reach 20 pounds—is a legendary tackle-buster, one of the world's great sport fish.

But the salmon and steelhead must have healthy gravel spawning beds to return to or the runs will not be perpetuated. Adult female fish will not drop their eggs in silt. No one can predict exactly how much damage this particular erosion from the Jersey-Jack project would wreak on the salmon and steelhead habitat, but it is indisputable that the rivers in the Pacific Northwest have been ravaged by events with a cumulative effect of gigantic proportions. No less than half of the entire Columbia River drainage has been shut off to migrating fish by dams and by blockages and sediment from logging, grazing, and mining. The habitat degradation continues, even though, as we have known since the great forester-naturalist Aldo Leopold wrote *Game Management* in 1933, good wildlife management depends on good habitat management.[3]

The Salmon River near the Jersey-Jack area has already been hard hit. No dams have been built in the region, but downstream impoundments have taken a heavy toll on the upriver fish runs, and habitat continues to deteriorate, mainly from logging and roading. The fragile stocks of native fish are way down, and the chinook salmon in the Salmon River has been declared a threatened species. Harold Thomas's Allison Ranch is square on the banks of the Salmon, and a good many of his guests come there for the fishing. "It would be terribly expensive for the Forest Service to do what they should do to prevent the erosion at Jersey-Jack," says Thomas, "and there's no sign they intend to. We saw what massive logging does to the spawning grounds when they logged in the South Fork of the Salmon in the early 1960s. We nearly lost those runs because of those landslides. We're looking at the same kind of thing here."[4]

Pyramid Lake is about 400 miles southwest of the Jersey-Jack area. People expect wild rivers in central Idaho but not broad, deep natural lakes in the sagebrush and juniper high desert country of Nevada. And so, whether it is your first visit to Pyramid Lake or your tenth or hundredth, you catch your breath as you come over a ridge and gaze out over this aquamarine sheet that stretches more than 30 miles off in the distance. Certainly that was the reaction of John Charles Frémont, whose expedition reached the lake in January 1844, making theirs the first known visit by white people: "It broke upon our eyes like the ocean. . . . The waves were curling in the breeze, and their dark-green color showed it to be a body of deep water. . . . It was set like a gem in the mountains, which, from our position, seemed to enclose it almost entirely." Frémont also gave the lake the name it bears today: "[W]e encamped on the shore, opposite a very remarkable rock in the lake, which had attracted our attention for many miles. It rose, according to our estimate, 600 feet above the water; and, from the point we viewed it, presented a pretty exact outline of the great pyramid of Cheops."[5]

Frémont was a newcomer to Pyramid Lake. Paiute people have lived there since at least 2000 years before Christ was born. Their name for themselves is "cui-ui-dakado," meaning "cui-ui eaters." The cui-ui, which lives nowhere in the world except Pyramid Lake, is ugly to the uninitiated—a plump, brownish gray sucker—but the juicy flesh of these easily caught, good-sized fish (adults range from 2 to 6 pounds) has always been a staple in the diet of these Paiute people. Their other key food source was the Lahontan cutthroat trout, a strain of which is native to Pyramid Lake. These fish, when smoked and dried, once formed the basis of a bustling commercial trade for the tribe throughout the Great Basin and over to the Pacific Coast. The large, salmonesque Lahontans almost certainly approached 60 pounds in size; we know that they exceeded 40 pounds, because a tribal member named John Skimmerhorn caught a 41-pounder in 1925.[6]

Other than a few small springs and ephemeral streams, the Truckee River is the only source of water for Pyramid Lake. The Truckee rises high in the Sierra Nevada as the outflow of Pyramid's sister lake, Tahoe, which is comparable in area and some 2400 feet higher in elevation. The Truckee River winds down the steep eastern flank of the Sierra through what is now downtown Reno to its terminus at the southern end of Pyramid Lake. The Paiutes placed their villages at the mouth of the Truckee because both the Lahontans and the cui-ui were migrating fish, living most of their lives in Pyramid Lake but moving up through the Truckee River system to spawn. The mouth of the Truckee served to funnel the fish to the Paiutes, with their nets, traps, and spears. Frémont's journal was expansive about this bounty:

> An Indian brought in a large fish to trade, which we had the inexpressible satisfaction to find was a salmon trout; . . . Their flavor was excellent—superior, in fact, to that of any fish I have ever known. They were of extraordinary size—about as large as the Columbia river salmon—generally from two to four feet in length. . . . They doubtless formed the subsistence of these people, who hold the fishery in exclusive possession. . . . These Indians were very fat, and appeared to live an easy and happy life.[7]

The discovery of gold in California four years after Frémont's visit led to a spillover of population to Nevada, the opening of the fabulous Comstock Lode in 1859, and early statehood for Nevada in 1864. Conflicts over land arose between Indians and the new settlers of western Nevada. To alleviate

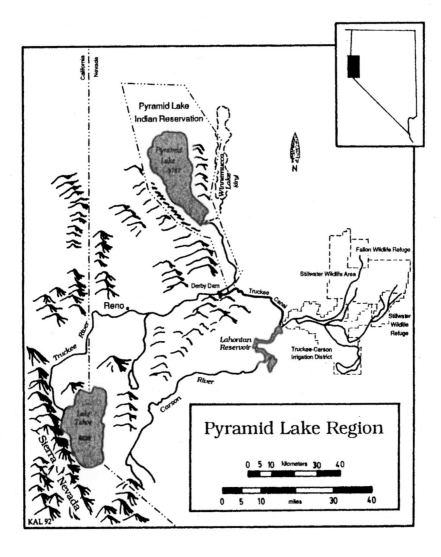

California | Nevada

Pyramid Lake
Indian Reservation

Pyramid
Lake
3787

Winnemucca
Lake
(dry)

N

Fallon Wildlife Refuge

Stillwater Wildlife Area

Derby Dam

Truckee Canal

Stillwater
Wildlife
Refuge

Reno

Truckee River

Lahontan
Reservoir

Truckee-Carson
Irrigation District

River

Carson

Lake
Tahoe
6229

Sierra Nevada

KAL 92

Pyramid Lake Region

| 0 | 5 | 10 | kilometers | 30 | 40 |

| 0 | 5 | 10 | miles | 30 | 40 |

tensions, in 1859 the Department of the Interior set aside the territory of the Pyramid Lake Band of Paiutes from settlement; this administrative action was confirmed by President Grant's executive order in 1874, which reserved 475,000 acres for the tribe. In recognition of the central place of Pyramid Lake in the existence of these Paiutes, the reservation is dominated by Pyramid Lake itself, with a strip of Indian land surrounding the lake and a 20-mile arm of land reaching up the lower end of the Truckee River. The late nineteenth century found the Paiutes' traditional way of life substantially unchanged, their millennia-old dependence on the lake's fishery still adequate to meet their needs. Indeed, the invention of an effective canning process allowed the Paiutes to expand their commercial use of the salmon-trout: by the 1870s, shipments of Lahontan cutthroat trout to restaurants and grocery stores across the country amounted to 25 to 50 tons each year.

Meanwhile, other Nevadans were undergoing frustrations of a kind found across the American West. Most sectors of the West, even the high desert land of Nevada, can support agriculture, but water must be brought in: beyond the 100th meridian (the north-south "dry line" running through the middle of the Dakotas and then through Nebraska, Kansas, Oklahoma, and Texas), annual rainfall by itself is insufficient to grow crops. In a few valleys, irrigation came fairly easily—water could be diverted from streams and transported through hand-cut ditches to nearby fields. More typically, however, potentially fertile farmlands were located on bench lands high above deep-canyoned rivers or in remote areas far from any watercourse. Further, western water comes at the wrong time of year. The big runoff from the mountains arrives in April, May, or June, at the front end of the irrigation season, leaving low flows for the key agricultural months of July, August, and September. Individual settlers were unable to raise private capital to build the dams needed for storing the spring floods for the dry summer months and to construct canals for transporting the water to faraway fields. So too did the small western states lack the wherewithal to fund water development.

Finally, westerners succeeded in persuading the federal government to support irrigation on arid lands. The Reclamation Act of 1902, one of the two or three decisive laws in the history of the American West, was the chosen means to provide funding for construction of grand-scale water projects. The 1902 act was sponsored by Congressman Francis Newlands of Nevada, who, according to congressional custom then as now, was entitled to have the first project in his home district. The Truckee-Carson Irrigation District, also called the Newlands Project, was begun promptly in 1903. It was designed to encompass some 350,000 acres of land near Fallon, within the drainage of the Carson River. Like all other reclamation projects, Newlands would be heavily subsidized by the United States government: the irrigators would receive free land and would pay only about

8 percent of the more than $10 million (in turn-of-the-century dollars) necessary to build facilities for storing and delivering water.[8]

The Newlands Project was such an ambitious undertaking that water from the Carson River would be insufficient. To make up the deficit, Derby Dam was built on the Truckee River, 35 miles upstream of Pyramid Lake. The squat, unimposing structure diverted 50 percent of the Truckee's flow out of the river channel. The water was transported southeast, via the Truckee Canal, to the Carson watershed and the farmers in the Newlands Project. The Paiutes at Pyramid Lake have a name for Derby Dam. They call it "the killer."

Before Derby Dam, Pyramid Lake was the second largest natural lake in the West, after the Great Salt Lake. The diversions reduced the lake's surface area by 25 percent, from 221 square miles to 167 square miles. The lake level dropped 70 feet. Vast amounts of former lake bed were left exposed, especially at the southern end, where the Truckee River feeds in. In most years, fish could not enter the Truckee River to spawn because its mouth had been transformed into a delta of mud flats and scattered trickles of shallow, warm water. Those fish that could work their way up into the Truckee River were confronted by Derby Dam, which had no operable fish ladders. The big Lahontans slammed up against the concrete wall again and again but to no avail. Unable to procreate, the native Pyramid Lake strain of Lahontan cutthroat trout died out, succeeded today by smaller, hatchery-reared fish with a similar, but not identical, genetic makeup.

The cui-ui is a hardier, more adaptable species and has done better. Some cui-ui have spawned in the few gravel stretches in the Truckee River below Derby Dam. In addition, it is a long-lived fish, having a life span of up to 40 years. Thus, cui-ui can survive if they can gain access to the spawning beds in the occasional years of high flows, when the fish can navigate the delta at the mouth of the Truckee River. In 1985, for example, 95 percent of the spawning cui-ui population was composed of fish born in 1969, a year of exceptionally high runoff, and the high water of 1986 permitted the species to revive itself by natural regeneration once again. The cui-ui is also able to survive in degraded water. This is an important asset in today's Pyramid Lake, which is more heavily saline than in years past because the reduced flow of water does not sufficiently dilute the minerals that have built up over millions of years in this lake with no outlet.[9]

The Newlands Project has wrought many other changes. Anaho Island was declared a national wildlife refuge in 1913; if the lake level continues to drop, a land bridge soon will connect the island to the shore, allowing predators such as coyotes to reach eggs and fledglings on one of the nation's few nesting colonies for the great white pelican. In its natural state, the Truckee River sometimes overflowed into a level valley floor to the east, creating a wetlands called Lake Winnemucca. This was prime habitat for migrating birds on the Great Western Flyway. Lake Winnemucca was declared a national wildlife refuge, but the designation was lifted after it became clear that there would be no more overflows from Pyramid Lake and that Winnemucca would dry up.

Ironically, the Newlands Project has itself contributed to a kind of substitute for Lake Winnemucca over in the Carson watershed. Originally, the Carson River spread out on the floor of the Great Basin, creating Carson Sink and associated wetlands. The flow of the Carson River is now used for irrigation, and the original wetland system has been drastically reduced. But unlike Lake Winnemucca, the area has not gone completely dry. Irrigation at Newlands has been notoriously wasteful—water has seeped through outmoded earthen transportation canals, flowed off improperly leveled fields, and been applied excessively by flooding of fields rather than by use of more efficient sprinkler or drip systems. Today, Truckee River water once bound for Pyramid and Winnemucca lakes is mixed with Carson River water, and much of it runs off the Newlands Project as wastewater into the Stillwater National Wildlife Refuge.

But Stillwater, seemingly a place of refuge for birds and other wildlife, has taken a grotesque turn. The irrigation tailwater from the Newlands Project carries highly toxic minerals leached out of the soils, and Stillwater has seen a buildup of many pollutants, including selenium, mercury, and arsenic. The situation has worsened since federal officials forced farmers in the Newlands Project to conserve water. These conservation measures were taken so that diversions from the Truckee River could be reduced to provide more water and better habitat for the cui-ui and Lahontan cutthroat trout; yet water conservation at Newlands, made in the name of wildlife protection in the Truckee, has helped create a death trap for wildlife in Stillwater. With less irrigation outflow from Newlands, the toxins have become more concentrated. Blue herons have dropped dead in flight, and white pelicans have developed deformities. In 1987, Tom Harris of the *Sacramento Bee* visited Stillwater and gave this description:

> A yard-wide band of death rings the massive, shallow and shrinking lake they call the Carson Sink, overwhelming evidence that the ecological system here is in complete collapse.
>
> Dead fish by the uncountable millions are washing up along the gooey shoreline, bobbing across the surface or decaying on the bottom, where bloating gases soon will pop great fetid masses more of them to the surface.
>
> Duck carcasses dot the shore. . . . [H]erons, egrets, grebes, geese, cormorants—all are represented among the carcasses.
>
> It is a wretching, reeking sight.[10]

The causes for this breakdown are complex and are not yet fully understood, but the main contributing factor seems plainly to be the chain reaction of events resulting from water development in the Truckee and Carson watersheds—this water, land, economic, and social engineering on a grand scale. All the while, as good, hardworking farmers in another basin irrigate with Truckee River water, the Pyramid Lake Paiutes face an unemployment rate exceeding 40 percent and are left with an uncertain supply of water, either for the fish and the lake that sustained them for 4000 years or for the irrigation that opened the West for settlement.[11]

The stresses in the Jersey-Jack area and at Pyramid Lake are contemporary manifestations of the age-old nexus between people and the land and its yield, a relationship that has always been the hallmark of society in the American West. Indian people in aboriginal times built their diets, economies, and religions on the swarming herds of buffalo and elk and the bank-to-bank runs of salmon and steelhead. The fleeting presence of the fur traders during the early nineteenth century was premised on the shipment of hundreds of thousands of beaver and otter pelts back to England, France, and Russia. The first wave of European settlers—one of the greatest human migrations in history—poured into California and other regions during the mid-nineteenth century in pursuit of gold and silver. In the late 1800s, stockmen came west to establish far-flung ranching empires based on the rich grasses of the prairies. Near the turn of the century, farmers put tens of millions of acres into crops.

The pattern of a culture reliant on its natural assets continues today. Nearly all western urban centers have engaged in protracted and bitter struggles over the importation of water from distant watersheds. The region is dotted with Elk Citys and Dixies—small towns dependent on timber harvesting, tourism, ranching, mining, or farming. The western population boom of the 1970s and early 1980s was fueled in large part by oil, gas, coal, and uranium development. Since World War II, recreation has emerged as a key economic factor and has outstripped most of the traditional consumptive resource uses. Recreation—skiing, camping, hunting and fishing, bird- and animal-watching, off-road vehicle use, and sightseeing—now is the second or third leading industry in most western states. Colorado state officials estimate that tourism in the state produced $6 billion in retail sales in 1991. A 1985 Stanford Research Institute International report on Wyoming's economy found that "travel and tourism are especially important to Wyoming because they generate net wealth for the state without using up natural resources or destroying the environment." In 1986, in the midst of a downturn in the extractive industries, *High Country News* concluded that "[t]raditionally, the rural Western economy is portrayed as a three-legged stool, resting solidly on mining and logging, agriculture, and tourism. Today the economy teeters precariously on tourism. . . ."[12]

There is also a more intangible side to this. Frederick Jackson Turner was speaking of psychic, as well as economic, values when he ascribed a central role to the frontier in the nation's history. The westward movement has always stood at least as much for freedom and the wonder of deep backcountry as it has for economic opportunity. It also has to do with the uncluttered, pastel high plains, with what contemporary Wyoming author Gretel Ehrlich has called "the solace of open spaces."[13]

Further, there has long been a spirituality about western land and its fruits. Navajos believe that their people came up from the earth, within the area bounded by the Four Sacred Peaks. Expansionists during the past century commonly invoked God's name, arguing that He had placed the abundant resources there for a reason and that it was contrary to divine will not to put water, minerals, and land to productive use. Those older ideas live in various fashions today, supplemented by the notion that the wildlands of the West rejuvenate the human spirit. The idea of government-protected wilderness, one of America's great contributions to intellectual history, came to its natural zenith in the American West. The big open country is a salve to western city-dwellers—it is what brought most of them west—and it infuses the region with a subtle but palpable informality.

The relationship between modern civilization and western lands is laced with crosscuts and ironies. This politically conservative region with deep strains of localism is mostly owned by the federal government; federal lands comprise 50 percent of the eleven western states (the Pacific Coast east to the Montana–Wyoming–Colorado–New Mexico tier of states) and 90 percent of Alaska. Much like Harold Thomas, corporate executives in Denver and Phoenix spend the winter planning an open-pit coal mine or a dam on a free-flowing river, then allocate two spring weeks to floating down through the mystical, red-hued walls of the Colorado Plateau. Indian councilpeople, struggling to reverse the seemingly intractable poverty on their reservations, will approve the mining venture and the water project, all the while determined to preserve the old ties to the earth. Loggers and cowhands may help to tear up some ground with clear-cuts or steer hoofs, but a clean and vital outdoors remains the fiber of their daily lives. Across the region, and in many sectors of the East as well, everyday citizens expect the western lands to generate wood products, metals, food, and electricity—and, as well, abundant wild animals; stretched-out, pristine vistas; wondrous watercourses; and a deep quiet that stirs in a near-primeval way the contemplation of centuries back and centuries ahead.

The West and the nation have struggled for generations to reconcile these and other changing and conflicting counterpressures. By the late twentieth century, however, agreement has emerged as to the root principles that should guide the West's land and resources. These are not just my, or any single group's, ideas but rather are broadly stated precepts—a mix of national policies, local prerogatives, market economics, social concerns, and environmental protection—held by most people concerned with the American West. The shared set of values encompasses these ideas:

1. Sustainable development should be employed so that resources will be available in sufficient quantity and quality for future generations.
2. Roughly equal respect should be given to the traditional extractive uses and to the more recently conceived nonconsumptive uses. Wildlife, recreation, and wilderness are "resources"—they, too, are a supply of something valuable.
3. Resource development should be conducted in a relatively level, consistent way in order to promote and preserve healthy, stable, and lasting communities.
4. Federal and state governments usually ought to receive a fair return when their resources are developed.
5. Government subsidies should be given to private industry only sparingly and under compelling, well-documented circumstances.

Stated even more broadly, a consensus exists that western resources generally ought to be developed but that development ought to be balanced and prudent, with precautions taken to ensure sustainability, to protect health, to recognize environmental values, to fulfill community values, and to provide a fair return to the public.

These principles have broad acceptance, but development in the West does not proceed in accordance with them. Rather, westwide, natural resource policy is dominated by the lords of yesterday, a battery of nineteenth-century laws, policies, and ideas that arose under wholly different social and economic conditions but that remain in effect due to inertia, powerful lobbying forces, and lack of public awareness.

The lords of yesterday trace to one of the extraordinary eras in all of history, the American westward movement of the nineteenth century. Initially, the mountains, heat, and scarcity of water and the sheer distance of travel across the Great Plains were daunting impediments to settlement. So too was Indian opposition. Nevertheless, as historian Walter Prescott Webb accurately observed, the American West, as compared with frontiers in other parts of the world, had an essential simplicity to its expansionist policy.

> The absence of the military, the proximity of the new land to the old, the ease of migration, and the absence of any attempt on the part of the government to regulate or control the process made the American situation the last word in simplicity. . . .[14]

The crucial ingredient in Webb's formulation was the *laissez-faire* policy of both the federal and state governments. The West held an array of natural goods that could support settlement of the region, boost the national economy, and assist mightily in establishing the young nation's place in the international trade community. The chosen means to achieve those ends was for the federal and state governments to open the gates, step back, and allow American ingenuity to take over. There was no commonly perceived need for any environmental policy. A recent survey, for example, named John Muir as the greatest Californian in history, but for most of his career (he died in 1914) Muir's brilliant philosophical ruminations over the value of wild places to humanity were sustenance for only a small group of followers. Westerners cared about the intangible products of their land but took them for granted because they were so abundant. Environmental constraints played at most a marginal role in the making of western public policy during the nineteenth century. The main thrust was to transfer public resources into private hands on a wholesale basis in order to conquer nature. Historian Vernon Parrington called it "the Great Barbecue."[15]

Government not only allowed nearly unfettered private resource development. It also subsidized it. The opening of the American West for settlement by non-Indians during the nineteenth century is often painted as a time of heightened individualism and self-reliance, and there is no question that those human qualities mattered a great deal during that intense time. Nevertheless, settlement was promoted and supported by perhaps the most extensive program of subsidies ever adopted by any government. More than 1 billion acres owned by the United States were given to private citizens and corporations free or for minimal filing fees. Railroads obtained 94 million acres directly and received an additional 37 million acres that had been transferred to states for the benefit of the railroads; these railroad land grants amounted to an area nearly the size of California and Washington combined. In addition to land, the United States dispensed free minerals, timber, range, and water. As with the Newlands Project in Nevada, Congress underwrote most of the massive western dams and reservoirs by passing reclamation acts, beginning in 1902, that extended billions of dollars in subsidies to water development interests.[16]

The states contributed mightily to the subsidies. They transferred to settlers and corporations, at little or no cost, most of the lands and minerals they had received from the federal government at statehood. Until the turn of the twentieth century, states engaged in no regulation whatsoever of hunting and fishing, whether for commercial or subsistence purposes. Western states took a passive, but decisive, stance in the key area of water. They allowed unrestricted diversions from all streams and lakes, without any payment to the government, and decreed that such appropriations would become vested property rights. Further, the states organized special water districts with favorable tax treatment so that irrigators and other water developers could promote and fund large water projects.

The issue of subsidies, a recurring topic in this book, deserves special mention here. "Subsidy" is a loaded term and is often used pejoratively, but subsidies can be a legitimate component of government policy. A subsidy— most commonly defined as government action that supplies capital, com- modities, or services at less than their market cost—is almost universally accepted as appropriate when there is some private market failure; a classic modern example is the funding of mass transit. Subsidies also are widely supported when necessary to further the public interest where a diffuse constituency is not organized, in market terms, to provide public benefits; instances include government funding of the arts, parks, and medical re- search. I will argue later that finely tuned, targeted subsidies sometimes ought to be extended to small ranchers, farmers, and timber mills to main- tain community stability and to preserve the cultural values afforded by those subcultures of the West. The real objection, in other words, ought not be to subsidies generally but to irrational or unexamined subsidies. The crux of subsidy policy is continuous and vigilant reexamination:

> "Federal programs aimed at supporting or improving the economic position of particular groups or industries should be constantly reevalu- ated in the light of changing circumstances. Whatever their initial justi- fication, subsidy programs should be so contrived as to eliminate the necessity for their continuation. The broad changes which must be expected in our economy require frequent revision in the scope and character of these programs if they are to achieve their purposes."[17]

It is not the point of this book, therefore, to second-guess federal and state programs during the formative years of the American West. Many of those policies had enormously beneficial effects for the nation, or at least for the vastly larger non-Indian population. The homesteading program, with all of its abuses, is justly acclaimed as one of the most progressive land distribution policies ever undertaken by any nation. The almost incom- prehensibly large subsidies to railroads may well have been excessive, but it is hard to deny that some extraordinary public incentive was required to achieve the widely held objective of connecting the coasts. Much the same is true with many of the early large-scale reclamation projects. Federal capital was necessary if the West was to be opened for the small family farm.

The fact that the nineteenth-century program may have been right for its own time does not, however, settle the question of whether it is right for these times. I have found five lords of yesterday that fit the needs of the frontier West but that are radical and extreme by modern lights. They exemplify public policy at a moment and a place when there seemed to be no end to nature's ability to produce still more material goods with few negative consequences. These lords of yesterday in no sense amount to a full listing of natural resource issues in the modern American West. There are pressing questions relating to water and air pollution, land use planning, the greenhouse effect, acid rain, nuclear energy, and toxic wastes. I have not included some of these subjects here because they are not distinctively western issues; that is, those concerns will be approached by a set of principles that by and large are as applicable in, say, Massachusetts and Ohio as in Colorado and Alaska. I also have excluded a few sets of issues that are distinctively western, such as the leasing of onshore and offshore oil, gas, and coal deposits. The central problems in mineral leasing do not trace to decisions made in another era—the mineral leasing laws have been substantially modernized—so the core conceptual issues vary from those presented by the lords of yesterday. Nevertheless, although the laws and policies taken up here do not encompass all western natural resource problems, they have a sweeping and pervasive influence in western society and are properly treated together because of the common themes that they raise. They are the heart of what can be called the law of the American West.

The first lord of yesterday is the Hardrock Mining Law of 1872, which dedicates more than half of all public lands to mining as the preferred use. Individual miners—or, much more often, mining corporations—can enter federal lands and extract hardrock minerals (gold, silver, copper, uranium, and many others) entirely free of charge. Further, this extraordinary law allows successful mining operations to obtain title to the land overlying the deposit; miners can receive as many 20-acre parcels as they wish, providing only that they discover valuable minerals under each. The hardrock statute, born of the California gold rush, is the vehicle for an array of health and environmental hazards, fraudulent practices, and land use problems arising from the some 1.1 million hardrock mining claims that blanket the western public lands.

The second and third lords involve the public rangelands and forestlands. In the nineteenth century, the federal government began the practice of allowing free and unregulated grazing of cows and sheep on the public domain. There is now a modicum of control on the 170 million acres of Bureau of Land Management lands where private grazing is allowed, but grazing fees are set at a fraction of their market value, and poor grazing practices have devastated western rangeland and the rivers that receive millions of tons of eroded soil annually. In the national forests, the Forest Service continues to push into remote, roadless areas such as the Jersey-Jack, still following its turn-of-the-century policy of treating logging as the dominant use of the forests in spite of changed public perceptions of the forests and clear evidence that many current government timber sales are unprofitable.

The final two lords of yesterday relate to water, which figures so prominently in the West. The Jersey-Jack area and Pyramid Lake, in other words, are typical of most western resource conflicts today because they implicate water in substantial ways. The fourth lord involves the dams and other development practices of the Pacific Northwest that have crippled the runs of Pacific salmon and steelhead. During the mid-nineteenth century, we set the stage for our policy toward salmon simply by doing nothing. Unrestricted netting and trapping, even dynamiting, were allowed. Unregulated dams on tributaries of the Columbia River—usually constructed in the name of "cheap" hydropower—destroyed spawning beds and choked off migration routes. Even passable dams with fish ladders account for a loss of about 5 to 13 percent of each run *at each dam*. Salmon bound for the area near Harold Thomas's Allison Ranch on the Salmon River, for example, must surmount eight dams and will lose three-quarters of their numbers during the upriver steeplechase. The problems for young fish traveling downstream to the ocean are even more severe. Fish biologists still have not found a reliable bypass system to prevent mortality for juvenile salmon and steelhead on their journeys to the ocean. Further, asserted demand for still more hydropower creates pressure to manage the dams on an even more intensive basis, which will bode even worse for these remarkable fish. In addition to the dams, land management practices such as those proposed in the Jersey-Jack area have cost us dearly in terms of loss of salmon habitat— and, therefore, loss of salmon.

The final lord of yesterday also deals with western water. The prior appropriation doctrine first announced by the California Supreme Court in 1855, along with associated water policies, is perhaps the area in which the law of the American West is most out of kilter. Like the Hardrock Mining Act, the essential notion behind prior appropriation is an exercise in simplicity: water developers have been allowed to tap into any western stream without charge and extract as much water as desired, so long as the water is put to a beneficial use—that is, a domestic purpose or a commercial use such as mining, farming, ranching, manufacturing, or power production. Diverters of water under this system obtain vested property rights that cannot be taken away unless the government pays full compensation. The oldest water rights are absolutely superior to those of all junior users; senior users need not share the resource, as was the law under the riparian doctrine accepted in the eastern states. Under the pure prior appropriation doctrine, western water users can, with impunity, flood deep canyons and literally dry up streams, as has happened with some regularity. Large water development efforts were subsidized by the federal and state governments.

Until recently, no consideration of any kind was given to the needs of fish, wildlife, or the streams or canyons themselves. Thus, projects such as Newlands and Derby Dam were not only allowed but also actively promoted.

The lack of symmetry between nineteenth-century methods and modern values is compounded by a related problem, the capture by large interests of the laws and policies that comprise the lords of yesterday. It was not intended to be this way. Congress envisaged the westward expansion as a movement for "the little man," for individual initiative. The Jeffersonian ideal of the small family farm was repeatedly invoked during the nineteenth century as the cornerstone of the westward movement. One problem, however, was that Jefferson conceived his theories on the East Coast; although he plainly grasped the immense potential of the West, as demonstrated by his achieving the Louisiana Purchase and commissioning the Lewis and Clark expedition, the evidence had not yet come in as to whether the small family farm would work in the West. As it turned out, many of Jefferson's ideas were impractical. For example, in most areas beyond the 100th meridian, the 160-acre plot envisaged in the Homestead Act of 1862 was larger than needed for a family farm (if irrigated) and too small for ranching. Big interests seized on the land and resource laws in a variety of ways, recounted in more detail throughout this book, and water developers, railroads and their landholding companies, timber companies, corporate ranches, agribusiness, and multinational mining companies took control of the economy of the West. Because of these forces, many of the main players in the western economy are located in urban centers, sometimes outside of the region, and have no concern for or accountability to the rural areas where the resource development occurs. As a result, the West has been imprinted with a lurching, up-and-down economy that cuts against the building of stable, lasting communities and often causes towns to stagnate after the trees, metals, or oil deposits drop in value or are mined out.

Reform has been stalled by several factors, some obvious, some much less so. Of course, to a considerable degree proposed changes are beaten back simply by the political and financial muscle wielded by the interests that have so much to gain by perpetuating the lords of yesterday. Yet we fundamentally misperceive the nature of the problem if we look only to the extractive industries. A larger, and more subtle, force is also at work.

The western economy has settled into the comfort of a unique kind of welfare system subsidized both by direct federal and state action and by the habit of writing off the extraordinary costs imposed on the environment and on dispossessed western communities such as Dixie and the Pyramid Lake Indian Reservation. To be sure, the industries are the direct beneficiaries, and their actions drive the system. But there is a trickle-down effect, and the subsidies permeate broad segments of the West's populace, often whole communities. Most westerners receive cheap water and electricity. Wages from the mills, mines, farms, and ranches—and from construction projects for dams and roads—end up in the markets, restaurants, gas stations, and clothing stores, and in the local school and park budgets, too. Banks pin their investment strategies on the long-settled system; many of their loans depend on it. Land developers and realtors push for one-time profits from the growth spurts stimulated by building another dam, excavating a new open-pit gold mine, or pushing up the timber cut another notch.

Going with the lords of yesterday has understandably been the accepted way for nearly a century and a half. The elaborate structure, however, cannot remain in place much longer. Government treasuries are at the breaking point. The costs to the lands and waters are coming due: growing numbers of rivers, aquifers, forests, rangelands, and farms are in decline. It is increasingly evident that the traditional reliance on the extractive industries cuts against the promising, emerging western economy based on recreation and tourism; scaled-back resource development; and, critically, light industries that are drawn by the region's lands, waters, space, and pace of life—and that are now able, through modern communications, to overcome the distance that once made location in the West impractical. Still, final change cannot come until westerners fully perceive the nature and magnitude of the current problems, look beyond their perceived short-term interests, and determine to alter the settled ways.

It will not be easy, and opposition has and will come from many quarters. Even though most westerners accept the shared set of values discussed above, it is hard to move from a settled system with its tangible financial returns to an uncertain future—even if there is good cause to believe that change will bring a better future, sustainable in terms of both the western economy and the lands and waters that westerners hold so dear. It is hard even when the day of reckoning moves, as it has, from the long term to the mid term to the short term.

In spite of their antiquity and pervasive influence, the lords of yesterday have operated mostly out of the sunlight. Public scrutiny into the full impacts of the lords of yesterday has been deflected by a mystique, instilled by the beneficiaries of the existing system, that these issues are so complex that they are beyond the ken of average citizens. The mining laws are the province only of the initiated. Forest and range policy can be comprehended only by those who can deal comfortably in millions of board feet and millions of animal unit months. The need for, and scope of, western water projects must be resolved by the superior knowledge of expert lawyers, economists, and engineers. We are, after all, talking about a matrix of law and policy that must support power grids spanning from Seattle to the San Francisco metropolitan area; a logging program covering ancient forests from the Rocky Mountains to the Alaska panhandle; and tunnels and aqueducts sending out Colorado River water to San Diego, Los Angeles, Las Vegas, Phoenix, Tucson, Salt Lake City, Albuquerque, and Denver and points east. These matters, the argument goes, must be left to experts.

This book operates on the opposite premise. To be sure, there is a point at which a forester must plan a timber sale, an engineer must design a dam, and a lawyer must draft federal agency regulations. But the public must make fundamental policy judgments before then. As matters now stand, most of those judgments were made long ago by a distant society and are embedded in state and federal laws. The laws, now with a momentum of their own, drive development. But the essential workings of the lords of yesterday are surprisingly uncomplicated. Remember the words of Walter Prescott Webb: the Gilded Age was highlighted by its simplicity.

The Jersey-Jack project is a case in point. It may well be wise to design a public timber program to benefit the Bennett Lumber Mill in Elk City and the jobs and people it supports. Or it may be that overly ambitious timber cutting now will lull Elk City into a false sense of security, leading only to an inevitable decline when the timber supply plays out or when the public is no longer willing to subsidize private communities with public resources. Perhaps, in terms of evaluating revenue flows, the Forest Service should pay much greater heed to the estimated $60 million that commercial outfitters generate annually for Idaho's economy on a statewide basis. Perhaps the Forest Service should adopt a lower, more moderate, harvesting level, one that can be sustained indefinitely. Perhaps the timber harvesting, whatever its level, can take place in a setting less fragile than the Jersey-Jack area.[18]

But the clear-cutting program in the Jersey-Jack region is not determined primarily by these kinds of considerations. Rather, timber harvesting in the national forests is driven by a national timber cut, which is set in Washington, DC. Congress decides on the level of the cut in the budget process, but it does so based on the expertise—and bias toward timber production—of the Forest Service and on heavy and persistent lobbying by the timber industry. In spite of recent laws mandating strict concern for noncommodity resources, the national allowable cut has, except for a recent and perhaps temporary dip, remained at 11 billion board feet annually for more than a generation. To meet the national goal, the Washington office of the Forest Service sends out harvesting targets to each Forest Service region, and each region then makes allocations among the national forests within it.

Thus, in the case of the Jersey-Jack project, the context for local decision making is set by orders from Washington, DC, to the regional forester in Missoula, who in turn gives directions to the forest supervisor of the Nez Perce National Forest. This lord of yesterday—the dedication of the national forests to timber harvesting and the setting of inflexible harvesting targets—skews the process and negates the possibility of a fair and principled balancing of the economic needs of Elk City and Dixie; the habitat of the elk, wolves, and salmon; and the beauty and mystery of the central Idaho high country. Distortions of a similar magnitude arise when decisions are made regarding mines, ranching practices, electric power projects, and irrigation dams.

Indian land and resource development must be considered in this context. One of the main occurrences in the American West during the past quarter of a century has been the reemergence of Indian tribes, who own nearly 5 percent of all land in the region, as a significant force in natural resource policy. Indian tribes once again have become an integral part of the western social, economic, and government structure. At Pyramid Lake and in hundreds of other places, western policy has merged with Indian policy. This in turn leads to still other dimensions of history, economics, law, and morality.

I wish to explore, then, a set of questions that, when fairly presented, are clouded with ambiguities and subtleties, with gray areas and close calls. But these questions are not fairly presented due to the lords of yesterday and the forces that perpetuate them. The law of the American West has become a classic case of what can happen when the normally salutary tendency of the law toward stability becomes subverted, when societal change far outstrips entrenched legal rules: when that happens, as legal scholar Roscoe Pound has observed, law can become "in very truth a government of the living by the dead."[19]

To be sure, there has been some progress. The past decade has been a dynamic time in the West, and as of the early 1990s, it is apparent that we have moved into a time of transition. In the pages that follow, I will recount a number of changes that have come to each of the fields governed by the lords of yesterday.

This spirit of reform has touched the two episodes examined in this chapter, and the nature of the progress suggests the extent and limitations of the recent activity. Some of the changes are not much more than cosmetic. The Forest Service, chastened by a 1985 court decision requiring the agency to take a second look, has completed a much more thorough environmental impact statement and made alterations that will give timber sales at the Jersey-Jack project a somewhat lighter touch. The essence of the project, however, is unchanged: a sprawling network of roads will still be punched into this fragile, pristine backcountry, and the sales will still turn out 76 million board feet of below-cost timber. Under the current decision-making regime, there was no real choice. The Nez Perce National Forest has been under able, environmentally conscious leadership since the mid-1980s, but the Nez Perce has been faced with relentless pressure to meet its share of the national cut. The timber must be produced, and the Jersey-Jack area is one of the few places in the Nez Perce National Forest where sufficient timber can be found.[20]

The current transition to a new framework is considerably more evident at Pyramid Lake. In 1990, Congress enacted promising legislation based on a settlement agreed to by almost all of the many parties. The Settlement Act is designed to protect Pyramid Lake and its fish, and to bring some justice to the Paiutes, by improving the flow regime in the Truckee River and establishing recovery programs for the Lahontan cutthroat trout and the cui-ui. Tribal, federal, and state wildlife biologists are hard at work to make the recovery programs on the Truckee succeed, and the same is true at Stillwater National Wildlife Refuge with biologists from the U.S. Fish and Wildlife Service. In the Newlands Project, conservation measures continue to be implemented so that less water will be drawn out of the Truckee; at the same time, The Nature Conservancy has headed up a water purchase plan so that farmers, if willing, can sell water rights and allow fresh Carson River water to flow into the refuge and prevent further toxic horrors. The city of Reno is expected to adopt a water-metering program to promote water conservation through market incentives.[21]

Yet there is still a very long way to go. The Settlement Act for the Truckee and Carson watersheds is contingent on further negotiations and actions involving the United States, Nevada and California, the city of Reno, the Sierra Pacific Power Company, and the tribe. The final returns will not be in until 1995 or 1996. Further, it is still unclear whether the conservation and water purchase programs will be fully implemented or whether the threatened Lahontan cutthroat trout and endangered cui-ui— even given a first-rate recovery effort—will have the staying power to eke out an existence from their depleted, battered habitat. The same is true with the birds and fish on the contaminant-laden flats of the Stillwater National Wildlife Refuge.

Even more to the point, the National Forest System is wracked with Jersey-Jacks, and the rivers of the American West are studded with Derby Dams. The same forces that created and sustained them fuel the other lords of yesterday as well. Transition time, yes; completed journey, no.

In *Beyond the Hundredth Meridian: John Wesley Powell and the Second Opening of the West*, which many would count as the greatest book ever written about the West, Wallace Stegner showed that the mountain men, the hardrock miners, and other early explorers were just the first era in the settlement of the region by non-Indians. They conquered the barrier of distance and, in the nation's eye, made the western half of the continent accessible. Then their government obtained most of the land from Indian tribes and foreign nations. The second era, of which Stegner wrote, involved the populating of the lands beyond the barrier of the dry line.

Now, of course, in spite of the obstacles of distance and aridity, we have settled the West. The task of this third era is to move beyond settlement and to achieve resource sustainability, economic stability, and social justice in a great land. To do so, we must cross a new meridian, this time not a geographic marker but a line of intellectual, social, and government commitment. This crossing involves gaining an understanding of the origins and content of old laws and policies and then juxtaposing them with the needs of modern society. That will allow us to sort out those that work and those that do not. We can then move beyond the lords of yesterday toward fundamental but measured and equitable reform. It is that exploration to which the remainder of this book is dedicated.

Chapter Two

The Miner's Law

The largest recent discovery of gold in the United States was made in 1988 in mile-high northeastern Nevada, about 45 miles out of Elko. If you go to a nearby bluff, you will be standing in the morning shadow of the 7500-foot Tuscarora Range, its juniper-studded slopes offering little cover but still holding snowpack until early spring. All around you is the compelling geology of the Basin and Range Province, where the terrain is composed of parallel north-south mountain ranges separated by broad, flat valley floors 5 to 30 miles wide. Clarence Edward Dutton, one of the first geologists to study the region, wrote that the Basin and Range Province, stretching from southern Nevada and Utah to southern Idaho, looks like "an army of caterpillars marching northward out of Mexico."[1]

Yet your attention is irresistibly drawn away from the long vistas of the Basin and Range country, away from the Tuscaroras, to the fascinating display of human and mechanized activity spread out below. Mining is proceeding at a furious pace. There is traffic everywhere, twenty-four hours a day, 365 days a year. Cranelike electric shovels gouge the rock, fractured and loosened by blasting, out of the pit wall, and front-end loaders fill 3-story-high haul trucks on 12-foot tires (the tires cost $15,000 apiece; a blowout can explode with the force of a stick and a half of dynamite). These giant haul trucks are latter-day beasts of burden in the fullest sense: at 190 tons per load, the fleet carries out a total of 325,000 tons of ore daily. Meanwhile, sprinkler trucks fight the relentless dust from all the disturbance. Miles upon miles of roads and packed-earth passageways weave through the pounded, gouged, and piled pits, tailings ponds, cyanide-doused "heaps," waste rock, and slashed-in-half hillsides.

The Goldstrike Mine has proved to be so fabulous that the operation is about to be taken to a new order of magnitude. Goldstrike's largest open pit—already 800 feet deep, excavated down so far that the massive mine vehicles are barely visible in the depths—will be expanded in every direc-

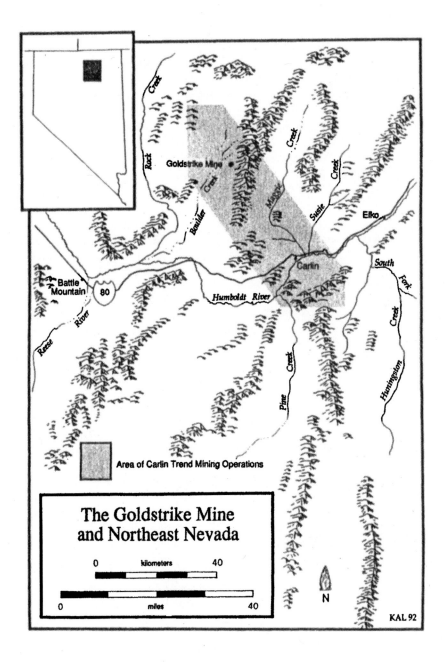

Rock Creek

Goldstrike Mine ●

Boulder Creek

Maggie Creek

Susie Creek

Elko

South Fork

Battle Mountain

80

Carlin

Humboldt River

Huntington Creek

Reese River

Pine Creek

Area of Carlin Trend Mining Operations

The Goldstrike Mine and Northeast Nevada

| 0 | kilometers | 40 |

| 0 | miles | 40 |

N

KAL 92

tion. The Betze Pit, as this new dig is called, will be canyon sized, nearly 2 miles long, three-fourths of a mile wide, and 1800 feet deep.

Numerous benefits accrue from the Goldstrike Mine. General Manager John McDonough is an earnest, straightforward man who takes his civic responsibilities seriously, as do other executives with the firm. To prevent formation of a separate "company town," Goldstrike has built 375 homes in Elko and provided 150 mobile homes and 100 apartments for the mine's 1200 employees and their families. The company has made major contributions to the Northern Nevada Community College in Elko and to other causes. Numerous business, education, government, and citizen groups supported the Betze Pit when the environmental impact statement was being prepared. Many of the comments were canned—Goldstrike was not bashful about mobilizing support for this rich project—but one is left with little doubt that Goldstrike has made many contributions to the Elko area. This letter from the chief executive officer of the Vitality Center is typical:

> I have been associated with Barrick Goldstrike Mines, Inc., for many years through their support of Vitality Center and our efforts in the community. Additionally, I have served on various community and statewide projects with Barrick employees.
>
> I have been consistently impressed with their concern for the community and welfare of our citizens. I feel secure in recommending support of any plans Barrick has to expand their operation in the Elko area.
>
> The expansion activities will have a positive economic impact on northeastern Nevada and will generate millions of dollars in revenue annually for the city, county, and state. . . .[2]

Since the pit is located on federal public lands administered by the Bureau of Land Management, one might think that Goldstrike would make lucrative returns to the federal treasury. This is especially so since American Barrick Resources Corporation, the Canadian firm that is parent to the Goldstrike, expects to make a $3 billion net profit from the known reserves; when the Betze Pit comes into full production, Goldstrike will move from its present position as the fourteenth largest gold-producing mine in the United States to being the richest gold mine in North America. Stock in American Barrick has been one of the most rapid gainers on the New York Stock Exchange. Yet Barrick, like scores of other companies extracting hardrock minerals estimated at $4 billion annually from federal lands, is required to make no royalty payments of any kind to the United States for developing these public deposits. So, too, is the federal land free for the taking, or effectively so—a fee of $5 or less per acre is required. Although the hardrock mining industry must pay income tax (in 1991, American Barrick paid $22 million for Goldstrike and its four other mines), the extraordinary subsidies given to mining companies operating on federal public lands allow the companies to avoid any payment for the valuable raw materials essential to their operations.

Hardrock mining has exacted other costs. Contamination of water and soil from acid mine drainage, heavy metals, arsenic, and mercury pose widespread and significant hazards to wildlife and human health. Hardrock mines on public lands already account for fifty Superfund sites, and many more are sure to be designated as scientists uncover more poisons from abandoned mines.

Today's mines operate in an atmosphere of increased awareness, and the technology for detection and prevention of contamination continues to improve. At the same time, the scale and methods of modern hardrock mining create environmental and health risks never before encountered. The Goldstrike Mine is not an isolated example: the landscape of the American West supports eighty to one hundred large open-pit gold, silver, copper, and molybdenum mines, many as large as Goldstrike's current operation.

In the case of Goldstrike, as with most other precious metal mines, cyanide is used to dissolve the gold from the ore after the material is trucked up out of the pit to high ground. This is accomplished by sprinkling a cyanide solution over piles of ore that cover 280 acres and rise up to 200 feet above the natural topography. The pit itself raises additional pollution issues. Mining is already going on far below the groundwater table, causing water to seep steadily into the pit. Pumping it out accounts for much of the staggering amount of electricity consumed by the mine—Goldstrike's annual power consumption is equal to that of a city of 100,000 people. When the Betze is mined out, which is expected to occur in the year 2000, groundwater will seep in and create a lake 1150 feet deep—two-thirds as deep as Tahoe, the tenth deepest natural lake in the world. But this will be a dead lake, fenced off to keep people and animals away from its nearly vertical sides that will create a drop of several hundred feet down to the water's surface.

No one knows exactly what this lake will be like and what will happen to the water, for there has never been a gold-mining project of this size. We do know that the water will be saline and that arsenic may well make the water undrinkable. Fish and other forms of wildlife will probably not be able to live there. The groundwater may be tainted by acid mine drainage.

The nearest natural watercourse to this future lake is Rodeo Creek, which feeds into Boulder Creek. Population in the area is low, but Boulder Creek is used by ranchers for irrigation. The creek and the aquifer are within the watershed of the Humboldt River, the corridor for the Overland

Trail and, today, Interstate 80. Elko, upstream, would not be affected by surface or underground seepage of this significantly degraded water into the aquifer. But the Humboldt, virtually the only water in this parched country, runs for 175 miles west of the Betze Pit, passing through Carlin, Battle Mountain, Winnemucca, and Lovelock. The problem is compounded because nine other major pit mines are already operating, or ready to start up, in this mineral-rich Carlin Trend in the Humboldt watershed. Glenn Miller, professor of environmental chemistry at the University of Nevada, speaking of the Goldstrike and Betze operations, says, "What we are getting are twenty years of tremendous economic benefits for Elko and enormous water problems for the next thousand years."[3]

Environmental problems accompany even small mining operations, which usually entail use of bulldozers and other mechanized earth-moving equipment. In the summer of 1984, sludge from a gold mine operation on the Fortymile River, a tributary of the Yukon River in Alaska, ate away at the river's salmon runs and at the subsistence economy of the Athabascans who lived in nearby downstream villages. There are similar concerns in dozens of Alaska drainages. John McPhee described the father-and-son mining outfit of the Gelvins in his account of interior Alaska, *Coming into the Country*:

> When the Gelvins departed, I was cleaning some grayling, five in all. I caught one with my fishing rod. The Cat caught the others. When Stanley dammed the river, and diverted it into the pipe, he took it out of its bed for a couple of hundred yards. Pools remained there, like low tide, and as they slowly drained they revealed the graylings' dorsal fins. I walked from pool to pool, trapping the fish with my hands. This pretty little stream is being disassembled in the name of gold. The result of the summer season—of moving forty thousand cubic yards of material through a box, of baring two hundred thousand square feet of bedrock, of scraping off the tundra and stuffing it up a hill, of making a muck-and-gravel hash out of what are now streamside meadows of bluebells and lupine, daisies and Arctic forget-me-nots, yellow poppies, and saxifrage—will be a peanut-butter jar filled with flaky gold.[4]

Public land mining twists off in other, very different, directions. On Stanley Creek about 10 miles from the scenic high mountain town of Stanley, Idaho, at the base of the Sawtooth Mountains, a midwestern schoolteacher lived for years in a fine log cabin on national forest lands. The teacher, like American Barrick, asserted an unpatented mining claim that, if valid, gives the holder "the exclusive right of possession and enjoyment of all the surface" within the claim. Unlike American Barrick, the teacher near Stanley was not a legitimate miner but rather was in pursuit of a summer residence, using the federal hardrock mining laws as a lever.

Uncounted thousands of other "miners" remain in summer homes on public lands across the West. In 1984, the Forest Service was finally able to evict the schoolteacher on Stanley Creek, but only after protracted administrative procedures that cost the United States some $10,000.⁵

All of these situations proceed under the auspices of the General Mining Law, or Hardrock Act, of 1872. The act may be ancient, but it is no dead letter. The Bureau of Land Management reports approximately 1.1 million active claims scattered across the federal lands. Most unpatented mining claims are at least 20 acres in size, and some run as high as 160 acres. Overall, about 25 million public acres—more than half the size of the state of Washington—are subjected to these elusive property interests that tie up mineral rights, frequently interfere with public use and access, and provide no returns to the public treasury. The meter is running: the BLM receives 90,000 new claims for recording each year. Further, environmental regulation of hardrock mining, although gradually improving, lags far behind government oversight of most other health and environmental hazards. From its inception, hardrock mining has been the highest and most preferred use of the public lands, and the old law extends to mining companies a "right to mine." Agency officials regularly stay their hands, cowed, even when human health is put at risk, by this broad-shouldered grant of power to the mining industry. Even with an operation as extraordinary as the Betze Pit, no serious thought is given to the possibility that the project should not be allowed to go ahead.⁶

The Hardrock Act remains afloat for a congeries of reasons. The mining industry heaps lobbying clout on top of inertia to stall reform. Towns like Elko receive substantial economic benefits so long as the mine keeps producing, and many of their citizens let their congressional representatives know about it. Proposed reforms typically raise constitutional questions, since the 1872 act created several species of vested property rights, and full compensation must be paid to the owners if valid claims are terminated. Further, for all of its failings, the old law has pockets of good policy—there are fears of disrupting the flow of needed minerals, especially strategic minerals such as copper, uranium, and molybdenum.

The act's proponents also make much of the independence and sturdiness of the small miner. The right—that word comes up often—of any American to head out over the ridge with a pack mule, or in a Jeep, toward the financial independence of the big strike or the spiritual freedom of several days' wages dug from the ground continues to burn bright in our national consciousness. Even though in modern times the great bulk of serious mining is conducted by corporations, the image of the small miner continues to hover over much of the debate.

Let us return to the observations of John McPhee, as good a conservationist as there is. After relating the Gelvins' bulldozer operation in bush Alaska and their plundering of the wildflowers and grayling, McPhee said this:

> [T]he relationship between this father and son is as attractive as anything I have seen in Alaska—both of them self-reliant beyond the usual reach of the term, the characteristic formed by this country. Whatever they are doing, whether it is mining or something else, they do for themselves what no one else is here to do for them. Their kind is more endangered every year. Balance that against the nick they are making in this land. Only an easygoing extremist would preserve every bit of the country. And extremists alone would exploit it all. Everyone else has to think the matter through—choose a point of tolerance, however much the point might tend to one side. For myself, I am closer to the preserving side— that is, the side that would preserve the Gelvins.[7]

The Hardrock Act plays out on the modern public lands in a range of ways other than those just described, and I will shortly return to the contemporary operation of the law and the modern reform movement. Discussion of current issues, however, is sterile without an appreciation of the era that generated this practice of holding open federal land and minerals to miners. The old times influence, and in many cases determine, our actions today.

Gold and Silver Open the West

When James Marshall made his gold strike at Sutter's Mill on the American River on January 24, 1848, the region of California had not officially become part of the United States, much less a federal territory or a state. The nation was in its greatest spate of land acquisition—more extensive even than the time of the Louisiana Purchase of 1803 or the Alaska purchase of 1867. During the presidency of James Knox Polk, from 1845 through 1849, the United States annexed Texas and obtained nearly all land west of the Continental Divide by means of treaties with England and Mexico. California, along with Nevada, Utah, most of Arizona and west- ern Colorado, and New Mexico, was acquired from Mexico by the Treaty of Guadalupe Hidalgo, which was not ratified by the Senate until March 10, 1848.[8]

The small number of Americans in California in early 1848, however, treated the area as their own before the acquisition from Mexico. The nation had long coveted the region, and Mexico had been vanquished in war. The discovery of gold flashing up to the naked eye from a stream bottom in the Sierra foothills carried an almost inevitable logic: the find confirmed all of the rampant rumors as bright fact.

The news of Marshall's discovery blazed throughout California communities. Within months, miners were working over every major stream that fed from the Sierra Nevada into the Central Valley. Miners operated as far north as Redding on the upper Sacramento River. By late summer and fall of 1848, aspiring miners began to arrive from Oregon, Hawaii, and Mexico.

But we accurately use the term "forty-niners" to describe those arriving in great numbers at the beginning of the gold rush. This frontier society existed before the advent of transcontinental communication. There was no telegraph system, no railroad, not even the pony express. As just one example, when the United States Senate gave its advice and consent to the Treaty of Guadalupe Hidalgo, it did not yet know of the epochal event that had taken place on the American River two months earlier. It took six months for word of the gold strike to travel back east.

Ocean voyagers making their way through the Isthmus of Panama or around Cape Horn began to arrive in droves in the spring of 1849. Overland travel to the gold country could not even begin until the spring thaw of 1849. The journey from Independence, Missouri, or some other jumping-off point would then take at least four months, usually more.

Most of these gold seekers failed to strike it rich. Many worked only for wages. Others toiled not in mining at all but as entrepreneurs or employees in the thriving business of supplying the mining camps. Still others, misfits or criminal outcasts in the communities they left behind, lived on the fringes of society in California.

Yet for pure opportunity, for a truly fresh start, there may well never have been anything to equal this vigorous, booming westward movement. The numbers, of course, involve some guesswork, but Rodman Paul, the leading historian on the gold rush, estimates that California's population was 14,000 in 1848, 100,000 by the end of 1849, and 223,000 by 1852. California became the first western state to join the Union in 1850. Because of California's gold production, the United States, which previously had been insignificant as a gold producer, turned out nearly half of the world's gold by the mid-1850s.[9]

The California gold rush triggered the opening of all of the American West, not just California. For some forty-niners and for scattered gold seekers a short time thereafter, the valuable metal came easily from the Sierra foothills. Miners on Nelson Creek scrambled out of that rugged canyon on the Middle Fork of the Feather River and traveled nearly 100 miles to a find on the North Fork, later named Rich Bar, in pursuit of a story that panned out:

> In a fortnight . . . , the two men who had found the first piece of gold had each taken out $6,000.00. Two others took out thirty-three pounds of

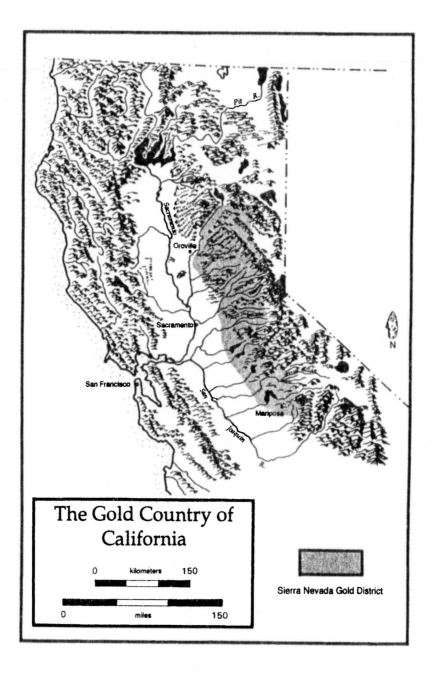

The Gold Country of California

0   kilometers   150

0   miles   150

Sierra Nevada Gold District

gold in eight hours. The largest amount taken from one pan of dirt was $1,500. In a little more than a week from its discovery five hundred men had settled upon the bar for the summer.

But few miners had such luck; of those who did, most promptly squandered their fortunes. The gold country miners fanned out to the Trinity Alps in northwestern California and to Oregon, Idaho, and Montana. Silver was discovered at the Comstock Lode in Virginia City, Nevada, in 1859. Major strikes were made in Colorado the same year. J. Ross Browne reported to Congress in 1868 that "[w]ithin the brief space of nineteen years our people have opened up to settlement a larger area of territory, valuable as a source of supply for nearly all the necessities of man, than has ever before in the world's history been brought within the limits of civilization in so short a time."[10]

The stampede to the West's mineral riches had a deadly effect on Indian tribes living in the regions of the major strikes. The rapid migration into the new state of California generated a demand for land to settle. In 1851, the United States negotiated a series of treaties with Indian tribes, who owned their aboriginal land jointly with the United States. In these treaties, the California tribes agreed to relinquish their homelands for much smaller parcels outside the path of settlement.[11]

California Indians, in performance of their obligations under the treaties, began moving to their substitute lands. The California legislature, however, wanted no treaties with Indians, no matter how favorable the bargain might be to the non-Indian settlers. The California lawmakers made their point clear to the United States Senate, which had yet to give the treaties its advice and consent. The Senate acceded to California's demands and never approved the treaties.

Most California Indians ended up homeless. Their historical lands had been overrun by gold seekers and other settlers, and they were denied the lands promised to them at the treaty negotiations. Eventually the federal government set aside small reservations, called rancherias, for California tribes and bands.

Tribes in Nevada, Oregon, Colorado, and elsewhere were removed by the relentless press of the gold rushes. A famous example with continuing ramifications involves the Black Hills of South Dakota, promised to the Sioux by the Fort Laramie Treaty of 1868. In 1980, the United States Supreme Court awarded the Sioux monetary compensation—but not land— for the illegal occupation, saying this of the 1874 gold rush in the region:

The discovery of gold was widely reported in newspapers across the country. [Lieutenant Colonel George] Custer's florid descriptions of the mineral and timber resources of the Black Hills, and the land's suitability for grazing and cultivation, also received wide circulation, and had the effect of creating an intense popular demand for the "opening" of the Hills for settlement. The only obstacle to "progress" was the Fort Laramie Treaty that reserved occupancy of the Hills to the Sioux.[12]

The treaty, of course, was insufficient to stem the tide, but the Sioux have refused to let the issue die. As one historian noted, "[t]he Sioux thus affected have not gotten over talking about that treaty yet." After the successful compensation suit, the Sioux continue to press for an exchange of those dollars for part of the Black Hills, an increasingly viable campaign that is just one of the many modern legacies of the gold and silver fever that swept across the land more than a century ago.[13]

Mining remained the dominant sector of most western societies for decades after the original rush in California. As of the mid-1860s, 25,000 men actually worked in California's mines; the state's population was 488,000. Thirty percent of all Nevadans were working miners, and in Montana and Idaho, the figures were 25 percent and 30 percent, respectively. Of course, the impact of mining was far greater than the numbers of active miners, for the industry required support from numerous callings, including assayers, equipment manufacturers, teamsters, and suppliers of clothing, housing, and entertainment. Only in the Utah Territory, where farming predominated, was mining of less than central importance.[14]

The basic government and societal units in the mineral regions were the mining camps that grew up spontaneously and autonomously. Most were located in remote, steep canyons where, over the eons, the gold had been washed down by the rush of mountain creeks. The streets were narrow, and the ramshackle cabins or tents were necessarily clustered together by the cramped environs. These rough-hewn camps, replete with bars and pool halls, were usually about 90 percent male, especially in the early days. Even with all of the inevitable embellishment, the mining camps were plainly marked with a unique swaggering, shoot-'em-up, bar-fight chaos.

But whatever ribald revelry prevailed during off-hours, the miners insisted on order when it came to washing the yellow metal out of gullies and ravines with pans, sluices, and Long Toms and, by the mid-1850s, from hillsides with the giant hoses that drove hydraulic operations. The requirements went well beyond the fact that outright claim-jumping was a good way to get strung up by a vigilance committee. These miners, like all businesspeople, needed a reasonably well defined structure—a set of accepted norms—to protect the hard labor and materials that they had sunk into their operations.

The resulting laws, the codes of the mining camps, were montages of Spanish rules transported north by Mexican miners, regulations from the

Midwest, improvisation bred of common sense, and local custom. Everywhere, the idea of "first in time, first in right" prevailed: a miner ought to have exclusive rights to a find that he had discovered, a principle also applied to the water necessary for mining. The codes set a specific breadth and length for claims. Claims typically had to be staked by erecting notices with the names of the claimants, accompanied by monuments driven into the ground or blazes struck on trees. Miners were usually limited to one claim. Elected recorders were the official repositories of claims information. The codes often provided for arbitration of disputes. Some mining districts allowed each disputant to choose an arbitrator, with those two to choose a third; arbitrators were usually required to be miners or residents of the mining district. Some camps, including the Sugar Loaf District in Colorado, had the good sense to prohibit lawyers from arguing cases. The Union District, also in Colorado, was even more explicit that disputes would be decided by local understandings, not legal technicalities: "[N]o lawyer shall be permitted to practice law in any court in the district under a penalty of not more than fifty nor less than twenty-five lashes and shall be forever banished from the district."[15]

A key element of the codes, or of the implied usages, was the rule that mining claims be worked diligently. The North San Juan District in California, for example, provided that any person expending $500 in money and labor would be entitled to a secure claim for the two years following the expenditure. The most common provision required at least one day's work per month during the mining season. If these diligence requirements were not met, the claim was forfeited and thrown open to relocation by other miners.[16]

The customary law in the camps became the benchmark for state law. An early California statute provided that "the customs, usages or regulations established and in force at the bar or diggings embracing such claims ... when not in conflict with the Constitution and laws of this State, shall govern the decision of the action." In 1864, the California Supreme Court explained the role of the mining codes:

> These customs ... were few, plain and simple, and well understood by those with whom they originated. ... And it was a wise policy on the part of the Legislature not only not to supplant them by legislative enactments, but on the contrary to give them the additional weight of a legislative sanction. These usages and customs were the fruit of the times, and demanded by the necessities of [the mining] communities. ... Having received the sanction of the Legislature, they have become as much a part of the law of the land as the common law itself, which was not adopted in a more solemn form. ... [T]here is no reason why Judges or lawyers should wander ... back to the time when Abraham dug his well,

or explore . . . the law of agency or the Statute of Frauds in order to solve a simple question affecting a mining right, for a more convenient and equally legal solution can be found nearer home, in the "customs and usages of the bar or diggings embracing the claim" to which such right is asserted or denied.[17]

The Rise of the Hardrock Mining Law

Yet even though almost all mining took place on federal public lands, by the mid-1860s there was no general federal mining law for hardrock mining in the West. A leasing system applicable only to lead had been adopted in 1807 but abandoned in 1846. A few special statutes provided for sales of mineral lands in designated geographic areas in the East, but they had no force in the western mining districts.[18]

This vacuum in the federal legal system created a variety of problems for the mining industry. There had been some early confusion as to who owned the great mineral deposits in the West: in 1853, the California Supreme Court suggested that the mines belonged to the state. It soon became clear, however, that minerals underlying the federal public lands, like the lands themselves, were owned by the United States. Since no federal statute authorized entry, the miners were trespassers.[19]

To be sure, there was an implicit understanding that miners were welcome on the public lands. The few federal lawmen in the West—fully cognizant of the lifeblood of the region and presumably solicitous of their own skins—took no action to prosecute these technical trespassers. President Lincoln reinforced the common understanding by extolling the mining industry in his State of the Union Address of 1864, saying that "numerous discoveries of gold, silver, and cinnabar mines have been added to the many heretofore known, and the country occupied by the Sierra Nevada and Rocky mountains, and the subordinate ranges, now teems with enterprising labor, which is richly remunerative."[20]

Nevertheless, the miners' disquiet steadily increased. Mining in easily accessible placers—loose deposits of ore in soil or gravel—began to play out by the 1860s. Work focused increasingly on the more labor-intensive lode deposits—minerals embedded in quartz or other rock. The role of small miners began to decline. The higher capital requirements for lode mining, which usually required deep tunnels, brought in eastern and foreign investors, and these sophisticated capitalists held concerns about the security of their operations. The edginess was heightened by Lincoln's seizure of the New Almaden mercury mine in California in 1863. The president took the action to eliminate a fraudulent claimant under a Mexican land grant, but the order was made on the express ground that the claimant was a trespasser on federal public lands.[21]

The miners also were frustrated by the lack of a mechanism for obtaining title to land, since homesteading was not allowed on mineral-bearing lands. The miners' precarious land tenure was illustrated by reports that the Central Pacific Railroad was angling to have its far-flung land grants extended to cover mineral lands. One leading writer of the era, John Hittell, heaped praise on the physical virtues of California and the sense of freedom in the new state but decried the rootlessness of the populace. Hittell attributed this largely to the "evil effect of the want of secure land-titles" in the gold fields and "the consequent unsettled character of the population," reminding us of the symbiotic relationship between mining and the general society.[22]

Today, we commonly refer to the General Mining Law of 1872 as the dominant law on hardrock mining. The 1872 act, however, is an amalgam of mining laws enacted in 1866 and 1870 plus several refinements of the ideas legislated by those earlier Congresses.

The trailblazing 1866 statute, the first federal legislation covering mining on the western public lands, reflected the remote and independent region to which mining was so important. There were only three western states—California, Oregon, and Nevada—at the time. The nearest state-house to the east of Carson City, hard up against the Sierra Nevada in the western part of Nevada, was Topeka, Kansas. Colorado, for example, was still a decade from statehood; Washington, more than two decades; New Mexico and Arizona, almost a half century; Alaska, nearly a century.

The champion of the Mining Act of 1866 was William M. Stewart, Nevada's first United States senator. Stewart, an original forty-niner who had been a successful mining lawyer in the camps of California and Nevada, cut an imposing figure in a variety of reports. He was a big man, and a photograph taken late in life shows him with a flowing, chest-length beard. As a courtroom lawyer cross-examining a witness of more than doubtful veracity, he claimed to have used a derringer to reinforce the obligations imposed by the witness's oath. This technique, it seems, was consistent with early Nevada civil procedure: "The old judge turned and grinned at me." As senator, he became a leading figure in Washington during his long career. In addition to his work on the mining laws, he contributed to the railroad acts, the post–Civil War reconstruction legislation, and the reclamation program. In 1871, he apparently declined an appointment to the Supreme Court that would have made him, after Stephen J. Field, the second westerner on the Court. Stewart also knew the mining business and parliamentary procedure cold, and both areas of knowledge stood him in good stead on Capitol Hill during the passage of his cherished mining legislation.[23]

Stewart's 1866 mining bill was partly an affirmative thrust to codify the miners' wishes and partly a defensive measure. Congressman George Julian of Indiana, with the backing of other eastern and midwestern lawmakers, had introduced legislation providing for the sale of mineral lands at public auction. Julian, supported by the secretary of the treasury, argued that the proceeds would help retire the debt incurred by the Civil War and that orderly sale by the federal government would best promote permanent settlement. There also was considerable agitation for a 3 percent or 5 percent federal tax on the proceeds of mining operations.[24]

Stewart was able to fend off those proposals with his personal qualities, firsthand knowledge of the gold fields, eloquence, and wonderfully Byzantine parliamentary maneuvering. Among other things, Stewart was able to bypass Julian's mining committee in the House by striking the entire text and inserting his provisions on mining, in a bill entitled "An Act Granting the Right of Way to Ditch and Canal Owners Over the Public Lands, and Other Purposes," which became the official title of the Mining Law of 1866. Instead of the easterners' provisions, he passionately and successfully argued for "the miner's law":

> The Legislature of California . . . in 1851 . . . after full and careful investigation wisely concluded to declare that the rules and regulations of the miners themselves might be offered in evidence in all controversies respecting mining claims, and when not in conflict with the constitution or laws of the State or of the United States should govern the decision of the action. A series of wise judicial decisions molded these regulations and customs into a comprehensive system of common law. . . . The same system has spread over all the interior States and Territories where mines have been found as far east as the Missouri river. The miner's law is a part of the miner's nature. He made it. It is his own bantling, and he loves it, trusts it, and obeys it. He has given the honest toil of his life to discover wealth which when found is protected by no higher law than that enacted by himself under the implied sanction of a just and generous Government.[25]

The 1866 act applied to lode, not placer, claims and covered only gold, silver, cinnabar, and copper. Yet Clyde Martz, the eminent Denver natural resource lawyer and scholar, has aptly described the law as "the miner's Magna Carta." First, it removed all doubts as to the status of miners as trespassers by ratifying past entries and by announcing the rallying cry that in the future, "the mineral lands of the public domain, both surveyed and unsurveyed, are hereby declared to be free and open to exploration and occupation by all citizens. . . ." Almost incredibly by today's standards, the 1866 act zoned a billion acres—nearly all of the American West—for mining of lode deposits. Placer deposits would be added four years later.[26]

Second, the 1866 act may have been a federal statute, but it was in large part an empty vessel to be filled by state law and local custom: mining would proceed "subject . . . to the local customs or rules of miners in the several mining districts," when not in conflict with the scant body of federal law. Third, a miner who had expended $1000 in labor and improvements was entitled to purchase, at the rate of $5 per acre, a patent (the terminology for a deed of public land or minerals from the United States) to the lode or vein and the surface overlying it. Thus, miners obtained the desired security: they could enter and mine at will and, if they made a discovery, obtain title to the deposit.

The principles of the 1866 act were extended to placer deposits in 1870. The General Mining Law was then passed on May 10, 1872. The act did not depart from the essential principles of the 1866 and 1870 laws, but even though Congressman Aaron Sargent of California assured his colleagues that "[t]his bill simply oils the machinery a little," the General Mining Law of 1872 supplemented the workings of the earlier laws in several respects. Western lawmakers were now firmly in the driver's seat—the legislative discussions are replete with statements by easterners who disclaimed any expertise on this body of western law and policy. The 1872 act was a faithful reflection of the needs of the western mining industry. One writer, comparing England's mining advance into British Columbia with early American procedures in Idaho, Montana, Oregon, and eastern Washington, captured the essence of United States mining policy by contrasting it with the British system:

> [W]e see, on the one hand, [British] government concentrated largely in the hands of an efficient executive, who made laws and organized administration on summary methods; on the other, [American] representative government, under hampering conditions, working tardily and painfully towards order, and meeting local or occasional reinforcement. Under the former society was from the first under control, and there was a tendency to restrain individuals for the benefit of society—a restraint at times verging to over repression; under the latter individualism was feebly controlled from above, but had to generate within itself forces of order, and it tended to undue license hurtful to society. The American system developed a country the more swiftly, the British the more safely.[27]

The Machinery of the Hardrock Law

The 1872 act remains on the books almost exactly as originally written. It may be helpful to summarize the essentials of hardrock mining law. After that general description, I will turn to the ways in which the law has been modified by events outside of the text of the law, the various problems that the law causes today, and the proposals for reform.[28]

The Hardrock Act provides that the federal public lands are "free and open" to mineral exploration. This right of free access, or self-initiation, should be thought of as Article I of the "miner's Magna Carta." As discussed in more detail later, this prerogative no longer applies to all federal acres—some lands have been withdrawn by presidents or Congress and set aside for special purposes, such as military bases or recreation lands, thought to be inconsistent with mineral development. But some 400 million acres, well more than half of the public lands, including most national forests, remain open for mining today. The statute requires no permit, lease, or other form of federal approval prior to entry. It is up to hardrock miners to decide whether an area should be mined. The miners, pick-and-shovel and corporate, have a "right to mine."

The 1872 act, which multiplied several times over the 1866 act's listing of covered minerals, applies to "all valuable mineral deposits." Congress has since removed several classes of minerals from the sweeping terms of the original law. Most fuel minerals (such as oil, gas, oil shale, and coal, but not uranium), commonly occurring fertilizer minerals (such as sodium, sulfur, and phosphates), and "common varieties" (such as ordinary gravel, sand, and cinders) have been placed under systems calling for lease or sale. Nevertheless, dozens of minerals are subject to the right of self-initiation guaranteed by the 1872 act: the major hardrock minerals include gold, silver, uranium, copper, molybdenum, iron, lead, aluminum, and the gemstones.

The 1872 law, of course, kept in place the deference to state and local law. It provided generally that hardrock miners would proceed "according to the local customs or rules of miners in the several mining districts, so far as the same are applicable and not inconsistent with the laws of the United States." Several other provisions made reference to the applicability of state and territorial law on the federal mineral lands.[29]

State and federal courts came to recognize certain rights of miners while prospecting, before a strike is made. During this period, a miner is protected by the doctrine of *pedis possessio*, which gives a miner exclusive possession of the ground in the area where the prospecting is being conducted. It allows a miner "room for work and to prevent probable breaches of the peace."[30]

Miners commonly make a location, which must "be distinctly marked on the ground so that its boundaries can be readily traced," when they begin exploration. Although the act provides that "no location of a mining-claim shall be made" until a valuable mineral is actively discovered, the courts have upheld prediscovery locations on the pragmatic ground that such a practice sets with some precision the extent of *pedis possessio* rights. Thus, early location—"staking a claim"—can prevent disputes over the area subject to exclusive prospecting rights of the miner first to begin work.[31]

Importantly, although *pedis possessio* rights protect a miner from other miners, they do not comprise constitutionally vested property rights as against the United States. The federal government, therefore, can unilaterally terminate the tenure of a miner in the exploration process without being required to pay any compensation to the miner. Thus, for example, Congress can place an area within a national park or wilderness area and prohibit mining without incurring any financial obligation to prospecting miners who have not yet made strikes.

All of these rules change in fundamental and remarkable ways when exploration rights mature into an unpatented mining claim at the moment a discovery of a valuable hardrock mineral is made. This bears careful attention, since the creation of an unpatented mining claim is the heart of the Hardrock Mining Act and one of the crucial aspects of property law in the American West.

The discovery of a valuable hardrock mineral—I will return to the definition of discovery shortly—transmutes the fragile *pedis possessio* prerogative into a sturdy vested property right, good against the United States and all other users. Each unpatented mining claim is 20 acres in size, except that as many as eight individuals may join together to form an "association" claim, which can total 160 acres. There is no limit to the number of claims a miner can obtain.[32]

An unpatented mining claim gives the miner, in the words of the 1872 act, "the exclusive right of possession and enjoyment of all the surface included within the lines of their locations." The courts have underscored the breadth of this unique real property interest:

> The law is well settled by innumerable decisions that when a mining claim has been perfected under the law, it is in effect a grant from the United States of the exclusive right of possession to the same. It constitutes property to its fullest extent, and is real property subject to be sold, transferred, mortgaged, taxed, and inherited without infringing any right or title of the United States.[33]

The miner can use the property fully so long as the activities are "reasonably incident to mining." This includes constructing a home, cutting timber, grazing cattle, and diverting water. The rights inherent in an unpatented mining claim do not properly include, as enterprising miners have found, the operation of hotels, saloons, or brothels.[34]

I said earlier that an unpatented mining claim, a constitutionally protected property right, is created "at the moment" a miner makes "a discovery." Appreciate the full beauty of this legerdemain. Discovery is almost

necessarily a solitary, anonymous event unattended by any formal recording or evaluation procedures. A lone miner makes a find, whether in an
Arizona back canyon or in Alaskan bush, and precarious *pedis possessio*
instantaneously becomes an unpatented mining claim. Just as important, a
miner can *say* that a find has been made and tie up the land as against other
miners, public users, and the United States. In actual practice, therefore, the
initial pounding of stakes in the ground, whether or not a valid discovery has
been made, often becomes the critical event. Bare locations, merely *pedis
possessio* as a matter of law, are customarily referred to as "unpatented
mining claims." On the ground, the stakes—and the fences and "no trespassing" signs that regularly accompany them—often take precedence over
the legal requirement of a discovery. "Don't tread on me."

Still, legally recognized vested property rights depend on a valid discovery. The Interior Department has traditionally been, as leading analyst
John Leshy puts it, "tender" toward hardrock miners in the administration
of the 1872 act. In the late nineteenth century, the Interior Department
developed the so-called prudent person test to determine whether the
magic moment of discovery had been reached. Under this test, a valuable
mineral deposit has been discovered if "a person of ordinary prudence
would be justified in the further expenditure of his labor and means, with
reasonable prospect of success in developing a valuable mine." In other
words, a miner has made a discovery if there is a reasonable prospect of
future success. This version of the "prudent person" test thus called for
subjective judgments as to future events. Miners tend to be optimists,
especially in formal judicial proceedings.[35]

Policy took a new turn in 1962 under the direction of Frank J. Barry,
Secretary of the Interior Stewart Udall's choice as solicitor, the Department
of the Interior's top lawyer. Barry, a fiery man who ardently believed in
revamping the mining laws, concluded that the prudent person test was still
in force but that it included a new element—present marketability. Under
the marketability standard, a miner had to prove a new and objective fact:
that the hardrock minerals could be mined and sold at a profit under
current market conditions.

The United States Supreme Court upheld Barry's interpretation in the
1968 *Coleman* case, which remains the leading word on the definition of
discovery and which illustrates many of the recurring problems in the
administration of the Hardrock Act of 1872. Alfred Coleman, who was
even more brazen than our midwestern schoolteacher near Stanley, Idaho,
argued that he had 720 acres of valid claims in the Angeles National Forest
in California. He based his supposed mining claims on a discovery of
quartzite. As the Supreme Court correctly put it, quartzite is "one of the
most common of all solid materials." You are likely to trip on it on an

average hike. Not coincidentally, one suspects, Coleman's home had been built near Big Bear Lake, a popular resort area "in a highly scenic national forest located two hours from Los Angeles." The Court approved Solicitor Barry's finding that no discovery can be made unless the deposit is currently marketable at a profit. The Forest Service removed Coleman from the property, an act that Coleman's lawyer pronounced to be "very high-handed and unAmerican."[36]

There is still plenty of room for miners, even of the Coleman genre, to prove a discovery. The miner need not actually take the ore to market. The only requirement is that it *could* be marketed at a profit. If it could be, a discovery has been made. A reminder of the difficulty of administrative oversight: there are 1.1 million alleged unpatented mining claims, 25 million acres in all, scattered across the West, and the Bureau of Land Management receives 90,000 new claims each year.[37]

It is not hard to keep this extraordinary property right alive. To protect an unpatented mining claim, the 1872 act requires a miner to locate the claim and conduct annual "assessment work"; in addition, since 1976, miners must also file annual reports with the Bureau of Land Management. The first requirement, location, may well have been completed by the time of a discovery: as noted earlier, miners usually stake out their claims on the ground at the time of initial entry in order to gain *pedis possessio* protection during prospecting. If not, the miner must then stake the claim and file documents with the county recorder. This routine task proceeds according to particulars set by state law, which are minimal. The federal filing requirement involves filling out a one-page form.[38]

The act's provision for annual assessment work raises a number of policy issues. The 1872 act attempted to embody the prevailing rule in the mining districts that claims must be worked diligently or suffer forfeiture. The statute set the rule that in order to keep an unpatented claim alive, "not less than $100 worth of labor shall be performed or improvements made during each year." In 1872, $100 worth of assessment work was a substantial undertaking: wages at the time were $.20 per hour, so the statutory requirement called for nearly two months' solid labor.[39]

Today, of course, the $100 standard is laughable. I know of three adjacent claims in California—which happen to lie astride a 2-mile stretch of fine trout stream—that are kept alive solely by an annual Fourth of July "work day," complete with several sticks of dynamite and perhaps rental of a Caterpillar tractor for a joyride. The requirement begs, and receives, widespread fraud: federal agencies can hardly take the time to disprove a notarized affidavit alleging a day or two's work, perhaps coupled with a bulldozer scrape or the purchase of a shovel.

There are powerful consequences for public land and minerals when miners claim a discovery, make a location, perform the annual assessment work, and file the documents with the county recorder and the BLM.

After a discovery, serious miners—the American Barricks and hundreds of other large and midsize companies—have their "right to mine," the near-absolute right to remove the minerals under the claims. They need make no payment to the United States. Indeed, if the United States wants to put the unpatented mining claim to another use, the federal government must compensate the claimant for the value of the minerals and the land.

Fraudulent entrants, and small miners with marginal claims, have tremendous inertia on their side after an asserted discovery. They can hold their claims, and usually can reside there, until the BLM successfully contests their claim in a formal administrative proceeding. Numerous stalling tactics are available. As one Forest Service mining officer told me in frustration: "I say 'take me to your discovery.' He does. I come in with a bulldozer, cut a trench, remove some minerals and get them assayed. They don't pan out and I notify the claimant. He says we should have taken samples further up the hill. And so on it goes. I have spent 10 or 12 years removing some of these guys." The government must pursue a $10,000 administrative proceeding, and possibly a subsequent court challenge, during which time the claimant is usually allowed to remain on the land.[40]

Furthermore, a claimant is not always thwarted even when the government wins a contest proceeding. If the land is still open for mining, the 1872 act entitles the miner to reenter the claim, thus instituting the entire process once again. To be sure, the BLM sometimes prohibits reentry by an administrative withdrawal of the land during the initial contest, but the Interior Department is understandably reluctant to withdraw lands in regions where minerals might possibly be present. For understaffed federal land agencies, it is like killing flies with a pencil eraser.

Holders of unpatented mining claims are not required to obtain full title to the land and minerals through the patent process, but the option is open to them. A miner who has made a discovery and put in $500 worth of assessment work in labor or improvements can acquire a patent. (The federal government has always used the term "patent" to describe the legal document transferring land out of public ownership: a patent has exactly the same meaning and function as a deed.) The fee is $5.00 per acre for lode claims, $2.50 per acre for placer claims. A miner who can "prove up" the claim receives not just the subsurface mineral estate but the overlying 20 acres of land, 160 acres for association claims. As is the case with unpatented claims, there is no limit on the number of patents per individual or company. A miner obtaining a patent is also entitled to an additional 5 acres of nonmineral land for use as a mill site.[41]

The issuance of patents has slowed since the 1920s and 1930s due to increased administrative scrutiny. In all, the government has issued about 65,000 mining patents, totaling nearly 3 million acres, but fewer patents have been obtained in recent years. The amount of patenting, however, is still significant: in 1990, the BLM issued 448 patents covering 7324 acres.[42]

The fraudulent claimant, of course, will virtually never go to patent. Filing would simply generate a protest and disturb the *status quo*. Even serious miners often have little incentive to seek a patent. Granted, full title has advantages because it eliminates most regulation by federal agencies, provides somewhat greater security, and in some cases may establish ownership to valuable nonmineral resources such as timber. Still, there are legal and expert witness fees (and perhaps risk) attendant to the patent proceeding. State property taxes will surely increase, and there may be zoning and regulatory disadvantages. For claimants of all ilk, the unpatented claim affords enough advantages that there is little call to rock the boat.

The final distinctive quality of the General Mining Law is its utter lack of any provision for environmental protection. The lands and waters have paid dearly, and the legacy continues long after mines have been abandoned. Approximately 50 billion tons of mining and processing waste have been left behind at mining sites. At highest risk are waters—rivers, lakes, and aquifers. A U.S. Bureau of Mines researcher estimates that 12,000 miles of rivers and streams and 180,000 acres of lakes and reservoirs have been adversely affected. The Western Interstate Energy Board has found that 1298 river miles in Colorado alone have been contaminated by mining wastes. Among the fifty mining sites included on the EPA's highest-priority list of hazardous waste sites is the largest Superfund site in the country, resulting from several large mines near the headwaters of the Clark Fork River basin in western Montana, where copper mining began in 1879 and continues today. The listed area covers the entire river, 120 miles long, and its floodplain from Butte to Missoula.[43]

The most prominent way in which wastes have polluted surface waters and groundwaters is through acid mine drainage. This process begins when minerals common in mining wastes—usually pyrite or other metal sulfide ores—combine with oxygen-rich water to form sulfuric acid. In addition to being highly corrosive, the acid can dissolve heavy metals such as lead, zinc, cadmium, and copper that are left in tailings piles or exposed through excavation. The solution flushes downstream, following the regular flow of the watercourse. When acid mine drainage is substantial, aquatic life virtually disappears and the river bottom becomes covered with a layer of reddish slime that often contains heavy metals. Acid mine drainage water can be 20 to 300 times more acidic than acid rain. The copper, gold, and silver industries, all prominent in the West, have the highest potential for creating substantial acid mine drainage. The Mining Waste Study Team of the University of California, Berkeley, explains one modern manifestation of the "right to mine," the idea embedded in old federal law that miners ought to be able to do as they see fit:

> Frequently, the surface waters several miles downstream of an abandoned mine discharging AMD [acid mine drainage] are totally devoid of higher forms of life. Beyond this vicinity, usually within ten miles, dilution of the drainage and precipitation of the [heavy] metals takes place. Downstream of this point the aquatic life is subject to chronic toxicity (that is relatively low concentrations of toxic metals over long periods of time). There is evidence that some organisms have adapted to this environment. However, massive sudden discharges sometimes take place, as might occur if a holding pond for AMD spills over into a river, and cause acute toxicity (that is, the effects occur over a short time period) and often result in fish kills.[44]

Reforms at the Edges

Those are the classic, unvarnished principles that have dominated mining for metals on the public lands since Senator Stewart's time. Nevertheless, various movements have softened the 1872 act as it was originally written. The primary developments are the transfer of some minerals from the "right to mine" regime to systems based on leases and sales; the removal of some land from the operation of the 1872 law; and the rise of administrative regulation to diminish some of the adverse environmental effects resulting from the policy of free access. These movements have all responded to changing public demands for varied uses of public lands and resources. Much of the public estate is still zoned for mineral development, but not all of it.

The most significant inroad on the 1872 act has been the removal of various minerals from the coverage of the Hardrock Act. The principal statute is the Mineral Leasing Act of 1920, dealing with the fuel and fertilizer minerals. Since leasing is an approach that is sometimes suggested when reform of hardrock mining is raised, it may be helpful to look at mineral leasing first.

The 1872 act was so broad—encompassing "all valuable mineral deposits"—that it covered a range of minerals that did not much fit the commonly used term "hardrock." Coal had been made subject to sale at public auction by statutes of 1864 and 1873, but nothing exempted oil from the coverage of the 1872 act. In 1897, Congress passed the Oil Placer Act, which confirmed the status of oil, gas, and oil shales as within the scope of the Hardrock Act. Those minerals, then, were subject to free and open mining—and to the vesting of absolute rights on discovery—without federal controls.⁴⁵

The demand for energy fuels boomed at the turn of the century. Industrial needs steadily increased. The gasoline car came into vogue in the 1890s, and production of the Model T began in 1907. The United States became a world power with growing military obligations. Western coal production rose from 2 million tons in 1873, the year of the most recent federal coal law, to 58 million tons in 1912. Even more dramatically, oil production in the public-land states jumped from 2 million barrels in 1897, when Congress confirmed oil and gas as being covered by the 1872 law, to 141 million barrels in 1912.⁴⁶

Theodore Roosevelt became president in 1901, and natural resource policy quickly became a principal concern of his administration. The rallying cry was conservation, by which was meant the reliance on expert planning to achieve efficient resource development; the avoidance of waste; and the safekeeping under federal stewardship of sufficient timber, mineral, and water resources so that products would be available for use by future generations. Roosevelt grew concerned about reports that large deposits of coal were being obtained not under the coal sale laws but by homesteaders and stock-raisers taking title to surface lands for agricultural purposes—and, not coincidentally in those days of widespread abuse of public land laws, to subsurface coal as well.⁴⁷

In 1906, Roosevelt withdrew from all forms of entry 66 million acres of known coal deposits, calling for conservation of federal coal through leasing. (A withdrawal, which amounts to a zoning requirement, prohibits some or all uses of designated federal public lands. Congress and the executive branch have used withdrawals, many of which have been highly controversial, to limit activities on the public domain, which was traditionally left open to entry for homesteading, mining, and many other uses. Withdrawals have been employed most often to close land areas to homesteading and mining, but lands have regularly been withdrawn from other uses as well.) Robert Nelson put Roosevelt's coal withdrawals in this larger context:

> [T]he conservation movement was itself a central part of the broader progressive movement. Progressivism arose from a wide discontent with many results of an unfettered individualism in nineteenth-century America, sanctioned under the free-market principles of classical liberalism. The classical liberal ideology offered a vision of rapid social and economic progress, wide individual opportunity for all, and wide personal liberty. . . . Nevertheless, . . . a crisis of confidence . . . had developed by the turn of the century. . . .
>
> In these circumstances Americans saw a necessity to turn to government to bring greater control over the new order.⁴⁸

All of these tensions were magnified with federal oil and gas reserves. Because oil and gas fell within the ambit of the 1872 act, companies were entitled to enter and obtain full title to vast basins of petroleum. If the United States needed the reserves (for example, for military purposes), the federal government would have to buy back the oil and gas even if it had not been extracted: under the Hardrock Act, title to all of the deposit would have passed to the companies at the moment a discovery had been made. These were hardly hypothetical fears, for then, as now, energy companies were nothing if not efficient. Indeed, as the director of the Geological Survey reported in September 1909, at the current rate of discovery activity on oil lands in California, "it would 'be impossible for the people of the United States to continue ownership of oil lands for more than a few months. After that the Government will be obliged to re-purchase the very oil that it has practically given away.' "[49]

President Taft acted immediately and withdrew from oil and gas development more than 3 million acres of public land in California and Wyoming. The move, coupled with a call for a leasing system for fuel minerals, drew a hail of controversy. One of the more temperate comments was made by Utah governor William Spry, who believed that any supposed shortages could best be resolved by private industry, not by federal action:

I have absolutely no sympathy for the bugaboo of mineral exhaustion. No man or set of men will assume to estimate the mineral deposits of this nation. Not until the surface of the entire United States has been honey-combed by the prospector and miner will any thoughtful man attempt to approximate the mineral resources of the nation, and then no man will have the temerity to fix a limit to which the sciences may go in discovering new processes of extracting and making useful the mineral deposits of Mother Earth.[50]

The legal attack on Taft's set-asides was based on the argument that the president had no constitutional authority to make unilateral withdrawals. Oil companies—which, after the Taft withdrawals, had continued to enter oil and gas fields and make locations that would be valid if the presidential withdrawals were voided by the courts—argued that Article IV of the Constitution lodged in Congress, not in the presidency, the power to "make all needful Rules and Regulations" respecting the public lands. The Supreme Court heard the issues in 1915 in the momentous *Midwest Oil* case. The Court acknowledged that Congress had primary authority on the federal lands. Nevertheless, the legislative branch had "impliedly acquiesced" in unilateral executive withdrawals because more than 200 presidential withdrawals of various kinds had been made over the course of eighty years and Congress had never objected. The Court, paraphrasing the maxim that necessity is the mother of invention, commented that "government is a practical affair intended for practical men." The Taft withdrawals stood.[51]

World War I and the complexity and emotionalism of hardrock reform delayed the enactment of a mineral leasing system. Dire predictions from western politicians abounded during the deliberation process. A few western congressmen, moved in part by the heavy weight of the continuing withdrawals, grudgingly swung over. One acknowledged that although the 1872 act remained desirable for gold, silver, and copper, "the system admittedly has broken down" with respect to oil and gas. Another, perhaps representing western sentiment more accurately, allowed that "I may hold my nose and vote for it." Eventually, on February 20, 1920, the Mineral Leasing Act, the first significant mining revision in half a century, was signed into law. Coal, oil and gas, oil shale, phosphate, and sodium were placed under the new leasing regime. Other fertilizers and geothermal energy were added later.[52]

The mineral leasing system, the major contrasting model for the self-initiation and patent approach taken in the 1872 act, has numerous special and technical provisions that apply to some leasable minerals and not others. But the following are the main features of leasing that distinguish it from the Hardrock Act:

1. There is no "right to mine." Permission must be obtained from the federal government to prospect or mine.

2. The United States receives an economic return in the form of royalties, rents, and bonus payments. Examples of royalties are 12.5 percent to 25 percent for oil and gas, depending on the amount of production; at least 12 percent for surface-mined coal; and 10 percent to 15 percent for geothermal steam. A bonus is also included in the bid, and leases are usually issued to the qualified bidder with the highest bonus bid, since the royalty is usually fixed by the BLM in advance.

3. The United States has discretion to decide which, if any, competitive bidder may proceed.

4. Each lease is for a fixed term—for example, five years for most oil and gas leases and twenty years for most coal leases. Usually, leases can be renewed if the miner is producing minerals in paying quantities.

5. The United States can require reasonably prompt development of the resource through lease provisions providing for cancellation if a lessee does not proceed with due diligence.

6. Provisions can be and are included in the lease to protect other,

competing resources and the environment. Thus, federal officials often set construction standards and prescribe access routes for roads, a principal cause of erosion and disruption of wildlife habitat. In some instances, helicopter access has been required. Highly specialized conditions can be imposed, such as the "winter access only" provision in some Alaska leases to protect the delicate tundra environment during the summer months. Reclamation (restoration of the mined-over area to a natural-looking condition) is required of lessees when the operation is completed.[53]

The leasing approach, then, was spawned by a crisis due to overextraction of public resources. It is premised on a fair monetary return to the United States and has evolved to include protections for the environment. The potential danger, of course, is that an inflexible bureaucracy could stifle necessary mineral production, since the government, not industry, makes the basic decision of whether, and on what terms, prospecting and mining will proceed. As such, the Mineral Leasing Act of 1920 has the same broad characteristics as the English system in British Columbia, discussed briefly above: there is "a tendency to restrain individuals for the benefit of society," and mining proceeds less swiftly but "more safely."[54]

The second broad area of reform in hardrock mining, already suggested, has been the withdrawal of substantial areas of public land from entry under the 1872 act.

The crosscurrents of history and public policy are no better evidenced than by the irony that the Hardrock Act—such a vivid emblem of the laissez-faire philosophy dominant in the nineteenth-century American West—was preceded by the space of just two months by the passage of the Yellowstone Park Act on March 1, 1872. Congress set aside the expanse in what is now Wyoming, Idaho, and Montana by declaring that the area was "hereby reserved and withdrawn from settlement, occupancy, or sale under the laws of the United States, and dedicated and set apart as a public park or pleasuring-ground for the benefit and enjoyment of the people. . . ." The "pleasuring-ground" of Yellowstone became the first national park, not just in the United States but in the world.[55]

Over the course of the succeeding century, many other areas of public lands were withdrawn from mining. Withdrawals for purposes of preservation proceeded fitfully for several decades after Yellowstone. Yosemite National Park was created in 1891. Theodore Roosevelt, employing authority entirely questionable at the time, established the first wildlife refuge at 5-acre Pelican Island off the coast of Florida in 1903. The action was taken to protect, of all things, birds. The withdrawal of Pelican Island did not directly threaten mining, but westerners knew a dangerous thing when they saw it. One legislator pronounced the president's action "the fad of game preservation run stark raving mad." In 1906, Congress passed the Antiquities Act, allowing the president to set aside areas in order to protect landmarks, structures, and "other objects of historic or scientific interest." The legislative history suggests that a cautious Congress intended only small withdrawals—roughly one section (640 acres) or less—but presidents beginning with Theodore Roosevelt began setting aside "national monuments" such as the Grand Canyon (271,145 acres), Death Valley (1,601,800 acres), and Katmai (1,088,000 acres) and Glacier Bay (1,164,000) in Alaska. These were later included in the National Park System, within which mining is generally prohibited.[56]

Congress did not stand by—it too began to make withdrawals for preservation, where hardrock mining was usually disallowed. The Roosevelt wildlife refuges were followed by congressionally created refuges. The National Park Service Organic Act of 1916 provided a policy umbrella for the wondrous regions that had already been declared—places such as Glacier and Rocky Mountain national parks, in addition to Yellowstone and Yosemite—as well as the many national parks that would be reserved in the future.[57]

The preservation withdrawals moved into a new dimension when Congress established the world's first legislatively sanctioned wilderness system with the passage of the Wilderness Act of 1964. Official wilderness initially amounted to just 9.1 million acres but has burgeoned—assisted mightily by the Alaska National Interest Lands Conservation Act of 1980, which designated 56.4 million acres as wilderness—to a national total of 95 million acres. Wilderness designation is now attached to 4.2 percent of all land in the country; 15.7 percent of all land in Alaska; 2.0 percent of all land in the lower 48 states; and 15.2 percent of all federal public lands. In ways discussed in more detail below, location of new hardrock claims in wilderness areas was prohibited as of January 1, 1984, and mining of preexisting claims can continue only under tight restrictions.[58]

Land has been removed from the purview of the General Mining Law for many purposes other than preservation. Indian reservations, where mineral leasing is in force under federal and tribal authority, have been established for 53 million acres. Military reservations include 23 million acres of land closed to mining. Various water and power projects have withdrawn 12.7 million acres. Over the years, executive officials have made literally thousands of withdrawals for scores of purposes.

There are no exact numbers on total federal acreage subject to withdrawals from mining. The records have not been consolidated. There are definitional problems: withdrawals include not only absolute bars to mining but also a range of restrictions that deter, but do not prohibit, mining and are difficult to classify neatly. Further, the ground is shifting: total public-land holdings are being altered as the state of Alaska and Alaskan natives select the more than 140 million acres of public land in Alaska to which they are entitled; in 1976, Congress ordered the Interior Department to review all withdrawals, so rescissions continue as withdrawals are reevaluated.[59]

Of one thing there is no doubt: the mining industry believes that the total quantum of withdrawn land is irresponsibly large. In 1975, in an article titled "Is Our Account Overdrawn?" two BLM employees argued that 73 percent of all public lands were unavailable to hardrock mining, that "[l]ands which have been put off limits to mineral exploration can no longer be considered as assets in our account." J. Allen Overton, president of the American Mining Congress, proclaimed that "[i]n magnitude, this is equivalent to putting a fence around every state east of the Mississippi except Maine and posting a sign: Progress Keep Out!"[60]

A later study by the congressional Office of Technology Assessment drew different conclusions. Leaving aside the especially complicated situation in Alaska, the OTA found that 15.7 percent of all public lands were "closed" to hardrock mining, 6.1 percent were "highly restricted," and 44 percent had "slight or moderate" restrictions. Regardless of whose statistics, if any, are accurate in this elusive area, there is no question that the geographic sweep of hardrock mining has been cut back considerably since Senator Stewart drafted the miner's law. Whether the reduction is characterized as an appropriate response to shifting values or as an overly zealous and shortsighted crimping of miners' prerogatives, or as some of both, there is no doubt that the reduction is in place and that it will be difficult for industry to dislodge it substantially.[61]

In addition to removing acreage and specified minerals from the scope of the Hardrock Act, Congress and the federal land agencies have adopted programs giving the environment some protection in areas where hardrock mining occurs. In 1955, Congress adopted the Surface Resources Act as an attempt to curtail fraudulent unpatented claims. First, the act allows federal agencies to make use of the surface of claims for other purposes, such as timber harvesting, grazing, and access routes to other public lands. The House report set out the reasons for the corrective action: "The fraudulent locator in national forests, in addition to obstructing orderly management and the competitive sale of timber, obtains for himself high-value, publicly owned, surface resources bearing no relationship to legitimate mining activity." Second, the Surface Resources Act was an attempt to get at the problem of would-be miners who blocked recreational access to their claims: "[A] group of fisherman-prospectors will locate a good stream, stake out successive mining claims flanking the stream, post their mining claims with 'No trespassing' signs, and proceed to enjoy their own private fishing camp." The 1955 act was another road sign that the mining law should accommodate multiple-use considerations, but it has not resulted in fundamental reform. In spite of the 1955 act, "recreational mines" continue to be a bane to sound land management. The act did not disturb the miner's right to land, as well as minerals, and therefore left inertia on the side of those who would abuse the privilege of mining public minerals.[62]

Another limited congressional venture into hardrock reform took place in 1976, with the Federal Land Policy and Management Act (the hapless acronym, FLPMA, is pronounced "Flip-ma"). Restrictions were placed on mining in roadless areas being studied by the BLM for their potential wilderness value. FLPMA also required recordation of hardrock mining claims—the filing of location information for all claims, including existing ones, and an affidavit stating that the annual assessment work totaling $100 has been done. The filing requirements, which, if not met, call for forfeiture of claims, provide for the first time information on which federal agencies can base inventories of mining claims on federal lands. Even though the FLPMA provisions did no more than require perfunctory filings, mostly duplicative of documentation already required by state statutes, mining lawyers made an all-out attack on the provisions, arguing that they were unconstitutional. A federal appeals court, however, found that the "[n]ames, addresses, and the other information that the challenged regulations require of those making filings . . . do not constitute the regulatory horrible that [the mining companies] attempt to vivify," and the Supreme Court upheld the filing requirements.[63]

A more notable series of events in mining law reform involves the attempts of the Forest Service, and later the BLM, to regulate hardrock mining activities directly.

As late as the 1960s and early 1970s, most hardrock mining went entirely unregulated. Forest Service authority arguably could be found in its 1897 Organic Act, which does not mention regulation of mining but gives the agency broad authority to "regulate . . . occupancy and use" within the forests. In addition, the General Mining Law itself provides that mining must proceed "under regulations prescribed by law," although the potential authority had never been exercised. Any regulation of mining by the Forest Service, however, was clouded by the agency's location in the Department of Agriculture and by the statutory designation of the BLM, in the Department of the Interior, as the administering agency for mining laws on all public lands, including the national forests. This did not deter conservationists from pressing the Forest Service to take action. More fundamentally, the nation's oldest federal land agency had come to view the unparalleled autonomy of hardrock miners as an impediment to orderly land management and was ready to act.[64]

In 1970, the Forest Service began working on mining regulations. The draft proposal—which, with a bow to politics and the Interior Department's authority to regulate mining, was couched in terms of regulating "the surface of [the] National Forest System lands," not minerals—was released for public comment in December 1973. Predictably, industry came up in arms, but the final regulations, effective in September 1974, were largely unchanged from the initial proposal. In general, the regulations require a miner to give notice to the agency before beginning any mining operation that could disturb surface resources. If the disturbance is "significant," the miner must file a "plan of operations," which must receive agency approval; while approval is pending, work may continue under agency guidelines "to minimize adverse environmental impacts." Reclamation is required after mining is completed. There are no provisions for fines or shutdown of mines in noncompliance.[65]

The Forest Service's action in this historically sensitive area, relatively modest though it may be, took institutional courage. Those regulations, however, apply only in the national forests, less than a third of the public lands open for mining. The Bureau of Land Management, which is responsible for mining on the more than 270 million acres under its jurisdiction, took seven years longer to act, expressing concern about its limited discretion under the Hardrock Act and about any provisions that might be unduly burdensome on small miners. The resulting BLM regulations, adopted in 1981, are even more lax than the Forest Service program. Most notably, mining operations disturbing fewer than 5 acres are effectively outside of the regulations—operators need only give notice to the BLM that they are going ahead with mining. These "notice" mines comprise 80 percent of all mines on BLM lands, and many of them hardly qualify as small: with a bulldozer operation, you can rearrange a very large amount of earth on 5 acres. For mines larger than 5 acres, operators must file a plan of operations, but the requirements for posting of bonds and for reclamation of mined-over land are vague. As with the Forest Service regulations, there are no provisions for fines or penalties or for shutdown of noncomplying operations.[66]

The 1872 Act at Work Today

These are the primary reform measures relating to the General Mining Law of 1872. The reform effort has been a cut-and-paste process, with virtually no changes to the act itself. Numerous environmental, land management, and economic problems continue to attend hardrock mining. The following discussion treats the current state of the hardrock mining system—still the miner's law—built on open access, free minerals, unlimited tenure, and rights to land as well as minerals.

Fraudulent occupancy and residency of public lands by supposed miners is less serious than it was, say, twenty-five years ago, but it remains a persistent and time-consuming problem. There are an estimated 3000 disputed structures on Forest Service and BLM lands in the western states, excluding Alaska, where there are uncounted thousands more. Illegal conduct in the mid-1980s was less open and notorious than that in the early twentieth century, when Ralph Cameron located a series of claims on the South Rim of the Grand Canyon, astride the Bright Angel Trail. Cameron, a United States senator from Arizona, built a hotel on the claims and charged tolls to hikers and guides wishing to use the popular trail leading down to the canyon floor. It took a series of legal actions stretching out over three decades to evict him. Then there was the ambitious and creative charlatan Merle Zweifel, who located paper claims across the West during the 1960s and 1970s. Among many other things, he was willing to file affidavits alleging that his aerial claim-staking service had located as many as 2000 claims per day. John Leshy described Zweifel's exploits in this fashion:

> Until his flamboyance, greed, and disarming candor about the game he was playing attracted so much attention that he could no longer be tolerated, the "old prospector," as he styled himself, filed mining claims on millions of acres of federal land all over the West. (He himself put the figure at 30 million acres, which included an unspecified amount of land claimed on the outer continental shelf.) When Congress authorized the Central Arizona Project in 1968, part of which required construction of an aqueduct from the Colorado River to Phoenix and Tucson, the old prospector was there, filing claims on 600,000 acres along the aqueduct route. When interest in oil shale development began to revive on Colorado's west slope after 1960, Zweifel surfaced with 465,000 acres of mining claims in the Piceance Basin. Acknowledging that he would never actively explore the land (because that would damage the scenery, he said) he exploited the Law's offer of free access to the federal lands with a vengeance, though the character of his claims reflected the German meaning of his name—doubt. His "real goal in life," he was reported as saying, was to "discredit bureaucrats and their hypocritical ways," though he also admitted that fighting large companies "is an enjoyment I can't pass up," and that—at last—"I do have a lust for money."[67]

There is no one on the scene today with quite the flair of Cameron or Zweifel, but there are still shenanigans—as evidenced by a continuing spate of occupancies by vacationers from the snowy East on BLM lands near the outskirts of Phoenix and Tucson during winter months. In addition, federal officials must wage a continuing backwoods campaign against widely scattered professional people, drifters, and eccentric miners who seek seasonal residence on isolated, scenic public property. The midwestern schoolteacher is finally evicted from the bogus claim near Stanley, Idaho; an occupant is moved out of a cabin in Oak Ravine, upstream from Belden in the Plumas National Forest in California, after a lengthy legal battle; clusters of occupants hole up in outposts like Galice Creek in southwestern Oregon and let the administrative machinery grind slowly along before moving on to some other canyon. They typically bluff the public off their "property," or, as happened recently in northern Idaho, exact a fee from campers. This is, of course, multiplied thousands of times over.[68]

The right of free and open entry and the ability to sit on a claim without mining it, except for the token $100 annual assessment work, can lead to holdups if the circumstances are right. Miners have demanded payment when roads or water projects were planned: if a "discovery" of a valuable mineral has been made (even though no serious mineral development has ever occurred), the claimant may hold a vested property right that must be compensated. Even if no discovery can be shown, it is cheaper for the highway or water agency to expend, say, $500 or $1000 to buy out a miner. The price can go much higher, as it did in 1989 when an inventive citizen staked claims at the proposed site of the Yucca Mountain high-level nuclear waste facility in Nevada and exacted a nuisance payment of $250,000. Similarly, legitimate mining companies often are forced to acquire paper claims before they can proceed with exploration or development. Claim holders, from frauds such as Merle Zweifel to small-time weekend miners, have been paid off, sometimes handsomely, to relinquish their claims. One BLM mining expert concluded that nuisance claims "increase uncertainties and costs and cause delays in often vitally needed prospecting and exploration activity." A House subcommittee was more blunt: "[S]peculators, intent on selling an interest in uranium claims to major energy companies and utilities, have developed a significant traffic in illegally held mining claims."[69]

A separate matter, implicating no fewer than 60 million acres, involves federally held subsurface rights. During the nineteenth century, the United States pursued a general policy of withholding from homesteading and railroad patents those areas where known mineral deposits existed. Once a patent was issued, however, later-discovered minerals belonged to the private owner. After the loss of federal coal deposits that led to the Roosevelt withdrawals in 1906, Congress passed various reform acts providing that federal patents for nonmineral purposes must contain a reservation of mineral rights in the United States. Thus, major land grants statutes, such as the Stock-raising Homestead Act of 1916, create "split estates," with surface ownership vested in the private owner and subsurface ownership in the United States. Any federal hardrock minerals under these split-estate lands are open for entry under the 1872 act.[70]

This situation has not pleased ranchers and farmers whose titles trace to the 1916 Stock-raising Homestead Act and who, like the Forest Service and the BLM, must allow entry into, and mining of, their grazing or agricultural lands. There are provisions for posting of bonds, for protection of permanent improvements, and for compensation for damages to crops or grazing land from open-pit mining, but the courts have not been particularly generous in awarding damages to surface owners. Their fields, too, are zoned for mining.

The difficulties with split-estate hardrock mining do not stop there. Nebraska state park officials arrived at work on February 5, 1981, to find stakes located by out-of-state uranium companies at Fort Robinson State Park; the United States had granted only the surface of the park to the state. Even more difficult problems have been created by the expansion of western towns and cities into former grazing lands. In 1983, the residents of Round Mountain, Nevada, learned that a mining company owned subsurface rights under the rural town and that the company might begin gold-mining operations. These incidents are not always in remote areas:

> Pausing for a moment, one can envisage an entire residential subdivision on Stock-Raising Homestead Act lands. There are many such developments today, and more are being built. In come the prospectors, bearing not only their 1916 picks and shovels, but their modern day bulldozers and draglines. They may not harm the permanent improvements; that much is clear. And they must make restitution for damages to "crops." So they set to work in the lawn areas of the suburb, and perhaps also in the parks, greenbelts, and other "unimproved" areas. On at least one occasion such activity, or the threat of it, has prompted Congress to take the unusual step of specific legislation withdrawing the subject minerals from location and leasing.

One recent episode of this sort took place in 1991 in Silver City, New Mexico, where Phelps Dodge was literally staking claims in the backyards of the Oak Grove subdivision before pulling out due to adverse publicity.[71]

Due in large part to sheer luck, the right of free access to subsurface minerals under private lands has caused fewer imbroglios than might be expected. Some of this relates to the lay of the land: hardrock minerals are geologically less likely to occur under the high plains agricultural and stock-raising land subject to the split-estate provisions. Where mineral deposits do occur in those regions, they are most likely to be coal, oil, and gas, which are subject to mineral leasing, not free entry under the Hardrock Act. The restitution requirements help, as does the fact that some owners are willing to sell their surface rights to a mining company that will pay generously for surface rights overlying a potentially lucrative deposit. But the right of entry to subsurface rights remains as a cloud over 5 percent of all private land in the eleven western states and Alaska.

Hardrock mining often has been given special dispensations in national parks, wilderness areas, and other areas set aside for their preservation resources. Mining is allowed, under agency regulation, in much of the Wild and Scenic Rivers System. Most national parks long have been closed to mining. However, six units in the park system—Crater Lake National Park, Denali National Park, Death Valley National Monument, Glacier Bay National Park and Preserve, Coronado National Memorial, and Organ Pipe Cactus National Monument—were left open. Finally, the Mining in the Parks Act of 1976 made mining on existing claims in the six units subject to regulation by the National Park Service as "necessary or desirable for the preservation and management of these areas." A study was ordered, with an eye toward buying up existing claims. As a result, although there are still some 2000 unpatented claims, there is little mining today in the parks.[72]

Wilderness has raised more controversy. The Wilderness Act of 1964, one of the strongest conservation laws ever enacted, described wilderness areas as "primeval" and stated, with a near-lyricism almost nonexistent in the statute books, that "[a] wilderness, in contrast with those areas where man and his own works dominate the landscape, is . . . an area where the earth and its community of life are untrammeled by man, where man himself is a visitor who does not remain." Congress had nearly codified the ideal of leading environmentalist David Brower, who, mixing his metaphors with obvious delight, once described wilderness as an area "where the hand of man has never set foot."[73]

But other sections limited the idealistic generalities of the 1964 act. The most prominent exception to the "primeval" and "untrammeled" character of wilderness involved the mining provisions of Section 3(d)(3), insisted on by western congressmen, especially Congressman Wayne Aspinall of Colorado, the powerful former chairman of the House Interior Committee. All existing claims were fully protected. All future patents would convey title to minerals only—no surface rights could be obtained, but wilderness would remain open for location of new claims for twenty years, until January 1, 1984.[74]

There has been little mining in wilderness areas, due to remoteness, harsh climates, and stiff Forest Service regulations. Still, pressures build. The Conundrum Creek drainage of Colorado's Maroon Bells–Snowmass Wilderness Area contains a marble quarry and an access road. In the Cabinet Mountains of northwestern Montana, U.S. Borax holds silver and copper claims that it believes may be worth $2 billion. ASARCO also has unpatented claims to silver there and plans to employ 350 people during production. The wilderness area is loaded with numerous species of wildlife that would be disrupted by mining, but the greatest concern is with grizzly bears, a threatened species in the Cabinets, who need solitude, especially during denning. In the Three Sisters Wilderness Area in the Oregon Cascades, U.S. Pumice Supply Company announced plans to develop a block pumice deposit. To stop the mining of unpatented claims, Congress was forced to buy out the company for $2 million. At least 10,000 claims lie dormant in wilderness areas.[75]

The mining industry, as well, has its objections to the outmoded hard-rock law. The combination of liberal *pedis possessio* and discovery standards means that a company is likely to be faced repeatedly with blotches of inactive but enforceable property interests during the exploration process. Even if there are not competing claimants, the law on *pedis possessio* and unpatented claims is cumbersome for most modern operations. The 20-acre size limit in the 1872 act was developed at a time when a significant part of mining involved following small but highly productive lodes for relatively short periods until they played out. Today, much larger target areas are needed for exploration. Aerial reconnaissance and mapping involving regions as large as 1000 to 100,000 square miles are employed to provide clues to the low-grade, widely disseminated deposits that companies usually must work today. Modern scintillation equipment is used to analyze large areas if radioactive deposits are being sought. Yet in most recent court decisions, judges have refused to budge from the old *pedis possessio* requirement that prospecting is protected only if the claims are "actually occupied."[76]

The problems for mining companies continue after exploration. A 20-acre parcel may make a splendid summer home, but it is arbitrary and confining to many mining operations, especially the large ones, such as American Barrick's Goldstrike. Development work—postexploration activities, including drilling to block out the deposit and other work necessary to begin actual production of minerals—may well require several thousand acres, especially if open-pit mining is involved. Companies are then required to locate large numbers (often hundreds) of small claims and to purchase the additional lands, if available. These costs of location and surface land purchases, unrelated to the production of minerals and unnecessary under a leasing system, have been explained as follows by Lawrence MacDonnell:

[T]here are substantial additional costs imposed by the system which has developed under the 1872 law, most of which are nonproductive.... Perhaps the most startling fact ... is the overwhelmingly greater cost imposed by the present location-patent system through the development stage.... The two major blocks of cost [in a hypothetical example given by the author] are claim location (30%) and additional land acquisition (60%). Most of these costs are nonproductive and do not contribute to gaining knowledge about the mineral deposit.[77]

Last, there is the recurring question of environmental protection.

To be sure, improved technology has made inroads into the chilling devastation wreaked by the first century and a quarter of mining in the West. The damage from acid mine drainage has probably decreased by about one-third since the early 1970s, when the Clean Water Act and other federal environmental laws were put in place. Mining of highly toxic minerals such as mercury and asbestos is far below historical levels; that fact, along with improved safety precautions, means that danger from those sources is significantly decreased.[78]

Today's production methods, however, have brought their own problems. The sheer magnitude of modern operations, especially open-pit mining, is such that we do not yet know whether current waste management techniques can prevent damage from sudden releases into surface waters or seepage of acid mine drainage into groundwater tables. In addition, as with American Barrick's Goldstrike Mine in Nevada, the new gold mining in the West uses a leaching method that includes spraying huge "heaps" of ore as much as 200 feet high with cyanide, which picks up the gold as it percolates through the heap. The cyanide-gold solution is captured, the gold separated, and the cyanide used again when possible. Heap-leaching is meant to take place on top of an impermeable liner, but the process is not foolproof. Liners can tear, and floodwaters can cause spills, resulting in cyanide contamination of streams or groundwater through percolation into the soil. Although the gold-mining industry proudly claims that there are no proven human deaths due to cyanide poisoning from heap-leaching, thousands of waterfowl, deer, and other wildlife have died because they mistook cyanide storage ponds for water bodies.[79]

Some mining companies have become acutely aware of these environmental and health problems and, undoubtedly, of the costs in attorneys' fees and shutdown time when operations are challenged. American Barrick has taken a great many steps to reduce the hazards from the Goldstrike Mine in Nevada. The McLaughlin Gold Mine in northern California, operated by Homestake Mining Company, and Coeur d'Alene Mines Corporation's Thunder Mountain Mine in Idaho have won kudos from environmental organizations. A smaller gold operation, the Mineral Hill Mine, reopened in the late 1980s amidst extensive consultation with the local community. The mine is located in Montana just north of Yellowstone National Park, on Bear Creek, a tributary of the Yellowstone River. Contamination of the Yellowstone would raise cries from locals and from conservationists coast to coast. The company hired John Hoak, an environmental scientist, respected businessman, and wilderness guide and packer in the area, to oversee environmental and regulatory affairs. The company adopted state-of-the-art practices to protect the water and wildlife, including eagles that nested in the area. Today, the Mineral Hill Mine, with Hoak as administrative superintendant, provides eighty-six jobs and is a model of an environmentally conscious mine.[80]

But waste management techniques have limits, and it is here that the 1872 act's "right to mine" comes into sharp focus. Some sites present such high risks, usually due to proximity to surface water or groundwater, that mining should proceed in a severely truncated fashion or not at all. Regardless of preventive technology, as the Environmental Protection Agency has emphasized, "[s]ite selection . . . is the single most important aspect of environmental protection in the mining industry." Yet under the General Mining Law, the fundamental decision to mine is made by private mining interests, not as a matter of public policy.[81]

The law has yet to catch up with the situation in the field. The regulatory system for health and environmental damage from hardrock mining is a patchwork quilt of state and federal agency authority that guarantees both gaps and overlap. The Army Corps of Engineers must issue a dredge and fill permit whenever an excavation or other disturbance affects the waters of the United States, which includes wetlands as well as lakes, streams, and creeks. The Environmental Protection Agency has ultimate authority over air and water pollution, but in most cases enforcement authority has been delegated to the states. In the case of air, enforcement is reasonably strict—hence the water trucks for dust suppression at the Goldstrike Mine in Nevada. State control over water pollution from hardrock mining is much more spotty. California, for example, has a strong regulatory system, while Nevada's is far more permissive. Everywhere, the funding for regulation of mining is very tight. In practical terms, the onus ultimately falls mainly on the Forest Service and the BLM for regulating hardrock mining on their respective land systems. These agencies review the miners' notices and plans of operation, prepare the environmental impact statements (or, far more often, much less stringent environmental assessments or analyses), and are most directly knowledgeable of, and involved with, these lands as a matter of their general land management responsibilities.[82]

The Forest Service's trailblazing 1974 regulatory program has wrought some progress. The mining industry fought the Forest Service's authority tooth and nail in court, but the program has been upheld, and most mining companies have developed acceptable plans of operation, working more or less cooperatively with federal land officials.[83]

Nevertheless, the Forest Service remains cautious in the face of the aura surrounding the historical right to mine. The agency's ambivalence about regulating hardrock mining is reflected in both official and informal statements. The preamble to the agency's mining regulations states that

> [t]he Forest Service recognizes that prospectors and miners have a statutory right, not mere privilege, under the 1872 mining law . . . to go upon and use the open public domain lands of the National Forest System for the purposes of mineral exploration, development and production. Exercise of that right may not be unreasonably restricted.

John R. McGuire, the widely respected chief of the Forest Service during development of the regulations, said, "The 1872 Mining Law does not permit us to refuse prospecting and mining . . . for environmental reasons." A district ranger, in the spirit one hears repeatedly in discussions of the 1872 act with Forest Service field officers, put it most directly of all: "When I am sitting down with a mining company and proposing changes in their operating plan or suggesting a $10,000 reclamation bond, there is, in the back of my mind, the worry—What do I do if they tell me to go to hell."[84]

The situation in the BLM is more dismal still. The soft agency regulations—which, as noted, effectively bypass mines that disturb fewer than 5 acres of land, about 80 percent of all operations on BLM lands—are combined with sporadic enforcement. The BLM rarely requires companies to post bonds, and then only when a company has a record of prior noncompliance, and it often fails to require reclamation. In 1989, the General Accounting Office rightly described mining on BLM lands as "loosely regulated." In all, there is little question that the BLM enforcement program is understaffed, that employees doubt their authority to regulate mining under the Hardrock Mining Law, and that the philosophy of the agency still is, as it always has been, to exercise its expansive discretion to favor, at nearly every turn, the production of minerals over any other competing objective.[85]

It may be that the Forest Service and the BLM, the primary potential regulators of hardrock mining on public lands, have ample authority under the Hardrock Act and other federal laws to impose stiff operating plans, issue shutdown orders, and require complete reclamation when mining is completed. Even the 1872 act provides that mining must proceed "under regulations prescribed by law," and common sense and court decisions, though not definitive, suggest that the federal agencies have broad regulatory authority. But we still do not know the full extent of agency authority because the mystique of the 1872 law and its perceived "right to mine" cause Forest Service and BLM employees to head for the door when it becomes time to declare that the location of a mine prohibits mining or that an obstinate company must be shut down because it has failed to comply with agency directives.[86]

Environmental regulation, then, has come to hardrock mining, but the specter of the 1872 act hovers over the agencies, so the setting and enforcement of environmental standards for these mining operations is less rigorous than with other comparable industries. The right to mine—real or perceived—permeates all of the many discretionary decisions made by federal and state officials and results in spotty, inadequate government oversight of these socially valuable but potentially destructive and dangerous operations.

An Approach toward Modernizing the 1872 Law

As one would expect, with such substantial concerns raised by all of the interest groups affected by the Hardrock Act, there have been continuing efforts at reform. Early on, amendments were sought mainly by the mining industry. In more recent times, industry has recognized the deficiencies in the 1872 act but has resisted change out of fear that the cure might prove worse than the disease. Rather, miners have been mostly on the defensive as moves to eliminate the "right to mine" system come from various quarters. To date, the power of the mining industry has proved adequate to the task of preventing fundamental statutory revision.

In the 1970s, a number of comprehensive public interest reform proposals were made. Washington senator Henry Jackson, Montana senator Lee Metcalf, Arizona congressman Morris Udall, Secretary of the Interior Rogers C. B. Morton of the Nixon administration, Hawaii congresswoman Patsy Mink, and the Carter administration all urged a leasing system for hardrock minerals. During most of the 1980s, little serious attention was given to hardrock reform, in light of the Reagan administration's staunch support of the 1872 act as written. And the mining industry was never hesitant to use its clout to beat back any winds of change. Morris Udall, a staunch environmentalist and a fine lawyer who knew the weaknesses of the mining law inside out, rose to the chairmanship of the House Interior Committee but also had to be reelected in his southern Arizona district, where the big copper companies hold a firm grip. In deciding not to assist hardrock reform legislation, Udall invoked his matchless wit and commented wryly, "I may not have seen the light, but I have felt the heat."[87]

The equation changed in the late 1980s. Major gold strikes, especially in

Nevada, led to the opening or reopening of numerous large mines and to sharply increased production. With more at stake for the big companies, some segments of the mining industry began to show interest in very limited technical changes to the 1872 law in order to eliminate *pedis possessio* limitations and other provisions that can unduly restrict modern operations. The press kept up a drumbeat of articles exposing the weaknesses of the old law; in particular, on the environmental side, the debate moved beyond fraud, patenting, and other land use issues to include the serious pollution problems that became ever more evident. Another factor involved the birth of a new organization in 1988, when the Mineral Policy Center was founded by Stewart Udall and other conservationists. Udall had long sought an overhaul of hardrock mining law. In 1969, when he left office as secretary of the interior, Udall had declared that "[a]fter eight years in this office [he held the position longer than anyone except Harold Ickes], I have come to the conclusion that the most important piece of unfinished business on the Nation's natural resource agenda is the complete replacement of the mining law of 1872." The Mineral Policy Center galvanized environmental support for legislative reform and quickly developed solid research capability, practical knowledge of the mining industry and its practices, the ability to disseminate information, and lobbying expertise.[88]

A final decisive event involved the uproar over the large-scale patenting in the late 1980s of oil shale claims, a giveaway fully worthy of the Great Barbecue days of the nineteenth century.

Oil shale contains organic matter called kerogen, which can be converted to synthetic oil (oil shale is one of the "synfuels") by heating the shale to 900 degrees Fahrenheit. The resulting oil shale is then upgraded by removing sulfur and nitrogen and mixing the oil shale with water.

There is no doubt about the potential commercial value of this "rock that burns." (It is said that the initial discovery of oil shale's fuel potential was made by a homesteader who used oil shale in construction of the fireplace in his new cabin, which burned to the ground when he lit the inaugural fire.) The world's largest deposits of oil shale are located mostly under federal lands in northwestern Colorado, northeastern Utah, and southwestern Wyoming. Yet in spite of decades of industry research and planning and extravagant federal subsidies during the 1970s, there has been little commercial production of oil shale. The shale is too deep, and the production costs, including both mining and the requisite large quantities of water, are too great.[89]

Oil shale was removed from the 1872 mining law and placed under a leasing regime in 1920, so it might seem that the final decade of the twentieth century is a late date for controversy over oil shale in the context of the Hardrock Act. The 1872 act, however, proved its tenacity once again. The 1920 Mineral Leasing Act grandfathered all "valid claims" under hardrock mining law. Before 1920, the companies had put stakes in the ground high above the shale deposits and taken some samples, but they had never done any mining for production. Ordinarily, there would seem to be no "discovery," which requires marketing at a profit, and the Interior Department and lower courts so held in the 1970s. The Supreme Court, however, reversed that decision in a five-to-four opinion, relying on administrative rulings in the 1920s that had set up a separate discovery test for oil shale. The old claims were good, mining or no mining. Afterward, a 1985 lower court found that the energy companies had met the legal requirements (basically just $100 of work per year per claim) to keep most of the pre-1920 claims alive. The companies had just established vested rights to hundreds of thousands of acres of public lands under the Hardrock Act without ever producing any significant amount of synthetic fuel for sale on the open market.[90]

In 1986, the Interior Department settled with the oil shale claimants. No fewer than 82,000 acres of federal land in the Yampa River and White River watersheds in northwestern Colorado were transferred out of public ownership for a filing fee of $2.50 per acre. The ensuing events were predictable. Within less than a year, one claimant turned around and sold 17,000 acres for more than $2000 per acre—a total sale price of $37 million. Local ranchers, who held a total of fifty grazing permits on the formerly public land, faced fee increases or outright revocation of their grazing privileges. This high desert piñon-juniper country, habitat for elk and for the largest mule deer herd in North America, was no longer public land, open as a matter of federal law to the public for hunting and hiking. The state of Colorado later succeeded in obtaining written guarantees that grazing, hunting, and public access for recreational use can continue under most conditions for twenty years, but no assurances have been made beyond that time. Nor is the oil shale episode over. Applications for patents to 270,000 more acres of land are still pending, and although technical issues still must be resolved, the 1872 act may well give the private claimants all rights to those lands.[91]

As a consequence of these various factors, there is the strongest sentiment in the air for deep, structural reform of any time since 1872. The most active legislator has been Congressman Nick Rahall of West Virginia, who has proposed legislation that would ban the patenting of mining claims, set strict reclamation requirements, and establish a fund to help clean up environmental damage from old hardrock mines. Senator Dale Bumpers of Arkansas and Congressman Peter DeFazio of Oregon have introduced measures that would go further by instituting royalty payments and setting stronger reclamation and bonding requirements than the Rahall proposal does. Bumpers also would give federal agencies express power to restrict mining, or prohibit it altogether, under specified conditions.[92]

Segments of the mining industry would like some technical changes in the 1872 act to facilitate their large-scale operations, but the Rahall, Bumpers, and DeFazio proposals are hardly what they have in mind. The trade organization, the American Mining Congress, has taken a hard line against any amendments that remotely resemble the approaches now being floated.

All corners of industry have raised the image of the small miner as the symbol of their tenacious defense of the old law. They paint a landscape of individual prospectors heading over the ridge, picking over the ground, making discoveries, and then turning the finds over to large companies for efficient and productive mining. They tie those discoveries into cherished American traditions. Consider these views of Clifton J. Hansen of Anaconda:

> There is something uniquely American about the location system. It was born of the frontier spirit when emphasis was on self-reliance, and it has remained a tool of individual enterprise throughout the years. The belief that a man is entitled to the rewards won by daring, ingenuity and a willingness to accept adversity is a fundamental aspect of our national character. The location system epitomizes that philosophy.[93]

The problem is that the old-time prospector with pickax and burro has virtually ceased to exist as a serious market participant. The decline of the small miner was well evident even by the time of the General Mining Law of 1872, as most of the easy surface deposits had played out. Indeed, western mining was a central focus of the union movement even during the nineteenth century because the field was dominated by large companies: most working miners were employees, not entrepreneurs. During modern times, the only moment when individuals had any realistic chance of making substantial discoveries was during the uranium boom on the Colorado Plateau in the mid-1950s, when $100 would buy a Geiger counter and a chance—albeit a slim one—to hit a big find. Today, a person can expect to make expenses and maybe wages, but the odds against any serious strike are astronomical. The mineral-bearing regions are well known and have been thoroughly worked over. As is the case with American Barrick's Goldstrike Mine in Nevada, most development is of low-grade, widely dispersed deposits, precisely the kind of capital-intensive work in which individuals and even small companies cannot participate. The Zortman-Landusky Mine in northern Montana, for example, is able to keep its massive strip mine operating even though it retrieves just 0.016 ounce of gold per ton of earth.[94]

The result is that small miners have made no recent major contributions to mineral production. The most thorough study of the subject was conducted for the Council on Environmental Quality by Professor Anthony Payne, who selected Nevada as a case study because of the widespread development that occurs there. Noting that the same conclusions could almost certainly be applied to the neighboring states of Utah, Idaho, Oregon, California, and Arizona, Professor Payne decried the "romanticism" promoted by "popular writers" and offered these conclusions:

> Several hundred to a thousand or more small miners in Nevada hold mining claims in the mining districts scattered through the state. A very small number of them make a living mining their claims. Many of them subsist on the hope that a company representative will come along and develop their claims. . . .
> The record of new mineral discoveries that have been made in the post–World War II period reveals that the role of the individual prospector and small miner has been very small. Only a few relatively minor deposits, mainly tungsten and barite, have been found by them, and the total production coming from these mines is minor.[95]

None of this means that good policy should ignore the small miner. Undeniably, there is a sense of freedom and opportunity here that is, and ought to be, preserved in the American West. Proper incentives for exploring for valuable minerals ought to be maintained. But the Hardrock Act, with all of its problems, goes too far and cannot fairly be justified by the need to provide incentive to the small prospector: the returns from such mining are simply too minimal. The miner's way of life ought to be preserved, but that goal can be achieved without tying up millions of acres of public property by the outmoded "right to mine" system.

Reasonable people should be able to agree on baseline ideas for governing hardrock mining on the public lands. Federal law ought to provide incentive and stability for serious, diligent mining operations on those lands deemed appropriate for mining. Those miners should be able to proceed with a minimum of extraneous concerns and should be secure in their operations. But there should be no "right to mine." Production of minerals, as opposed to exploration, should not proceed until there has been a public interest determination that the net public benefits of mining outweigh those of not mining. In no case should a miner receive title to the land. The environment should be protected by laws with real teeth in them. The system ought to have no truck with persons seeking to achieve goals other than mining. The public should receive a fair economic return, so long as it is not unduly burdensome on a mining operation. As Lawrence MacDonnell has put it, the system should be economically neutral—that is, "neither artificially subsidizing nor unduly hindering normal mineral activities, so that such activities may proceed in a manner which accords with the rewards inherent in mineral production itself."96

The Hardrock Act fails to meet even one of these objectives, except to the extent that the free access policy, coupled with the promise of no royalties and the possibility of a land patent, offers incentive. Even that benefit, however, must be balanced against detriments to industry in the form of continuing hassles over nuisance claims and outmoded location and claim size requirements.

Industry has traditionally objected to the adoption of hardrock leasing as a method for reforming the 1872 act. Leading mining lawyer Don Sherwood argues that a leasing system would be "an administrative jungle." Others believe that the payment of royalties would render many marginal operations uneconomical. But federal leasing of energy fuels— and of hardrock minerals on acquired and Indian lands—has not crippled our ability to produce energy. Indeed, the nation's impressive response to the 1973 Arab oil embargo was made under a leasing regime.97

A congressional shift to a leasing system would plainly achieve the goals of securing the use of land for serious mining operations, prohibiting use by nonminers, and ensuring environmental regulation. There is nothing intrinsic in a leasing regime that would jeopardize incentives or violate the principle of economic neutrality; such undesirable results would accrue only if the system were designed improperly. Incentive to prospect can be preserved by allowing easy acquisition of large-acreage prospecting permits at a nominal fee. Economic neutrality can be guaranteed by a royalty or fee structure that imposes little or no burden on marginal operations while imposing a reasonable, fair payment for mining companies turning profits. Importantly, there is no magic in royalties *per se*: for example, a scheduled payment on net profits, rather than on gross extraction, would not burden marginal operators but would require large, producing operators to pay their fair share for the use of public resources. Nothing here discourages the small miner from heading over the ridge or the multinational corporation from conducting state-of-the-art reconnaissance. Indeed, leasing literally would unclutter the landscape for real mining operations.

Yet leasing may not be a politically viable alternative because of industry's vehement (that is far too pale a term) opposition. An alternative approach, which also would reach the desired policy objectives, would involve a permitting process in which exploration permits would be freely issued. If a find were made, actual mining could proceed only after an administrative determination that the public interest weighs in favor of mineral production on the site in question. If so, the company could go ahead with production, with no fixed termination date, so long as the company diligently produces paying quantities of minerals. A fair return would be made to the Treasury during production, and, at all times, suitable environmental protections would be in force.

This permitting approach would differ from leasing only in its details. Both would call for deep, structural reform. Yet both systems would meet both the public interest and the legitimate interests of serious miners.[98]

The ultimate problem, of course, is that the meter keeps running under the current system. Hard, vested rights against the United States, other miners, and public users are asserted every day by people who allege hypothetical "discoveries" under the ground. If some activity other than mining is the highest and best use of the land, then the United States must pay dearly; recent examples include the $2 million payment to U.S. Pumice Supply Company for its unused block pumice unpatented claims in Oregon's Three Sisters Wilderness Area, a $3000-per-acre buyout of the dormant patented claims near the White Cloud Peaks in the Sawtooth National Recreation Area in Idaho, and the payoff of $250,000 for claims asserted at the site of the Yucca Mountain nuclear waste facility. If the government cannot make the payment for budgetary reasons, the fence stays up. Under a leasing or permitting system, the land never leaves public hands, and the minerals remain with the United States except when mining companies are diligently removing them. The 1872 act's legerdemain of creating an instant and permanent transfer of both land surface and subsurface minerals is a blunt instrument unnecessary for the legitimate miner and exploitive of the public lands.[99]

Congress needs to give attention not only to future mining operations but also to the existing 1.1 million patented claims. The approach follows from the policy goals suggested above: actual, working mining operations ought to be supported and encouraged, and shadow miners should be ousted. Holders of unpatented claims should be offered—in place of their unpatented claims—leases or permits that fully protect their right diligently to produce valuable minerals. If a miner refuses the new arrangement, or does not proceed to meet realistic, modern diligence requirements, that miner's use of public land should be terminated. Such a congressional transmutation of an unpatented claim into a lease allowing full development of the deposit would be upheld by the courts because there is no "unconstitutional divestment" of the right to mine: the miner's "rights of use, enjoyment and disposition . . . remain undiminished." The real miner would hardly skip a beat.[100]

Senator Stewart succeeded in zoning all of the public domain for miners. He was right for his time—he faithfully met the call of the remote society he knew and loved so well. To say that today's call is different and more varied is no attack on the mining industry or on nineteenth-century figures like Senator Stewart. To the contrary, any fair reform of the 1872 law is bottomed on the idea that too much of the old law has been twisted by nonminers and opportunists: the legitimate interests of working mining operations ought to be protected at every turn. By allowing that protection—but only that—we can turn away from a public land estate blotched with environmental abuse and 25 million acres of property rights that have long failed to comport with the diverse needs of the modern American West.

Chapter Three

The Rancher's Code

The waters of Camp Creek gather in the rounded, low-lying area around the Maury Mountains and Hampton Butte in central Oregon. The small stream flows northward through open rangeland for some 40 miles, mostly at an elevation between 5200 and 4000 feet, until it discharges into the Crooked River. This is the arid eastern two-thirds of Oregon, not really of the Pacific Northwest but of the high plains country found throughout the Rocky Mountains. Average annual precipitation in the Camp Creek drainage is just 12–14 inches.

Peter Skene Ogden, the intrepid British fur trapper for the Hudson's Bay Company, led a hunting party up the Crooked River in December 1825. In his journal, the first written account of the region, he observed that the banks were "well lined with willows" and rejoiced at the fine feed for his horses: "The Soil on this Fork [is] remarkably rich in some parts [and] the Grass seven feet high." Ogden believed the Crooked River system to be a potential bonanza for the beaver men, saying, "I doubt if we should find another equal to it in any part of this country." A half century later, in 1875, the deputy surveyor of Oregon examined Camp Creek, describing the valley floor as a "meadow" and noting several marshes. The surveyor's notes also pointed out the abundance of bunchgrass on the uplands of the Camp Creek watershed.[1]

Excessive grazing of cattle since the 1880s has worked over Camp Creek in almost incredible ways. There are few beaver, no willows to speak of, and no 7-foot-tall grasses at all. The creek itself runs not through a grassy meadow but on a hard-packed floor at the bottom of deep cut-banks. The timing of the runoff has been thrown off: water shoots out during the spring melt, and little is held for late summer and fall. In 1905, just one generation after the surveyor general's report, Israel Russell of the United States Geological Survey had this to say of the meadow that so recently had been the Camp Creek valley:

> [Its] surface is intersected by arroyos, or small canyons, through which water flows during the wet season. Joining the main trenches are several branches, each of which has the characteristics of a young stream-cut canyon. The main trench, which follows the longer axis of the valley, ranges from 60 to 100 feet in width, is approximately 25 feet deep, and has vertical walls throughout the greater portion of its course. . . .
>
> The change . . . probably coincides with the introduction of domestic animals in such numbers that the surface covering of bunch grass was largely destroyed, and in consequence the run-off from the hills accelerated.[2]

A "trench" 25 feet deep and up to 100 feet across. If you stand on Camp Creek's rocky bed today, you can visualize the immense amount of earth that was driven downstream during the radical down-cutting of the last two decades of the nineteenth century. You will be standing between the sheared-off banks, 50 feet away on each side. The banks rise up 20 or 25 feet. You can imagine the former meadow surface at the tops of the cut-banks high above your head, at the roof level of many houses. If you fix on a point upstream, say, 100 yards away, you can begin to comprehend the volume of soil and rock driven downstream—the equivalent of several neighborhoods of houses full of material—just on that one short, 100-yard stretch of stream.

The erosion of Camp Creek continues. Topographical maps show "Severance Reservoir" on Camp Creek about 7 miles up from Crooked River. A rancher named Ned Severance built this impoundment by putting in a dam across the creek in 1952, creating a 40-acre reservoir. It was 65 feet deep in places and was considered a fine trout lake by locals.

There is no longer a Severance Reservoir. By 1977, just a quarter of a century after the dam had been built, it had become completely filled with sediment carried into it by the flow of Camp Creek. In other words, if you stand on top of the earthen dam and face downstream, the trickle of Camp Creek will slip over the dam and drop down 40 or 50 feet below you to the channel. If you turn around and face upstream, you will be standing about a foot above a flat meadow of 40 acres, the former lake surface. Camp Creek, which runs along the top of this new meadow, has stacked up a million tons of sediment behind the dam.

All of this is due to cattle and sheep or, much better put, to the poor management of cattle and sheep by human beings. In the 1880s and 1890s,

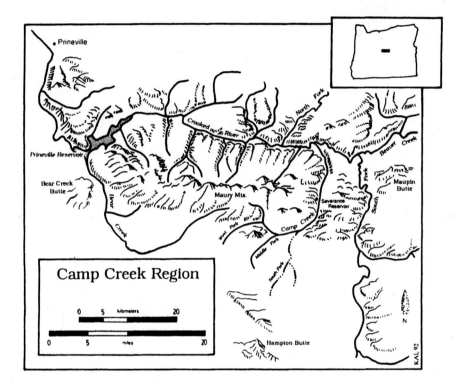

Camp Creek Region

Prineville

Prineville Reservoir

Bear Creek Butte

Crooked River

North Fork

Beaver Creek

Maupin Butte

Maury Mts.

Severance Reservoir

Camp Creek

South Fork

West Fork

Middle Fork

South Fork

Bear Creek

Hampton Butte

0 5 kilometers 20

0 5 miles 20

N

KAL 92

ranchers took over the public domain rangeland and introduced thousands
of cows, and significant numbers of sheep, into the Camp Creek valley.
Understandably, when cows see green and smell water, they head for it.
After all, riparian zones—the "green strips" along streams and creeks—
produce twenty-five times more vegetation per unit of ground than do
upland sites. And stream bottoms are cool. If you let them, those cattle will
pound down the banks, crush the beaver dams, root out every last stalk of
forage, and then wallow in the mud that is left. Some of them will literally
stay on all spring and summer, drinking what water is left and losing
weight steadily as the hot sun bakes down. Some cows will move into the
uplands to graze, or be driven there by ranchers who locate a spring or
build a water tank. Those animals will concentrate in spots in the uplands
and give that ground a pounding, unless they are kept moving.

Even the Shoshone Indians who lived in the valley as long as 6000 years
ago did not observe how the Camp Creek range system was formed, but
range scientists have no doubt how it occurred and how it was later
transformed. This was a living stream system, always building and changing through the accumulation of small events. Willows, reeds, sedges, and
rushes took root in the rich soil of Camp Creek's bottomland. As earth was
carried down by the stream, this vegetation caught still more soil. Sediment
would build up against, say, bulrushes growing in the stream bottom. A
tiny islet would develop, and it would catch more soil to grow more rushes.
The islet would grow up and spread out each year; eventually, it would
reach one shore and, having formed a small peninsula, nudge the stream off
in a new direction, thereby creating a meander in the channel. At other
times, change would come more violently, as when the high spring runoff
leaped a bank to establish a new channel. There was no single, trench-
bound Camp Creek. This was a stream that shifted and meandered
throughout a long, broad meadow, always rejuvenating itself with earth,
fresh water, and the resultant celebration of green.

Camp Creek, therefore, was an elaborate holding and filtering system.
The broad, marshy meadowlands trapped sediment. The vegetation also
slowed and caught water in its matrix of meanders, soil, and plants. Cool
water seeped into the groundwater table, the top of which blended with the
root systems of the plants. The blue ribbon of Camp Creek was only the
visible tip of a vast, interconnected aquifer.

A healthy riparian system, such as existed in the Camp Creek valley
before the 1880s, produces a range of economic benefits. It cools and
purifies water. It is a deep and efficient reservoir—much like a great
sponge—that stores water without evaporative loss and feeds it back into
the stream conveyance channel, ensuring a reliable supply of water to
downstream users during summer and fall and in dry years. Further, if

proper land management practices are followed, cattle can graze in these exceptionally nutritious areas.

A riparian zone can also be a festival of wildlife species, and Camp Creek once was exactly that. Canada geese, wigeon, and green-winged teal nested there. The great blue heron coasted in on its 7-foot wingspread to feed on insects and minnows. Native rainbow trout lived in the water all year, and salmon and steelhead pushed up several hundred miles from the ocean to spawn. Raccoons prowled the stream bottom, and deer and elk stole down from the uplands at the close of day to drink. Beaver, which Peter Skene Ogden found so plentiful, were exceedingly important to the integrity of the old Camp Creek system. Pools behind the beaver dams stored water and spread it out, expanding the reach of the riparian zone.

The uplands above the Camp Creek valley were once covered with protein-rich bunchgrasses. The lush tallgrass alluded to by Ogden was probably Great Basin wild rye. There were other bunchgrasses—bluebunch wheatgrass and Idaho fescue. The deep root systems of these plants held the soil in place. Rainfall soaked into the soft ground cover and slowly percolated down to the groundwater table. There were no sheets of surface water to force down large sediment loads.

Poor ranching practices destroyed all of this at Camp Creek. When cows beat down the stream banks and destroyed the vegetation in the riparian zone, the creek's flow scoured out soil and rocks. This activity was particularly rapid in the spring. Camp Creek has a languid flow most of the year, but it can be a raging torrent, fifty times larger, in March and April, when the snow melts off. Unimpeded by vegetation, the big spring flow gouged out the exposed stream bottom, and the process snowballed as rocks and boulders tore down the channel. In many stretches, the scouring effect continued until the stream bottom cut down to bedrock. With no spongy soil to hold the water, the groundwater table was not recharged. The top of the aquifer declined, dropping below the reach of streamside trees. Valuable willows, whose root systems helped stabilize the soil, died out. The flow pattern radically changed. The snowmelt, much of which was once stored by the riparian zone, flushed down the rocky chute in a rush, leaving little or no flows for the dry months of summer and fall. Hundreds of animal species were driven out.

The uplands, the other component in a rangeland system, were also integrally involved in the deterioration at Camp Creek. Ranchers simply turned their cattle loose on the open public range in the early spring and rounded them up in the fall. The cows overgrazed the bunchgrasses on the uplands and pounded down the native plants with their hoofs. None of this was necessary. New growth in these grasses occurs at the "growing point" near the base of the plant, where new cells develop. Light grazing can actually promote growth: removing as much as 40 percent of a plant's leaves and stems is much the same as pruning for these wild grasses. In addition, the sharp hoofs of cattle can chip up the turf, loosen it, and promote water storage and seed regeneration. But these beneficial effects accrue only if the animals are present in the right numbers and if they are kept moving.[3]

With native grasses being driven out of Camp Creek's uplands, a low canopy of juniper, sagebrush, and rabbitbrush moved in. These invaders, with their broad, shallow root systems, hastened the departure of the bunchgrasses by successfully competing for scarce water. The protective ground cover on the uplands was now gone, and the transformation of the Camp Creek watershed was complete. Rainwater, instead of seeping into the soft ground, washed unprotected soils down to the creek. The trench was now crisscrossed with small gullies and arroyos. Uncountable tons of sediment from the once-green bottomlands. Uncountable tons from the uplands.[4]

There are Camp Creeks all across the American West—thousands of them. To be sure, factors that determine the amount of erosion—soil types, vegetation, gradient, and volume and regularity of stream flow—will differ from locale to locale. Camp Creek, for instance, is unusual because of its native tallgrasses; the tallgrass prairies were found mostly near the 100th meridian in the heart of the country and in the Central Valley of California. Nor is the sediment load of the little drainage in central Oregon necessarily typical; the soils of Bear Creek, the watershed adjacent to Camp Creek on the west, are considerably more stable, so erosion in Bear Creek, though substantial, is less than in Camp Creek. General regional differences also can be drawn—the ravages of overgrazing tend to be somewhat less severe, for example, in Montana and somewhat more severe in New Mexico. Nonetheless, Camp Creek fairly represents the current state of the western range.

The problems symbolized by Camp Creek are of daunting magnitude. Overgrazing has put nearly 10 percent of all land in the American West in a state of severe desertification. Desertification is not, as the term may suggest, the wholesale advance of sand dunes. Rather, the process operates in blots and splotches to eliminate the ability of arid lands to support life. The chief characteristics of desertification are loss of topsoil through erosion and wind, salinization of surface water, and loss of native vegetation. Water storage is also affected. Poor ranching practices not only have cost us the vast natural storage capacity of riparian zones but also have contributed (along with soil erosion from irrigated agriculture, a matter taken up later in this book) to the clogging of the West's great public works reservoirs: all across the region, sediment loads are filling up these artificial lakes. Prineville Reservoir on the Crooked River, for instance, was built in

1962 but has already lost about 15 percent of its storage capacity to sedimentation from Camp Creek and the other streams in the watershed. As one standard source has said, "Perhaps nowhere have the harmful effects of erosion on water supplies and vegetation been more acutely felt than on the Western ranges."[5]

The western range contributes only a small amount of our national livestock production. Private lands in the East, which grow many times more forage per acre, account for 81 percent of all livestock production in the United States. Western private lands produce just 17 percent of the country's livestock production; the federal public lands, a scant 2 percent. Yet more acres of the eleven western states are dedicated to cattle ranching than to any other use. Leaving aside private grazing lands, the Bureau of Land Management and the Forest Service administer grazing permits on no less than 258 million acres of rangeland, an area that would encompass all of the land within the three Pacific Coast states of California, Oregon, and Washington and most of Nevada as well. Silt-clogged Severance Reservoir on Camp Creek stands as a mute testament to the hundreds of millions of tons of earth washed down annually from the overworked western range. Still, the United States continues, as it always has, to provide heavy subsidies to ranchers: as of 1991, federal agencies charged a fee of $1.97 per month per cow for grazing on public lands, compared with an average fee of $8.70 on private lands.[6]

Inevitably, the situation has spawned citizen concern based on ecological and economic grounds. Edward Abbey, author of *The Monkey Wrench Gang*, was not typical on this issue—the fire-and-brimstone Abbey was typical of nearly nothing—but he spoke for a growing phalanx of westerners:

> Overgrazing, I think, is much too weak a term. Most of the West, and especially the Southwest, is what you might call "cow-burnt." Our public lands are infested with domestic cattle. Almost anywhere and everywhere you go in the American West, you will find herds—*herds*— of these ugly, clumsy, shambling, stupid, bawling, bellowing, stinking, fly-covered, shit-smeared, disease-spreading brutes. They are a pest and a plague. They pollute our springs and streams and rivers. They crowd and overcrowd our canyons and valleys and meadows and forests. They graze off the native bluestem and grama and bunch grasses. They trample down the native forbs and shrubs and cactus in the Southwest. They spread the exotic cheat grass and the Russian thistle and the crested wheat grass. *Weeds.*[7]

Abbey's solution was straight to the point. Remove cattle from the public lands. Every last cow from every last acre. The message took. By the late 1980s, some environmentalists had taken up the war cry, "Cattle-free by '93." Soon a new slogan evidenced even more immediacy and perhaps even more lyricism as well: "No moo by '92."

Abbey and others are correct about the magnitude of the problem, but they are almost surely wrong about the remedy. People like Wayne Elmore and Allan Savory have mounted impressive cases for the idea that the problem is not cattle but poor cattle and land management. In many instances, the Camp Creeks of the West can be rejuvenated with good stewardship practices, and ranchers can continue to graze cattle in substantial numbers, thus supporting not only ranchers but also the struggling ranching communities that offer a great many benefits to the western scene. We will return to the innovative proposals of Elmore and Savory, but first we need to go back and examine another lord of yesterday, the takeover of the public range by private ranchers. The code of the rancher has very different terminology and legal characteristics from the miner's law, but the degree of control by a capturing industry remains much the same.

The Rise of Private Range Rights

Cattle had been introduced into California and Texas during the late eighteenth century as the Spanish missions were established. These hardy, rangy Spanish cattle were later popularly known as Texas longhorns. Cows arrived in the Willamette Valley of Oregon with British settlement in the early 1800s. Wagon trains traveling over the Oregon Trail usually brought European strains of cattle with them.[8]

The number of cows in the Far West jumped with the population boom spurred by the California gold rush. Most would-be miners drawn west by gold eventually moved into other occupations, usually farming and ranching. Oregon cattle were driven south from the Willamette Valley over the Siskiyous to meet the demand in California. Then, during the 1850s and 1860s, drives radiated out of California's Central Valley to support communities growing up around gold and silver strikes in Nevada, Oregon, Montana, and Idaho.

Not until the period immediately after the Civil War, however, did it become apparent that ranchers would be the second great wave of settlement after the miners. Longhorns from Texas were driven north and west, sometimes in herds totaling tens of thousands. Six hundred thousand longhorns were moved out of Texas in 1871 alone. The figures are rough, but there were probably no more than 3 or 4 million cattle in the West, mostly in Texas, in 1865 when the war ended. Two decades later, the figure was 26 million, along with nearly 20 million sheep. The diminished range resource, coupled with excessive hunting, drove out the buffalo, the main competitor for forage.

This cattle kingdom, as it is so often called, required that each rancher control large amounts of rangeland. Even in the early halcyon days, when nutritious native grasses still predominated, a single cow required 3–10 acres, depending on the region. It took thousands of acres to make a spread, but the General Homestead Act of 1862 allowed a maximum of 160 acres, far too small for a going cattle operation. Thus, ranchers would acquire additional parcels from other homesteaders or from relatives—or from dummy homesteaders paid off to make false proof under the 1862 act. This land would be the base ranch, the heart of the operation, holding a residence, barns, corrals, and hay pastures. The acres in fee ownership, however, were small in comparison with the total land controlled by a rancher, since the deeded land was always supplemented by large blocks of public grazing land.[9]

The base ranch had a key function other than providing a central land area: it served to establish water rights. The need was not so much for stock watering, since the animals do not require much water for drinking. The far greater call was, and is, for water to farm. Although cows and sheep graze mainly on unirrigated rangeland, irrigated crops such as alfalfa play an integral role in most ranching operations. Animals need to be brought down from the high country in the winter. Sometimes they graze on winter range, but more often they live on feed produced from irrigated pastures. Thus the need for large amounts of water for fields on base ranches all across the arid West.

Most base ranches were homesteads located on rich, creekside bottom-land. Virtually all surrounding land would be federal public domain land, and in the spring, summer, and fall ranchers would turn loose their stock to graze on tens of thousands of acres of higher land above the base ranches. The public domain rangeland was unregulated and available free of charge. In this manner, a very small number of ranchers gained control over the land and water in entire watersheds. One respected observer writing in 1884, during the heyday when the present system was set in place, offered the following scenario as "the most widely used method of establishing a ranch":

> Select a site on a river near a woods—for on the plains woods are scarce—in as accessible a location as possible. Include within the tract as much timber as possible, as this is one of the necessities of life. It is one of the primary reasons for preventing over-settlement. Then, since the Government permits only one such homestead to a person, the ranchers acquire through the exercise of this same privilege by various members

of their families, as well as their employees, other distant—even far distant—homesteads on the same basis. They [the ranchers] then purchase these lands from them.

By this method one can succeed in preventing, almost completely, the intrusion of settlers, and can enclose an area of land sufficient to assure one's existence and the development of a rather large herd. This method of operation succeeds best the farther one gets away from railroad lands. The author knows a group of eight ranchers in the neighborhood of Yellowstone National Park, who are partly in Montana and partly in Wyoming, some six days distant on horseback from a railroad and who thereby have succeeded in protecting themselves from the invasion. On a range sufficient to raise and permit the increase of their herds, they have today altogether around 150,000 head of cattle.[10]

The cattle ranchers had competitors for their kingdom. These were not so much the miners; their prospecting was mostly in the foothills and mountains above the plains. Further, their diggings were not much threatened when stock moved into the lightly forested uplands during the summer months. Nor did Indian holdings ultimately stand in the way. The large blocks of land set aside for the Indian tribes initially posed problems because the reservations were off-limits. The cattle ranchers ran stock on Indian lands anyway. At the Pyramid Lake Indian Reservation in Nevada, for example, long before Truckee River water was diverted from the lake to non-Indian farmers, ranchers ran thousands of head of cattle on tribal lands as early as the 1860s, in spite of continued protests from the Paiutes and federal Indian agents. Finally, the cattlemen, with the help of other interest groups, achieved the passage of the General Allotment Act of 1887. The Dawes Act, as it is also called, resulted in the sale of 90 million acres of the 140-million-acre Indian estate and allowed low-cost grazing leases on the remaining reservation rangelands.[11]

The transcontinental rail lines had some effect on the grazing empire. The railroad grant acts, beginning in 1862, benefited transcontinental giants such as the Central Pacific, Union Pacific, Northern Pacific, and Southern Pacific, which cut great east-west, checkerboarded swaths 20, 40, or even 80 acres wide. The grants transferred to the railroads every alternate section of land (a square mile) out to the designated width for each mile of road built. In the case of the Central Pacific–Union Pacific road completed in 1869, for example, the companies received every alternate section—half of all the land—in a belt 40 miles wide from Omaha to San Francisco. But those lands had been designated in advance, and the cattle barons could locate elsewhere. Besides, railroad land was usually for sale or lease, and the even-numbered sections within the grant areas remained in federal ownership, open for free grazing.[12]

The cattle ranchers' real opponents were the sheepherders and the homesteaders, the "yeoman farmers" favored by federal policy since Jeffersonian days. They were the intended beneficiaries of the General Homestead Act of 1862, designed to open the West to settlement by small family farms. All public domain land was open for homesteading in 160-acre parcels unless expressly withdrawn from settlement for some specific purpose such as a military base or Indian reservation or, later, for a national park or forest.[13]

The ranchers were using public land at the passive sufferance of the United States, which had never given them formal permission to run their stock. Official federal policy, responding to powerfully held national beliefs, kept the public domain open for homesteading by the small family farmer.

This did not sit well with the large ranchers wanting exclusive control over vast areas of public domain lands. Sheepherders were repeatedly on the wrong end of violent tactics. Cattle interests killed two Mexican sheepherders and clubbed to death 300 of their sheep near Craig, Colorado, in 1896. The Oregon Sheep Shooters Association was organized in the early 1890s to keep sheep out of most of the far-flung Cascade Forest Reserve (which since has been divided into several smaller national forests) that blanketed the Cascade Range from the Columbia River south to the California border. Slightly to the east, tensions were high in the region that encompasses Camp Creek. The corresponding secretary of Crook County's Sheep-Shooting Association of Eastern Oregon wrote this letter to the editor in response to an editorial in the *Oregonian*:

> I am authorized by the association (The Inland Sheep Shooters) to notify the *Oregonian* to desist from publishing matter derogatory to the reputation of sheep-shooters in Eastern Oregon. We claim to have the banner County of Oregon on the progressive lines of sheep shooting, and it is my pleasure to inform you that we have a little government of our own in Crook County, and we would thank the *Oregonian* and the Governor to attend strictly to their business and not meddle with the settlement of the range question in our province.
>
> We are the direct and effective means of controlling the range in our jurisdiction. If we want more range we simply fence it in and live up to the maximum of the golden rule that possession represents nine points of the law. . . . When sheepmen fail to observe these peaceable obstructions we delegate a committee to notify offenders. . . .
>
> These mild and peaceful means are usually effective, but in cases where they are not, our executive committee takes the matter in hand, and being men of high ideals as well as good shots by moonlight, they promptly enforce the edicts of the association. . . . Our annual report

shows that we have slaughtered between 8000 and 10,000 head during
the last shooting season and we expect to increase this respectable
showing during the next season providing the sheep hold out and the
Governor and the *Oregonian* observe the customary laws of neutrality. . . . In some instances the Woolgrowers of Eastern Oregon have
been so unwise as to offer rewards for the arrest and conviction of sheep-
shooters and for assaults of herders. We have therefore warned them by
publication of the danger of such action, as it might have to result in our
organization having to proceed on the lines that dead men tell no tales.
This is not to be considered as a threat to commit murder, as we do not
justify such a thing except where the flock-owners resort to unjustifiable
means of protecting their property.[14]

The Johnson County War of 1892 is the most famous example of the
conflict between large ranchers and homesteaders. Tensions had been
building in northern Wyoming for years. A husband and wife were lynched
in 1889 because they filed for homesteads on public lands within a large
pasture treated as his own by a cattleman. In November 1891, two men in
Johnson County were ambushed and shot to death, supposedly for cattle
rustling. In retaliation, cattle theft by the homesteaders in fact increased:
"[M]any homesteaders who would not steal from neighbors thought nothing of rounding up calves belonging to some far-distant cattle baron, and
applying their own brands." The large companies sent in so-called regulators, fifty-two hired gunmen from out of state, to shoot down the
homestead-rustlers. The regulators killed two suspects and set fire to a
ranch, but the local citizenry called in federal troops, who arrested the
outsiders. Witnesses failed to appear, apparently due to intimidation by the
cattlemen, and the prosecutions were dismissed. The Johnson County War
and other killings were the exception, but the goal of excluding homesteaders by nearly any means was not: threats and property destruction
aimed at small farmers and ranchers were commonplace.[15]

Coercion and violence, however, were only part of the reason why
ranchers were able to lay *de facto* claim to so much of the open public land
of the West. Simple possession mattered a great deal, especially when it was
coupled with the senior water right in the area. In such cases, "range
rights" were recognized as a matter of custom for all land actually grazed
within the drainage in which the base ranch was located; it was not
uncommon for range rights to apply to 30 or 40 square miles. These
customary range rights, although necessarily different in their particulars,
grew up in circumstances not dissimilar from those that gave rise to mining
claims in the early mining camps.

Ranchers often solidified control of the range by fencing the public acres
where their stock roamed. Fencing boomed in the late 1870s, when barbed

wire was perfected, providing a relatively inexpensive means of enclosing vast areas. The practice of fencing off public lands was made illegal by the Unlawful Inclosures Act of 1885, but the magnitude of the problem was demonstrated by the General Land Office's 1886 report identifying 375 illegal fencing units covering 6 million acres of land. The government's power to protect the public lands in this manner was upheld in *Camfield v. United States*, in which the defendant had enclosed 20,000 acres of the public domain. Nevertheless, the Unlawful Inclosures Act was only a partial success. Obtaining evidence in remote areas was expensive and time-consuming, prosecutors' offices were short-staffed, and some lower court judges refused to enforce the statute against the large livestock interests.[16]

The established cattle industry was highly successful in persuading state legislatures to adopt laws furthering its interests. In 1886, Texas enacted a law recognizing range rights by making it a felony to drive cattle onto the "accustomed range" of another. The other western states passed similar laws. The common-law rule, which required owners to fence in their animals or be responsible for damage caused by their stock, was reversed. Reflecting the western custom of allowing stock to roam at will, ranchers were not liable for damage caused by their animals, thus forcing land-owners to build fences to keep the ranchers' stock out.[17]

These and other state laws were all valid on the federal public domain because the United States had never passed any statute to the contrary. In 1918, the United States Supreme Court reviewed an Idaho law, passed at the instigation of the cattle industry, prohibiting sheepherders from allow-ing their animals to graze on any range previously occupied by cattle. The Court upheld the state law: "The police power of the State extends over the federal public domain, at least when there is no legislation by Congress on the subject."[18]

"At least when there is no legislation by Congress." In other words, states could set out rules for range rights when there was a void in the federal laws, as was the case during the nineteenth century. There was a significant limit to this: local customs and state statutes could set binding rules as to ranchers and other private parties, but they could create no rights in federal property. Ranchers possessed only a "privilege," not a right, to graze their stock on the federal lands.[19]

At the same time, federal officials plainly knew of, and condoned, private ranching on the public commons. In a leading statement on the question, the Supreme Court ruled on the rights of a sheepherder who wanted to graze his stock on 900,000 acres of public land in an area interspersed with 350,000 acres of deeded land owned by a cattleman. The Court found that the sheepherder could drive his sheep across the private land to reach the checkerboarded public land:

> We are of opinion that there is an implied license, growing out of the custom of nearly a hundred years, that the public lands of the United States, especially those in which the native grasses are adapted to the growth and fattening of domestic animals, shall be free to the people who seek to use them, where they are left open and uninclosed, and no act of government forbids this use. For many years past a very large proportion of the beef which has been used by the people of the United States is the meat of cattle thus raised upon the public lands without charge, without let or hindrance or obstruction. The government of the United States in all its branches has known of this use, has never forbidden it, nor taken any steps to arrest it. . . .
> . . . The owner of a piece of land, who had built a house or inclosed 20 or 40 acres of it, had the benefit of this universal custom, as well as the party who owned no land. Everybody used the open, uninclosed country which produced nutritious grasses as a public common [on] which their horses, cattle, hogs, and sheep could run and graze.

Still, this "implied license," although it reflected an important western custom, created no legal obligation for the United States to allow it to continue.[20]

It is interesting to ponder why the cattlemen, with their immense political power, were unable to obtain vested rights in the public rangeland, as miners were able to do with public minerals by means of the Hardrock Act of 1872. The basic problem seems to have been that public antagonism toward large ownerships in the West burgeoned during the late 1870s and 1880s, the very time when the ranchers were solidifying their *de facto* control of the western range. The extravagance of the donations to the railroads had become fully apparent. Hostility had been fueled by acquisition of more than 20 million acres of public land by alien capitalists. In Colorado, Lord Dunraven owned 60,000 acres near Estes Park. The Marquis of Tweeddale consolidated an estate of 1,750,000 acres. The antimonopoly sentiment of the 1880s and 1890s promoted land disposal and westward expansion, but the intended beneficiaries were family farmers, not large stock concerns. Populism was on the rise, and large interests such as the cattlemen were required to operate mainly in the back rooms of public policy, not in the white light of open congressional debate.[21]

Congress, therefore, left ranchers with an unwritten privilege rather than with a Magna Carta such as that achieved by the hardrock miners a generation earlier. At the time, the cattle industry was unruffled by this. They had the state laws. More importantly, they had their own code, built on manipulation of the land disposal laws, physical possession of the federal range, intimidation, illegal fencing, and customary recognition of range rights among themselves. As leading historian Walter Prescott Webb put it: "The cattle kingdom worked out its own means and methods of utilization; it formulated its own law, called the code of the West, and did it largely upon extra-legal grounds." And from that day until this, westerners have heard ranchers speak with unwavering certitude of their "right" to the public rangeland.[22]

The rapid ascension of the ranch cattle industry was replete with ambiguities, which persist today. To be sure, the chosen means were by turn impolite, shady, and vicious. But there is also a great deal to admire. Western ranch hands have put in more backbreaking hard work than most bodies could begin to bear. Cattle and sheep operations, large and small, have bred family and community values that are at the cultural bedrock of the rural West. It is mainly ranch land that accounts for the open, big sky country that so distinguishes the region. And the ranches were born of ingenuity of the highest degree, whether it meant inventing barbed wire, developing the system of range rights, finding ways to capture scarce water, instituting the system of thousand-mile cattle drives to market, or taking any of the myriad other steps necessary to build a workable, economical system of raising domestic animals in an arid, barren terrain utterly different from the green pastures of the eastern states. Thus, Walter Prescott Webb could properly refer to the extralegal devices of the cattle industry in one breath and, in the next, describe the ranch cattle industry as "perhaps the most unique and distinctive institution that America has produced."[23]

The Costs of Overgrazing: Adjustments to the Rancher's Code

By the mid-1880s, cattlemen controlled the land they needed, but the ground and the vegetation were absorbing a terrible beating. In 1886, Theodore Roosevelt, who later would make his mark on grazing and other resource policy as president, traveled through the plains country. He wrote of the life of the cowboy and the "free grass" offered up by the United States. He also issued this warning:

> But scantiness of food, due to overstocking, is the one really great danger to us in the [northern Great Plains], who do not have to fear the droughts that occasionally devastate portions of the southern ranges. In a fairly good country, if the feed is plenty, the natural increase of a herd is sure shortly to repair any damage that may be done by an unusually severe winter—unless, indeed, the latter should be one such as occurs but two or three times in a century. When, however, the grass becomes cropped down, then the loss in even an ordinary year is heavy among the weaker animals, and if the winter is at all severe it becomes simply appalling. The snow covers the shorter grass much quicker, and even when there is

enough, the cattle, weak and unfit to travel around, have to work hard to get it; their exertions tending to enfeeble them and to render them less able to cope with the exposure and cold. . . . The cows in calf are those that suffer most, and so heavy is the loss among these and so light the calf crop that it is yet an open question whether our northern ranges are as a whole fitted for breeding. When the animals get weak they will huddle into some nook or corner and simply stay there till they die. . . .

Overstocking may cause little or no harm for two or three years, but sooner or later there comes a winter which means ruin to the ranches that have too many cattle on them; and in our country, which is even now getting crowded, it is merely a question of time as to when a winter will come that will understock the ranges by the summary process of killing off about half of all the cattle throughout the North-west.[24]

Roosevelt proved to be prophetic. The die-off during the hard winter of 1886–1887 produced stock losses of staggering proportions. From all accounts, it was an almost incomprehensible scene. "These terrible blizzards, with continued snow and bitter cold which kept the grass buried under sheets of ice, killed hundreds of thousands of cattle." "When it was over, 70 percent of the cattle in eastern Montana lay frozen, stacked where they died in piles in willow thickets along various streams. Dugouts and old shacks were stuffed with carcasses of cattle that had jammed into any refuge offering protection from the bitter storm." "Without fences the range stock could have drifted ahead of the blizzards. Many might have been saved by finding shelter in some stream bottom or dry coulee. As it was, they wandered downwind until they could go no farther, then died huddled against the barbs by the tens of thousands." The big die-off of 1886–1887 was followed by several drought years in most regions of the West.[25]

In the twentieth century, the essence of federal range policy has been a series of attempts to resuscitate the range from the condition it reached in the late 1800s. These efforts have proceeded in the face of ranchers who continue to assert their "right" to graze herds without regulation. Western writer Owen Wister, in general a fervent admirer of ranch society, saw the dark side this way:

The unthinking sons of the sage brush ill tolerate a thing which stands for discipline, good order and obedience; and the man who lets another command him they despise. I can think of no threat more evil for our democracy, for it is a fine thing, diseased and perverted—namely, independence gone drunk.[26]

The first corrective measures taken by the federal government were made at the instigation of Gifford Pinchot, who was named chief of the

Division of Forestry in the Agriculture Department in 1898. The appointment made Pinchot the top government forester, but this ambitious, brilliant leader had a problem: the forest reserves, which had been established by presidential executive orders beginning in 1891, were housed in the Department of the Interior. Pinchot's main order of business was to gain control of those lands through a wholesale transfer of the national forests from Interior to Agriculture, a goal he achieved in 1905 with the support of Theodore Roosevelt after seven years of public oratory and behind-the-scenes maneuvering.

Pinchot was a forester, and, of course, it was control over the timberlands in the national forests that stirred his soul first and foremost. But the Transfer Act of 1905, which lodged such great power on his desk, allowed him and his president to accelerate their work on several projects relating to conservation. This was a holy crusade:

> When the natural resources of any nation become exhausted, disaster and decay in every department of national life follow as a matter of course. Therefore the conservation of natural resources is the basis, and the only permanent basis, of national success. . . .
> . . . The planned and orderly development and conservation of our natural resources is the first duty of the United States.[27]

Pinchot moved quickly to implement his conservationist philosophy in the area of grazing policy. His opportunity was greater than commonly realized: about one-third of the national forests are open rangeland, and another third are lightly timbered, where grazing is possible. Thus, when Pinchot introduced a Forest Service regulatory program for grazing in 1906, he was able to influence nearly 100 million acres.

The 1906 program modified the tradition of free and unregulated grazing on lands within the national forests by requiring a permit and a fee of $.05 per animal unit month (AUM). An animal unit is one cow or horse, or five sheep or goats, so the initial monthly fee was $.05 per cow or $.01 per sheep. An AUM, the accepted measuring stick for livestock consumption, is more forage than one might think: each AUM amounts to about 800 pounds of grass. The initial Forest Service permits were issued automatically to existing users, almost always for the number of AUMs requested.

Pinchot's 1906 program may have been modest by today's lights, but it was incendiary to the cattle industry. Several western legislatures passed memorials denouncing regulation of the federal range. "Pinchotism" was front-page news in western newspapers, and the chief of the Forest Service was labeled a dictator and a carpetbagger. Many forest rangers, who had thrived on the support of their local communities, suffered harassment.[28]

The legal question of Forest Service authority to require permits and

fees—Pinchot had no express congressional permission to regulate grazing, only general statutory authority to regulate "occupancy and use"
within the national forests—came to a head in litigation involving Fred
Light, a longtime rancher in the Roaring Fork River valley in Colorado. In
the 1880s, Light and his wife had built a rough-hewn log cabin and ever
since had run their sheep in what was later declared the Holy Cross Forest
Reserve. Light had opened summer range never previously grazed and was
a widely respected figure in the region. He and others were livid not just
over the fees and permit requirement but also over the Forest Service's
implicit assumption that it was not bound by the state fence laws: private
landowners in Colorado (and all other western states) were required to
build fences if they wished to keep other ranchers' stock off their land, but
the federal agency asserted the right to require a permit for grazing on
unfenced land. When the new rules were announced, Forest Service officials from the local area and from Denver met with local ranchers to
explain the necessity for the program. "But Fred Light, as leader of the
association and the opposition, under his code, could not back down."[29]

Light's refusal to obtain a permit became a test case for the Forest
Service program. It was a *cause célèbre* in Colorado and in ranching circles
nationally. The stock associations contributed to the payment of Light's
attorneys' fees. So did the Colorado legislature. Finally, the United States
Supreme Court agreed to hear the case and, in 1911, ruled for the Forest
Service in a milestone opinion. The Court acknowledged that there "grew
up a sort of implied license that these lands, thus left open, might be used."
The justices found, however, that the government's "failure to object . . .
did not confer any vested right" on Fred Light or "deprive the United States
of the power of recalling any implied license." Noting that "[t]he public
lands of the nation are held in trust for the people of the whole country,"
the justices ruled that "the United States can prohibit absolutely or fix the
terms on which its property may be used." The Court ruled in a companion
case that the Forest Service could enforce the grazing program by imposing
administrative fines on ranchers who failed to obtain permits.[30]

The courtroom struggle over, Light acceded graciously and obtained
federal permits for his animals. Other ranchers grudgingly followed. After
the passage of a decade, Forest Service grazing regulation became an
accepted part of western ranching. The actual payments, after all, were
only a fraction of market value. In fact, regulation did little to reduce the
intensity of grazing. Domestic stock use of the national forests rose from 14
million AUMs in 1908 to an all-time high of 20 million AUMs in 1920.
Further, and fundamentally, the pioneering work of the Forest Service had
no effect outside of the national forests. Public domain land remained open
to free and unregulated grazing for nearly three decades.

It took larger national events to bring regulation to the public domain lands in the form of the Taylor Grazing Act of 1934. The Great Depression had settled in, driving down beef and lamb prices. The severe, protracted droughts of the early 1930s helped create the Dust Bowl. Soil erosion became aggravated by water but most dramatically by wind. The ground had been overutilized not only by cattle and sheep but also by sod-busting farmers. A traditional Pawnee Indian, looking at a newly plowed-over field in the Great Plains, observed, "Wrong side up." The plumes of dust in the western half of the country were described by one Washington, DC, insider as "the most impressive lobbyist" on Capitol Hill. President Franklin Roosevelt and his aggressive, reform-minded interior secretary, Harold Ickes, pushed hard for regulation. Even western congressmen came to agree. They included Edward Taylor of Colorado, a states-righter who had fought against Pinchot's initiatives in the national forests and whose name would adorn the legislation bringing federal control to public domain grazing for the first time.[31]

The Taylor Grazing Act established 80 million acres of land in grazing districts that would be administered by the new Grazing Service in the Department of the Interior. Two years later, the act was amended, and the land within grazing districts was roughly doubled. At that point, virtually all federal grazing land finally had been brought under regulation.

The Taylor Act, however, was a compromise heavily influenced by western stock interests, and it amounted to an even lighter touch than the minimal regulation enforced by the Forest Service in the national forests three decades earlier. Grazing fees were set at a low level, the $.05 per AUM standard adopted by the Forest Service in 1906, in spite of a 1934 Forest Service fee nearly three times as high. Statutory preferences ensured that permits would almost always go to existing stock interests and that 1934 stock levels would almost always remain undisturbed. National and local advisory boards, composed of ranchers, were established by amendments to the act and wielded enormous influence over the grazing program. The Grazing Service was woefully underfunded; its total of sixty employees in 1935, for example, virtually excluded the possibility of any on-the-ground management, evaluation, or enforcement. The new agency could do little more than rubber-stamp decisions made by the advisory boards dominated by ranchers, the very group that the Taylor Grazing Act supposedly had been enacted to regulate.

The Taylor Grazing Act also implicitly confirmed the livestock industry's attitude toward the rangeland of the American West. There was no room for policy initiatives to protect the mule deer, trout, ducks, and raccoons that once inhabited the riparian zones of Camp Creek and other western streams, much less the animals that directly competed with cattle and sheep: the wild horses and burros that were shot and sold for their hides or the eagles and coyotes that were regularly poisoned. With the Taylor Act, the rudiments of range management were instituted, but "range" meant land dedicated to domestic stock. And it meant public land still controlled by private industry, by the rancher's code.

These failings continue to hamper the Bureau of Land Management, created in 1946 by consolidation of the Grazing Service and the General Land Office. T. H. Watkins and Charles Watson have observed that

> [l]ike the public domain itself the Bureau has from its beginning suffered from an overdose of neglect. It was founded by the minions of the Two-Gun Desmonds of the West to be nothing more than an interim caretaker of the land while they figured out some way of getting that land out of federal ownership, and the agency was for years deliberately kept short of money and manpower. Even now, when the Bureau has acquired the image of a steward of the land instead of a disinterested observer, it is understaffed, underfunded, and underpowered.[32]

The Taylor Grazing Act, mild though it may have been, led to a series of recriminations by the stock industry. In 1946, when the Grazing Service (shortly to become the BLM) attempted to move grazing fees in the direction of market value, western congressmen friendly to cattle interests slashed the agency's budget in half. Minimal oversight was nearly restored to no oversight. Congressional field hearings were held in various western cities when the Forest Service sought to cut back the number of AUMs in the national forests. Bills were introduced in Congress in 1947 and 1948 to transfer the public grazing lands to the states. Similar proposals were made in 1952 and 1953. Broader-based western support never materialized, in part because of a remarkable series of some forty articles by native Utahan Bernard DeVoto, writing his "Easy Chair" column for *Harper's Magazine*. Decrying the proposed "landgrab," DeVoto described this chapter of the stock interests' crusade to rule the public range:

> A few groups of Western interests, so small numerically as to constitute a minute fraction of the West, are hellbent on destroying the West. They are stronger than they would otherwise be because they are skilfully manipulating in their support sentiments that have always been powerful in the West—the home rule which means basically that we want federal help without federal regulation, the "individualism" that has always made the small Western operator a handy tool of the big one, and the wild myth that stockgrowers constitute an aristocracy in which all Westerners somehow share.[33]

The late 1950s and 1960s brought no major developments in federal range policy. Ranching practices were left to the discretion of ranchers.

Fees inched up but still fell even further behind market value. The fact that
the range remained in poor condition—and was holding steady at best—
was widely recognized, but industry continued to control the BLM and
western congressmen who chaired key committees and subcommittees. In
the 1970s, however, the *status quo* was altered by a relative newcomer to
the federal rangelands—the conservation movement. The conservationists
in turn brought in the judiciary, which previously had been enlisted only by
the Forest Service in the early test cases and by private ranchers seeking to
confirm their range rights.

The environmentalism that took hold during the several years on each
side of 1970 brought a new set of priorities and, as importantly, new
procedures. The legislative centerpiece was the National Environmental
Policy Act, passed in 1969 and made effective on January 1, 1970, in order
to usher in the new decade on a note of heightened consciousness toward
the environment. NEPA, which had the full support of President Richard
Nixon and Senator Henry Jackson, chairman of the Senate Interior Committee, may well have been intended by many of the legislators who voted
for it to be little more than a fuzzy and unenforceable policy statement.
Indeed, much of NEPA is general, nonbinding policy. NEPA, for example,
asserts in ringing phrases that "it is the continuing responsibility of the
Federal Government to . . . fulfill the responsibilities of each generation as
trustee of the environment for succeeding generations" and to "assure for
all Americans safe, healthful, productive, and esthetically and culturally
pleasing surroundings." Those lofty goals, however, are watered down by
language in the same section that NEPA's policy should be carried out by
using "all practicable means, consistent with other essential considerations
of national policy." Those are time-honored code words for any bureaucrat with a mission that would be inconvenienced by much attention to
environmental issues.[34]

But stuck away in another section of NEPA was a seemingly innocuous
provision that all federal agencies must prepare a "detailed statement" for
all "major Federal actions significantly affecting the quality of the human
environment." The court decisions since have indeed required "detailed"
environmental impact statements, or EISs, and the EIS requirement has
been applied to a wide range of administrative activities that might have
severe environmental consequences. Grazing on the public lands, for example, was never mentioned in NEPA's relatively sparse legislative history,
but court-mandated EISs have played a role of considerable importance in
modern federal grazing policy.[35]

The idea that courts might hear citizen lawsuits involving grazing issues
was near-revolutionary even in 1970. Just as the stock interests had controlled the public range during the nineteenth century by the exercise of
possession and harassment, and just as they controlled the range during

modern times through the intermediate step of controlling administrative policy, so too had the stockmen held sway over the judiciary on a *de facto* basis. It was not corruption. Rather, there simply was nothing in the laws that held out any handle to anyone but ranchers or, occasionally, federal or state officials. Before 1970, there had never been any significant lawsuit implicating grazing brought by a citizen outside of the ranching community. Sheepherders had sued cattle interests, and vice versa. States had brought prosecutions to enforce violations of state-created range rights. Ranchers had sued the United States to attack increases in fees or decreases in AUMs. The only cases with public overtones were the test cases brought by Gifford Pinchot's Forest Service against Fred Light and others. Those decisions, it bears remembering, were handed down in 1911. Implicitly, the judiciary traditionally had recognized that the 270 million acres of federal grazing lands existed to serve the stock interests.

Developments of the 1960s and 1970s outside of grazing law—often outside of natural resource law generally—opened the federal courts to other individuals and groups. The Supreme Court adopted the so-called hard look doctrine of judicial review, meaning that federal judges would give serious scrutiny to decisions of administrative officials under the Administrative Procedure Act's prohibition against "arbitrary and capricious" actions. Citizen groups possess standing (that is, they meet the requirement that any person or organization bringing suit against a federal agency have a minimum stake in the outcome of the suit) if they have a "special interest in the conservation and sound maintenance" of the federal land area in question, a standard that can be met simply by showing that some members of the group use the area. Responding to the need to allow the citizenry access to the courts to ventilate grievances, Congress waived federal sovereign immunity for most lawsuits, other than those involving title to federal lands, so that public organizations seldom would be stymied with the hoary rule from Old England that suits against the sovereign were impossible because "the King can do no wrong." Even with the emergence in the late 1980s of a more conservative Supreme Court, these and other similar developments, technical on one level but evincing profound pressures for open government on another, allow unprecedented scrutiny both by federal judges and by groups never before associated with public grazing issues.[36]

Conservationists plugged NEPA's "detailed statement" requirement into these judicial-access principles to achieve the first serious outside review of overgrazing on the federal lands. In 1973, the newly created Natural Resources Defense Council filed suit to contest an EIS that the BLM had completed to evaluate its grazing program. The EIS was "programmatic," meaning that it described the BLM's national, overall programs and had no detailed on-the-ground analysis. The Natural Resources Defense Council argued that such a general document was insufficient and that EISs must zero in on specific impacts at the local level. In December 1974, a federal judge agreed, saying that assessing national impacts in a programmatic EIS was useful but that it was not sufficiently "fine-tuned" and could not replace local EISs sensitive to "individual geographic conditions." But Judge Thomas A. Flannery's opinion rested on more than NEPA. He also decried the condition of the range itself and the lack of management and recognized that the public lands exist for purposes in addition to cattle raising:

> [T]he BLM Budget Justification for fiscal year 1973 estimated that only 16 percent of the BLM managed grazing land was in good or excellent condition while 84 percent was in fair, poor or bad condition. In addition, plaintiffs present evidence from both private and governmental sources demonstrating that serious deterioration of BLM lands is taking or has taken place. In its first annual report, the Council on Environmental Quality reported that overgrazing had dramatically affected the public lands.
>
> Much of this land, particularly the vast public domain, remains in desperate condition, as wind, rain, and drought have swept over them and eroded their exposed soils. Although the effects of overgrazing in rich pastures or prairie farmland can be quickly corrected, the process is often irreversible on the limited soils and arid climate of much of the public lands. [CEQ, Environmental Quality 182 (1970).]
>
> Unfortunately this situation has not been rectified since that date. A recent Bureau of Land Management report entitled Effects of Livestock Grazing on Wildlife, Watershed, Recreation and Other Resource Values in Nevada (April 1974) documents the serious damage being wrought on the environment. The report, compiled by a team of BLM resource managers, states flatly that wildlife habitat is being destroyed. "Uncontrolled, unregulated or unplanned livestock use is occurring in approximately 85 percent of the State and damage to wildlife habitat can be express[ed] only as extreme destruction." Overgrazing by livestock has caused invasion of sagebrush and rabbitbrush on meadows and has decreased the amount of meadow habitat available for wildlife survival by at least 50 percent. The reduced meadow area has caused a decline in both game and non-game population. In addition, there are 883 miles of streams with deteriorating and declining wildlife habitat, thus making it apparent, according to the report, that grazing systems do not protect and enhance wildlife values [citations omitted].[37]

Ultimately, the BLM was required to complete 144 grazing EISs, a process that was about three-quarters complete by the late 1980s. It has been expensive: on-site analysis of the state of the public range in this fashion may exceed $100 million. Still, the starting point for rational land planning and management is a reliable resource inventory, and these EISs have brought in a great amount of valuable information. As George Cameron Coggins, Parthenia Evans, and Margaret Lindberg-Johnson have put it, "Future historians may date the beginning of modern rangeland management from December 1974 when a federal district court ordered the BLM to comply with NEPA."[38]

The next major event in federal range policy occurred in 1976, with the passage of the Federal Land Policy and Management Act. FLPMA finally consolidated and modernized the hundreds of laws relating to the BLM. FLPMA also articulated the mission of the BLM, for so many years the stepchild among federal land agencies. Perhaps paramount, the six-year passage of FLPMA through Congress amounted to a national referendum on what has always been the central philosophical issue regarding the federal public lands: should America's landed estate, nearly one-third of all land within the nation's borders, continue to be owned by the United States, or should it be sold off to the states or private parties? The very first section of FLPMA was a congressional declaration requiring that "the public lands be retained in federal ownership."[39]

FLPMA dealt with nearly the full range of issues involving BLM lands. As noted earlier, it required that information concerning hardrock mining claims be filed with the government. Its provisions on grazing, enacted in response to a broader public conception of the values of rangeland as well as the lobbying of the stock interests, reflected new times in grazing management. The range was declared subject to multiple-use management for recreation and wildlife as well as for domestic animals. The planning and enforcement authority of the BLM, including the power to levy fines and reduce AUMs, was clarified. Ranchers were given additional security: most permits were set for ten years, and permit holders were to be compensated for their investments in range improvement if their permitted acres were put to another use. Importantly, although FLPMA dodged the increasingly volatile issue of below-market grazing fees by calling for a study of the problem, the act confirmed existing law that ranchers had no vested rights in the lands on which their stock grazed.[40]

Two years later, Congress revisited range management in the Public Rangeland Improvement Act of 1978 (PRIA). Ranching interests succeeded in achieving a grazing fee formula guaranteed to keep rates well below market value. On the other hand, with the poor state of BLM rangeland ever more apparent, in PRIA Congress identified range improvement as the highest management priority, mandated that range plans be "tailored to the specific range condition of the area to be covered by such plan," and directed that review of the plans be aimed toward determining whether "they have been effective in improving the range condition of the lands involved."[41]

During the late 1970s, BLM officials in the Carter administration began to implement stock reductions in response to the shiny new FLPMA-PRIA policy mandates and the range condition data generated by the court-ordered EISs. But the reduction program was short-circuited. In 1979, industry succeeded in achieving the McClure Amendment, a rider to the appropriations bill, which effectively gave a two-year phase-in period for any reduction of more than 10 percent. Then came the much-heralded Sagebrush Rebellion of the early 1980s.[42]

The rebellion's basic constituency was composed of ranchers fed up with the increased federal oversight and threatened stock reductions accruing from the 1974 *Natural Resources Defense Council, Inc. v. Morton* decision, FLPMA, and PRIA. The stock interests and their allies wanted a sell-off of the public lands, especially BLM lands. At first, the proposal was for the sale to be made straight to industry, but the formula was modified to call for transfer to the states as stalking horses for the stock interests, to whom the land would promptly be reconveyed. The sale idea went nowhere. President Ronald Reagan announced, "I am a Rebel," and then appointed James Watt—so plainly a Rebel that he scarcely needed to proclaim it—as interior secretary, but Congress was not much interested in "The Great Terrain Robbery," as some have called it. Scattered bills were introduced but never taken seriously. Nevada filed a lawsuit, arguing that the United States was just a "temporary trustee" of the public lands for the state and that the federal government's policy of permanent retention, set out in FLPMA, was unlawful. A Nevada federal judge concluded that "beyond doubt" the United States owns the public lands and that it is up to Congress to decide how to manage them.[43]

The Sagebrush Rebels, though unable to convince Congress to sell off the federal lands, had little trouble achieving a less radical objective: persuading the Interior Department of the 1980s that it ought to take a hands-off policy toward grazing. The centerpiece of the Watt administration's grazing policy was the so-called cooperative management agreement (CMA) program. The stated goal was to provide CMAs to "exemplary" ranchers so that they would have increased security and management latitude. CMAs, which were to remain in effect for ten years, would leave nearly all decisions, including the setting of AUMs, with the ranchers. This program, too, was halted by the judiciary. In 1985, a federal district court declared that the CMA approach illegally circumvented the BLM's statutory obligation to care for overgrazed public range:

> The cooperative agreements unlawfully abdicate the Secretary's statutory duty to prescribe for ranchers the appropriate number of livestock

which may be grazed on each public land allotment or the permissible grazing seasons. The agreements also fail to retain necessary governmental authority to enforce overgrazing prohibitions by cancelling, suspending, or modifying permits on abused public allotments.[44]

The ruling on the CMAs prevented a formal long-term transfer of authority over the public range to the ranchers, but the Interior Department has been able to achieve much the same result through benign neglect. In spite of the impressive amount of on-the-ground data showing the poor condition of the land, BLM officials have continued the time-honored system of deferring to the ranching industry. The stock reductions proposed during the 1970s have been abandoned. Few management requirements have been imposed.

This system of passive resistance has proved difficult to attack in court. Judges feel reasonably comfortable evaluating the legality of a formal, written policy such as Secretary Watt's CMA proposal. They are less well equipped to assess a nonpolicy. The Natural Resources Defense Council challenged the grazing program of the BLM's Reno District, comprising some 1.5 million acres of rangeland. In its EIS, the BLM had studied the region and solemnly noted the pervasive effects of grazing but nonetheless had ratified the existing AUMs and range practices. Judge James Burns knew that this was business as usual, candidly stating, "Plaintiffs are understandably upset at what they view to be a lopsided and ecologically insensitive pattern of management of public lands at the hands of the BLM." Still, finding no firm legal handle in the policy statements in FLPMA and PRIA, he ruled in 1986 that a federal judge should not be a "rangemaster" and left the matter with the BLM and the political process. The appellate court affirmed this hands-off judicial approach.[45]

The ranchers' ability to preserve the *status quo* continues on other fronts. In February 1986, President Reagan signed an executive order extending indefinitely the current grazing fee of $1.35 per AUM, as against an average fair market value of $6.35. In doing so, Reagan ignored the advice of his financial watchdog, Office of Management and Budget director James Miller, who recommended that the subsidy be extended "for only one year in order to 'maintain the pressure on Congress to seek a permanent solution for the problem.' "[46]

Congress took no action as a body during the 1980s, but an upsurge of reform sentiment was evidenced when the House Government Operations Committee filed an angry report in May 1986. The report, put together by a subcommittee headed by Democrat Mike Synar of Oklahoma, decried the grazing fee subsidies and criticized numerous aspects of the current program, including the fact that an unknown number of federal lessees are able to sublease their below-market grazing rights at a profit. The report also reflected the continuing concern of many members of Congress, especially those from eastern states, that subsidies to public land ranchers give them a market advantage over other meat producers. As the Synar Subcommittee on Environment, Energy, and Natural Resources put it:

> The livestock industry consists of more than producers who graze livestock on public rangelands. (As the Committee notes, less than 2% of American livestock producers use public rangelands.) On the other hand, it is *not* just public rangeland users who are affected by hard economic times. . . . Yet it is *only* the users of public rangelands who enjoy a unique Federal grazing fee subsidy amounting to about $1,435 per permittee.[47]

Synar's focused efforts, complemented by lobbying from the large national environmental groups, bore some fruit later but only in the House of Representatives, which by comfortable margins passed bills calling for grazing fee increases in both 1990 and 1991. The 1991 measure also called for abolishing the pro-industry BLM grazing advisory boards and for authorizing the BLM to use grazing fee receipts not only for funding traditional range improvements to benefit ranching but also for improving wildlife areas, protecting wildlife habitat, and funding on-site monitoring of ranchers. The Senate, with the Energy and Natural Resources Committee dominated by pro-producer western senators, had not acted as of the early 1990s.[48]

Reform Begins to Brew in Ranch Country

While Washington, DC, remained in gridlock, giving most of its attention to grazing fees, other movements began to coalesce in the West. These close-to-the-ground developments, led by progressive federal land managers and forward-looking ranchers, have centered on the land itself and have struggled to accommodate both ranching and a healthy range. These advances may well hold the best hope for an enduring resolution to the seemingly intractable problems on the western range.

For tangible evidence of the possibilities, we can return to Camp Creek in Oregon, where this chapter began—where the soils, water, and wildlife have been so thoroughly worked over since the 1880s and where silted-up Severance Reservoir stands as vivid proof of how this trampled-down, gullied-out watershed is literally slipping toward the sea.

On upper Camp Creek and on Bear Creek, its neighboring watershed to the west, range specialists have carried out one of the oldest and most exhaustive studies of rangeland conditions in the world. Wildlife biologist Harold Winegar instituted the project in 1965 under the joint auspices of the BLM and the Oregon Department of Fish and Wildlife. Initially, about a mile of upper Camp Creek—then a rocky, deep-cut trench—was fenced: this "exclosure" kept all cattle out. For more than a decade, the project has been run and substantially enlarged by Wayne Elmore of the Prineville office of the BLM.[49]

Elmore, a wildlife biologist and riparian ecologist born and schooled in Oklahoma, has expanded the original upper Camp Creek project to 5 miles of fenced stream. He also has succeeded in obtaining exclosures on about 70 miles of Bear Creek and other watersheds in the BLM's Prineville District. Further, Elmore has taken the findings at Camp Creek and Bear Creek elsewhere, lecturing across the West on the potential benefits to be gained from good riparian management. A big, likable man with a bushy beard, Elmore is a considerable raconteur. He likes to tell the story about the time he was showing slides to his office staff on how native grasses can collect sediment and thereby build up stream bottoms. He flipped to a slide showing a side view of himself against the backdrop of Camp Creek. As he recounts it, his secretary noted his athletic but ample girth and commented, "Looks like you've been collecting a little sediment yourself, Wayne."

His sense of humor, and more than a little bit of courage (he once rode rodeo bulls), have come in handy because it is not easy going to tell western ranchers where and how to graze their stock—no matter how salutary the results. Elmore has endured continued resistance from BLM higher-ups responding to complaints from angry rancher-constituents. Other cattlemen have taken more direct routes. One tried to haul the strapping Elmore out of his pickup truck by his shirt. Another showed up in the lobby of the Prineville BLM office toting an 8-foot fence post, telling the receptionist that he wanted to see Elmore because he had a place where he would like to insert the post. Fortunately for Elmore, the western range, and, not incidentally, the livestock industry, all of these efforts failed, because the results of his range management program show the promise that is held out if we are able to alter the age-old, unilateral right of private ranchers to control the public range.

If you go to the exclosures on upper Camp Creek today, you can see the revival of the watershed. Before the management program began, virtually the only vegetation in the riparian zone was a superficial covering of Kentucky bluegrass. This cover was quickly consumed by the cattle that were turned loose in the early spring. With the animals excluded, native riparian vegetation returned—woolly and Nebraska sedge, redtop grass, three-square rush, water hemlock, and willows. They have caught sediment, and Camp Creek has started to rebuild itself within this stretch.

Remember that Camp Creek once was at rooftop height above the current channel. The gradual collection of silt has not brought the streambed back up that far, but after twenty years of protection the creek is at door-top level: there is now 6 feet of new earth. You walk not on hard-packed dirt and rocks but on a surface that is noticeably spongy. The smell of wild mint is in the air during the late summer. There is an old fence post, but you see only a nub of 3 or 4 inches. The stream bottom has slowly risen to submerge the rest of the post.

There are many other changes. Trout have not yet returned, but little dace now dart around in the stream. There are eight beaver dams. Mule deer tracks are regularly sighted. Before the project, waterfowl were rarely seen, and nesting was unknown. Today, there are several nesting pairs of ducks; songbirds are abundant. The riparian zone feels like a sponge because it is one. The water table has risen steadily. Just 1.0 cubic foot per second (cfs) of water enters the exclosure from the unfenced region upstream. After receiving seepage from the management area, the stream carries 2.4 cfs of water. In the dry years of 1977 and 1981, Camp Creek was entirely dry except for the stretch within the BLM exclosure. All of this has occurred with no structures except the fences—no expensive dams, rock-filled baskets called gabions, or riprap. Those kinds of projects were not needed to hold water or stabilize banks. As Elmore says: "Nature is ten times the stabilizer that our engineers are. We don't tell the stream where it needs help. We let the stream tell us."

The exclosure at Camp Creek has been operated to keep cattle out of the streambed, but in many other projects domestic stock has been allowed to graze in the rejuvenated, highly productive riparian zones. One example is Bear Creek, Camp Creek's sister drainage to the west, where the results of good management have been at least as dramatic. The watershed produces more water than Camp Creek, and the sediment buildup of 6 feet or more has produced a meandering channel holding trout up to 20 inches long. Also, the trench cut by erosion at Bear Creek was shallower than in the neighboring watershed, so the riparian zone has spread out more. You can visualize how the water table, fed by the reviving green zone, has steadily risen back up. All along the managed area of the stream, 100 feet out on each side, are sagebrush and juniper skeletons. There is now too much water in the soil for these invading dryland plants. Bunchgrass and wild rye, the old tallgrass of Peter Skene Ogden's day, are moving back in. In one 600-acre pasture, a rancher once obtained just 72 AUMs by turning his cattle out in June and rounding them up in September. Now he runs 313 AUMs of cattle in the same area from mid-February through mid-March. Then the cattle are rotated through pastures in the uplands while the riparian zone flourishes during the spring-summer growing season.

Wayne Elmore, of course, is not alone. There are growing numbers of range professionals in the Forest Service and the BLM who are determined to bring the range back into acceptable condition. To be sure, both agencies have many miles still to travel. A go-slow attitude predominates in many of the field, regional, and national offices. This is particularly true in the BLM, but both agencies remain too susceptible to pressure from obdurate ranchers who seek to throttle the efforts of reform-minded range conservationists. In a 1988 report, the General Accounting Office cited two main reasons for the snail's pace of restoring riparian areas on public lands: reductions in staff specializing in riparian work and the fact that "many of the field staff responsible for riparian improvement work, primarily in BLM, do not believe their work will be supported by agency management if it is opposed by ranchers using the public rangelands." Still, if you spend time with professional federal grazing officials at any level, and if you keep up with the rising number of agency enforcement actions, you come away with a clear sense that a new determination has been born and that it is building steadily.[50]

Developments of equal importance involve the ranching community itself. They are personified by Allan Savory, founder of the Center for Holistic Resource Management in Albuquerque, who is an extraordinarily successful popularizer of concepts of modern rangeland management. A native of southern Rhodesia (now Zimbabwe), Savory has applied his knowledge of the high plains of his homeland to the western rangelands of the United States. Both are what Savory calls "brittle" environments—arid or semiarid regions where rainfall is sporadic and most of the plants, usually bunchgrass types, die off at the end of the growing season. In such brittle environments, Savory argues, grazing ungulates are essential to the health of the system. They eat the dead top material, thereby stimulating growth in the plants. Their hoof action chips up the soil, allowing seeds to germinate and water to be held:

> You have all no doubt watched cattle or bison graze. I will bet that as they grazed you didn't see them kick up any dust, nor did you see them put a foot down on a coarse plant. They tread carefully and slowly. This does not always do the job required. Watch the same animals when they are "herding" as natural wild populations fearing predation do when moving. They kick up dust and trample all over coarse plant material. It is this behavior that is so vital to the soils and plants and all the other life dependent on them in our brittle environments.
>
> This is why early American settlers did not meet up with large wildlife herds in the East, which is largely non-brittle, but met them in the brittle environments of the West, where the communities of soils, plants and all animal life had developed a mutual interdependence which led to high

productivity and stability. Where herding ungulates were largely missing
in environments leaning toward brittleness in post-Pleistocene periods,
the grasslands that developed tend to be less stable and productive.

So, removing the cattle won't do any good unless there are other
herding animals to replace them.[51]

For Savory, therefore, the real issue is timing of grazing, not numbers of
stock. He believes that if animals are brought in at the right time of year
and managed well—kept moving and given "just one bite at each plant"—
the range can be revived. In many cases, Savory argues, as many or more
head of stock as before can be grazed on a spread that has become healthier
because of the improved management.[52]

Importantly, Savory's holistic resource management (HRM) puts
ranching in a broad context. Ranch families are urged to engage in comprehensive goal setting, which includes not only beef or lamb production but
also quality-of-life issues—the wildlife, beauty, and general land health of
their ranches. On those ranches where the HRM approach has worked, the
participants usually reflect back to the early goal-setting sessions—around
the kitchen or dining room table, with coffee, taking the time to dream
about what they want a full ranch life to be. When it does work, the
approach yields increased profits, a healthier environment, and personal
satisfaction.[53]

The charismatic Savory—he is a brilliant teacher and lecturer—has
become a lightning rod. Some range scientists say that he promises too
much, that some soils are simply too unstable to accommodate cattle at all.
Such areas, they say, need to be closed off for at least a generation. Others
dispute the purity of his analogy between cattle and buffalo. Wayne
Elmore, for example, says, "You don't *need* livestock to regenerate a range
system, but 95% of the time you *can* regenerate a system if livestock are
there." Others make the point that the HRM approach does not always
work precisely because it takes so much work—from the initial goal setting
through the increased vigilance and labor out on the ground. Still, although
it may be that Savory overextols the reach of his approach, growing
numbers of ranchers have become enthusiastic converts. Many who have
adopted Savory's method claim that they have found substantial improvements in range conditions within eighteen months; the added costs in
personnel (to keep the cattle moving) and range improvements (mainly
fencing and employee salaries related to herding) are exceeded by increased
revenues in the fourth, third, or even second year. Riparian zones are so
productive that their increased growth offsets the new expenses. Rotating
the stock through the uplands, rather than allowing the animals to congregate, promotes the return of the nutritious native grasses.[54]

As might be expected, much of what Elmore and Savory say is not truly new. Savory's emphasis on the "timing" of grazing, for example, has its precedents: Gus Hormay and other range scientists and managers have long advocated "rest-rotation" grazing, in which cattle were rotated through a four-pasture system, and other specialized grazing systems that combine periods of use and nonuse. But Elmore and Savory have sharpened the debate and accelerated the possibilities for progress through their on-the-ground work and, not incidentally, the publicity accruing from their personalities and sense of commitment. Further, the times are ripe for real progress because of the increased attention given to the state of the western range by litigation and legislation since the mid-1970s.[55]

Ultimately, the approaches of Elmore and Savory show so much potential because of three fundamental ideas. First, cattle ranching must be viewed holistically, with a determination that all elements of a range ecosystem will be healthy and vigorous. Such an approach promotes both domestic stock-raising and the other rangeland resources, including water, wildlife, and recreation. Second, cows simply cannot be turned loose in the spring and rounded up in the fall. Too many costs, in the form of a degraded range, result from that traditional way of ranching. This intensive range use must be carefully planned and managed. Third, the controversy over the health of the western range ought not to be a war against the ranchers. We must eliminate this lord of yesterday—unregulated grazing of domestic cattle on the public range—but that objective need not override western ranchers and the societal benefits they produce.

The latter is no small point. The repeated emphasis on raising grazing fees and reducing stock numbers, as opposed to the Elmore-Savory approach of promoting good management, backs ranchers into a financial corner. Heather Smith Thomas, a family rancher near Salmon, Idaho, puts it this way:

> Some people are saying that these Western ranches aren't needed, that they're only a small part of the beef industry and if they go broke it won't really matter. But that's not true.
> Ranching is the major industry in a lot of Western communities, and the economic future of those communities, and by ripple effect the state. . . . This isn't just a remote situation that affects only a few Western ranchers. . . .
> . . . [I]f ranches like ours become uneconomical, if we are forced or priced off federal lands, most of these ranches would be sold for subdivisions. Without the range permit, they are not functional as ranches, and the only market for them would be to developers who would cut them up into summer homes and "ranchettes."[56]

If the Elmore and Savory ideas can aid the livestock industry, why do so many ranchers remain unreconstructed? Why does the erosion continue and the land remain far below its potential productivity? When those questions are asked, one gets a number of replies. First, the industry is in a trough, and ranches—especially small ones—are cash poor. Even if projections show that the returns may well outstrip the costs, there is a fear that the expense of better management would be good money thrown after bad. Second, it takes a different kind of work and a different approach to the world to rotate the animals through several pastures. Ranchers are hardly lazy, but many do tend to be set in their ways. Third, when it comes to the federal government, for generations the ranch community has let simmer a thick stew of fierce independence, paranoia, bad experiences with federal agencies, and firsthand knowledge of local traditions. Federal initiatives simply are not welcome. An outsider may conclude that Wayne Elmore knows the Camp Creek drainage better than any person alive—and he may, at least as far as a comprehensive understanding of cows, soil, water, plants, and wildlife is concerned. But Elmore grew up in Oklahoma and works for the federal government. Period. One Camp Creek rancher, who speaks for much of the western ranching industry, sees Elmore as a surrogate for the national bureaucracy: "I run cows here and I always have. Elmore just wants his bird sanctuary."

But there is another reason why ranchers object to initiatives for change, and it is here that we can begin to appreciate the actual stakes. The predecessors of today's ranchers built their operations at a time when the public lands were free and unregulated. After the Taylor Grazing Act of 1934, existing ranchers always were given grazing preference for the lands that their stock had historically used. The new BLM leases have always run with the base ranch, and AUMs have been kept at historical levels. Whenever a ranch changes hands, the federal grazing permits are bought and sold as an integral part of the spread.

This pattern has become a critical aspect of ranch real estate transactions. Western ranch sales typically are premised on AUMs, not acreage. Ranches sell, in other words, not at $1000 per acre but at $1000 per AUM—$2000–$3000 in some areas, including parts of Colorado and New Mexico. Purchasers know that public land AUMs are not as secure as AUMs on deeded land, and some discount may be made for public AUMs. Still, the federal grazing leases are capitalized into the value of the ranch. Although by law these resources belong to the public, in market terms western ranchers have literally *bought* these AUMs. Understandably, they rage at the idea that some of "their" AUMs might be eliminated.[57]

These economic forces are the most powerful reason why ranchers have so tenaciously opposed any reductions in AUMs. A cut in AUMs will cut the sale price of the ranch proportionately. Further, ranches are usually valued for loan purposes based on AUMs, and the appraised value will drop if the AUMs drop. A decrease in AUMs thus will reduce a rancher's ability to raise capital and will weaken the security on existing loans. Of course, any sharp rise in the grazing fee could also directly affect the financial viability of a ranch. Politically, proposals to reduce AUMs or to increase grazing fees have translated into lobbying by the banking industry as well as the ranch industry. As Charles Callison, longtime observer of range policy, has told me: "It's one thing when western congressmen hear from the ranchers. But they really leap into action when the bankers start getting on the telephone." The Elmore-Savory regime of intensive management, therefore, may be designed to improve the financial well-being of western ranches as well as the ecological health of the range, but many western ranchers see it as a federally imposed stalking horse for the environmentalists' stock reduction–fee increase program. And they tell their bankers about it.[58]

Elmore, Savory, and other advocates of intensified management also raise their share of suspicion among conservationists. Indeed, the phrase "intensive management" has become something of a buzzword. Environmental leaders argue that riparian exclosures for cattle also tend to exclude recreationists and wildlife, even when fences are constructed to allow for passage by people and by animals other than cows. They believe that ranchers, rather than using exclosures around riparian zones, should keep their stock out of stream bottoms by more vigilant herding. Similarly, upland fencing should be kept to a minimum. There is also opposition to manipulative techniques such as chaining and chemical defoliating, designed to drive out undesirable invading plant species in the uplands. Elmore and Savory would make minimal use of such techniques or eschew them altogether, but other range managers favor them in some situations. There is no doubt that we are far from consensus on these matters and that the implementation of improved management practices will be accompanied by disputes over particulars.[59]

Conservationists working on rangeland issues also show a deep-set skepticism that the call for increased management is anything other than a subterfuge for increasing the AUMs on a hypothetically improved federal range. They are especially critical of the colorful Savory and his holistic resource management. Steve Johnson of Defenders of Wildlife has walked some ground in Arizona where Savory's methods have been adopted. Although he recognizes that five years may not be enough time to evaluate the merits of HRM, Johnson argues that Savory is guilty of "extravagant promises" and that "HRM bears a stronger resemblance to a religion than to a scientifically based method of land renewal." And, to be sure, the validity of Savory's method is most in doubt in the parched Southwest, where thin, fragile soils have been so badly punished in some areas that grazing must be drastically cut back or eliminated altogether, perhaps for many years, perhaps permanently. Indeed, it is exactly on this point that Elmore and Savory (and the range specialists they each represent) part ways. Savory seems to suggest that virtually all of the western range needs as many or more cows as it now holds. Elmore thinks that some areas—although a small part—need to be removed from cattle grazing altogether.[60]

Leaving aside personalities, exceptionally fragile and abused areas, and the details of implementation in specific watersheds, there is growing recognition that improved management can rebuild most western riparian zones and uplands and still maintain cattle at or near current levels. There are many examples, but none is better than the Deseret Ranch in northeastern Utah. This huge 220,000-acre spread is all private land, but after 100 years of heavy use it began to show symptoms of the widespread desertification that characterizes most of the public range. In 1979, the ranch embarked on a program of management that kept cattle out of the creek beds except for short periods in the early spring and that rotated herds through four different upland pastures each spring, allowing plants to recover fully from grazing. Within eighteen months, the vegetation was visibly reviving. The land health of the upland range has improved as native bunchgrasses have moved back in. The same is true with Deseret Ranch's riparian zones: as at Camp Creek, sagebrush-lined washes have been replaced by plant communities characteristic of riparian areas, and some long-dry creeks have running water all year long. The profit margin of the ranch has increased steadily. Cattle numbers have increased from 4500 to 5700 head. Elk have doubled from 750 to 1500, enough to support a profitable private hunting program in this serene high country.[61]

Deseret Ranch, Camp Creek, and Bear Creek are just some of the many success stories cropping up across the West. Steve Gallizioli is an Arizona outdoors writer long critical of poor grazing practices. In making the following comments, he happened to be writing about one of Allan Savory's sessions, but he evidenced an emerging awareness among ranchers that there needs to be a new vigilance toward the range:

> Significantly the ranchers at the school I attended (most of the 38 people were either ranchers or in related fields) were an enthusiastic and appreciative bunch from all over the west, several from Arizona. They seemed to have as much concern for proper land use as I did and were eager to go home and begin the hardest part of an HRM program—the long hours and days with paper, pencil and maps to develop even a preliminary land use plan.
>
> I came away from Albuquerque much encouraged about the possibility of actually restoring our worn-out and bleeding rangelands. I'm

sure over the next few years you're going to be hearing a lot more about Holistic Resource Management and what it portends for healthier eco-systems and for the wildlife dependent on those ecosystems.[62]

The combination of determined federal oversight and improved ranching practices by a growing sector of the ranch community is young, basically tracing to the late 1970s and early 1980s. Yet it would be wrong to ignore its promise and force. Ed Marston, publisher of *High Country News*, put it well when he wrote that he feels

> a sense of profound relief because there is—at last—evidence of sustainable, unstoppable movement to recover a lost land. The movement appears sustainable and unstoppable for two reasons. First, because I believe for a variety of reasons that both the Forest Service and the ranchers are ready for a new approach to the range. And second because the push for change is coming from what the media call "everyday" people [in Forest Service and BLM field offices and in western communities].[63]

Toward a Proper Regard for the Range

Achieving reform in grazing policy is a different matter from reforming the General Mining Law of 1872. For hardrock mining, the key is to make statutory changes that will, among other things, eliminate the "right to mine" and the patenting process and strengthen and consolidate environmental regulation. To be sure, administrative policies toward mining, especially in the BLM, need to change to comport with contemporary values, but the first and most critical step involves the United States Code.

The context for grazing reform is much more diffuse. The problem is not with the statutes. The congressional words written in FLPMA and PRIA during the reforms of the 1970s are still in place and fairly sparkle with the values this modern society expects of government policy involving natural resources. There will be no sell-off of the public lands. There is no vested right to graze cattle or sheep—any rights are fixed-term contract provisions in the grazing leases. The federal range must be kept open for a wide spectrum of uses, and all users ought to take good care of the ground. There are now ample data on which to base reasoned management.

But actual range policy, as carried out by the BLM and to a considerable extent by the Forest Service, still bears the mark of the 1880s. Too many decisions are effectively made by the hard-line element of the cattle industry. The range is run for cows. The range itself is recovering at a glacial pace, if at all. The number of AUMs on BLM lands holds at 13.5 million, not much below the number of AUMs on the BLM range in 1936, two years after the Taylor Grazing Act was passed. Sixty-eight percent of all BLM rangeland is described as poor or fair—and "fair" is administratively defined as land supporting less than one-half of its historical carrying capacity. Fifteen percent of all land is in decline, 64 percent is stable, and only 15 percent is improving.[64]

The reasons for the disparity between societal demands—as reflected in federal law—and actual range conditions are not hard to identify. The cattle industry developed a powerful legislative capacity more than a hundred years ago. Cattle interests held a hammerlock on state legislatures and, as importantly, were able to stave off any federal control. When change was forced by the Dust Bowl days, stockmen drew up the Taylor Grazing Act to preserve the *status quo* to the greatest extent possible. Today, progressive laws like FLPMA and PRIA cannot be implemented on BLM lands because the BLM is kept down—the Forest Service has five times more funding per acre than does the BLM.[65]

By comparison, conservationists, off-road vehicle enthusiasts, hunters, and fishers are unable to exercise power on these issues in the pervasive manner that the ranchers do. These citizen groups are new to public range policy and by their nature are far less organized than industry. Even national organizations such as the Natural Resources Defense Council and the National Wildlife Federation are able to devote only a relatively small portion of their resources to grazing issues. Monitoring of administrative activity is even more difficult than lobbying on Capitol Hill because senior, old-line BLM personnel steadfastly and effectively resist change and because the sheer numbers of decisions to be overseen require great amounts of field-work. The public interest groups, in other words, can gear up reasonably well for a sweeping legislative initiative such as the enactment of FLPMA, but they almost entirely lack the ability to influence the thousands of significant policy decisions made every year in the BLM and Forest Service field offices. Indeed, most grazing decisions are made not on Capitol Hill but in the trenches—in hundreds of field offices scattered across the West. These include what are in a sense the most important decisions of all: to allow by default this grazing allotment, that grazing allotment—and the one over there also—to go ahead for yet another year under what amounts to no management. For the cattle industry, administrative lobbying at that level is literally part of the cost of doing business.[66]

But this lack of access by public interest groups to the decision-making process is coupled with their own analytical failure, which is equally fundamental. The conservation groups have had a fixation on grazing fees and the number of AUMs—"overgrazing"—as the key problems on the federal range. However, an impressive body of evidence indicates that the root concern is neither subsidies nor numbers of cattle. Rather, the real lord of yesterday is poor cattle management.

Federal policy ought to focus on land health and sound land management and move away from the battlefields of AUM reductions and grazing fee increases. As for the numbers of AUMs, the evidence is strong that—at least on most of the western range—the real evil is not too many cattle but too many poorly managed cattle. Similarly, the current preoccupation with subsidized fees misses the heart of the problem. The total grazing subsidy on all federal lands is about $37 million annually, only a nick out of a budget that casts out subsidies to more segments of our citizenry than could ever be counted. There is no reliable research on whether a raise in fees would cause a decline in the number of cattle, but even if it did, range conditions would remain unimproved unless range management practices were improved. The ranch cattle industry is undeniably in trouble, and to this writer at least, the stress imposed by sharply higher fees does not merit the marginal and uncertain returns. An unknown but considerable number of ranches would likely go out of business altogether, directly affecting the communities to which they contribute. The crunch would be most severe on small ranchers, such as those in northern New Mexico, most of whom are Hispanic grazers who can trace their families' tenure to before the Treaty of Guadalupe Hidalgo of 1848. Over time, the fees should edge up toward market levels, but subsidies are not central to the key task of healing the ground.[67]

If some environmentalists must take on faith the promised benefits from better management, the livestock industry must also take some chances. Good range practices require initial investments, and although some federal funding is made available for range improvements, the onus of financing good range management ought to be on the ranchers. They will benefit financially and, under FLPMA, will be compensated for the value of authorized range improvements such as fences if the land is ever put to another use.[68]

The best edge for change, then, is the federal agencies, who must work with the responsible ranchers and crack down on the irresponsible ones. The BLM and the Forest Service are the institutions best positioned finally to bring to an end the rancher's code—the practice of turning cattle loose in the spring and rounding them up in the fall. Both agencies should make the first, critical land management decision by deciding which acres can properly be used for grazing and which cannot, either permanently or for a period of years. For those areas where domestic grazing will be allowed, federal officials should then insist that sound management plans be adopted within a realistic time frame, no more than one to two years: among other things, cattle should be excluded from all riparian zones for most of each year, and stock should be rotated through upland pastures. Ranchers should be encouraged to adopt goal setting and integrated planning and management. These approaches usually lead to an acceptable plan from the standpoint of federal law. When a rancher refuses to move with deliberate speed, the agencies can and should exercise the power they have under existing law: to revoke the permit of any rancher who refuses to propose a plan or to comply with an approved plan.[69]

There is also a place for legislation. Congress should adopt a policy statement calling for strong land management practices. Such action might technically be redundant, but this is an appropriate time to reaffirm the progressive policies set out in FLPMA in 1976 and PRIA in 1978. Congress should also terminate the BLM advisory boards, which are dominated by hard-line ranchers and wield far too much power. Legislation should provide modest budget appropriations for low-interest loans to accomplish range improvements in relatively rare cases in which ranchers cannot afford them; for additional BLM staff; and for public education and research.

Granted, these proposals will take time to implement. But range policy—perhaps more than is the case with any of the other lords of yesterday—is an area rife with subtlety and complexity. Then again, perhaps the main returns will come quickly enough. In many cases, the range ought to begin to heal, even to the layperson's eye, within eighteen months. In 1934, the Taylor Grazing Act stabilized a range in poor condition. Three generations later, we are close to achieving the combination of scientific information and political awareness necessary to begin to improve the public range from its current stable, but still poor, condition.

The federal range has long been conceptualized as, and used as, a place to graze cows. We now know that it is much more than that. It is fragile: if its cover is not protected, it can lift up and blow away. It houses other animals: elk, antelope, and wild horses and burros also have grazing needs; trout require clean, cool streams; and wildfowl must have nesting places in green marshlands. It has wonders: it is the principal monument to the sense of space that is the soul of the American West. Ranchers have contributed much to the West, and they deservedly hold a prime place among those with access to the public rangeland, but they have no right to a monopoly or to practices that injure the ground. If we look first to the needs of these long-neglected lands, the western range will provide benefits aplenty.

Chapter Four

Forests for the Home-Builder First of All

The trouble over the proposed Jersey-Jack logging and roading project in the Nez Perce National Forest in Idaho, where Harold Thomas, Emmett and Zona Smith, and others oppose the development near Dixie, is emblematic of a historic crisis point for the Forest Service. All across the West, there is deep and broad criticism of federal logging and the accompanying road systems that would cut into the far corners of the national forests. The *Denver Post* argued that

> the Forest Service would be wise to rethink its priorities—especially since it costs so much more to cut down a tract of forest than it does to manage it for dispersed recreation.
>
> Colorado and its tourism-dependent economy stand to benefit from such a change in policy. . . . [T]he Forest Service should consider whether the sales of marginally valuable timber—often in steep, remote areas that never have been logged before—will ever offset the loss of wilderness character on those lands.

The *Idaho Statesman*, referring to the "big blowout" landslides on the South Fork of the Salmon River, which Harold Thomas believes the Jersey-Jack project may replicate, editorialized:

> When the heavy rains of 1964 to 1965 came, the hillsides became the riverbed, clogging the gravel used for salmon spawning. Gone was one of the state's premier salmon streams.

Do we need another such lesson? ...

Logging will continue to occupy a paramount place in Idaho's economy, as it should. But that needn't mean sacrificing the assets such as water quality that make the forests so valuable to everyone. If we must err, let it be on the side of protecting the environment, which is so important to this and future generations.[1]

One of the most notable aspects of the furor about Forest Service logging and roading is that the opposition comes from so many different quarters. Emmett and Zona Smith and Harold Thomas simply are not environmentalists in the way the term is commonly used. The same is true of most of the tens of thousands of hunters, fishers, trappers, berry pickers, rock hounds, and everyday westerners who have risen up because their favorite creek, meadow, grove, or ridge line has been torn up. As one Forest Service official told me, "I get concerned, I honestly do, when I hear from environmentalists. But I'm more or less used to them. What has really gotten to me lately has been the complaints from the coon and turkey hunters." Jeff Sher, one of the leading journalists specializing in regional issues, summed up the phenomenon in these terms:

> Roads, and whether we should continue to build them at our current breakneck pace into the last untouched strongholds of the mountain West, have become a major issue in the West.
>
> The West's remaining roadless lands in most cases are not as spectacular as the areas we already have set aside to please our sense of aesthetics or satisfy our growing thirst for outdoor recreation. They do not quite rival Glacier National Park or Yellowstone. But many of them are spectacular enough that, were they not so near existing parks and wilderness areas, they almost certainly would already have been granted protected status.
>
> Furthermore, many of these lands, partly by virtue of the fact that they are *not* the most spectacular and well known, do provide the best hunting and fishing and backcountry solitude that remain in the lower 48 states. For that reason, many westerners view preservation of these lands in an untouched state as crucial to the preservation of their outdoor-oriented lifestyle.[2]

Increasingly, opposition has begun to come from constituencies historically supportive of development on public lands. Ranchers and farmers dependent on the national forests for their irrigation water have criticized Forest Service clear-cutting because it increases erosion and causes the snowpack to melt more quickly, resulting in an early season runoff, when the key irrigation demand is in late summer. More and more small towns and their chambers of commerce, seeing their future in recreation and tourism rather than in logging, have urged a go-slow approach to timber harvesting. Western states that traditionally have opposed restrictions on cutting public forests now tend to see the issue differently. Several state and local governments have sued the Forest Service, or appealed forest plans administratively, in order to curb cutting in the national forests. Pointed questions are now regularly raised in state administrative agencies, especially fish and wildlife departments. An *Arizona Daily Star* reporter surveyed western state agency offices and found, contrary to the historical pattern, that "today, it is the federal government rushing to cut timber, and the states urging a slowdown."[3]

So many disparate elements have become involved because national forest issues, along with disputes over water, are the most visible points of conflict over western natural resources. This is due in part to the vast amount of land in the national forests. Federal public lands constitute 46 percent of all land in the eleven western states and about two-thirds of the land in Alaska. Although the lands administered by the Bureau of Land Management are more extensive than the national forests, the Forest Service oversees a huge domain: 163 million of the 191 million acres in the National Forest System are located in the eleven western states and Alaska. National forest lands are few on the eastern plains of Montana, Wyoming, Colorado, and New Mexico, but all of those states have major concentrations of Forest Service lands in their western, more mountainous, portions. The other region of the West where national forest lands are disproportionately sparse is in the Great Basin (Nevada, western Utah, southeastern Oregon, and southwestern Idaho). Still, in spite of these areas where there are few national forests, about 18 percent of the total land area within the eleven western states is administered by the Forest Service. In all, the greatest concentrations of national forest lands are found in Idaho (39 percent of all land in the state), Oregon (25 percent), Washington (21 percent), Colorado (22 percent), California (21 percent), Montana (18 percent), and Arizona (15 percent). Southeastern Alaska also holds large amounts of Forest Service lands. The Tongass and Chugach national forests total 22 million acres and comprise about 6 percent of the nation's largest state.[4]

But the special qualities of the national forests go beyond the sheer number of acres involved. The national forests affect more people in more ways than any federal or state land system. The forests build 1 million homes annually. The Forest Service maintains 310,000 miles of roads— more than any other jurisdiction in the world. The national forests host no fewer than 200 million recreational visitor days each year, double the amount for the national parks. The current trail system totals 93,000 miles, far more than maintained by any other federal or state agency. Most of the

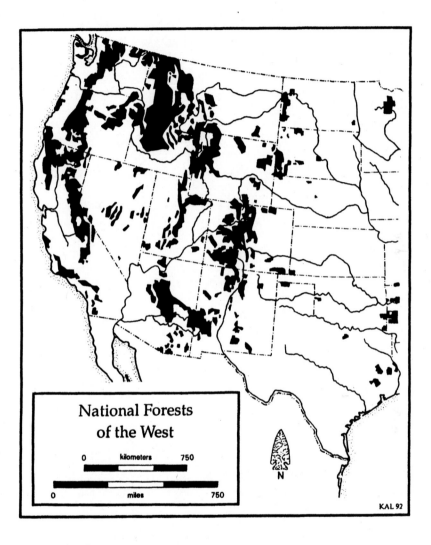

National Forests
of the West

| 0 | kilometers | 750 |

| 0 | miles | 750 |

N

KAL 92

Rockies, the Sierra, the Cascades, and numerous smaller mountain ranges are national forests. Thus, the high country under the jurisdiction of the nation's oldest land management agency is the spine of the American West: the national forests produce snowpack for more than half of all water runoff in the West, and the vast majority of the country's major ski areas are within the national forests. The national forests also supply hardrock and energy minerals; provide forage for domestic stock; create some of the finest habitat in the world for wild animals; and hold most of the official, congressionally designated wilderness in the lower forty-eight states, as well as tens of millions of acres that are wilderness with a small *w*. All across the West, towns are located within, or adjacent to, national forests, and their economics and life-styles often are dramatically affected by Forest Service decisions. However you articulate it, the national forests are on any short list of ingredients that make the American West a distinctive region.[5]

The physical characteristics and laws of the national forests guarantee that these lands will generate more controversy than do lands under any other land management system. The national parks contain some of the nation's most spectacular scenery in world-famous "crown jewel" parks such as Yellowstone, Grand Teton, Grand Canyon, Yosemite, Glacier, Rocky Mountain, and Olympic. The National Park System, however, is less than half the size of the National Forest System, and almost three-fourths of all national park acreage is in Alaska, mostly in remote areas; in the eleven western states, there are 17 million acres of national parks and 141 million acres of national forests. Even more fundamentally, national park legislation prohibits many uses, thus preempting most potential disputes. Timber harvesting is barred, as is hunting. The parks are off-limits to both hardrock mining and mineral leasing, with the exception of special legislation applying to a small number of parks. Livestock grazing is allowed on a very limited basis. To be sure, the national parks are magnets that draw hordes of visitors, and the parks raise questions about the impact of overcrowding. Still, the virtual exclusion of the traditional extractive industries ensures that national park policy will have fewer participating interest groups, and will stir fewer passions, than national forest policy. Indeed, many of the most controversial issues in the parks involve external threats, in which resource development in adjacent national forests affects the parks. A leading example, discussed later in this chapter, is the Greater Yellowstone Ecosystem, where timber harvesting and roading in forestland surrounding Yellowstone National Park threaten the habitat of elk, grizzly bears, and other animals that move in and out of the park.[6]

Disputes over the national forests also are more pointed than is the case with BLM lands. Unlike the parks, these lands are more extensive than the

Federal Public Land Systems	Acreage*			
	11 Western States	Alaska	Remaining 38 States	Total
National forests	141	22	28	191
Bureau of Land Management lands	178	92	2	272
National parks	17	55	7	79
National wildlife refuges	7	76	7	90

* In millions of acres.

SOURCES: The national forest statistics are from U.S. Department of Agriculture, Forest Service, *Land Areas of the National Forest System*, pp. 14–31 (1990). These figures include acreage in the national forests, national grasslands, and research-experiment areas. The Bureau of Land Management statistics are from U.S. Department of the Interior, Bureau of Land Management, *Public Land Statistics: 1990* (Aug. 1991). The national park statistics are from Sierra Club, "National Park System" (San Francisco: Sierra Club Books, Oct. 1984 and Supp. Nov. 1988). These figures include all lands under the National Park Service jurisdiction. The statistics on national wildlife refuges are from U.S. Department of the Interior, Fish and Wildlife Service, "Annual Report of Lands under Control of the U.S. Fish and Wildlife Service as of September 30, 1990" (1990).

National Forest System, and, of course, BLM lands have been held open for all forms of development (see table). But BLM lands are more clearly "leftovers"—those acres not homesteaded or set aside for national parks or forests—and thus public attention has been trained on them infrequently. The national wildlife refuges are less extensive than the forests; they, like the BLM lands, have failed to capture the public imagination as firmly as the national forests have.[7]

None of this is intended to understate the importance of the other public land systems. In total, the federal lands comprise a near-majority of all land in the West and play key roles all across the region—whether it be the majesty of the high plateau of Yellowstone, the descent of a flock of Canada geese to the marshes at the Stillwater National Wildlife Refuge south of Pyramid Lake in Nevada, or the classically western open-range country at Camp Creek in central Oregon. Still, the national forests remain the crucible for disputes over the public lands and resources of the American West.

The lord of yesterday that governs the National Forest System—the dedication of these lands to the production of commercial wood products as the first and dominant use—arises from a wholly separate set of traditions than did the laws governing hardrock mining and grazing. Those *laissez-faire* policies were first achieved on a *de facto* basis by westerners, who then obtained the express or tacit approval of Congress and federal officials: the lords of mining and grazing arose in the West.

Timber policies had opposite origins. Theodore Roosevelt and Gifford Pinchot, in one of the greatest and most daring achievements in conservation history, set aside—over the vehement opposition of the timber industry—three-quarters of the current National Forest System. Today, in a double twist of irony, environmentalists decry Pinchot as the source of the centralized timber targets that drive inflated harvests throughout the national forests, while the timber industry looks kindly on the once-despised Pinchot as the philosophical parent of high-yield forestry in the national forests. Pinchot, as able and visionary a public servant as there has ever been, was chief of the Forest Service from 1898 through 1910, author of several works on conservation, and, later, governor of Pennsylvania. He never sat in Congress, but no one has made a bigger part of the law of the American West.

The Unmanaged Forests

The United States fell heir to an almost incomprehensible array of challenges, from the conceptual to the practical, when it obtained title to the real estate stretching from the Mississippi all the way to the Pacific. The principal acquisitions were the Louisiana Purchase from France in 1803 (523 million acres), the Oregon Compromise with England in 1846 (180 million acres), the war with Mexico and the resultant Treaty of Guadalupe Hidalgo of 1848 and Gadsden Purchase of 1853 from Mexico (a total of 534 million acres), and a purchase from the new, land-rich but cash-poor state of Texas in 1850 (79 million acres). The 365 million acres comprising Alaska were obtained from Russia in 1867, and Hawaii was annexed in 1898.[8]

By the turn of the century, therefore, the total land area within the national boundaries stood at its present total of 2.3 billion acres. More than two-thirds of it had been obtained in the sixty-four years of expansionist policy that ended in 1867. The United States exercised government authority over this vast new estate. The federal government also held land title to most of the West. Except for the land within Texas (which, as an independent republic, had insisted on retaining title to its real estate on admission) and land grants made by foreign nations before their withdrawal, the United States owned it all, subject only to obligations to Indian tribes. About half of the new empire contained standing timber, some of it scrubby, some of it among the most valuable commercial timber in the world.

Through the 1880s, federal timber was effectively open for the taking, much as was the case with federal minerals and rangeland. An 1831 law made it a crime to "cut, destroy, or remove live oak or other trees" belonging to the United States, but the statute was unenforceable: there were far too many acres and settlers for the handful of federal employees to monitor. The statute remained on the books, but by the mid-1850s the General Land Office, due to both logistics and sympathy for the settlers, had adopted an approach of enforcing the timber trespass law against only commercial operators, not individual homesteaders. Even then, the government never prosecuted the few timber companies that were detected but rather required them only to pay the stumpage value for their timber trespasses.[9]

In addition to outright theft of timber, there was rampant abuse under the homesteading laws. The fraudulent schemes were so varied and colorful that no summary can do them justice, but two patterns were predominant. The great General Homestead Act of 1862 allowed a good-faith settler to enter a parcel and receive a free federal patent (that is, a deed) to 160 acres of public land after residing on, and farming, the land for five years. One device was simply to obtain permission to enter a parcel of timberland, cut the timber (purportedly clearing it for farmland), sell it, and move on: "Oops, I guess I won't be farming and homesteading this land after all." There were much more elaborate schemes in which timber speculators hired dummy purchasers, who would sign fraudulent affidavits stating that they were good-faith farmer-settlers and then turn around and sell the patents to the speculators for a modest fee. Government officials could barely begin to monitor the flood of patent applications. The fraud was most pervasive in the Pacific Northwest, where the spruce, cedar, redwood, and Douglas fir stands amounted to green gold. The most luscious account of the fraudulent schemes, titled *Looters of the Public Domain*, is by Steven A. Puter, the "king of the Oregon land fraud ring." Fortunately for historians, Puter had time on his hands, so he could spin out in detail the intrigue behind his land ring: he wrote the book from a prison cell.[10]

Fire also ravaged the federal timberlands. The situation was especially serious in the dry Southwest. Fires started by settlers were a main concern of Franklin Hough, appointed in 1876 as the first chief of forestry in the Department of Agriculture. In his 1882 report, for example, Hough concluded that "fully one-third of all the timber accessible among the mountains in [Colorado] has been burned over and killed by fire within the last six years." Hough's successor, Nathaniel Egleston, agreed. His 1884 report decried the fires caused by miners scouring the Rocky Mountains for gold and silver—"[t]he worst enemy of the woodlands in Colorado is the careless prospector." Egleston quoted a correspondent in Colorado who estimated the total impact of development on the forests of the southern end of the Front Range in Colorado: "About one-quarter of the area of the cleared forest land in this county has been destroyed by fire. The remainder, or one-half of the whole area of forests, has been cleared for fuel and mineral purposes, and chiefly for lumber and railroad ties."[11]

Endless though the nation's natural bounty must have seemed, limits began to appear. In the public's eye, the diminution of public resources was personified by the railroad land grants, which not only allowed the railroads free timber for construction but also transferred to the railroads 131 million acres of land. In 1877, Secretary of the Interior Carl Schurz warned that "[t]he rapidity with which this country is being stripped of its forests must alarm every thinking man. It has been estimated by good authority that, if we go on at the present rate, the supply of timber in the United States will, in less than twenty years, fall considerably short of our home necessities."[12]

Schurz, Chief Foresters Egleston and Bernhard Fernow, Interior Secretary John Noble, and other officials in Washington, DC, urged that government forestlands be reserved—set aside from homesteading and other forms of disposition. Opposition ran deep, for westerners were steeped in the idea that the public lands existed to fuel the Great Barbecue. Finally, in 1891, a House-Senate conference committee moved to amend the General Revision Act by adding Section 24, a little-noticed, seemingly innocuous provision authorizing presidential withdrawal of forest reserves. Such withdrawals would put specified public forestlands beyond the reach of the homestead laws. When the conference committee report went back to the Senate and the House in the hurried last days of the session, members were assured that the president would not go too far, and if he did, that Congress could simply override him and adopt a statute reopening the area for homesteading. The act passed on March 3.[13]

The 1891 provision created no forest reserves by itself—it only authorized presidential withdrawals. President Benjamin Harrison, however, moved quickly and, on March 30, 1891, set aside the first forest reserve. The Yellowstone Timberland Reserve, now mostly within the Shoshone National Forest in Wyoming, was contiguous to Yellowstone National Park on the east and southeast. A month later, Harrison set aside the White River Plateau Reserve (embracing the headwaters of the White, Yampa, and Grand rivers in Colorado), and by the end of 1892 he had reserved a total of 13 million acres of forestland. In 1893, President Cleveland added another 5 million acres to the new system.

At this point, Cleveland initially refused to set aside additional forest reserves, taking the position that the priority ought to be to give proper protection to the existing reserves. The 1891 act had given the president unfettered power to create the reserves but had provided no funding to administer the reserves. Timber trespass and fire remained the biggest problems. Chief Fernow reported that "areas once heavily timbered have been turned into fire-swept barrens." Still, national leaders pressed for the creation of more forest reserves. The National Academy of Sciences had created a National Forest Commission, of which Gifford Pinchot was a member. After studying the matter, the commission recommended bold action—the creation of thirteen new reserves totaling 21 million acres. As a symbolic matter, the commission recommended to President Cleveland that he make the reserves on Washington's birthday, 1897, and Cleveland went along with the idea.[14]

The Washington's Birthday Reserves, which doubled the federal forest system at one fell swoop, raised a clamor of protest across the West. The new reserves were symbolic, all right—but to the captains of industry, they were symbolic of a George other than Washington. The Seattle Chamber of Commerce complained that "King George had never attempted so high-handed an invasion upon the rights" of American citizens. Local news-papers picked up the drumbeat and opposed any further reservations in their regions. The *Plumas National-Bulletin* in the Sierra Nevada high country in northern California spoke for many western towns when it editorialized that "[t]he Forest Reserves proposed for this county, if made permanent, would retard, if not wholly arrest, the development of the county's resources. Our people, therefore, are right in protesting, as they are doing, against the wrong sought to be inflicted upon Plumas county."[15]

The Washington's Birthday Reserves in 1897 brought federal forest issues to the front and center in a complex political milieu that included the perceived western birthright to plunder federal land and resources, the growing desire of western towns and cities for unspoiled watersheds for their water supplies, the need to preserve timber stands for future con-sumptive use to replace cutover stands in the Great Lakes region, the forestry profession's belief in the value of professionally managed public forests, the need of individual settlers for timber, and the nuts-and-bolts desire to get some funding for the reserves. Another key segment of public opinion was the tide of populism, whose proponents viewed big timber companies with a zealous affront normally reserved for the railroads. Such sentiments were evident even in the prime timber districts. Congressman Binger Hermann of Oregon feared that weak federal oversight would allow the companies to "denude the public forest reservations," while Congress-man William Hall Doolittle of Washington warned: "You might just as well turn a dozen wolves into a corral filled with sheep and expect the wolves to protect the sheep as to expect your timber to be protected if you permit the lumbermen to go upon the reservations at all."[16]

The many players broke out into three camps: those who wanted an end to all federal control so that the forestlands could be opened for *laissez-faire* development; those who wanted to continue reserve status and allow timber harvesting only by settlers, not by timber companies; and those who wanted to retain reserve status and allow commercial harvesting on a controlled, government-supervised basis. Essentially, the latter view won out as events moved quickly during the first half of 1897. Congress attempted to repeal the Washington's Birthday Reserves in March, but President Cleveland pocket vetoed the provision on his last day in office. The antireserve forces in Congress lost a key supporter when Charles Wolcott of the U.S. Geological Survey persuaded Senator Richard Pettigrew of the virtue of the reserves. Major compromise legislation was enacted by President McKinley's signature on June 4, 1897.[17]

The 1897 Organic Act was to remain the basic charter of the Forest Service for almost eighty years. It provided both funding and management authority, directing the secretary of the interior to "make provisions for the protection against destruction by fire" and delegating to the secretary extraordinarily broad authority "to regulate . . . occupancy and use" of the reserves. The sale of timber was allowed, but to appease those many members of Congress who did not want to throw the forests open to the timber industry, the Interior Department was allowed to sell only "dead, matured, or large growth of trees"; further, all sold trees had to be "marked and designated . . . and removed under the supervision of some person appointed for that purpose by the Secretary of the Interior." In contrast to national parks, most of which are federal enclaves, states retained jurisdiction over persons within the reserves. Water diversions were allowed within the forests. Mining interests obtained statutory assurance that the Hardrock Mining Law of 1872 would be operative within the reserves. Presidential authority to create new reserves was retained, but it was now defined: "No national forest shall be established, except to improve and protect the forest within the boundaries, or for the purpose of securing favorable conditions of water flows, and to furnish a continuous supply of timber for the use and necessities of citizens of the United States."[18]

In retrospect, it is clear what was most important about the 1897 Organic Act: it recognized broad federal power, both by allowing the president to make future reserves and by granting to the management agency the power to sell trees and to "regulate occupancy and use" within the forest. The act, therefore, reversed the passive federal presence on federal timberland and created a mighty engine for an activist administrator with access to the president's ear.

Enter Gifford Pinchot.

The Grand Master

Pinchot became chief of the Division of Forestry in the Agriculture Department on July 1, 1898, at the age of thirty-three. He would dominate federal resource policy for more than a decade, until his departure in 1910. Pinchot's policies continue to be debated. His name is commonly invoked in congressional hearings, and public policy conferences on the national forests are invariably chockful of references to Pinchot, his historical views, and how he might react to today's issues. One must be cautious about typing Pinchot: his policies and beliefs were multifaceted and cannot be reduced to any one pat formula. For these reasons, it is worthwhile to look closely at Pinchot, his accomplishments, and his views.

One can string out a bevy of strong adjectives, each accurate, to describe Pinchot—brilliant, patrician, knowledgeable, manipulating, charismatic, arrogant, and savvy all come to mind. Stewart Udall, former interior secretary, called Pinchot's Forest Service "the most exciting organization in Washington," and it was. Pinchot's policies were so forceful that he managed to offend nearly every private group, from ranchers to timber companies to preservationists. But whether he had to go around or over his opponents, he achieved most of his goals. Perhaps most notable was the reservation of an additional 148 million acres of national forests, about three-quarters of the current system. To do that, he needed a president willing to sign the necessary executive orders, and in Teddy Roosevelt he found one. Pinchot had Roosevelt's ear on the nation's natural resource issues by day but also spent many an off-hour with the president:

> One of the most spectacular of Pinchot's many hikes with Roosevelt occurred late one afternoon after a telephone call from the President suggesting a walk. Pinchot went from his office to the White House dressed as he was. The third member, Robert Bacon from the Treasury Department, a former banker, appeared in a derby hat, patent-leather shoes, and a cutaway coat. Because it had been raining hard, they soon found themselves wet to their knees as they walked along the Potomac River. When, with darkness coming on, their path was blocked by a canal, the President suggested that Pinchot and he swim it; but Bacon protested at being left behind. All three placed their wallets and other valuables in their hats, put the hats on their heads, and swam across. Pinchot and Bacon both held umbrellas in their left hands. "And then," said Pinchot, "we walked back to the White House with much merriment." As soon as Pinchot reached home the comment of Mary McCadden, his childhood nurse, proved that such escapades were not uncommon. As his sleeve brushed her hand she quickly exclaimed: "Drenched! You've been out with the President."[19]

Pinchot had attended Yale in the late 1880s. After graduation, he studied forestry in Germany and France, where, unlike in the United States, the profession was well established; in Germany, foresters had managed commercial forests as tree farms for centuries. He returned to America and for three years obtained on-the-ground experience by managing the forest on George Vanderbilt's estate in North Carolina. As a private consultant, he also developed a management plan for a large private forest in New York.

In spite of his early emphasis on private forestry, Pinchot always had kept an eye on the public arena. He participated in the new American Forestry Association and was the youngest member of the National Forestry Commission, which was so influential in the passage of the 1897 Organic Act for the national forests. Indeed, Pinchot had long seen himself as a trailblazer in a whole new sphere of natural resource policy. In the 1880s, a college friend asked Pinchot what he intended to do after graduation. Pinchot replied, "I am going to be a forester." "What's that?" his friend inquired. Pinchot responded, "That's why I'm going to be a forester."[20]

On entering government in the Department of Agriculture in 1898, Pinchot's main problem was that he had no forestlands to manage. The forest reserves were over in the Interior Department. For seven years, Pinchot argued, coaxed, strategized, wheedled, and—well, one might wish that there were a verb form for "tenacity." Finally, on February 1, 1905, Congress transferred the 63 million acres of forest reserves from Interior to Agriculture. Pinchot, the Grand Master, was at long last chief government forester in fact as well as name.

Even before the Transfer Act, Pinchot had relentlessly lobbied Roosevelt for a massive expansion of the federal forest system. The president was only too glad to comply by creating new forest reserves, but as he did, the opposition intensified. Congressman John Calhoun Bell of Colorado spoke for many of his western colleagues when he complained that forest reserves in the western states were usually set aside at the request of organizations "with headquarters in some codfish district of Massachusetts or Maine." Objections to the creation of new reserves were heightened by Pinchot's successful efforts to regulate grazing on the reserves and to institute the grazing fee system. "Then," as leading historian Harold Steen put it, "the storm broke" in early January 1907, when Roosevelt withdrew a large area of prime Douglas fir land in the northern Cascade Range in Washington. Legislation was introduced and rapidly pushed through both houses, prohibiting any further presidential forest withdrawals in the key western timber states of Colorado, Idaho, Montana, Oregon, Washington, and Wyoming. Since the bar against future reservations was attached to the annual appropriations bill, Roosevelt was forced into signing away an important measure of his power to implement his conservation policy. On March 4, 1907, he did.[21]

But in the meantime, Pinchot, Roosevelt, and others had been busy. During late January and through February, Pinchot and his subordinates had been burning the midnight oil—laying out maps of the public lands of the West on office floors, reviewing the work of boundary surveyors, and inking out vast new forest reserves. Apparently they used blue or black ink, but one can imagine that had they been invented at the time, green felt-tip pens would have been the order of the day in those exultant sessions. They drew up presidential proclamations to comport with the marked-up maps. Amidst great celebration in Forest Service and White House offices, Roosevelt signed off on "the midnight reserves," no fewer than thirty-eight executive orders on March 1 and 2, proclaiming more than 16 million acres of new forest reserves in the prohibited states—prohibited, that is, as of March 4. As Roosevelt recalled in his autobiography, "[T]he opponents of the Forest Service turned handsprings in their wrath." Those were the days of days in the history of the conservation movement.[22]

The midnight reserves turned out to be Pinchot's swan song. Roosevelt was succeeded in 1909 by William Howard Taft. Pinchot and Taft soon were at odds on a number of conservation issues. Matters came to a head over the controversy between Pinchot and Richard Ballinger, Taft's interior secretary. Although the national forests had been transferred to Agriculture, Interior continued to manage all mineral resources, including those in the forests. Pinchot charged Ballinger with misconduct in the issuance of coal patents to corporations in Alaska. Taft sided with Ballinger, and even today there is no agreement among scholars as to whether Ballinger engaged in any wrongdoing. But the Ballinger-Pinchot dispute sealed Taft's conviction that Pinchot was too much of a loose cannon for his taste. Pinchot, too, was disaffected and was in no mood to smooth the waters with the new president. On January 7, 1910, Taft fired Pinchot, the only instance in which a Forest Service chief has been removed from office.[23]

The Grand Master was gone, but his ideas continued to burn bright. Perhaps his most famous statement is in the so-called Pinchot Letter, written on February 1, 1905, the day when the forest reserves were transferred from Interior to Agriculture. Pinchot himself authored the document, but in a technique used by clever administrators before and since, Pinchot's words were styled as a letter from Secretary of Agriculture James Wilson to Pinchot. If you want to get your marching orders set out correctly, write them yourself.

The Pinchot Letter, embodying as it does the philosophy of the Forest Service's *ne plus ultra*, is in a certain sense the most important legal or policy statement ever made about the national forests. When the Multiple-Use Sustained-Yield Act was passed in 1960, the Forest Service described the act as embodying Pinchot's maxim, "the greatest good for the greatest number." Even today, in the Forest Service's official explanation in the

Federal Register of its current regulations, the agency defends its goal of "maximizing net public benefits" by explaining that the concept is the same as Pinchot's "greatest good" formulation. The Pinchot Letter is prominently placed in the federal compilation titled *The Principal Laws Relating to the Establishment and Administration of the National Forests and Other Forest Service Activities*. The Pinchot Letter, which remains gospel for Forest Service personnel, reads this way:

> In the administration of the forest reserves it must be clearly borne in mind that all land is to be devoted to its most productive use for the permanent good of the whole people, and not for the temporary benefit of individuals or companies. All the resources of forest reserves are for *use*, and this use must be brought about in a thoroughly prompt and businesslike manner, under such restrictions only as will insure the permanence of these resources. The vital importance of forest reserves to the great industries of the Western States will be largely increased in the near future by the continued steady advance in settlement and development. The permanence of the resources of the reserves is therefore indispensable to continued prosperity, and the policy of this Department for their protection and use will invariably be guided by this fact, always bearing in mind that the *conservative use* of these resources in no way conflicts with their permanent value.
>
> You will see to it that the water, wood, and forage of the reserves are conserved and wisely used for the benefit of the home builder first of all, upon whom depends the best permanent use of lands and resources alike. The continued prosperity of the agricultural, lumbering, mining, and livestock interests is directly dependent upon a permanent and accessible supply of water, wood, and forage, as well as upon the present and future use of these resources under businesslike regulations, enforced with promptness, effectiveness, and common sense. In the management of each reserve local questions will be decided upon local grounds; the dominant industry will be considered first, but with as little restriction to minor industries as may be possible; sudden changes in industrial conditions will be avoided by gradual adjustment after due notice, and where conflicting interests must be reconciled the question will always be decided from the standpoint of the greatest good of the greatest number in the long run.[24]

All of the many strains of Pinchot's deeply held beliefs are evidenced in the Pinchot Letter. The influence of progressive populism and Pinchot's revulsion toward the land grabs of the nineteenth century—his writings are peppered with references that forest policy ought to be directed toward "the little man," not "the big man"—are reflected in the mandate that the forests be used "for the whole people." Pinchot's disdain for any waste of public natural resources is manifested in the letter's references to wise use and "businesslike regulations." His dedication to conservation and sustained-yield practices is lodged in his formulation of the greatest good "in the long run." His much-praised administrative policy that key decisions be made in the field, by forest rangers talking "around the campfire" with local citizens, is the basis for the letter's statement that "local questions will be decided upon local grounds."

Another premise of Pinchotism cuts against his populist views. Pinchot was essentially antidemocratic in believing that scientists, not politicians, could best decide how the forests ought to be run. After all, this is a letter about "administration" and "management" (Pinchot wrote elsewhere that "[t]he first duty of the human race is to control the earth it lives upon"), and there is no doubt that federal administrators—especially the recipient of the letter—would decide what was "the greatest good." And although it is never expressly mentioned, the letter surely presumes that federal land-ownership is a good and essential thing. As Pinchot said years later: "I say again, and I say it with all the emphasis I can muster, that the forests of the United States will never be safe . . . until the great majority of our forests are either government owned or government controlled. And I mean by the federal government."[25]

The last, and by no means least, foundation for the Pinchot Letter was the judgment that the national forests were to be used for utilitarian purposes and that timber production was the preeminent use. To be sure, Pinchot saw grazing, water development, and other commercial uses as being entirely legitimate, but these lands existed "for the benefit of the home builder first of all." "The greatest good of the greatest number" sounds like, and has been used to justify, multiple-use management, but the Pinchot Letter is better understood as standing for dominant-use management, with timber production as the dominant use in the national forests. Pinchot had been profoundly influenced by the Germanic tradition of intensive forest management, and he saw the national forests as the great proving ground in America for his profession of forestry. In his autobiography, Pinchot elaborates on this new science:

> The purpose of Forestry, then, is to make the forest produce the largest possible amount of whatever crop or service will be most useful, and keep on producing it for generation after generation of men and trees.

Even more succinctly, Pinchot said simply, "To grow trees as a crop is forestry."[26]

This is not to say that Pinchot failed to see beauty in the forests. Although their relationship later soured, Pinchot and John Muir, the great naturalist and founder of the Sierra Club, initially got along well. On occasion, Pinchot rhapsodized about the natural beauty of the West. He called Montana a "fairy land," philosophized that "there is a freedom in the pathless woods, if you are there on your own feet and on your own resources," and asked: "But who shall describe the Sequoias? Their beauty is far more wonderful than their size. When the black marks of fire are sprinkled on the wonderfully deep richer ocher of the bark, the effect is brilliant beyond words."[27]

When it came to the implementation of policy, however, Pinchot resolutely followed a utilitarian path. He opposed the famous 1894 provision in the New York Constitution setting aside the Adirondack Forest Reserve from development, which Roderick Nash has properly paired with the creation of Yellowstone National Park as "milestones in the . . . history of American wilderness preservation." Pinchot backed the 1906 Forest Homestead Act, which allowed the patenting, or deeding, of millions of acres of potential agricultural land within the national forests. Pinchot was against national parks unless they were made available for development. Thus, he opposed the creation of Glacier National Park and others because they would be off-limits for timber harvesting, water development, grazing, and railroad construction. He insisted that the term "forest reserves" be abandoned, as it was in 1907, in favor of the term "national forests" to make it clear that commercial uses were emphasized in the forests. And in one of the premier natural resource disputes in the history of the West, Pinchot set himself off against Muir in the 1910s by supporting the flooding of Hetch Hetchy Valley in Yosemite National Park in order to slake San Francisco's thirst for water. Further, with the exception of a few asides of the kind mentioned in the preceding paragraph, Pinchot's published works are nearly devoid of any mention of noncommodity uses—and, as I say, Pinchot was not a retiring man: had he believed that preservation had a place in the national forests, he would have told us so in no uncertain terms. His was simply not an era when recreation, much less aesthetics, was emphasized in forest policy, and Pinchot had no inclination to advocate such an approach.[28]

It is an open question as to how Pinchot would design forest policy under modern conditions. Respected Forest Service observer Glen Robinson believes that Pinchot, were he alive today, would hold fast to his turn-of-the-century devotion to timber production:

More timber products are now demanded. . . . But any notion that Pinchot would be shamed by the agency's present timber policies must be rejected out of hand. If anything, Pinchot would react adversely, not to the service's timber orientation but to its increasing attention to preservation and other "nonproductive" uses.[29]

My guess, on the other hand, is that Pinchot might have adjusted his views on timber domination in the national forests. For all of his arrogance, Pinchot understood generational change and seems to have realized that he could hope to set only broad guidelines, not rock-hard rules, for future societies. His talk of "the long run" evokes transcendent future needs, demands, and values. In his 1910 book, *The Fight for Conservation*, he argued for the Forest Service's right to make new policies by stressing that "[t]he public welfare cannot be subserved merely by walking blindly in the old ruts. Times change, and the public needs change with them." He quoted Chief Justice John Marshall's discussion in *McCulloch v. Maryland* of a living, evolving Constitution that grows to meet new societal challenges. Thus, Pinchot might well have believed that dominant-use status for timber production could properly be altered by new minds and a new consensus, so long as the later generation would comply with the unwavering rules of Pinchotism—retention of public forests in federal ownership, conservation for yet more generations, and distribution to a broad range of people, not just large economic interests.[30]

Perhaps. But two essential things involve no guesswork at all. The Grand Master dedicated the national forests to timber as the first use, and that dedication has remained firmly lodged in place.

The Forest Rangers and the Quiet Years

Pinchot's stormy departure marked the end of the frenetic, mission-shaping days of the national forests. The next three decades, until the onset of World War II, would be staid, almost somnolent, compared with the controversial times that had gone before and that would follow. During the era from 1910 to about 1940, the Forest Service worked from the firm foundation set by Pinchot and built an image, nearly a mystique, that has no real parallel in any other federal agency. The Forest Service became personified by the forest ranger, who grew into an institution, much like the Texas Ranger or the Canadian Mountie. Even today, the goodwill and aura of romanticism generated during this era, still exemplified by the forest ranger, remain valuable assets of the Forest Service.

One reason for this long stretch of smooth sailing was that there was little demand for federal timber. Stumpage prices remained chronically low. For all of Pinchot's public pronouncements about using the national forests for timber production, and for all of his detailed instructions to rangers in the agency's bible, *The Use Book*, the actual harvest of timber from national forests remained inconsequential. Until World War II, annual harvests rarely exceeded 1.5 bbf (billion board feet) and averaged about 1 bbf—less than 10 percent of the annual cut of approximately 11 bbf in modern times. About 125,000 acres were cut each year—less than one-fifth of 1 percent of the 75 million acres of the national forests' commercial timberland and well under one-tenth of 1 percent of all land then in the national forests. By way of comparison, timber companies annually removed 50 bbf from 10 million acres of private land during this time. The Forest Service thus could make its cut from "easy" lands— highly profitable stands that would jeopardize few recreational or environmental values. There simply was no basis for any controversy. The cuts were essentially invisible, swallowed up by the vast backwoods.[31]

Not only did the Forest Service stay clear of controversy but the agency also served society admirably in the West through its affirmative programs. The Forest Service continued Pinchot's policy of selling timber primarily to local mills. This approach responded to community needs while avoiding competition with private timber owners on national markets, which would have reduced prices even further. The forests served a valuable watershed function for municipal water supplies, with the pristine woodlands producing steady supplies of clean water. The national forests also held out an allure for recreation, and the Forest Service responded. Recognizing, in Chief Henry Graves's words, that "[t]he western National Forests are . . . the natural public playgrounds for most of the country west of the Mississippi," the agency launched programs for construction of campgrounds, summer homes, and improved trail systems. Tourism increased markedly; for example, recreation visitor days tripled between 1917 and 1924. In 1924, Aldo Leopold, then a Forest Service employee, succeeded in convincing the regional forester in Albuquerque to set aside from development more than 700,000 acres in the Gila National Forest in New Mexico. It was the birth of the wilderness ideal, the first time any government in the world had dedicated land solely for the purpose of leaving it in its natural, wild state. By the end of 1925, five more areas in other national forests had received wilderness protection. This administratively created wilderness system expanded to 14 million acres during the 1930s under the leadership of Bob Marshall (like Leopold, a founder of The Wilderness Society) before Marshall's death in 1939.[32]

Fire fighting was perhaps the single activity that did the most to win the gratitude of the Forest Service's public. For rural westerners, forest fires were apocalyptic—wildly frightening, out-of-control rampages that destroyed property and killed human beings. Most mining camps were wood frame and canvas towns. Grazing ranges, timber stands, watersheds, and wildlife populations could be wiped out. Even a middle-sized fire, whipped by a stiff wind, can outrun a person on foot.

In literally every year there were major fires, but 1910, when the combination of a dry year and electrical storm lightning strikes torched forests across the West, was one of the worst. In Montana's Bitterroot Valley, a farmer reported that on one day the cinders were so thick that "[i]t got so dark . . . at three o'clock in the afternoon the chickens went to roost." A baseball game in Hamilton was called in midafternoon due to darkness. In Idaho and Montana, the raging summer fires burned 3 million acres and took the lives of seventy-eight fire fighters and eight civilians.³³

In this setting, the Forest Service's programs of fire protection research and on-the-ground implementation took on real importance. Studies of the history of forest fires conducted during Pinchot's administration laid part of the groundwork for understanding the problem. When Henry Graves took over as chief, he sought out timber industry money for an endowed chair in fire protection at Yale University's School of Forestry. Graves also went directly to Congress for research funds and in 1915 established the Branch of Research, which emphasized fire protection.

There was also a great deal of work and ingenuity on the ground. Fire fighters took to the Pulaski, a combination ax and hoe devised by Forest Service ranger Edward Pulaski, which remains in wide use today. Fire lookouts, often with telephone hookups, bloomed on mountain peaks strategically selected for observation. Across the West, rangers and their staffs cut trail systems into the rugged mountain country. Crack fire-fighting crews sprang up. One of the most famous was the Lolo National Forest's Remount Depot, which served the timber-rich country of eastern Washington, northern Idaho, and western Montana. Like other crews of the day, the Remount Depot relied on community organization and made mule packing a high art:

> Ever since the Forest Service began, pack animals had transported equipment in the newly created Forests. Now, with the concerted effort to control fires in land so inhospitable that only animals could serve as transportation, the packer and his working horses or mules became all important. As an early writer put it, "As the Forest Service grew, so did the job of packing."
>
> All equipment—nails, telephone line, lumber, cable, food, and tools—was hauled up the new trails, mainly on horses hired from local ranchers for 50¢ a day per animal. At first, the pack stock was herded loose, not led, by a $60-a-month packer on his own horse leading a "bell mare." Gradually, mules began to be used more than horses, and the Forest Service purchased more of its own pack stock. The crews of firefighters, some trained, some off the streets of Butte or Spokane, walked to fires up these trails, sometimes taking several days to get there. The Forest Service equipped itself to respond as quickly as possible to every fire reported in order to prevent another 1910.³⁴

Forest rangers were the focal point for Forest Service policy. The first forest ranger was Bill Kreutzer of Colorado, who was signed on in 1898, when the forests were still managed by the Interior Department. Kreutzer's charge was a model of simplicity, at least on paper: he was, all by himself, directed "to protect public forests" throughout Colorado "from fires or any other means of injury." Presumably, Kreutzer well understood his limitations in personally protecting more than 10 million acres across the state, and early on, he developed the community relations skills that typified the rangers. At the turn of the twentieth century, beetles were killing off the stands of pine trees near Ward, in the Front Range of Colorado. Kreutzer directed a large timber harvest to eliminate further spread of the beetles. Citizens of Boulder objected, but Kreutzer found a way to allay their concerns:

> Bill took the group to the area and explained to their satisfaction why the clear cutting had to be done. To distract the attention of the chief objector he cut open the bark of an infested pine, collected a handful of the larvae of the beetles, and ate them.
> He induced the lady to taste them, others did likewise, and in the general interest aroused over their palatability the committee's objections to the cutting were partly allayed. Just whether the bug eggs were responsible for the change, Bill doesn't know, but the committee members soon departed, with everyone willing to give Bill and his rangers a free hand to fight the beetle infestation as best they could.[35]

Then, as now, the people of Boulder were suckers for anything organic.

Pinchot extolled the virtues of management in the field, close to the ground. He believed that the best policy was developed "around the campfire": "The old Land Office custom of referring pretty much everything to Washington for incubation and ultimate decision was definitely out." Pinchot placed tremendous emphasis on building a first-rate corps of rangers through recruiting, training, delegating responsibility, and, not incidentally, romanticizing the office of the ranger. The forest ranger became embedded at the heart of western lore—a technician, community organizer, and outdoorsperson, all in one. Pinchot loved to tell of an examination given by Fritz Olmstead to his prospective rangers in the Bitterroot Valley in Montana. It included proof of the ability to pack mules, run compass lines, and perform other essential tasks. In addition, the examination "also included two other highly practical tests. The first was: 'Cook a meal.' And the second: 'Eat it.'" In *A River Runs Through It and Other Stories*, Norman Maclean adds another dimension to this hardy breed:

> They still picked rangers for the Forest Service by picking the toughest guy in town. Ours, Bill Bell, was the toughest in the Bitterroot Valley, and we thought he was the best ranger in the Forest Service. We were

strengthened in this belief by the rumor that Bill had killed a sheepherder. We were a little disappointed that he had been acquitted of the charges, but nobody held it against him, for we all knew that being acquitted of killing a sheepherder in Montana isn't the same as being innocent.³⁶

The Forest Service thus enjoyed a honeymoon with the public of more than half a century, from Pinchot's day until well into the 1950s. During that time, the agency built up capital that still has not been fully expended. But a new paradigm began to emerge in the early 1940s, when the market changed in fundamental ways. Patiently waiting to fulfill the new demand for commercial wood products were the agency's foresters, who manned all levels of decision making in the Forest Service. It was time to activate Pinchot's dormant agenda of dedicating the forests to the primary task of harvesting timber.

Production and Controversy

World War II triggered fundamental changes in the national forests. Today, warfare is conducted with metals such as steel, aluminum, and molybdenum and with sophisticated computer and laser systems. In the 1940s, however, lumber was a main element in military matériel. The Forest Service's 1942 annual report set out the diverse purposes for which wood products were required:

> Billions of feet of lumber are needed to house the expanding American armed forces and the growing army of workers in war industries. Wood and wood derivatives are needed for ships, wharves, airplanes, gunstocks, explosives [nitroglycerin was made from glycerol extracted from wood, and turpentine was the fuel for flamethrowers], and a host of other war materials and facilities. Some 8 billion board feet of lumber is the estimated 1942 requirement for boxing and crating war materials, agricultural products, and essential civilian goods. Orders for Army beds will call for from 30 to 40 million feet of hardwoods this year. A million feet a day will be needed for Army truck bodies.³⁷

The chief was not overstating the point. It took three trees to equip and maintain one American soldier. Colonel F. G. Sherrill, who headed up the Materials and Equipment Section of the Army Corps of Engineers, said that wood products were "the most vital material for the successful prosecution of the war" and that the timber industry "was therefore the most important war industry in the country." The annual cut from the national forests jumped from the historical average of 1 billion board feet to 3.3 bbf in 1944.³⁸

After the war, the need for timber continued to increase but for very different reasons—to satisfy the demand for wood products to create paper, plastics, and, most of all, housing to support the postwar economic surge. The Forest Service had anticipated these developments and, even before the war had ended, laid plans for responding to a vigorous postwar economy. In 1944, the second Roosevelt, ever looking forward, called in Pinchot, now seventy-eight, to discuss the role of natural resources in the peacetime economy.[39]

By the late 1940s, it was clear that there was yet another reason why the national forests would be under greatly increased pressure to produce more timber. Just as the wood products industry had been forced to move west in the late 1890s because forests in the Great Lakes region had been logged over, in the 1940s and 1950s industry had to look to public lands to fulfill a timber demand that could not be met from a private timber base long subjected to poor logging practices. For generations, companies had followed what longtime Forest Service employee Leon Minckler called "one-shot" forestry. Companies "high-graded" timber stands, removing only the most valuable trees and taking no steps to regenerate the remaining stand.[40]

Even worse, it was common practice for forest owners to clear-cut whole parcels, fence line to fence line, and then refuse to make the necessary expenditures to keep the land in production. The situation was most critical in the Douglas fir, cedar, spruce, redwood, and true fir forests in the moist western side of the Cascade and Sierra Nevada ranges in Washington, Oregon, and northern California, the three highest timber-producing states in the country. These stands are extraordinarily valuable but only if long-term expenditures are made and good forest practices are followed. A few timber companies—Weyerhaeuser is the best example—had the requisite foresight, but most did not. With no plans for restocking and no remaining seed trees to provide for natural regeneration, blackberry, alder, and other brush species took over. The companies sold the land to farmers or subdividers, relinquished it at tax sales, or just let it sit. The physical results of such "cut-and-run" forestry are still evident to the naked eye across the Pacific Northwest. The policy results of losing productive timberland, and forcing an increased burden on the national forests, remain with us as well.[41]

The professional foresters who controlled the Forest Service were more than willing to step up the beat. The annual cut gradually increased to 4.4 bbf in 1952, when Richard E. McArdle became chief. McArdle, determined to increase the harvest, emphasized the need for a greatly expanded road system. He also saw the forests as places that existed mainly for the production of commercial wood products:

> Millions of acres of wild forest land must await an adequate road system before they will return their full worth in forest products and in growing

capacity. As those acres now stand, undeveloped, a large part of their growing capacity is continually being wasted by fire, insects, diseases, and wind.[42]

Both the cut and road construction boomed during McArdle's ten-year administration. Timber production reached 12.1 bbf in 1966. In all, twice as much timber was cut during the sixteen years between 1950 and 1966 as had been cut during all of the previous forty-five years since the Transfer Act of 1905 (see figure on page 138).[43]

During the twenty years after World War II, another set of developments, in direct conflict with the timber boom, was set in motion. The nation began to move west, and easterners could now easily reach the public lands by air or by the newly constructed system of interstate highways. Thus, the postwar timber boom was paralleled by a recreation boom: total recreational visits to national forests increased from less than 10 million in 1948, roughly the historical level, to 190 million in 1976, a twentyfold increase. These visitors came for many different recreational pursuits. Some wanted highly developed recreational facilities, most notably ski areas. The first ski run in the national forests was established in Sun Valley, Idaho, in 1936; by 1973, there were 218 ski areas. Other visitors wanted to view the scenery from their automobiles or from roadside turnouts. Still other kinds of recreation—guided river runs and hunts— were less elaborate; the much-expanded Forest Service campground system was even less so. And there were millions—literally—of backpackers, hunters and fishers, and day hikers.[44]

All of this gradually brought the Forest Service under intense public scrutiny. The roads and clear-cuts began to encroach on the locals' favorite groves, streams, trails, meadows, and vistas. Drive-through motorists took note. And nearly everyone flying into western towns and cities like Missoula, Boise, Eugene, Portland, and Seattle were taken aback by the extensive clear-cuts that they looked down on.

This was a new set of issues for the public, the timber industry, and the Forest Service. Congress responded cautiously. The Multiple-Use Sustained-Yield Act, passed in 1960, for the first time officially recognized recreation as a proper use of the national forests. The 1960 act, which the Forest Service saw as a holding action affirming its past policies, was little more than the most general policy statement. It avoided the setting of any priorities by listing the five basic uses of the forests in alphabetical order: "outdoor recreation, range, timber, watershed, and wildlife and fish." The 1962 report of the Outdoor Recreation Resources Review Commission more clearly signaled the increased awareness of the noncommodity values of the public lands. The ORRRC, chaired by Laurance Rockefeller, who had furthered numerous conservation causes in Jackson Hole, Wyo-

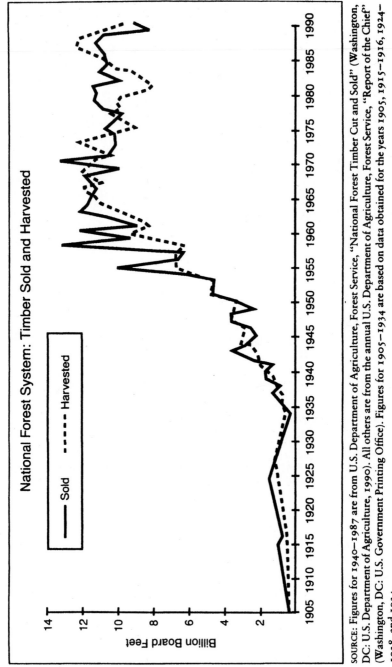

National Forest System: Timber Sold and Harvested

— Sold   - - - - Harvested

Billion Board Feet

1905 1910 1915 1920 1925 1930 1935 1940 1945 1950 1955 1960 1965 1970 1975 1980 1985 1990

SOURCE: Figures for 1940–1987 are from U.S. Department of Agriculture, Forest Service, "National Forest Timber Cut and Sold" (Washington, DC: U.S. Department of Agriculture, 1990). All others are from the annual U.S. Department of Agriculture, Forest Service, "Report of the Chief" (Washington, DC: U.S. Government Printing Office). Figures for 1905–1934 are based on data obtained for the years 1905, 1915–1916, 1924–1928, and 1934.

ming, recommended numerous major policy initiatives, among them a national wilderness system; a national trails system; a wild and scenic rivers system; and the establishment of a Land and Water Conservation Fund, a congressionally funded program for land acquisition. Due in part to the advocacy of Interior Secretary Stewart Udall, all of the principal recommendations became law during the 1960s.[45]

Striking the most profound chords was the historic Wilderness Act of 1964. The work of Aldo Leopold, Bob Marshall, and others had succeeded in setting aside national forest lands as administratively declared wilderness during the 1920s and 1930s, but wilderness activity had been stalled since Marshall's death in 1939. Indeed, during the 1950s the Forest Service seemed to be backtracking on wilderness preservation. In Oregon, designation of the old-growth French Pete Valley as wilderness was lifted to allow for potential logging. In New Mexico, part of the Gila Wilderness Area—the first entry in the agency's system—was removed from wilderness status. Other intrusions on wilderness areas drew regional and national attention.[46]

Howard Zahniser, executive director of The Wilderness Society, and other conservationists argued that these actions proved their central thesis: that congressional designation was essential because the Forest Service could revoke its own administrative classifications at any time. Zahniser drafted proposed legislation, and Senator Hubert Humphrey introduced it in 1956. The bill, which developed the largest legislative record of any conservation measure up to that time, was staunchly advocated and bitterly opposed. But after concessions were made to miners, ranchers, and other economic interests, the Wilderness Act—still one of the most idealistic pieces of federal legislation ever adopted—became law on September 3, 1964. The 9.1 million acres that the Forest Service had designated as wild areas were made "instant wilderness areas," the initial units in the National Wilderness Preservation System. It was the first time in history that any national legislature in the world had mandated that land must be maintained in a pristine state.[47]

The Wilderness Act had virtually no immediate effect on the Forest Service's timber program. Much of the land was above timber line, "wilderness on the rocks." The small percentage of forested land in the new system tended to be sparsely timbered holdings in steep, remote areas, where access for logging would be difficult at best. The amount of timber that would realistically have been cut was so small that the agency could easily make adjustments by increasing the cut on nonwilderness land. Thus, although the Wilderness Act was a monument in public land policy and although subsequent additions to the wilderness system would include timber stands of significant commercial value, the 1964 act did little to prevent the impending collision between the proponents of timber dominance and of recreational use in the national forests.

Beginning in the late 1960s, criticism of the Forest Service accelerated. It took many forms and flared up in many places. Major controversies erupted over, among other incidents, the "big blowout" on the South Fork of the Salmon River in 1965, the landslides on the Siuslaw River on the Oregon coast during the 1970s, and, as discussed later, the clear-cutting of eastern hardwoods in the Monongahela National Forest in West Virginia during the late 1960s and early 1970s. The most telling events, however, took place in the Bitterroot National Forest in north-western Montana. The Bitterroot situation set a new context by galvaniz-ing a diverse western constituency, sparking a major congressional investigation into forest practices in the national forests, and laying the foundation for the comprehensive legislation that controls the national forests today.

The Bitterroot River flows directly north through Missoula. The valley is flanked by the Bitterroot Range on the west and the Sapphire Mountains on the east. The Bitterroot National Forest comprises almost all of the high country, and well over half of all land, within the watershed. Missoula is home of the University of Montana, and the small towns in the scenic valley are dependent on ranching, logging, and farming. The Bitterroot River is one of Montana's blue-ribbon trout streams.

The Forest Service, responding to national pressures for a higher timber harvest, increased the cut in the Bitterroot during the late 1950s and the 1960s. To meet the new harvest level, the Forest Service engaged in exten-sive clear-cutting, in which all trees within a specified area are removed. In addition, the agency plowed terraces on steep clear-cut slopes so that young trees would have contoured benches on which tree-planting ma-chines could be operated. This intensive management required a greatly expanded road network.

Criticism mounted, and in 1969, Dale A. Burk wrote an influential, award-winning series of articles for the *Missoulian*. Burk's articles dem-onstrate vividly the many quarters of society affected by timber harvest-ing in the national forests. One third-generation logger, believing that the harvesting program could not be justified on a sustained-yield basis, argued: " 'They're ruining our timber stands for the next three genera-tions. They're taking out all the timber and pretty soon there won't be any more to log. . . . Most people working in the woods feel that the Forest Service is setting the forest back 150 years.' " Farmers and ranchers complained that excessive logging was destroying the watershed. Bill Lovely, who operated a 700-acre ranch, including 100 acres in hay, found that the clear-cuts caused the snow to melt off early, thus denying him water in the late summer, when it was needed for irrigation: "Now the water is coming down in the early spring, at the least desirable time." Marvin Bell of Hamilton, another rancher, charged that a destructive spring runoff in 1966 had washed out a headgate and eroded stream banks: "That never happened before. The water is coming down too fast because too large an area in the watershed has been disrupted." Further, as Lovely put it, the high rate of erosion made dams for storage ponds a fruitless endeavor: "[I]t would be senseless to build a small high country dam just to have it silt in."⁴⁸

Burk also catalogued complaints from former Forest Service personnel. G. M. Brandborg, who had been forest supervisor of the Bitterroot for twenty years, found that current cutting practices violated sustained-yield principles: the allowable cut of ponderosa pine, the most important commercial species in the area, was 18.3 million board feet each year in the Bitterroot, but the Forest Service was cutting an average of 25 million board feet annually.⁴⁹

The Bitterroot clear-cutting aroused a bevy of complaints based on fishery impacts and on aesthetic grounds. The Bitterroot Valley is a place where logging matters to the economy, but it is also country where residents revel in the outdoors, most of which is managed by the Forest Service. And *terracing?* One can well imagine that Bill Bell—the legendary old forest ranger in the Bitterroot who was found not guilty, although perhaps not innocent, of killing a sheepherder—would have recoiled at the idea of terracing and probably would have found it, well, effete.

Senator Lee Metcalf of Montana appointed a commission to study the Bitterroot. The commission consisted of seven members of the faculty of the University of Montana School of Forestry and was headed by the forestry school's dean, Dr. Arnold W. Bolle. In a 1969 letter to Bolle, Metcalf observed that "the Bitterroot is a typical mountain timbered valley and the results of such a study might well be extended to recommendations national in scope."⁵⁰

The Bolle Report, as it has come to be called, was released on November 18, 1970. Bolle is a quiet, dignified, courtly man not given to strong language, and it would require uncommon courage for a professional forester—and a sitting forestry school dean—to speak out in public on such issues. But Bolle's experience with the Bitterroot had deeply disturbed him and his colleagues, and the report reflected it. The unanimous report upbraided the Forest Service in no uncertain terms:

—Multiple use management, in fact, does not exist as the governing principle on the Bitterroot National Forest. . . .
—Quality timber management and harvest practices are missing.

Consideration of recreation, watershed, wildlife and grazing appear as
afterthoughts. . . .
—The Forest Service . . . needs to be reconstructed so that substantial,
responsible, local public participation . . . can "naturally" take place.

The report also criticized the Forest Service's "overriding concern for
sawtimber production" and the "economic irrationality" of the agency's
timber management policies.[51]

There were outcries elsewhere. The Forest Service, responding to complaints from the West Virginia legislature and Senator Gale McGee of
Wyoming, appointed agency task forces to study the Monongahela National Forest in West Virginia and four national forests in Wyoming. The
Service also issued an official report on its timber practices nationwide.
Senate criticism mounted: at one point, Senator McGee called clear-
cutting "a shocking desecration that has to be seen to be believed." Then,
in March 1972, the Public Lands Subcommittee of the Senate Interior
Committee issued its influential report, commonly referred to as the
Church Report, after Idaho senator Frank Church, the subcommittee
chairman.[52]

The Church Report set out guidelines that would later become the road
map for the National Forest Management Act of 1976. The report called
for a decrease in clear-cutting and addressed the broader issue of where
timber harvesting—by clear-cutting or any other method—should be allowed. The 1972 report identified four classes of land where timber harvesting should not be permitted: highly scenic land, land with fragile soils,
land with low reforestation potential, and land where reforestation or
environmentally acceptable harvesting would be uneconomical.[53]

Congress let the matter sit there, directing the Forest Service to take
remedial action. The agency, under its able chief, John McGuire, began a
major overhaul of its timber program. But by the mid-1970s, the third
branch of government had begun to assert its duty to take a "hard look" at
administrative action, including public land and environmental matters.
The judiciary changed the calculus, not by ruling on the Bitterroot or
another forest in a major public lands state but by addressing issues in West
Virginia in a manner that directly affected the American West.

For years, the Izaak Walton League of America had opposed the extensive clear-cutting in West Virginia's Monongahela National Forest. The
league, which traditionally eschewed litigation, had become sufficiently
frustrated and angered by the impacts on wildlife and by the Forest Service's intransigence that it sued to stop clear-cutting altogether. It relied on
the long-ignored language from the 1897 Organic Act stating that the
Forest Service was authorized to sell only "dead, matured, or large growth

of trees" that had been "marked and designated" before sale. The league took the position that the 1897 Congress, deeply suspicious of the timber industry, had intended to place tight restrictions on timber harvesting in the national forests by allowing harvesting only of fully mature trees—and that the Forest Service was cutting trees in the Monongahela that might be "economically" mature but not "physiologically" mature. Similarly, the league argued, clear-cutting did not meet the Organic Act's "mark and designate" requirement for each tree because the agency marked trees only around the perimeter of a sale, as opposed to practicing selective cutting, in which every tree to be harvested is marked.

On August 21, 1975, the United States Court of Appeals for the Fourth Circuit agreed with the Izaak Walton League on every count. The ruling effectively blocked the clear-cutting program in the Monongahela because the economics of clear-cutting dictated that less than physiologically mature trees be cut and that entire areas, rather than individual trees, be marked. The case was also a landmark because the court stated so succinctly the changes that had overtaken the Forest Service:

> For nearly half a century following its creation in 1905, the National Forest System provided only a fraction of the national timber supply with almost ninety-five per cent coming from privately owned forests. During this period the Forest Service regarded itself as a custodian and protector of the forests rather than a prime producer, and consistent with this role the Service faithfully carried out the provisions of the Organic Act with respect to selective timber cutting. In 1940, however, with private timber reserves badly depleted, World War II created an enormous demand for lumber and this was followed by the post-war building boom. As a result the posture of the Forest Service quickly changed from custodian to a production agency.[54]

Standing alone, the banning of clear-cutting of hardwoods in West Virginia's national forests is of little moment for national timber policy. The Forest Service administers only a small amount of land in West Virginia, and hardwood timber is in much less demand than softwoods, which the housing industry depends on for construction lumber. The problem was that the reasoning in the *Monongahela* case applied to the western softwood forests as well. Most of all, for the industry it would be a disaster for clear-cutting to be outlawed on the rich Douglas fir stands of the Pacific Northwest. Environmentalists promptly sent out a warning by obtaining an injunction against clear-cutting in the Tongass National Forest in Alaska.[55]

The forest products industry immediately went to Congress to obtain a repeal of the offending language from the 1897 act. It turned out not to be that easy. Conservationists responded in full force by using the clear-cutting issue as a lever to open a far-ranging congressional debate, not only on clear-cutting but also on all forest management practices. Senator Jennings Randolph of West Virginia offered omnibus legislation, drafted by environmentalists, that would have severely restricted Forest Service timber operations.[56]

The National Forest Management Act of 1976 (NFMA), enacted fourteen months after the *Monongahela* decision, was a compromise, but one so comprehensive as to amount to a new Organic Act for the Forest Service. Unquestionably, Congress wanted it both ways: it wanted to keep the annual cut at a productive level, and it also wanted serious, substantial environmental protection. But the thrust of the legislation was plainly toward the protective side. From Pinchot's day on, the implicit byword in the national forests had been "leave it to the experts." The tone of the NFMA, on the other hand, was set by Senator Hubert Humphrey, who, even though he introduced the "industry bill" in opposition to Randolph's "environmental bill," believed that "fundamental reform" was needed. Humphrey stated: "We have had 15 years since the 1960 Multiple Use and Sustained Yield Act was passed. Much has happened, and as we look at what has transpired, the need for improvement is evident." He identified the central problem as the predominance of timber production over protection of other resources. Humphrey declared:

> The days have ended when the forest may be viewed only as trees and trees viewed only as timber. The soil and the water, the grasses and the shrubs, the fish and the wildlife, and the beauty that is the forest must become integral parts of resource managers' thinking and actions.[57]

The NFMA restricted clear-cutting but did not prohibit it. The reason, as became evident during the congressional debates, was that clear-cutting has a legitimate place in forest management. Most notably, Douglas fir is shade intolerant throughout most of its range; that is, young trees require direct sunlight and usually will not regenerate under a canopy. Thus, clear-cutting provides seedlings with needed sunlight in a way that selective cutting cannot. The reasoning does not apply to most other species, but because of the commercial importance of Douglas fir, any idea of an outright ban on clear-cutting vanished quickly. The act did provide that clear-cutting must be the "optimum" method of harvesting whenever it is employed; that cuts must be shaped to the terrain to the extent practicable; and that cuts must be consistent with "the protection of soil, watershed, fish, wildlife, recreation, and esthetic resources."[58]

The NFMA has numerous other important provisions, all laced with qualifications but all placing a new level of restraint on the Forest Service.

Among the most significant are these. All timber cuts, clear-cuts included, must be performed in a manner that will protect streams from changes in water temperature and deposits of sediment that would "seriously and adversely affect water conditions or fish habitat;" ensure that soil and watershed conditions will not be irreversibly damaged; and ensure that harvested lands can be restocked within five years. The NFMA requires the Forest Service to protect biodiversity by providing for "diversity of plant and animal communities." The act prescribes a relatively lengthy rotation age (the number of years between stocking of new trees and harvesting) by essentially adopting the *Monongahela* court's rules that trees generally cannot be cut until they have reached biological maturity. A technical, but exceedingly important, provision is the NFMA's mandate that the Forest Service must follow "nondeclining even flow," a conservative variant of sustained-yield management that discourages the accelerated liquidation of old-growth stands. The act also contains opaque language suggesting that sales be tested by economic standards, thus casting doubt on the practice of below-cost sales.[59]

But it turns out that the wheels of forest policy, like those of law, grind exceedingly slowly. The NFMA had no immediate bite. Rather, Congress, recognizing the complexity of the issues, directed that the mandates of the NFMA would not go into effect immediately but would be implemented through individual forest plans adopted by each national forest. The 1976 act stipulated that the Forest Service must "attempt to complete" the plans by late 1985, but completing the plans proved no mean task. Planning remained on hold until an independent, congressionally mandated Committee of Scientists made recommendations to the Forest Service on regulations to implement the act. Regulations were adopted in 1979. Then the planning process began in earnest, replete with numerous congressional procedural directives, including greatly expanded inventories, to provide a detailed scientific data base; extensive public input, to ameliorate a perceived lack of sunshine; interdisciplinary teams, to counteract the domination by foresters; and a comprehensive consideration of all resources, to combat the emphasis on timber production. The nationwide planning process has been costly (conservative estimates place the price tag at $100 million) and time-consuming. Mike Sullivan, vice president of the Industrial Forestry Association, based in Portland, may not have been far from the mark when he concluded that "[i]t is the most ambitious centralized planning effort ever undertaken in the free world."[60]

The NFMA has wrought some constructive changes. The interdisciplinary teams have brought in new perspectives, the detailed inventories have provided a wealth of new on-the-ground information, and in a few cases the planning process has provided something of the town meeting approach that the congressional drafters seem to have intended. The Forest Service has developed the so-called New Forestry, designed to tailor timber harvesting to be more protective of species diversity, watersheds, and views. But one thing has not changed a whit: although the actual timber harvest temporarily dropped during the recession of the early 1980s and although the planned cut was reduced by Congress slightly in the early 1990s, the national annual allowable sale quantity has remained substantially steady at 11 billion board feet, exactly where it was when the Bitterroot controversy began to boil in the mid-1960s and where it has remained ever since. In essence, the NFMA and the Forest Service have probably produced the best national forest system possible under a regime of cutting timber at the current intensive level. The question now has become whether the land can tolerate production at this rate, however well managed.

The New Context for Decision

It is now apparent that a raft of new forces—institutional, scientific, economic, legal, political, and philosophical—have come to bear during the late 1980s and early 1990s. Scrutiny on the Forest Service has ascended to yet another level—higher than during the 1960s, higher even than during the NFMA deliberations in 1975 and 1976. The 1990s are a volatile time for the West's most distinctive lands, one that likely will determine exactly how entrenched is the lord of timber domination. The following is an assessment of the current situation and of the likelihood of change.

Throughout the 1980s, a series of personalities, events, and perceptions sharpened public consciousness on environmental matters, especially those related to health and conservation. In the early years of the decade, the policies of Secretary of the Interior James Watt and EPA administrator Anne Burford drew widespread attention and criticism. In the case of Watt, the issues were excessive mineral development on the inland public lands and on offshore oil and gas fields; inadequate protection of the National Park System; and a generally shrill, vitriolic rhetoric on almost any subject relating to the environment. In the case of Burford, public anxiety rose in response to her lax enforcement of federal laws on water and air pollution and on toxic waste dumps. The burgeoning federal deficit caused the public to grow ever more wary of government subsidies. The Reagan administration's drive to return authority to the states had an unintended effect in the environmental arena by creating more watchdogs in the statehouses. Late in the decade, global issues began to make what seems to be an indelible imprint. Acid rain, the depletion of the ozone layer, and the greenhouse effect are no longer viewed as abstractions that can await another day for action. Many of these developments are not tied directly to the national forests, but cumulatively they have created a public awareness that has directly affected forest policy.

A main by-product has been the transformation of environmental organizations. The national groups that have given the highest priority to the national forests—The Wilderness Society, the Sierra Club, the Natural Resources Defense Council, the National Wildlife Federation, and the Sierra Club Legal Defense Fund—have virtually remade themselves. Spurred by dramatic increases in membership, they have assembled large technical staffs with impressive credentials in many different disciplines. They have developed a skilled cadre of litigators to enforce the environmental laws; indeed, since the early 1970s, virtually every reform in public lands forest management has been sparked by citizens' suits holding the Forest Service to its statutory obligations. The national environmental organizations also have built highly varied public information programs, ranging from press contacts to lobbying to production of magazines and videos, that allow them to participate in a serious way in the shaping of public opinion.[61]

Take The Wilderness Society as an example. Founded in 1937 by an eminent group that included Aldo Leopold and Bob Marshall, the society operated out of a shoebox for nearly thirty years. Even the lengthy campaign to enact the Wilderness Act of 1964 was largely the work of one person, Howard Zahniser. Numbers tell part of the story of The Wilderness Society's growth over the past three decades. By the late 1970s, membership had hit a high of 75,000, and the budget had grown from tens of thousands of dollars to $1.5 million. The new money allowed the society to hire experienced professionals as the staff expanded to twenty-six employees. Today, membership has quadrupled to a current count of 310,000, the budget has mushroomed to more than $16 million, and the society houses 126 employees.[62]

In 1984, the society moved beyond wilderness issues *per se* and identified reform of the national forests as its first priority. Its professional staff, housed on three floors of a Washington, DC, office building, consists of foresters, economists, biologists, other scientists, and lawyers (for legal and policy analysis—the society uses outside attorneys when it is involved in litigation). It regularly brings in leading figures from politics, academia, and the business world for consultation. From top to bottom, the society has attracted a first-rate staff. One measure of the newly acquired stature of the conservation movement is the society's ability to hire Gaylord Nelson, the prominent former United States senator from Wisconsin, as counselor.

George Frampton, the president, or chief executive officer, was a clerk to Supreme Court Justice Harry Blackmun, a Watergate prosecutor, and a Washington lawyer for ten years.

The Wilderness Society turns out a stream of quality publications, including its magazine, *Wilderness*; books and pamphlets on subjects such as biological diversity, the old-growth economy in the Pacific Northwest, national forest planning, and the Forest Service budget; formal written comments on individual forest plans; and continuing policy papers on issues of the moment. The Wilderness Society also has several full-time staff members dedicated to legislative and administrative lobbying. The society's emphasis is not just on Washington, DC, however. It has fifteen field offices, from Boston to Atlanta to Denver to Anchorage, to implement policy on regional and local issues. The same kinds of observations, allowing for various individual differences, can be made about each of the major national conservation groups involved in forest policy and law.

Similar trends can be seen, on a smaller scale, in the regional and local organizations emphasizing the national forests. The Oregon Natural Resources Council (ONRC) is a leading example. It, too, pursues a regular publication program and engages in extensive advocacy work, which has contributed, among other accomplishments, to the Oregon Wilderness Act of 1984, adding 850,000 acres to the wilderness system. In 1980, the ONRC had four employees and a budget of $105,000. A decade later, it has twelve employees and a budget of $600,000.[63]

A second set of new developments in recent years is the increasing criticism of the Forest Service from sectors traditionally supportive of intensive development on the public lands. Thus, as discussed in the introduction to this chapter and as alluded to elsewhere, complaints are heard with some regularity from ranchers, farmers, small businesspeople, and state and local governments. A majority of the members of these groups probably still supports current cutting practices, but concern is significant and growing—and on numerous specific local issues (Bitterroot is just one example), it has amounted to real hostility. Given the fact that these constituencies historically formed much of the core of support for intensive extractive policies on federal lands, the increasing ferment among them is of considerable importance.

A third development helping to set a new context is the dramatically increased use of economic analysis. The idea that many of the sales in the Bitterroot were unprofitable was a point of attack in both the Bolle Report and the Church Report, but there was no number-crunching of the kind we see today. Nor, it should be said, was the early 1970s a time when government subsidies raised hackles in the way they now do. Even the debates regarding the NFMA did not train much attention on the issue of below-cost sales. To be sure, eminent resource economist Marion Clawson testified in favor of curtailing timber harvesting on economically marginal lands and submitted his study concluding that "expenditures for timber management are being made in regions, on forests, and on sites where timber values are so low that areas should be abandoned for timber growing purposes. . . . [T]he growing of more timber [in these areas] is not economically sound." Nevertheless, as with the Bitterroot, the emphasis in Congress was on the environmental destruction caused by clear-cutting. Thus, although most of the key legislators expressed concern about below-cost sales, the NFMA itself made only brief and ambiguous mention of economic viability of timber sales.[64]

The debate changed fundamentally on June 3, 1980, when the Natural Resources Defense Council (NRDC) released its study, *Giving Away the National Forests: An Analysis of U.S. Forest Service Timber Sales Below Cost.* The report, the first comprehensive analysis of the subject, concluded that "substantial amounts of federal timber are being sold at prices which do not recover the expenditures which the Forest Service makes to enable the sales to occur." The Forest Service responded the same day (there is now often a certain civility in these matters, such as providing advance copies to one's opponents), challenging the accounting procedures used by the NRDC. The basic point made by the Forest Service and industry—and it is a fair one—is that an annual cash flow analysis, such as that used by the NRDC, does not tell the whole story. It is wrong, the Forest Service and industry argue, to count all road costs, the most expensive item in timber sales, as expenses against the revenues from a particular sale. In future years, roads will serve other purposes—access for hunters and fishers, motorcyclists and snowmobilers, wildlife biologists conducting research, and state wildlife personnel stocking streams, and even for other timber sales in later years. Thus, the reasoning goes, those benefits should be recognized, and the road costs for the initial sale should be reduced accordingly and spread out over future years. Fair enough.[65]

The problem is that a great many sales in the national forests end up in the red even when such considerations are factored in. Numerous studies have been conducted since the NRDC's by a wide variety of groups: the General Accounting Office, the congressional research arm; The Wilderness Society; various congressional committee and subcommittee staffs; the Society of American Foresters; Resources for the Future; and the Forest Service. The analysis has steadily grown more sophisticated. In 1987, the Forest Service unveiled a new accounting system—even the acronym, TSPIRS, is a mouthful—that includes a host of additional factors and holds out the promise of shedding further light on this complex subject. But one can doubt whether the general conclusions reached to date will change.[66]

The results are these. The National Forest System as a whole makes money—quite a bit of it—on its timber program. The Wilderness Society, for example, found that the Forest Service nationwide spends about $700 million each year on timber sales and that the average annual gross receipts for the three years studied were $965 million, or an average annual net return of $265 million, a perfectly respectable showing.

But one gets a very different picture when the country is broken down into three areas: (1) Forest Service Region Six (composed of the two top timber-producing states, Oregon and Washington) and northern California; (2) Region Eight (the southern region, which contains highly productive stands of southern pine); and (3) everything else (national forests in the East, the Great Plains, the Rockies, the Southwest, Alaska, and most of California). In shorthand, Region Six and northern California make money hand over fist, Region Eight performs satisfactorily, and "everything else" is wracked with below-cost sales—nearly every national forest loses money. In dollars, Region Six and northern California make about $385 million annually, Region Eight makes approximately $30 million, and the others lose a total of about $150 million each year. In even terser shorthand, for this is a book about the West, the Douglas fir trees in western Oregon and Washington are green gold, and the lodgepole pine stands in the Rockies and the Southwest are bathed in red. In Forest Service circles, the words "Region Six" are intoned respectfully and solemnly. The words "the Rockies" cause everyone to head for the door.[67]

The fourth factor helping to create a new climate is the increased attention given to scientific analysis. Traditionally, forest research had concentrated mostly on fire protection and on methods for increasing timber production. During the past generation, however, government and foundation funding for forest research has both increased and diversified, with a resultant boom in scholarship from scientists in government, the conservation organizations, and academia. Two areas of emphasis bear special mention. First, there is a much greater appreciation of the effects of logging and road building on rivers and streams through landslides, erosion, changes in water temperature, and alterations of runoff. This new level of awareness contributed, with other factors, to the 1987 amendments to the Clean Water Act, which included a stepped-up program to combat the long-ignored problem of nonpoint source pollution (point source pollution comes from a discrete source, such as a pipe; nonpoint source pollution is diffuse and includes runoff and sediments from ranching, irrigated agriculture, and logging operations).[68]

Another key area of scientific research involves a deepening understanding of the fundamental role of biological diversity in the health of land systems. Based on Aldo Leopold's adage that the first rule of intelligent tinkering is to save all the pieces, biological diversity, according to Elliott Norse, operates on "three levels, the most familiar being the middle one, species diversity, the wealth of species. . . . Genetic diversity and ecosystem diversity—the levels of biological diversity below and above species diversity—are . . . less known but no less important." Biological diversity has implications for timber harvesting because clear-cutting and the elimination of old-growth forests can disrupt or destroy animal and plant species.[69]

The fifth factor altering the debate over the future of the national forests emanates from a surprising source, the nearly incomparably loyal (one imagines the slogan "We bleed Forest Service green") ranks of the agency itself. In 1989, Jeff DeBonis of the Willamette National Forest in Oregon, the top timber-producing forest in the system, wrote an "open letter" to Chief Dale Robertson, criticizing timber dominance in the agency. The dynamic DeBonis then left government service to found a nonprofit organization, the Association of Forest Service Employees for Environmental Ethics. The AFSEEE publishes a quarterly newsletter, *Inner Voice*; has increased its membership, which can choose to remain anonymous, to 2500 Forest Service employees (out of a total of 35,000); asserts the ethical obligations of the Forest Service to protect the land and of agency employees to speak out; and generally has made the point that the Forest Service is not monolithic and that a great many of its employees—far beyond the membership of the AFSEEE—are saddened in the heart and mind by the overcutting of the national forests.[70]

Jeff DeBonis spoke out on behalf of field employees against the Forest Service company line, but as everyone who deals with the agency knows, Gifford Pinchot's agency has become laced with conscientious doubters from top to bottom. In a wholly unprecedented move—a bolt out of the blue for this lockstep organization—the forest supervisors of Region One (the northern Rockies) sent a formal set of grievances to Chief Robertson in November 1989. The letter stressed the supervisors' loyalty to the agency and to its mission but made it plain that both were being severely compromised by the lords of yesterday as embodied in the high timber cut:

> These are troubling times for many of us. The values of our public and our employees have been rapidly changing and have become increasingly divergent, increasing the level of controversy surrounding management of [the] National Forests. . . . Many people, internally as well as externally, believe the current emphasis of National Forest programs does not reflect the land stewardship values embodied in our forest plans. Congressional emphasis and our traditional methods and practices continue to focus on commodity resources. We are not meeting the quality land management expectations of our public and our employees. We are not being viewed as the "conservation leaders" Gifford Pinchot would have had us become. . . .

In the summer of 1990, forest supervisors in Regions Two, Three, and Four sent a similar message. Rather than shock waves, these "supervisors' letters" reflected the slow waves of fatigue and knowing frustration rolling through a corps that holds the torch of idealism as high as any group of public employees ever has.[71]

In September 1991, these events accelerated still further. John Mumma, regional forester for the northern Rockies, which includes the Nez Perce National Forest and the Jersey-Jack area, had been forced to resign. Mumma, the first biologist ever to rise to regional forester in any region, had balked when it came to meeting, year in and year out, the timber targets mandated by the Forest Service's central office in Washington, DC. Mumma had received the news from his forest supervisors all across Montana and northern Idaho: the ground cannot take this pounding. And Mumma knew the same thing from reviewing forest plans, talking to his people on the ground, and walking the forests on his own. It was his job to know these things, and he took his job seriously. He traveled to Washington, DC, to testify before a House subcommittee on September 24, 1991. During the tense, emotion-laden oversight hearings, the tough-minded Mumma broke down, tearfully saying, "I'm here today with a heavy heart—a heart that's in shock at what's happening in the national forests." He continued:

> My [forest] supervisors and district rangers in the Northern region recognize that we cannot meet my timber targets. I also believe that my superiors in the Forest Service recognize that I cannot meet my targets or sell more timber.
>
> I did work on trying my best to convince everyone that we were doing everything possible within the law. I have done this since I have been the regional forester in the Northern Region. I have done everything I can to meet all of my targets.
>
> I have failed to reach the quotas only because to do so would have required me to violate federal law. . . .
>
> I love my job, I love my career, and I love the national forests—often at the expense of a Mother's Day, a child's birthday, a visiting relative. I was always committed to my job first. My employees call me a workaholic.
>
> I am just a person who loves his work, because it means so much to all the citizens of the Northwest, the nation and ultimately, the future generations of all Americans.
>
> Now I feel betrayed, not bitter, but deeply hurt. I have until the end of October to decide to move back to Washington or retire.[72]

The sixth and last development that has shaped a new framework for debate on the national forests is intangible but no less important. The American West has undergone enormous change since World War II, both in the cities, many of which have become heavily urbanized, and in the rural areas, which have seen a great amount of extractive resource development. In the West, more than in any region in the country, development proposals historically have gone unquestioned. That is no longer the case. The new attitude includes, but goes beyond, environmental concerns *per se.*

The people of the American West have acquired a much deeper sense of the distinctive qualities of the region. This appreciation has been bred in no small part by the vigorous body of regional literature that has thrived during modern times. Writers such as Wallace Stegner, Bernard DeVoto, John McPhee, Vine Deloria, Jr., Barry Lopez, Terry Tempest Williams, Edward Abbey, Gretel Ehrlich, Ivan Doig, Leslie Marmon Silko, James Welch, William Kittredge, and many others have brought home the idea that the land, society, and way of living in the West are different and special and need to be appreciated as such. There is an emerging determination— bred of social, as well as environmental, judgments—to respect and protect the fragile distinctiveness of the region. And surely that includes the 160 million acres of national forests that matter so much to the American West.[73]

Thus, many forces, old and new, converge on the national forests. Two places that demonstrate the large issues in vivid terms are the Greater Yellowstone Ecosystem and the "west-side" Douglas fir forests of Oregon and Washington in Region Six of the Forest Service.

The Greater Yellowstone Ecosystem

Congress set aside Yellowstone National Park in 1872 as the nation's, and the world's, first national park, to be used "as a pleasuring-ground for the people." Encompassing more than 2.2 million acres, mostly in Wyoming but also reaching into Montana and Idaho, the park is extraordinarily diverse, containing renowned geysers and mudpots, Yellowstone Lake, expansive high plateau forests, the headwaters of several major river systems, and inspiring waterfalls in the Grand Canyon of the Yellowstone River. The park also is one of the last strongholds of the grizzly bear and has major populations of elk, bighorn sheep, antelope, bison, moose, and eagles.

Development inside the park is tightly curtailed, but it is now apparent that the park cannot be considered in isolation because its resources are significantly influenced by events on nearby lands. In particular, most of the park's magnificent wildlife species migrate in and out of the park and its surrounding lands. Since wildlife vitality turns on habitat, and since the "park's" animals range far beyond the park's boundaries, a broader perspective is required. Accordingly, the public and many decision makers have come to think in terms of the Greater Yellowstone Ecosystem. The ecosystem encompasses some 13 million acres, mostly federal public lands, including the seven national forests that girdle the park, Grand Teton National Park, three national wildlife refuges, and BLM lands.

The ecosystem lands outside of the park are themselves spectacular. They include the Teton Range, holding the Grand Tetons, which have marked the centerpoint of the West since the time of the fur trappers; the jagged, formidable Wind River Range to the southeast; the more rolling, welcoming Absaroka Mountains to the northeast; the Madison, Gallatin, Yellowstone, and Snake rivers, among the world's greatest trout streams; breathtaking high mountain valleys, notably Jackson Hole to the south and the Paradise Valley on the Yellowstone River to the north; and, as a final reminder of the ecosystem's jarring diversity, the phantasmagoric red rock points and spires of the North Fork of the Shoshone River out to the east, formations that one expects to see only in the Four Corners region of the Southwest. All of this is prime habitat for animals.

The economy reflects the land. The ecosystem is dotted with towns like Jackson, West Yellowstone, Bozeman, Livingston, Gardiner, and Pinedale, which depend on hunting, fishing, guided tours, and the guest ranch and motel business. Of course, in addition to direct employment, a turnover effect is felt in the drugstores, gas stations, restaurants, general stores, and banks. Jobs are also created by mining, ranching, and timber harvesting, but the recreation economy exceeds all of these, even in combination: more than 80 percent of all jobs in the ecosystem are created by recreation. If one excludes the two national parks, the results are not much different. In looking only at the national forests, the most conservative estimate of recreation jobs is by the Congressional Research Service, which has concluded that recreation is "the major economic activity" on federal lands in the ecosystem, creating about two-thirds of all jobs resulting from activities in the national forests. Timber produced less than 10 percent of the jobs created by the national forests.[74]

Cautions need to be made. The number of jobs alone does not always tell the full story, since wages in the extractive industries tend to be higher than for recreation jobs, many of which are service positions. Further, regionwide statistics can mask agonizing local situations. For example, Dubois, Wyoming, in the southeastern part of the ecosystem, has long been a timber-dominated town, and many of its residents—including a vigorous grass-roots organization of loggers' wives, Women in Timber—have been shaken by the recent closing of the Louisiana-Pacific mill. It is hoped, and many believe, that the slack will be picked up by the growing recreation sector of the economy in Dubois, which, at the northern end of the Wind

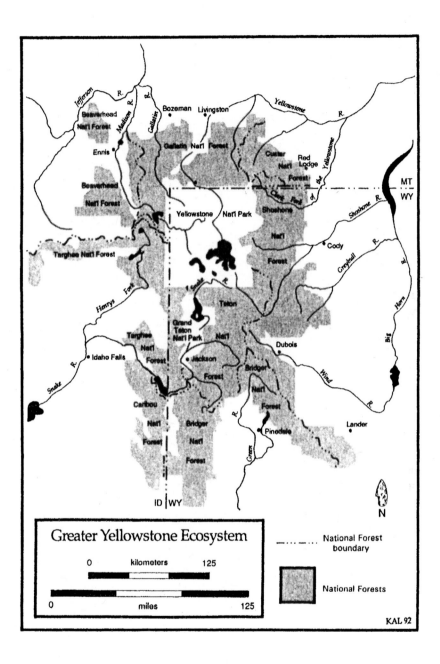

Greater Yellowstone Ecosystem

| 0 | kilometers | 125 |

| 0 | miles | 125 |

·—·—·— National Forest boundary

National Forests

N

KAL 92

River valley, is well situated for tourism. In any event, in spite of these qualifications, recreation remains easily the largest contributor to the eco-system's economy, whether measured in jobs, total wages, or total economic benefits.[75]

Yet the Forest Service continues to push extractive development in the ecosystem. Current forest plans would increase the timber cut by 20 percent. The seven forests in the ecosystem have always lost money on logging; from 1979 through 1984, the forests lost a total of $7.4 million annually on their timber programs, and the same trend continues in force. The great majority of future sales, using any method of accounting, will be below cost. Many of the sales are in highly scenic country, often on steep, unstable slopes where logging and roading would cause extensive erosion into the streams. Winter range for elk would be adversely affected, as would prime grizzly bear habitat in four of the forests. Grizzly recovery in the Greater Yellowstone Ecosystem has become one of the most sensitive and poignant wildlife issues in the country. Grizzlies are both an indicator species for scientists and a powerful symbol for ordinary citizens: as two House subcommittee chairmen noted in transmitting the Congressional Research Service report, "in the public's mind, grizzly bears are the most important indicator of the Ecosystem's health."[76]

Forest Service plans for the ecosystem simply do not add up. By the agency's own figures, recreation produces 80 percent of the estimated total economic benefits from the ecosystem forests, while timber provides just 10 percent. Yet the projected Forest Service budgets will spend three-fifths on timber harvesting and one-fifth on recreation. One is left with a sense of an agency struggling, in spite of all the elaborate pretense of extended analysis, to justify a predetermined result.[77]

Yellowstone depicts the current situation brightly because of the rare qualities of the ecosystem, but as with the Jersey-Jack roading and logging complex, the same dynamics are at work throughout the Rockies. A few forests in northern Idaho and northwestern Montana can turn profitable sales, but economic justification for the timber programs in Colorado, New Mexico, and Arizona is, if anything, even more tenuous. There ought to be some timber sales in the national forests of the Rockies, but the great majority of existing sales go well beyond any acceptable margin of social and economic utility.

The Ancient Forests of the Pacific Northwest

The other major region important in analyzing the current situation in the western national forests is the Pacific Northwest. The most reliable sources estimate that there are about 2.5 million acres of old growth left in the region, roughly 13 percent of the original ancient forest domain of 19 million acres. This is virtually the only old growth in the nation—nearly all other forested land has been cut over. The ancient forests of the Northwest are all located on public lands, a small part of them in national parks, under BLM jurisdiction, or in wilderness, but most of them are designated as general forestland in the "west side" National Forests.[78]

The situation in the Northwest is very different, and considerably more complex, from that in the Rockies, and one can sense the difference just by spending time in the ancient forests. Whereas the lodgepole and ponderosa pine forests of the intermountain West are spare, open, and sunny, the Douglas fir stands of Oregon and Washington are tight and closed in, not just by the giant standing trees but by the tangled understory of twisty vine maple and the ground cover confusion of liverworts, mushrooms, wildflowers, mosses, and ferns of all kinds and sizes. The forest floor, too, is littered with downed trees, often waist-high, crisscrossing each other, rotting, and playing host to fungi, bacteria, mosses, new vine maple shoots, and, in their cavities, small ground animals. The forests are so thick that light seems to come into the old stands of trees from the sides as much as from the sky. The sun pours down mainly into canyons and the streams at the bottom; it seems to spread out from there, picking up a deepening green hue as it works its way back into the depths.

Everywhere is green, and everywhere, too, is water, dripping, running in rivulets and flows, rising up as vapor. The arid West is far away. This old-growth country west of the crest of the Cascade Range receives moisture from the Pacific Ocean—anywhere from 40 to 250 inches of rain each year. Bogs and marshes lurk in every available hollow and bowl. The forest floor, when it is not standing water, is thick, spongy, and bouncy.

One has a powerful realization that this is truly a three-dimensional forest: a tremendous amount of biomass is located in its upper reaches. The gigantic living trees, some of which may have been standing for 300, 500, or even 800 years, force their near-perfectly straight bulk up beyond a straining line of sight, perhaps as high as 250 feet. At midlevel and lower level are the stumps and snags that constitute broken-off halves, quarters, and tenths of trees and are home to bats, eagles, owls, and goshawks.

The essential policy tensions flow from these physical facts. The old-growth trees are obviously of enormous value—sometimes, it turns out, $15,000 per tree—standing on the ground, unprocessed. There are no below-cost sales here (although some do occur in the "east side" forests of Region Six, where conditions more resemble those in the Rocky Mountains). Rather than cutting, bucking, and loading five or six trees on a logging truck, a logger can take one or two chunks from an ancient tree and have a full load. The trees are so large that mills can cut any size of lumber,

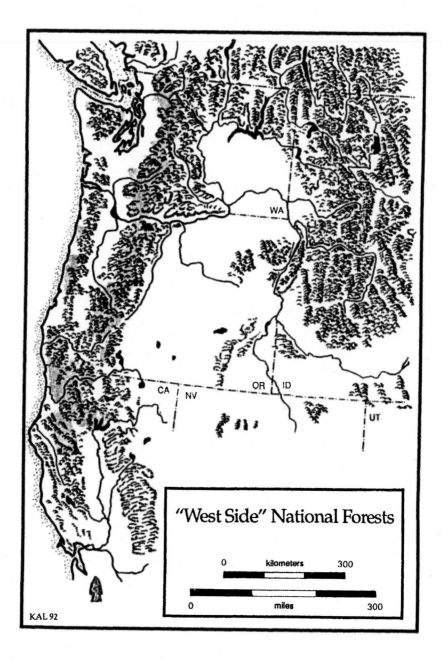

"West Side" National Forests

0   kilometers   300

0   miles   300

KAL 92

up to the most prodigious support beams. The big trees are completely straight and result in little waste. The grain is clear and the fiber strong. These stands, especially where the ground is level and the access good, are a timber executive's dream. Moreover, they can help fuel a state's economy, and, as noted, contribute a net of one-third of a billion dollars annually to the federal treasury.

But there is a downside. Old-growth forests contain as much as 475 tons of wood fiber per acre. As one can readily see from the rotting downed timber, those trees literally become soil. What will soil productivity be after two cuttings? Water in the old-growth system is held by the rich ground carpet and gradually filtered down to the streams. How will removal of the trees affect the ground cover—and the streams? The stands are a unique, complex, three-dimensional community of plants and animals. How will intensive logging affect that community? These ancient forests—in their primeval condition—matter greatly, on a number of counts, to the Northwest's economy and spirit. How much will be lost, commercially and spiritually, when too great a part of them has passed on? And at the current rate of logging, it will not be long: by about the year 2023, all unprotected old growth will have been logged, leaving about 1.2 million acres, 6 percent of the original ancient forests in the Northwest, in wilderness and other kinds of protected status.[79]

The northern spotted owl (*Strix occidentalis caurina*) became front page news in the mid- and late-1980s, but the foundation for the owl's prominence in defining the environmental, economic, and social future in the Pacific Northwest had been laid long before. Importantly, even though the owl is seen by some as a gimmick drummed up by environmentalists, the central role of the northern spotted owl was established not by environmentalists but by independent scientists for reasons of biology and the sustainability of the ancient forests.

The spotted owl became a concern in the scientific community in the early 1970s. In 1973, biologists from Oregon's State Department of Fish and Wildlife, the U.S. Fish and Wildlife Service, the Forest Service, the Bureau of Land Management, and Oregon State University formed an interagency group called the Oregon Endangered Species Task Force. The task force, recognizing the importance of the ancient forests for spotted owl habitat, recommended that 300 acres of old-growth forest be retained around every known nest site. During the late 1970s and early 1980s, scientific research continued to uncover information about the habitat needs of the spotted owl; the Forest Service and the BLM (which, in Oregon, has substantial stands of old-growth timber interspersed with Forest Service and private lands) gradually developed more detailed management prescriptions.[80]

By then, the National Forest Management Act of 1976 (NFMA) had been passed, mandating the Forest Service to "provide for diversity of plant and animal communities." The 1979 NFMA regulations, proposed by a blue-ribbon Committee of Scientists, further refined a legal approach for protecting species diversity as required by the NFMA. The chosen mechanism was the concept of "indicator species," based on the idea that it would be impossible to inventory all species (inventorying western big-eared bats, red-backed voles, and white grubs is neither cost-effective nor fun). Rather, the agency has identified animals and plants that can realistically be inventoried and that, because of their characteristics, act as surrogates for the animal or plant community as a whole. The health of the indicator species speaks for the health and diversity of a whole land system.[81]

The species chosen to be the proxy for the ancient forests is the northern spotted owl. Spotted owls, along with as many as thirty or forty other birds and mammals, have specialized habitat requirements and a food chain that can be fulfilled only by an old-growth system. Among other requirements, the spotted owl, a nocturnal animal, nests only in the broken-off tops of snags. Its food supply (in addition to being cute and fuzzy, this owl is a good-sized bird and a wicked predator) depends on animals such as the red-backed vole, which lives only in the cavities of rotted-out downed timber; the red-backed vole in turn depends almost entirely on fungi found only in old-growth forests. The food chain, and chain of dependence, ties into numerous other diverse animal and plant species and inorganic substances. The science here is young, and we still have much to learn, but the spotted owl is the best lens we have through which to view the food chain, which in turn allows us to view and understand the whole old-growth system.

The relatively recent emphasis on biological diversity is in large part a function of the rapid acceleration of species loss. The priority now being given to biological diversity is a response to the realization that human beings have extinguished hundreds of thousands of animal and plant species during the past century alone and that the process of extinction is continuing at the alarming rate of thousands of species per year. Maintenance of biological diversity allows for development of new food sources; preserves gene pools for genetic engineering; preserves a broad inventory of animals, fungi, and microorganisms for biological pest control; keeps available a source of new medicines; and fulfills more abstract ethical obligations of stewardship. Arching above the whole debate are the words and thoughts of the great conservationist Aldo Leopold, who struggled long and hard over a land ethic and biological diversity and over the way forests lose their vitality:

In Germany there is a mountain called the Spessart. Its south slope bears the most magnificent oaks in the world. American cabinetmakers, when they want the last word in quality, use Spessart oak. The north slope, which should be the better, bears an indifferent stand of Scotch pine. Why? Both slopes are part of the same state forest; both have been managed with equally scrupulous care for two centuries. Why the difference?

Kick up the litter under the oak and you will see that the leaves rot almost as fast as they fall. Under the pines, though, the needles pile up as a thick duff; decay is much slower. Why? Because in the Middle Ages the south slope was preserved as a deer forest by a hunting bishop; the north slope was pastured, plowed, and cut by settlers, just as we do with our woodlots in Wisconsin and Iowa today. Only after this period of abuse was the north slope replanted to pines. During this period of abuse something happened to the microscopic flora and fauna of the soil. The number of species was greatly reduced, i.e., the digestive apparatus of the soil lost some of its parts. Two centuries of conservation have not sufficed to restore these losses. It required the modern microscope, and a century of research in soil science, to discover the existence of these "small cogs and wheels" which determine harmony or disharmony between men and land in the Spessart.[82]

In 1986, the spotted owl and biological diversity surged into the public consciousness when the Forest Service released proposed management guidelines on the spotted owl. The guidelines called for 550 spotted owl habitat areas, each holding up to 2200 acres of old growth. Logging of old growth would continue apace, at the rate of 60,000 acres per year. Even by conservative estimates, the proposal would have allowed the harvesting of 25 percent of all existing spotted owl habitat within fifteen years and approximately 60 percent after fifty years. This spotted owl management plan—as controversial an issue as the Forest Service has ever addressed—generated 40,000 letters from the public. Both industry and environmentalists went up in arms, industry leaders claiming that the proposal would cost thousands of jobs, environmentalists pointing to studies showing that the plan might well end the spotted owl's chances for survival within just twenty-five years.[83]

The Forest Service released its final spotted owl guidelines in 1988. These called for protection of 3000 acres for each nesting site—ten times the area recommended by the original task force in the 1970s—and stipulated that the Forest Service would review the adequacy of these measures within five years. During the administrative appeals from the 1988 plan, however, new scientific evidence showed that more would be needed to protect the northern spotted owl—and its ancient forest habitat. In 1989, the Forest Service, the BLM, the U.S. Fish and Wildlife Service, and the

National Park Service established the Interagency Scientific Committee to "develop a scientifically credible conservation strategy for the northern spotted owl."[84]

A great deal was riding on the Interagency Scientific Committee, and its members were carefully chosen. The chairman was Jack Ward Thomas, chief research wildlife biologist with the Forest Service. Thomas, a big, open man, brought impeccable scientific credentials and a demeanor that was at once both genial and no-nonsense. Timber industry people could argue that the real issue was the economic cost of protecting the owl, but the charge of the Interagency Scientific Committee—the "Thomas Committee"—was not economic. It was to develop recommendations for saving the spotted owl based on good science, and there never was any doubt that the six men were eminently qualified to do just that.

The Thomas Committee released its assessment in the spring of 1990. It advocated the protection of large tracts of old growth, which it called "habitat conservation areas." The report rejected the approach, previously advocated by the Forest Service, of designating reserves just big enough to support single owl pairs. Instead, it required that the habitat conservation areas be designed to accommodate large, multipair colonies of owls. In all, the Thomas Committee report upped the ante to a range of 4.2 million to 4.8 million acres of land where logging would be prohibited. The political stakes were higher than ever, and the Bush administration sought to undermine the Thomas Committee by appointing a task force to develop a more acceptable report. The attempt failed, though, when after two months the task force concluded that the Thomas Committee report was "one of the best reports on an environmental issue that has ever been issued."[85]

The spotted owl controversy has become embroiled in litigation, and the courts have handed down dozens of decisions, almost all in favor of the environmental plaintiffs. Even before the Thomas Committee's report was published, the Seattle Audubon Society and other groups sued the Forest Service in the most far-reaching of the many suits, claiming that its 1988 spotted owl guidelines violated both the NFMA and NEPA. In 1989, Federal District Judge William Dwyer granted a preliminary injunction on 135 timber sales pending the final decision in the case. The appeals court upheld Judge Dwyer's ruling in the *Seattle Audubon* case in 1990.[86]

Just days later, the Forest Service vacated the 1988 spotted owl guidelines and announced that it would proceed in a manner "not inconsistent" with the more restrictive Thomas Committee report. Not for long. According to George M. Leonard, associate chief of the Forest Service, work in that direction was halted by a cabinet-level directive. In May 1991, Judge Dwyer issued a scathing opinion finding that the Forest Service had violated the NFMA by not completing an acceptable spotted owl management plan. Dwyer's opinion castigated the Forest Service for its "deliberate and systematic refusal" to comply with federal wildlife laws and also placed blame on "decisions made by higher authorities in the executive branch." The landmark opinion, later upheld on appeal, prohibited any further timber sales in spotted owl habitat until the Forest Service had complied with the NFMA and released suitable owl management plans.[87]

The U.S. Fish and Wildlife Service (FWS), which has responsibility for administering the Endangered Species Act (except for marine species, which are under the auspices of the National Marine Fisheries Service), has also been at the center of the controversy over logging in the Pacific Northwest. In 1987, environmental groups petitioned the FWS to list the northern spotted owl as a threatened species in Oregon, Washington, and northern California (a threatened species is one whose existence is not yet endangered but soon will be if recovery actions are not taken). The FWS denied the petitions, even though the health of the owl population was such that the agency could cite no scientific evidence warranting its refusal to act. Indeed, the FWS's chief expert on population viability had advocated listing the owl, and a General Accounting Office investigation revealed that the FWS, because of the economic ramifications of a possible listing, had altered scientific evidence in a peer-reviewed report in order to avoid any listing. But the FWS should not have been considering economics: the Endangered Species Act, perhaps this country's most stringent environmental law, requires that listing decisions be made solely on the basis of biological information.[88]

Environmental groups took the U.S. Fish and Wildlife Service to court, bringing one of the few moments of levity to the struggle by naming the unsuspecting owl as the plaintiff. In *Northern Spotted Owl v. Hodel*, Federal District Judge Thomas Zilly in Seattle ruled in 1988 that the FWS had acted arbitrarily in denying the petition to list and ordered the agency to reconsider its decision. In June 1989, the FWS listed the northern spotted owl as a threatened species in Washington, Oregon, and northern California but failed to provide full protection under the Endangered Species Act by refusing to designate the habitat that is "critical" for the survival and recovery of the owl. In February 1991, environmental plaintiffs—no, the owl itself—won a major victory in *Northern Spotted Owl v. Lujan*, when Judge Zilly held that the Endangered Species Act obligated the FWS to designate critical habitat for the owl. In May 1991, the FWS proposed a critical habitat designation of 11.6 million acres. This number was reduced to 8.3 million acres in August 1991. Finally, in January 1992, the U.S. Fish and Wildlife Service issued its final critical habitat determination, encompassing 6.9 million acres of federal, state, and private land—a 4.7-million-acre reduction in eight months.[89]

This "critical habitat" designation underscores how the Endangered Species Act both broadens and consolidates these issues. Previously, before threatened species status was invoked, the dispute proceeded along two tracks—the Forest Service's obligations in the national forests and the BLM's duties toward its old-growth stands. The Endangered Species Act, however, deals with species, not land bases, and encompasses private as well as public lands—and the U.S. Fish and Wildlife Service makes the decisions on a recovery plan for all lands designated as critical habitat.

The U.S. Fish and Wildlife Service makes most of the decisions, but not all of them. Under the Endangered Species Act, a project may be allowed to harm, or even extinguish, a species if five members of a special seven-person committee (composed of six high-level federal officials and one state representative) decide that the project should go ahead. This committee, commonly called the "God Squad," had been assembled only three previous times, all in the late 1970s, and had never superseded an FWS determination.[90]

In September 1991, the director of the BLM invoked this committee procedure by filing for an exemption under the Endangered Species Act for forty-four BLM timber sales in spotted owl habitat. Under the act, the committee could grant an exemption only if it found that (1) there were no reasonable and prudent alternatives to the sales, (2) the benefits of the sales clearly outweighed the benefits that would accrue from an alternate plan to protect the species, (3) the sales were of regional or national significance, and (4) the federal agencies had not made an irretrievable commitment of resources with the intent of encouraging these sales. On May 14, 1992, the committee voted to approve exemptions from the Endangered Species Act for thirteen of the forty-four petitioned sales (of course, the decision, while dramatic, was narrow and did not affect other BLM sales or any Forest Service sales). John Knauss, undersecretary of commerce, provided the necessary fifth vote only after Interior Secretary Manuel Lujan, Jr., agreed to force the BLM to undertake long-range planning to protect the spotted owl. Knauss felt that without such a concession, the exemptions would be largely symbolic. "What's missing is a long-term solution. In the absence of any other instructions from this committee, we'll be here a year from now attempting to resolve the 1992 sale program."[91]

Still, exceedingly tough judgments are yet to be made before we reach any long-term solution. The science seems to support a conservative approach. Research still is not sufficient to provide definitive guidance as to the habitat requirements of the many species dependent on the ancient forests. Thus, Andy Carey, a Forest Service wildlife biologist, made this observation:

> There is a whole system of animals and plants that is unique in old growth. Until we have further research, we can't say exactly what nega-

tive effects that cutting all the old growth would [cause], other than you'd probably get rid of all the owls and negatively affect some of the other species. We don't know if the effect would be so bad as to drive these animals to extinction in the Northwest or merely reduce their numbers.

The Society of American Foresters reached much the same conclusion in a formal report:

> With present knowledge, it is not possible to create old-growth stands or markedly hasten the process by which nature creates them. Certain attributes, such as species composition and structural elements, could perhaps be developed or enhanced through silviculture, but we are not aware of any successful attempts. Old-growth is a complex ecosystem, and lack of information makes the risk of failure high. In view of the time required, errors could be very costly. At least until substantial research can be completed, the best way to manage for old-growth is to conserve an adequate supply of present stands and leave them alone.[92]

In an effort to address the multiple values of old-growth ecosystems, two congressional committees asked four scientists in the summer of 1991 to provide an independent assessment of options for managing federal forests in the Pacific Northwest. The Scientific Panel on Late-Successional Forest Ecosystems (eventually dubbed "the Gang of Four") matched Forest Service biologist Jack Ward Thomas, chair of the Thomas Committee, with three highly respected university professors. John Gordon was Dean of Yale's School of Forestry and Environmental Studies. Jerry Franklin of the University of Washington and K. Norman Johnson of Oregon State University were first-rate scholars who had ample real-world experience through consulting and service in federal and state government. The report delivered a sobering message: "There is no 'free lunch'—that is, no alternative provides abundant timber harvest *and* high levels of habitat protection for species associated with late-successional forests." In order to give fish and wildlife species even a moderate chance of survival, timber production would have to drop by well more than half of historical and planned levels.[93]

Needless to say, however, the debate in the Pacific Northwest has not been only about science, the northern spotted owl, and its habitat of ancient forests. The timber industry traditionally has been a mainstay of the region's economy, and its dislocation caused by a reduced cut has understandably been an overriding concern. Industry, environmental organizations, the Forest Service, and university professors have all weighed in with analyses. Inevitably, the projections often conflict, and no one can pretend to forecast the economic effects of ancient-forest protection with any final certainty. We seem to have reached a point, however, at which some general conclusions can fairly be drawn.[94]

The timber industry in the Northwest has been in transition for more than a decade, for reasons largely unrelated to the spotted owl or any other environmental factor. The one-time bonanza of old-growth cutting on public lands is nearly over (remember that virgin stands on private lands had been liquidated by the first half of the century). In response, some companies have moved their operations to the South; southern pine cannot grow as large as Douglas fir, but it grows much faster, allowing rotations of twenty to thirty years, as opposed to sixty to eighty years for Douglas fir. In addition, southern pine is attractive because it can be harvested on level, easily accessible ground, whereas most of the remaining old growth is on relatively steep terrain. The timber companies that have remained in the Northwest are moving from an old-growth economy to a second-growth economy by retooling their plants to handle smaller trees more efficiently. As one former logging manager at Weyerhaeuser Corporation put it: "[A]s to old growth, everyone has gored that fatted calf long enough. Weyerhaeuser made a fortune from old growth, but you can't cut the last one and say, 'Gee, that was nice. What do we do now?' "[95]

The timber industry in the region, then, has pulled in its wings. In 1980, it employed close to 102,000 people. Eight years later, employment had fallen by 14 percent, to 88,000. This loss in jobs was not a result of insufficient timber supply—output of finished lumber actually increased by 19.2 percent during that period. Rather, cutbacks in employment were caused by the timber industry's determination to become more competitive by increasing efficiency. The continuing drive for leaner operations, in order to process second-growth timber, will cause still more layoffs. As Judge Dwyer found in 1991, after hearing extensive evidence: "[J]ob losses in the wood products industry will continue regardless of whether the northern spotted owl is protected. A credible estimate is that over the next twenty years more than 30,000 jobs will be lost to worker-productivity increases alone." Further, exporting unprocessed logs rather than milling them in the United States has cost more jobs than has protecting ancient forests.[96]

Nevertheless, no statistic or trend can obscure the fact that a major reduction in timber harvesting to protect the ancient forests will cause pain, and plenty of it. The issue will not be decisive for the timber industry, or the economy of the Pacific Northwest in general, but there will be severe impacts on individual communities. Some mills will lay workers off, and some will shut down entirely. In early 1992, the federal government estimated that as many as 32,000 jobs could be lost as a result of spotted owl protections. Although estimates by environmental groups of job losses are predictably lower than federal estimates, even the environmentalists admit that without mitigation measures, as many as 13,000 jobs could be lost. In most cases, these jobs affect whole families, and a ripple effect is felt through the community where the mill is located.[97]

Attention is turning to ways to soften these impacts. Typical is a 1990 Forest Service report that outlined a number of ways to mitigate the effects of decreasing the old-growth harvest. One proposal, a ban on log exports overseas, would create about 15,000 new jobs in the "value-added" processing of raw timber in the United States—examples include cutting two-by-fours and manufacturing more finished products, such as door and window frames. This export ban, if implemented, could compensate for many of the jobs lost due to ancient-forest protection. The Forest Service also recommended expanded job programs for repairing the damaged ancient forests, including reforestation of cutover areas and rehabilitation of damaged riparian areas. Job retraining would be made available for workers moving to new occupations.[98]

But these new jobs may often be unsatisfactory to laid-off loggers, truckers, or mill workers. The wages may be lower and the work less fulfilling. Some of the new jobs may smack of welfare. The work may require a move away from a rural community to a city where a plant is located. There is no denying the economic, social, emotional, and community costs.

Ultimately, however, there is an inevitability to this. Timber-dependent communities in the Northwest are in much the same position as other towns across the West that are struggling with the transition away from heavy dependence on extractive industry. In the case of old-growth logging, the inevitable "fall-down" (the precipitous drop in harvest when the big trees have been cut) has already taken place in many areas and will sweep through the rest of the region over the next two decades. Protecting the ancient forests only slightly hastens a process—the phasing out of the logging of the Northwest's virgin forests—that has been under way since World War II and accelerating since the early 1970s. Logging will continue to be a staple in the region, but its dominance has already ended, and its influence will decline for the next decade or so until it stabilizes. Equally important for today's timber-influenced communities will be to build up their potential for sustainable resource development, recreation, tourism, and light industry. Preserving the wondrous ancient forests assists, not detracts from, that inevitable process.

Toward Reforming the National Forests

In talking about reforming the national forests, it is important to recognize that agency competence is not one of the problems. The literature on state, federal, and even international bureaucracies commonly uses the Forest

Service as a model of administrative excellence. An objective person dealing with the agency will almost always be taken with the expertise, efficiency, knowledge, and collegiality of Forest Service employees. The agency is extraordinarily well equipped to fulfill its policy objectives.[99]

The difficulty comes with the policy goals for the national forests, far and away the most important of these being to maintain a high-level timber harvest. The Forest Service will ensure amenity values, first-rate timber-harvesting practices, unroaded backcountry, fish and wildlife protection, economically justifiable sales, and even protection for the spotted owl— and it probably will do those things better than any other government or private entity—*to the extent permitted by an allowable cut of 11 billion board feet.* The quality of all Forest Service programs is limited by the cut. National forest policy flows directly from the cut.

Timber domination was set in place by Gifford Pinchot, made inevitable by the force of his personality and ability, brought to fruition by World War II and its aftermath, and locked in place during the 1960s. The NFMA has made for a better forest system, but only so far as permitted by the overriding structure of maintaining the allowable harvest. The goal of maintaining the cut is set out in no congressional statute, but administrative agencies in fact make laws, and effective agencies make the firmest laws of all. Gifford Pinchot directed that the national forests be managed "for the home builder first of all," and that dictum, contained in a letter, of all places, became law. It has remained a law as fixed and powerful as any found in the statute books.

Several factors, taken together, explain why timber domination has proven so durable in a time so different from the Grand Master's.

The first reason for the continued heavy emphasis on timber production in the national forests, a factor often emphasized by environmentalists, involves the Forest Service's institutional personality—the fact that the Forest Service is controlled by foresters and that foresters are trained in silviculture, the science of raising trees as a crop. If we were starting fresh and staffing the National Forest System anew, it would make no sense, given the diverse mission of the forests, to favor the forestry profession over, say, biology, economics, range science, hydrology, mining engineering, ecology, geology, political science, and several others. Further, there ought to be room for generalists, those who have no specialized training but who have always contributed so much to the making of public policy in nearly every field.

Nevertheless, foresters dominate the Service, from Washington, DC, to the ranger districts. Agency records show that foresters amount to nearly 50 percent of all professional employees. Together, foresters and civil engineers (most of whom work primarily on timber road surveying, design, and construction) represent almost two-thirds of all professional employees. With the exception of the last chief, R. Max Peterson, who was a civil engineer, all chiefs of the Forest Service have held forestry degrees, and nearly all regional foresters have been professional foresters. The domination of a federal agency by a single profession in this manner is very rare; the only parallel I know of is the staffing of the Department of Justice by lawyers. The comparison probably explains the phenomenon: just as law agencies are essentially "single-use" offices, so too was the Forest Service conceived of as a single-use office in its formative years. This has been leavened. The leading national forestry schools now offer a much broader education, and the agency is opening itself up to other perspectives. But the emphasis on forestry in the Forest Service has yet to be dislodged.[100]

A second reason for timber domination in today's setting is related but somewhat different. Forest Service policy is due in part simply to habit, an understandable and human attitude of agency veterans who followed set-in-stone internal policies before the broad-based changes of the past twenty years. The logic and practicality of the Pinchot Letter ran deep with Forest Service employees, and it has not been easy for them to believe that such a basic organic document has been overridden in fundamental respects by the NFMA.

A third factor is set out in Randal O'Toole's book *Reforming the Forest Service*. O'Toole, an environmentalist but first and foremost an economist, pooh-poohs the forester-domination rationale offered by conservationists. Rather, he argues that all administrators, whatever their field, are driven to maximize their budgets. By bringing in large amounts of funds, they enhance their performance and receive the many different rewards (including promotions and new job opportunities) that accrue from good job performance. Thus, according to O'Toole, the main incentives for Forest Service professionals are related not to timber cutting *per se* but to activities that will maximize their budgets.[101]

O'Toole points to several laws that give Forest Service officials artificial incentives to cut timber. Suppose (as is the case, for example, with recreation in the national forests) that an agency receives an annual appropriation from Congress for a particular activity. Proceeds from the activity then go back to the Treasury. Such a program gives an incentive to the agency to spend only up to the appropriated amount.

The budgeting process for timber harvesting works differently. The Forest Service receives a direct appropriation from Congress for administering its timber program. Seventy-five percent of the proceeds from individual timber sales, according to a general funding statute, go to the Treasury, and 25 percent go to local counties in lieu of taxes (because state and local governments cannot tax federal lands). So far, there is no incentive to cut timber other than as expressly permitted by the timber budget in the direct appropriation. But as O'Toole explains, 75 percent of the proceeds do not in fact go to the Treasury. Rather, the Knutson-Vandenburg (K-V) Act of 1930 modified the general statutory scheme and allowed the Forest Service to keep a significant part of the Treasury share for reforestation costs. In 1976, the NFMA expanded the uses of these K-V funds to include precommercial thinning, wildlife habitat management, and other activities. The Forest Service has broad latitude to set the amount of K-V funds on each timber sale; they are determined separately for each national forest but usually range from $5 to $30 per thousand board feet. Importantly, the 1976 amendments to the original Knutson-Vandenburg Act give the agency such flexibility that these K-V funds amount to nearly wholly discretionary money for the Forest Service. It matters not whether the sales are profitable: the Forest Service gets its K-V funds off the top, out of the Treasury's share, which is reduced accordingly. *But the K-V funds are available only if timber is cut.*[102]

Other timber-oriented programs work outside the normal appropriations process and give the Forest Service incentives to maximize its budget by logging, regardless of whether the timber sales are profitable. They include funds for brush disposal, road maintenance, and salvage sales. In all, these funds, with K-V, amounted to $200 million in 1986, thus increasing the Forest Service's direct appropriation of about $1 billion by 20 percent. The funds are then distributed, by a Forest Service formula, to the Washington office, the regional offices, and the forest supervisors' offices, giving officials at every level budgetary incentives to make timber sales regardless of whether they are cost-effective. The Treasury may not make money on below-cost sales, but the Forest Service does.

A fourth factor contributing to the current level of harvest is congressional pressure. During the 1980s and early 1990s, members of Congress have been fighting out the essence of national forest policy—namely, the level of the national cut—in the relative anonymity of the annual appropriations process. These disputes have been waged through the budget process rather than through direct substantive legislation because, at least until the 1990s, Congress as a whole has been unwilling to reenter the thicket of timber policy. The focus has been on the Forest Service budget for timber administration and, in particular, on the roads budget. The main advocates for a lower budget (and a lower cut) have included Congressman Bruce Vento (D-MN), Congressman Sid Yates (D-IL), Senator Warren Rudman (R-NH), and former congressman John Sieberling (D-OH). Seeking to increase the roads budget, or keep it at the same level, have been Senator Mark Hatfield (R-OR), Congressman Les AuCoin (D-OR), and former senator James McClure (R-ID). One by-product has been a series of instructions from Congress directing the Forest Service to beef up its accounting system on below-cost sales. More fundamentally, however, the maneuvering within the budget process has worked to keep the cut up, roughly at the level of the Forest Service's requests, due in no small part to the widely respected Hatfield's position as senior Republican on the Senate Appropriations Committee. This is the way much of real forest policy has been made, regardless of the provisions of the NFMA or the plans for each individual national forest.[103]

A final factor supporting a substantial timber program in the National Forest System is simply that these lands hold major commercial timber resources, especially in the Northwest and the South, that should properly be used to fulfill part of the nation's need for timber. Further, there is honest concern, as there ought to be, over the many western communities dependent on public timber. The Forest Service, using the criteria of a community with at least 10 percent of its employment in the timber industry and at least 50 percent of its supply dependent on the national forests, counts 234 such timber-dependent communities—one of which is Elk City, Idaho, 45 miles from the proposed Jersey-Jack logging project. Some dispute the Forest Service's definition and question whether local communities ought to be supported by subsidized sales, but fair-minded observers ought to agree—regardless of which specific policies they advocate—that powerful equities weigh in favor of these small towns. These factors do not justify timber production at the current level, but they do underscore the fact that a substantial timber-harvesting program is a proper and desirable aspect of national forest policy.[104]

Given this setting, what action, if any, ought to be taken?

The judicial decisions in the Pacific Northwest have raised such large issues that Congress will almost certainly have to take some definitive action. Congress is the right forum because of the institutional limitations of the Forest Service and because the real issue is a congressional-level matter: the mission of the national forests for the foreseeable future. The timber industry and other extractive users argue that the forests should continue to be used for "wise use," which, like multiple use, has come to be a code word for giving priority to logging, mining, and grazing. Reformers argue for what can be called "public use"—continuing to allow extractive uses but giving priority to recreation, watershed, and wildlife.[105]

Congressional action, with many bills pending, is proceeding on two tracks. The first focuses on preserving some of the dwindling stands of the Northwest's ancient forests. An industry bill introduced by Senator Bob Packwood would prolong the current timber sale level. Bills by Senator Brock Adams and Congressman Jim Jontz would set aside large reserves of old-growth forests.[106]

The second track involves the appropriations process. Congress lowered the cut to 9.3 billion board feet for fiscal year 1991 and reduced it further for 1992, to a range of 7.1 billion to 8.4 billion board feet. Most reductions will come in the Northwest. It is still too early to know whether this portends a downtrend away from the cut of 11 billion board feet that has held sway since the mid-1960s. Further, even if ancient-forest logging is reduced in the Northwest, the question remains whether industry and some elements in the Forest Service will succeed in using the budget process to shift the Northwest's deficit in the timber targets to other regions and increase the cut elsewhere, thus perpetuating the basic problem—the unrealistically inflated annual cut.[107]

Many technical issues must be addressed, but the framework for a lasting resolution is not difficult to sketch out. The forests cannot sustain the current high-level cut of 11 billion board feet, and the harvest must be reduced significantly, probably by about half.

Reducing the cut by roughly one-half follows from a variety of indicators. As discussed earlier, the 1991 report of the congressionally appointed Scientific Panel on Late-Successional Forest Systems, written by Jack Ward Thomas and three university scholars, concluded that the cut in the Pacific Northwest—which produces nearly half of the harvest from the National Forest System—must be reduced from the recent annual level of 4.5 billion board feet to no more than 1.7 billion board feet to achieve a "medium to high" probability of sustaining the ancient forests of the Northwest and their dependent species. Across the rest of the National Forest System, below-cost sales are rampant: more than half of all timber is sold below cost. These unprofitable sales are commonly offered on marginal lands, where the environmental toll is highest.[108]

Halving the annual cut is good resource and economic policy. Private forestlands in all parts of the country, badly overcut during the first half of the century, are coming back into production and can replace much of the diminished supply from the public forests. Recycling of paper products is beginning to take hold and is reducing the demand for pulpwood. Further, the economic benefits of not cutting are becoming ever more clear. The Forest Service's most recent ten-year program acknowledges what economists have been saying for years: that a lower cut can provide higher net economic benefits because "high recreation and wildlife and fish outputs more than compensate in value for the value of lower timber outputs." Nor would halving the annual cut eliminate the national forests as a substantial supplier of wood products. A reduced cut of 5 billion board feet, after all, would produce enough lumber to build 500,000 new homes each year.[109]

A decrease in the national cut should be phased in over five or six years in order to afford protection for dependent timber communities. Further, extending subsidies to some of those communities through below-cost timber sales can be acceptable public policy, so long as the subsidies are the products of careful, informed choices. That is not the case with most below-cost sales today. Rather than reacting to the circumstances of those communities that have a clear need for the sales, the Forest Service has used dependent communities as one of many rationales in its campaign to meet the annual timber targets. Instead, the justification for below-cost sales to support dependent communities should come up from the ground, with a hard look at the trade-offs in terms of wildlife, watershed, and recreation, all of which have substantial economic values themselves. Thus, different strategies will apply in different communities, depending on local economic needs and opportunities for environmentally sound harvesting. But in all cases, the watchwords ought to be that legitimate, longtime community reliance on the national forests is a proper concern and that reductions in harvest will be phased in so that the local economy will have time to readjust.[110]

There are other issues to be addressed by remedial legislation. The phasedown of the cut should be coupled with generous retraining programs. Special protection, through set-asides of large blocks of land, should be given to the ancient forests of the Northwest. To complement these approaches, Congress should, as Randal O'Toole has persuasively argued, repeal the K-V fund provisions and other funding mechanisms that give the Forest Service budgetary incentives to cut timber when good resource management would dictate otherwise. Environmental groups should support logging at the new, lower level in order to allow a reasonable degree of stability for industry and communities. Logging is a legitimate use of these public lands, which can comfortably sustain timber harvesting in the range of 5–6 billion board feet.

But the overriding point, one we can no longer ignore, is that the Forest Service's cut can no longer be maintained at its current level. The system is bursting at the seams with forced sales—cuts made to meet a quota flowing from Washington to the regions to the forests to the forest rangers. Much has been made of the below-cost sales, the "economic irrationality," as the Bolle Report said of the Bitterroot. The problem, however, goes deeper than economics. In its search for timber stands to meet the cut, the Forest Service has repeatedly moved into areas where cuts are wrong not just economically but also scientifically: they cloud streams, wreck elk and fish habitat, and often fail to regenerate properly because the slopes are too steep, the soil is too thin, or the sun is too hot. And too many of the forced cuts are wrong socially. Whether or not a cut proves out at the cash register, it may be wrong to wipe out a grizzly's den or to clear-cut the old veterans that, standing since the Magna Carta, have built up a green cathedral for a host of animals, including our own species.

Setting the cut at a sharply reduced, sustainable level is a straightforward approach that avoids the necessity of enacting a complicated regulatory program. And it will work. The Forest Service can be counted on to manage on-the-ground timber harvesting in an environmentally acceptable way. The problem has been an excessive harvest level, not Forest Service expertise.

The recent era, especially in the 1980s and early 1990s, has marked nothing less than the plundering of an extraordinary public asset. Led, ironically, by a truly distinguished agency, public policy has spun out of control and been made to run counter to the best social and economic interests of the nation and the American West. We have now reached a point at which a new direction is at hand. By focusing on the central significance of the annual timber cut, Congress can move toward public use and serve both compelling modern realities and the truest spirit of Theodore Roosevelt's and Gifford Pinchot's great conservation actions.

Chapter Five

"The River Was Crouded with Salmon"

Jim Yahtin's father roused him from his sleep in the early morning gloaming. Even at the age of seven, Jim was already showing the strong shoulders and thick neck that he would carry all of his life. He snuggled back down once, but his father's tugs persisted. Outside, the little village was beginning to stir with a low-level commotion of murmuring and rustling. Jim knew his early morning routine and began getting to it.

Sitting cross-legged on the floor, the boy unbraided his hair, brushed it clean, and combed it. He knew the reason: "When you let your life wander off loose, evil will latch on to it." His grandmother peeked in, saw that it was time, and began her methodical rebraiding. That done, Jim pulled on his leggings and long-sleeved shirt. It was late spring and down by the river the day would be hot, but there was a modesty about all of the people. You had to keep your body covered: the women in particular, but the men and boys also.

This was his third year of fishing. His father had taught him how when he was five, and now he was expected to participate in catching fish for the family, enough to last through the winter until the next spring. He ate dried salmon for breakfast and then walked down the rocks to the edge of the river.

Even though his father did most of the paddling, it was laborious for the boy to help force the log boat across the current to the fishing station on the far side of the river. Still, he was glad that his family fished here at Big Eddy rather than at Celilo Falls, his cousins' fishing place—and the place, too, of a young girl he did not then know but later would marry. Celilo Falls, a morning's journey upriver, was where the fishing was the best but where the whole river crashed through the narrows and the furious white-water currents were most treacherous of all. Big Eddy was safer, better.

After ten minutes of paddling, the boy and his father made it across, and they scrambled up the slick rocks to the family's scaffold. They were now on the north side of the river, which ran east to west. The sun was still down behind the smooth, rounded hills. The father went to his net, leaving the boy to do his business.

Jim climbed out on the outreaching scaffold. He took his long-poled hoop net and lowered it past a rock ledge that was about 4 feet below the river's surface. Out farther, the main current ran from his left to his right, but here, in this backwater eddy, some of the currents circled back and ran right to left. He fixed his set net by wedging the hoop against some rocks. He held the pole in his right hand; in his left hand he held a string that was attached to the net. Two minutes later, feeling tugs on the string, he dropped the string, grabbed the pole with both hands, pulled the net up, and forced the fish up onto the log-and-driftwood scaffold.

The bright silver chinook salmon weighed 25 pounds, not half as heavy as the stocky boy, but it was much more than half his height. When he held the struggling fish up to show his father, its snout was at his shoulder, its tail flapping at the floor of the scaffold. The father nodded, and the boy clubbed the fish, walked to the shelter house, and put the fish inside, where it would be hidden from the sun, just now beginning to rise over the far hills.

They would fish for only a few hours because they quickly reached the father's self-imposed limit and there would be no need to continue. They had kept about twenty fish, almost all between 20 and 25 pounds. This was the best size; the women at the camp on the other side of the river, who would do the cleaning and drying, could not make good use of the really big salmon, the ones that grew to 70 pounds or more, heavier than the boy. The big fish did not dry as well because the slices were too heavy and would drop off the drying racks. Twice, as the boy knew he would, the father shook his head, and twice the boy wrestled fish nearly his equal from his net and dropped them back into the eddy. At midmorning they worked their boat, now much deeper in the water, back to the camp.

There were a good many things that the boy, or even his father, could not know. They did not know that two years before—in 1846, "the year of decision," as Bernard DeVoto later would call it—Great Britain had signed a treaty transferring all of the Northwest, including most of the reach of the

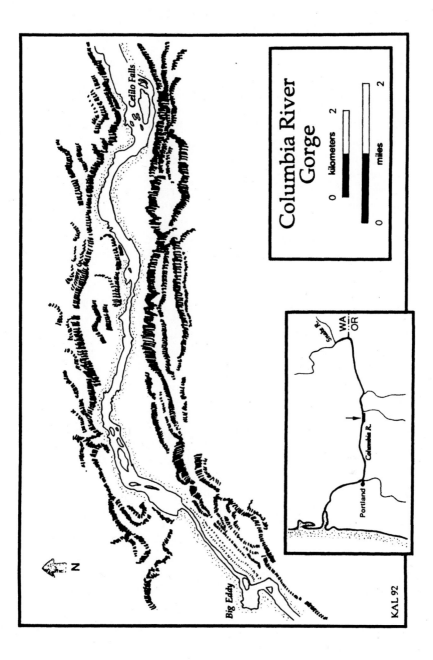

Columbia River Gorge

kilometers
0   2

miles
0   2

Celilo Falls

Big Eddy

N

Snake R.

WA
OR

Columbia R.

Portland

KAL 92

great river, which the white people called the Columbia, to the United States. They could not know that as they worked their set nets in the spring of 1848, the United States was solidifying its position in the West through the Treaty of Guadalupe Hidalgo with Mexico. They could not know that in just seven short years, in 1855, men named Isaac Stevens and Joel Palmer would come to their Sahaptin-speaking people and insist that they sign what Stevens and Palmer called a treaty, and that the treaty would mean that the tribes and bands would have to relinquish most of their ancestral lands and that, although they would be allowed to travel to the Columbia to fish at their "usual and accustomed places," their residences would be confined to much smaller inland reservations. And they could not know that the boy's very identity would be changed, for as they fished that morning his name was just Yahtin, pronounced "Yah-*teen*." Years later, in the 1860s, when the powerful young man enlisted in the United States Army to fight the Paiutes—which he willingly did because the Paiutes had killed some of his own people as well as the whites—the army found it necessary to add "James."

These were all things that James Yahtin and his father, named Wunn-o-ah-chi, did not know and could not have predicted. People like Isaac Stevens and Joel Palmer did know about the policy initiatives that had happened by that spring morning, or were about to occur, and could have predicted some of the things to come. But there were a great many things that Wunn-o-ah-chi, Jim Yahtin, Isaac Stevens, and Joel Palmer could not remotely have foreseen.

Wunn-o-ah-chi was born at almost exactly the time that Lewis and Clark came down the Columbia River, in 1805. The arrival of Lewis and Clark was a crackling, lightning-bolt event for the Indian society of 50,000 people that lived in the Columbia River basin. Word of these new visitors spread immediately—within a year, to everywhere, to everyone. Reactions among the people ran the full gamut—these explorers were devils, they were inconsequential, they were saviors. But the white people made little impact on the 260,000-square-mile basin during the next half century. The Hudson's Bay trappers came and traded. Although wagons began to move across the Oregon Trail in the early 1840s, not many people were involved, by the standards of either the Indians or the whites. By the 1846 England–United States treaty, by the spring fishing season of 1848, by the 1848 Mexico–United States treaty, by the 1855 Indian–United States treaty, even by Oregon statehood in 1859, the whole Northwest was still a back eddy. Indian people had been killed off in droves by the European diseases that the new arrivals carried with them, but tribal societies still functioned well and were mostly intact. The river was completely intact, and so were the great salmon runs.

The century and a half after 1848 would have astounded each of the four men. None of them, of course, could have foreseen the settlements and populations that would come, but beyond that, they could not have imagined what would happen to the River of the West, which figured so prominently in each of their lives and dreams. They could never have imagined that in less than a century after that spring fishing day, the family fishing rock at Big Eddy would be buried under 40 feet of water, as would Celilo Falls. Big Eddy to Celilo Falls, a 9-mile stretch that was perhaps the greatest fishing ground in the world. Big Eddy to Celilo Falls, where Indian people from all over the Columbia River basin came to fish. Big Eddy to Celilo Falls, from which radiated the religion, philosophy, and economy of an entire people. Big Eddy to Celilo Falls, where Jim Yahtin and Wunn-o-ah-chi's ancestors had fished for 11,000 years, where their two generations were preceded by 550 earlier generations. And not just Big Eddy and Celilo Falls but nearly the whole main-stem Columbia—nearly a thousand miles of raging river, now a series of slack-water lakes behind great concrete dams. Not one of them could have imagined such a thing.

There would be a great toll on the river, and also on Indian people and societies and on the fish themselves. Perhaps the amazing thing is that either still has a chance. There are still undammed places where in good years salmon and steelhead runs seem to fill up the rivers. There are still places where Indian fishing carries on. Indian people take their boats out on the pool high above the old fishing rocks and scaffolds at Big Eddy and Celilo Falls. They still take fish and can still feel some current. And there are other places, such as near Sherars Bridge on the Deschutes River in Oregon, where Delbert Frank—Jim Yahtin's grandson—and Frank's grand-children can fish much as people did in the spring of 1848. The scaffolds are constructed from cut lumber, not fir poles and driftwood; the hoops are made of steel instead of vine maple; and the net is fabricated from nylon or monofilament rather than hemp made from the little green-leaved willows. As you stand on the south bank of the Deschutes and look across at the Indian fishermen working the nets and the scaffolds, you do not see people dressed like Jim Yahtin or Wunn-o-ah-chi, and you do not see as many fish or as many big fish coming up out of the foam. Still, you know that you are seeing something traditional, real, and important.

But none of what you see at Sherars Bridge changes the fact that a great deal has been lost and what remains is in great jeopardy.[1]

The Fish and the Rivers of Old

Pacific salmon and steelhead, which were found in virtually every river on the Pacific Coast from Monterey Bay to the Bering Peninsula, preceded

Indian people by at least a million years. There are five species of Pacific salmon—the chinook, or king; the coho, or silver; the sockeye, or red; the chum, or dog; and the pink, or humpback. A sixth species, the steelhead, is a sea-run rainbow trout. All are anadromous fish; that is, they are born in fresh water, spend part of their lives in the ocean, and return to fresh water to spawn.[2]

In many ways the chinook is the most remarkable of all. It is the largest. Many of the chinook ran to 75 pounds, and the famous Columbia River "June hogs," or "Royal Chinook," bound for Canada reached 125 pounds (the Canadian runs no longer exist because the upper thousand miles of the Columbia was made impassable by the Grand Coulee Dam). The chinook travels the longest migration routes, up to 10,000 miles; lives the longest, up to five years; is the only salmon species with numerical and commercial importance in virtually every significant watershed from the Sacramento to the Yukon; and is prized for both commercial and sport purposes. It also is the species in greatest danger of extinction and thus has been particularly singled out for enhancement efforts of different kinds. The chinook salmon—much like the deep, misty ancient forests—has become a symbol of the Pacific Northwest.

The range of Pacific salmon and steelhead was enormous, and in spite of dams and other kinds of development that have reduced their inland habitat, these anadromous fish still penetrate vast areas. Historically, the largest-producing rivers were the Columbia, the Yukon, the Fraser River in British Columbia, and the Sacramento. Today, the Yukon is the champion, followed by the Fraser and the Columbia, whereas the runs in the Sacramento have dwindled to a small fraction of historical numbers. There are numerous other salmon-producing systems—as many as 2000 in Alaska and 1500 in British Columbia—but this discussion will emphasize the Columbia, the Sacramento and Klamath-Trinity systems of California, the Oregon and Washington coastal streams, and the rivers of the Puget Sound region of northwestern Washington. Stocks from these rivers, however, mix in the ocean with fish from British Columbia and Alaska so the more northerly rivers are an important element in the management of salmon originating in Washington, Oregon, and California.

From the Mexican border to the Canadian border, only two rivers break through from the interior of the American West to reach the Pacific. One is the Klamath River, which drains a relatively small area in California and Oregon east of the Sierra Nevada and Cascade ranges. The other is the Columbia.

The Columbia River basin is second in size among American watersheds to the Mississippi-Missouri basin. Encompassing 260,000 square miles, the headwaters of its various tributaries are found in eastern British

Columbia, Montana, Idaho, Wyoming, and Nevada. The big fish never reached Montana or Wyoming because of impassable conditions, but they did make it up to northeastern Nevada. The Salmon River chinook of central Idaho begin their lives in small tributaries under the Continental Divide.

A chinook salmon hatches, along with as many as 5000 other fry, in a specially constructed nest called a redd in a cold, swiftly flowing mountain stream. The fry may remain in the river for a year or two. Then, as fingerlings 2 to 6 inches in length, they descend the river in stages, hiding under stones and in shaded areas by day, carried by the current or swimming at night, to avoid numerous predators—larger fish, aquatic insects, crayfish, and birds. This down-migration will take as long as four months.

The fish, now smolts, cross the Columbia River bar and enter the Pacific Ocean. Most chinook "turn right" and head north; other species of salmon and steelhead tend to head south, but none travels as far north as the chinook. An adolescent chinook migrating northward moves in a broad counterclockwise sweep, following the continental shelf in a narrow zone about 25 miles from Washington, Vancouver Island, and the panhandle of Alaska and swimming out into the open ocean in a wide circle past Kodiak Island. The fish then disperse over their winter feeding grounds on the broad continental shelf of the Gulf of Alaska, preferring to feed in deep water, near the bottom. There they spend the greater part of their life cycles, far from the redds of their origin. They are opportunistic feeders, pursuing almost anything that does not pursue them. Chinook salmon rapidly mature into predators and are particularly fond of other fish, shrimp, squid, and krill. In turn, chinook are preyed on by larger creatures such as tuna, swordfish, sharks, seals, sea lions, and killer whales.

As the fish approach maturity, they begin to move back into coastal waters to the south, in response to an inner timetable not yet fully understood. After a few years of feasting, the fish will have developed a supply of fat that stores valuable energy reserves for the long journey upriver, for Pacific salmon cease feeding when they enter the river. Fish whose spawning streams lie relatively near the ocean are smaller, and their flesh is lower in oil content than that of the prized upriver stocks.

Even before Indian fishers and the intensive development of the Northwest's rivers, the fish confronted a seemingly impassable obstacle course in the rivers. They can surmount waterfalls of 10–15 feet, often making repeated leaps until they succeed. To do this, the fish time their runs for periods of high runoff, which reduce the height of the falls and allow the salmon to "climb" the torrent. Captain Charles Wilkes visited Willamette Falls in 1841 and wrote:

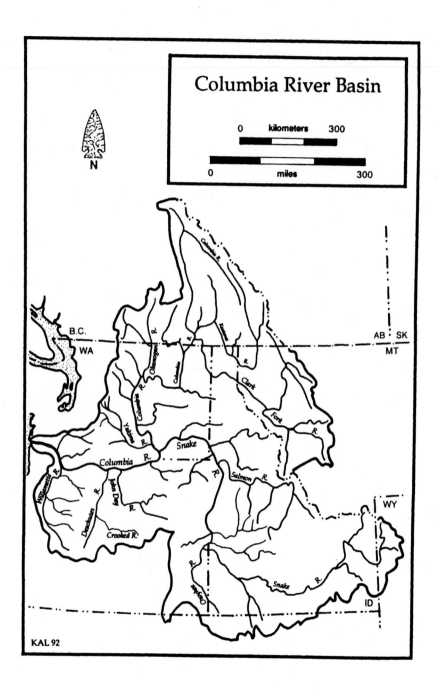

Columbia River Basin

N

0   kilometers   300

0   miles   300

B.C.
WA

AB · SK
MT

Columbia R.
Kootenai
Okanogan R.
Columbia R.
Columbia
Clark
Fork
R.
Yakima R.
Snake R.
Columbia R.
Salmon R.
R.
Willamette R.
John Day R.
Deschutes R.
R.
Crooked R.
WY
R.
Owyhee
Snake R.
ID

KAL 92

The salmon leap the fall; and it would be inconceivable, if not actually witnessed, how they can force themselves up, and after a leap of from ten to twelve feet retain strength enough to stem the force of the water above. About one in ten of those who jumped, would succeed in getting by. They are seen to dart out of the foam beneath and reach about two-thirds of the height, at a single bound: those that thus passed the apex of the running water, succeed; but all that fell short, were thrown back again into the foam.

The fish also face seals and sea lions at the mouth of the river and, higher up, bears, eagles, and ospreys.[3]

Eventually, after turning out of the main stem and into subbasins, the surviving fish in the run reach the mouth of their home tributary. There, returning fish often congregate in a dense mass, apparently in a holding pattern, as if they were somehow "taking turns" entering the home creek. At this point, the fish are no longer the bright specimens of the ocean or downriver stages of their lives. They have run into so many rocks, logs, and gravel bars in the smaller streams that their skin is bruised with white blotches. Further, the upstream journey can take several weeks, and their ocean fat has been depleted, causing rapid physical deterioration: the fish age a human equivalent of forty years in a mere two weeks. A delay of even a week may thus severely weaken the vitality of an upriver stock for years to come.[4]

Ascending the home stream, the fish may seek out the very gravel bar where they were born. In a spawning procedure almost as ritualistic as the spectacular mating dances of certain birds, the fish prepare nests, lay and fertilize eggs, and then die. (The exception is steelhead, which may make one or even two additional migrations.) The stream becomes littered with dead or dying fish, food for scavengers that eagerly await the event. For generations, leading nature writers have been moved by this final stage in the Pacific salmon's life and have drawn lessons from it. Bruce Brown wrote of the salmon's contribution to land health in the Northwest:

> Gifted with the ability to move from one medium to another and then return again to exactly the place where their lives began, the wild [salmon] have played a crucial role in the development of the general ecology of the Pacific Coast of North America. In a region that has been reworked by waves of glaciers for the last million years and which otherwise counts leaching rains as its predominant meteorological phenomenon, the wild salmon serve as nature's principal means of returning nutrients from the sea to the land. Through their passionate, seemingly perverse death, they give life not only to their own progeny, but also to a host of predators and other dependent species. They are, in short, an engine of general enrichment, and an important element in the long-range stability of the Pacific Coast ecosystem.[5]

David Rains Wallace offered this perspective:

> We are affected when a dog travels hundreds of miles to go home;
> salmon have traveled [thousands of miles and] millions of years. That
> they die after spawning makes the quest seem all the more heroic, and all
> the more tragic the possibility that the quest will be thwarted by dams
> which will silt up and become useless in a century or two.[6]

The size of the historical runs was nothing short of fabulous. When the
Lewis and Clark expedition crossed the Divide, moving down the Clearwa-
ter to the Snake and the Columbia, they were astonished by what they saw.
Among many other comments in his journal, William Clark wrote that the
river "was crouded with salmon." As one chronicler of the expedition
commented, "[t]hey had never witnessed such a piscatorial spectacle before and would never again." John Muir, during his travels in the Alaska
panhandle, observed, "The stream was so filled with them there seemed to
be more fish than water in it, and we appeared to be sailing in boiling,
seething silver light marvelously relieved in the jet darkness."

A common metaphor in the early reports is that salmon were so thick
that a person could cross a stream by walking across their backs. This is
understandable hyperbole, which one person explains this way: "[L]ike all
folk memories it has its truth. Nature has never practiced excess so dramatically as at the peaks of the great salmon runs. Observers in the last century
reported that the rivers would appear to boil, agitated to overflowing by
the bodies of the big fish." My impression is that during a run, a person
crossing a small stream would literally have to kick the moving, slippery
fish out of the way to get firm footing, an experience I had one lucky
September day on a small spawning creek on the northern side of Mount
Rainier.[7]

Before the Europeans, native people all along the Pacific Coast depended on the fish for their primary source of subsistence and for barter—
they relied on salmon more than the Plains Indians depended on buffalo.
The Columbia River gorge country (from the Bridge of the Gods, near the
current site of Bonneville Dam, up to Celilo Falls) was at the heart of the
salmon-based society of the Columbia basin. The Indian people revered
the salmon and devised rites to ensure the continuance of the cycle; the
"first salmon" ceremony at the beginning of the runs was a major religious
festival. During the height of the spring and fall runs, representatives of
tribes from all over the Northwest gathered for exchange in its broadest
sense:

> From downriver, the coast and Puget Sound came dried clams and
> mussels, whale and cedar products, shells (especially precious dentalia),

beads, canoes, baskets and, after the whites arrived, such trade goods as the beloved Hudson's Bay Company blankets. From the south came baskets, obsidian, wocus (water-lily seeds), Indian tobacco and slaves. From the plateau to the east came animal robes (including buffalo), meat, kouse and other plants, pipestone, feathers and, after 1730, horses and plains-style garments. Ideas were also exchanged; the Long Narrows–Celilo Falls area became a major communications center where diverse cultures made alliances and shared stories, religions, politics and history in peace.[8]

Indian fishermen were adept at the daring and picturesque job of fishing at the Celilo Falls torrents. From a platform or slippery rock overhanging the current, a tribesman (only men were allowed to fish) would adroitly maneuver a long-handled dip net in the churning waters below. Sometimes a fisherman would be lowered down the sheer face of the rock in a basket, waiting there motionless before lunging for a leaping fish with spear in hand. Imagine how precarious an Indian fisherman must have felt, hung in a reed basket from a platform perched over the rushing rapids, struggling with a 30-pound chinook at the end of the long-handled spear or net. No wonder all fishermen at Celilo were required to wear safety ropes.

These societies used far greater quantities of salmon than is commonly realized. For years, a 1940 estimate made by J. A. Craig and R. L. Hacker had been considered the standard figure: their calculation was that the 50,000 Indians in the basin harvested 18 million pounds annually before arrival by Europeans. In 1973, G. W. Hewes revised the estimate upward, to 22 million pounds. Then, in 1986, the Northwest Power Planning Council conducted a comprehensive study and nearly doubled the Hewes estimate, to 42 million pounds per year. Today, in contrast, the total commercial catch of salmon and steelhead in the basin is just 5–8 million pounds annually.[9]

The size of the Indian take required tribes and bands to take conservation measures and establish systems for allocating the harvest. They had rigid prohibitions against any waste of salmon and took actions, including closures, to ensure that the runs would be sustained. At the most sought-after sites, each platform or rock was a property right, passing by inheritance to family members. Other Indians were allowed to fish, but if a rights-holding fisherman was not taking enough fish, he would slap his buttocks twice as a signal to the others to stop fishing. Peer pressure was usually strong enough to guarantee that all of the law ways would be respected, but if they were not, designated leaders would enforce them by suspension or permanent withdrawal of fishing rights.[10]

Things moved with great speed for Indian people at midcentury. The three great events—the treaty with England in 1846, the treaty with

Mexico in 1848, and the discovery of gold in California in 1848—made imminent what was already inevitable. Homesteaders and miners were on the way, so the Indian tribes had to be confined to clearly defined, and preferably small, reservations. California became a state in 1850 and, as noted in chapter 2, was able to exercise extraordinary clout in Congress on the Indian issue: United States officials in the field negotiated treaties, but the Senate, under pressure from the new state, never approved them. Almost all California Indians were simply moved onto small lands called rancherias. An exception was the Hoopa Valley Indian Reservation in northwestern California, which was established on the Klamath River.[11]

Treaty negotiators in the Columbia River basin followed a different course. Congress created the Oregon Territory in 1848 and split off the Washington Territory as a separate unit in 1853. Oregon would not become a state until 1859; Washington, not until 1889. Indian-white conflicts flared up in various localities as settlers began to encroach on Indian land.

Federal officials in the 1850s knew full well that the land in fact was Indian land and settlers had no legal right to enter. The United States had eliminated any English or Mexican claims in the West, but under settled principles of American law, each Indian tribe continued to possess title, shared with the United States, to its aboriginal lands. Congress could simply confiscate tribal land and treat the tribes as conquered nations, as it did in much of California, but that was the exception. Treaties were the preferred course, in some measure because of moral considerations, in at least equal measure because many tribes had substantial military capability. It was largely beside the point that the United States could prevail in an all-out war: such a course was expensive, both in United States citizens and in money, on the far frontier. Thus, national policy was to deal with tribal leaders through the device of negotiated treaties. Once persuaded to relocate to reservations, the Indians could be subdued much more easily, and their former land could be opened for settlers.[12]

Isaac Stevens, appointed in 1853 as governor of the Washington Territory by President Franklin Pierce, quickly became one of the most important figures in the nineteenth-century Northwest, and as will be seen, his treaties were to live on into the late twentieth century. Stevens was an energetic, dynamic man who prided himself on results. He was not an Indian hater—his writings, public and private, contain numerous favorable references to Indian people. But the Northwest had to be opened for settlement, and his first priority was to deal with the tribes in order to get them out of the way.[13]

Stevens, with Oregon territorial governor Joel Palmer as a colleague when Oregon Indians were involved, moved with rapid-fire efficiency.

Despite huge distances and rudimentary forms of transportation, from late 1854 through the end of 1855, Stevens negotiated treaties with the numerous tribes and bands in the Puget Sound region; with the mid–Columbia River tribes; with the Nez Perce in what is now Idaho; and with the Salish and Kootenai tribes in what is now Montana. He obtained clear title to most of Washington, much of Oregon east of the Cascades, much of central and northern Idaho, and northwestern Montana.[14]

Stevens was a sophisticated man who knew in advance that the tribes would not relinquish their right to fish. The speeches at the negotiations underscored the Indians' resolve. Because Stevens clustered together so many tribes and bands at each treaty session, the talks were carried on in the Chinook jargon, a *lingua franca* of just 300 words that the many tribes used for trading purposes. This inevitably bred imprecision, but there can be no fair doubt that the tribes insisted that they be allowed to continue to fish at their historical sites; in return, they grudgingly agreed to relinquish the greatest part of their ancestral lands (most of the treaties involved cessions of 80 percent to 95 percent of all tribal lands). Ultimately, all of the Stevens treaties contained nearly identical provisions: in addition to fishing on the streams on their reservations, the tribes would also have "[t]he right of taking fish, at all usual and accustomed grounds and stations ... in common with all citizens of the Territory." The reservations were inland and did not include Big Eddy and Celilo Falls, but access to the old fishing sites was assured.[15]

Stevens made the concession because there would have been no treaties without it. But he must have believed that in time the tribes would dwindle or die out and that the guarantee of fishing rights at the traditional stations was a short-term promise. Beyond that, he must have assumed that the great runs would go on indefinitely and that the rivers would remain "crouded with salmon," holding enough fish for the Indians and all of the new immigrants alike.

He was wrong on both counts. A century and a quarter later, the tribes proved that it was not a short-term promise by enforcing Stevens's promise in the Supreme Court. Stevens's second idea—the lord of yesterday asserting that the salmon and steelhead runs were invincible—began to unravel during the very next decade.

The Era of the Free-for-All

The process of canning was invented in France in 1809. In an era when refrigeration was limited to iceboxes, canning—first in glass bottles, later in tin—was a significant advance in preserving meat, fruit, and vegetables.

Napoleon used canned goods to supply his troops in the field, and for merchants, canning allowed much wider distribution of their products. The first successful canning of fish occurred in New York in 1819. Salmon was canned in Scotland in the 1820s, but the first salmon cannery in America was established in 1864 by the Hume brothers—R. D., George, and William—and Andrew S. Hapgood on the Sacramento River. It was a small operation, set up on a raft in the river.[16]

In 1866, the Hume brothers and Hapgood shut down their canning business on the Sacramento River—the pollution from hydraulic mining had devastated the runs—and moved to the unspoiled and nearly uninhabited lower Columbia. In 1867, the Hume brothers' cannery began production. There was already a small trade in salted salmon packed in barrels, but the canneries revolutionized commercial production of Columbia River salmon. During its first season, the Hume brothers' cannery put out some 4000 cases of canned salmon. Each case consisted of fifty-eight 1-pound cans and sold for $16. Demand was inexhaustible, and, so it seemed, was supply: by 1883, forty canneries were operating on the Columbia, packing 634,300 cases that year, fully two-thirds of the entire harvest of salmon on the Pacific Coast. Nearly all of the canned salmon was the best-quality chinook, which was available in such abundance that the canners were not interested in lower-quality fish. Francis Seufert gave this description of the Canadian-bound "June hogs," or "Royal Chinook," packed by the Seufert Brothers Company:

> Because of their size, when you packed them into cans, only one slice of salmon was necessary to fill the can. When the customer purchased this can of Royal Chinook salmon and took it home and emptied it, he found just one nice chunk of salmon the size of the can, rich in oil, fine color, excellent texture and superb flavor. This salmon really deserved to be called Royal Chinook. It had no peer in the canned salmon markets of the world.[17]

The Columbia River chinook catch by non-Indians in 1883 was 43 million pounds. It was the peak year of inland chinook fishing. Never before, and certainly never since, has such a harvest of chinook been matched. (The 1986 Northwest Power Planning Council estimate of an annual aboriginal harvest of 42 million pounds, if correct, was for all five salmon species and steelhead, not just chinook.) From 1883 on, the chinooks were in steady, and eventually disastrous, decline.[18]

During the last three decades of the nineteenth century and, even as the runs began to decline, into the early part of the twentieth, the Columbia was a frenzied free-for-all of salmon harvesting. The canneries took all of the fish that anyone would supply to them. During the fishing season, from

April to October, port towns like Astoria were beehives of activity. Entry into the fishing fleet was easy; until 1888 the canneries, to encourage more fishing, provided both the boat and gill nets in exchange for a percentage of the catch. For independent fishers, the canneries paid ready cash. Indians and Scandinavians did most of the fishing, and during peak periods of the runs nearly everyone else joined them. Even the town parson would cancel Sunday services to go fishing with his flock.[19]

The fish hardly had a chance. They were caught with harpoons and hooks and in nets, traps, and weirs—on occasion they were even dynamited. Some of the more enterprising fishers would build large V-shaped traps of piles and netting, extending them far out into the estuary. If a trap was placed suitably close to the river bar, the owner would get the first chance at incoming fish and perhaps, if lucky, capture most of an entire run. In Puget Sound around this time, an entire run of sockeye salmon was obliterated when tens of thousands of fish wedged themselves so tightly in a trap that they all suffocated before the owner, who could not process them all, was able to release them.[20]

A trademark of the era was the fish wheel, introduced in 1879 or 1880, a creaky but effective device that mechanically dipped fish out of the river. Tended by a single operator and kept in constant motion by the current, it resembled a Ferris wheel, with several fish dippers, or baskets, on each wheel. These fish wheels, some fixed on rock formations, others floating and mobile, were deadly efficient when well located: the largest operator, Seufert Brothers, had twenty-seven wheels at the peak of operations, and one wheel took out 417,000 pounds of salmon in 1906.[21]

While the fish wheels operated inland in the Bonneville-Cascade Locks and the Dalles–Celilo Falls area, gill nets were dominant on the lower Columbia, near the mouth of the river. These devices, too, were highly proficient. A gill net is a rectangular net, buoyed on the upper edge by cork floats, that is stretched across a section of river (or across an entire small stream) and fixed at each end. The fish, unable to see the mesh, especially at night, swim into the net and are unable to back out when their gills are caught in the mesh. In 1883, an Astoria gill-netter could bring to the cannery as many fish as could be caught, and an assembly line of nimble-fingered Chinese cannery workers would strip, clean, and slice a 40-pound fish in less than a minute. If the nets caught species other than the prized chinook, the fish were hauled in anyway and dumped overboard at dockside. If more chinook were caught than could be processed at the canneries, they were summarily dumped back into the river, where the tide would eventually disperse their carcasses over the shoreline—food for gulls, eagles, seals, and the typhoid bacillus. If weary fishers wanted to escape the omnipresent stench of a cannery town on a Saturday night, they would go to an Astoria dance hall, where, if they lacked the price of admission, they could simply toss the ticket-taker a freshly caught chinook.[22]

Thus, the Great Barbecue of the late nineteenth century—a phrase ordinarily applied to the opening of the inland federal public lands to miners, ranchers, railroads, and timber trespassers—now played itself out on the once-great salmon runs. During the late 1880s, the depredations began to be reflected in the diminished size of the spring and summer chinook runs, and the fishing effort necessarily expanded to include other, less-desirable species and runs. Nevertheless, the industry, once Oregon's third largest, fell into decline, and only the hardiest few survived. The same phenomenon, with variations, occurred all along the Pacific Coast. The canning industry on the Sacramento River, for example, saw a revival in the 1880s, when hydraulic mining was regulated, but then fell into decline, with the last cannery closing in 1919. In his incisive analysis of the salmon fisheries in California, *The Fisherman's Problem*, Arthur McEvoy made this observation:

> Here was the fisherman's problem in laboratory form. Access to salmon was free to anyone who could put a gill net into the water or who had capital to build a cannery. The industry's gauntlet simply permitted too few fish to escape upstream to spawn new ones for future runs. Any fisher or any canner who might have left a salmon in the water so as to conserve the resource would simply have given that fish to competitors. As the fishery collapsed, the industry moved northward more or less bodily, workers and capitalists together, to exploit as-yet-undamaged runs in the Pacific Northwest and Alaska. Enough stayed behind, however, making just enough money from the crippled fishery to stay in business, to ensure that the stock did not recover on its own.[23]

The destruction was appalling to some sensibilities, even in that age of conspicuous bounty. In 1894, the Oregon Fish and Game Protector reported, "[I]t is only a matter of a few years under present conditions when the chinook of the Columbia will be as scarce as the beaver that once was so plentiful in our streams." Guardians of the public interest recognized the problem fairly early and tried two approaches. The first led to some early and tentative attempts at state regulation. The Washington Territory, for example, introduced gear restrictions in 1871, and Oregon followed suit in 1878. In 1877, Washington began regulating the duration of the fishing season, and Oregon acted accordingly the next year. Catch limits were first imposed on the British Columbia Fraser River salmon fishery in 1882, and in 1889 the federal government of Canada began to require licenses of all non-Indian salmon fishers. The Alaska Territory adopted catch and season regulations in its White Law. The second approach was to augment the supply. In 1877, at the request of and with partial financing by the canners, an agent of the United States Fish Commission opened a salmon hatchery on the Clackamas River in Oregon. There were no apparent effects on the size of the runs, however, and the hatchery was soon abandoned.[24]

These early gestures at bringing law to the harvest and propagation of salmon runs, however well intentioned, had almost no lasting effect. The catch, gear, and season restrictions of the nineteenth century, universally disregarded and sporadically enforced, were seen as a joke by fishers and enforcement officers alike. Willful violators were prosecuted only when a particularly objectionable violation was accompanied by publicity sufficient to make it hard to ignore. Hatcheries never became a factor during this era. The situation drove thoughtful people to despair. In 1908, President Theodore Roosevelt, in the same spirit as when warning about the western rangelands in the 1880s, lamented the ineffectiveness of state regulation of this common-pool resource:

> The salmon fisheries of the Columbia River are now but a fraction of what they were twenty-five years ago, and what they would be now if the United States Government had taken complete charge of them by intervening between Oregon and Washington. During these twenty-five years the fishermen of each state have naturally tried to take all they could get, and the two legislatures have never been able to agree on joint action of any kind adequate in degree for the protection of the fishers. . . .

In an address to the American Fisheries Society in 1892, Dr. Livingston Stone of the United States Bureau of Fisheries declared his pessimism:

> Not only is every contrivance employed that human ingenuity can devise to destroy the salmon of our west coast rivers, but surely more destructive, more fatal than all is the slow but inexorable march of these destroying agencies of human progress, before which the salmon must surely disappear as did the buffalo of the plains and the Indian of California. The helpless salmon's life is gripped between these two forces—the murderous greed of the fishermen and the white man's advancing civilization—and what hope is there for the salmon in the end?[25]

Dr. Stone's speech was delivered only twenty-six years after large-scale commercial fishing had begun in the Pacific Northwest. It was also just forty-four years after the spring morning when Jim Yahtin had pushed off with his father, Wunn-o-ah-chi, to fish at Big Eddy. In 1892, Jim Yahtin, who by now had married Yessessi, a Rock Creek Indian from Celilo Falls, was still fishing at the old family station. But by now he could look downstream and, in a stretch of just 1¹/₂ miles, see five permanent fish wheels and four wheels mounted on floating scows, all intercepting fish bound for Big Eddy. He could also see, up on the bluff, the rambling buildings of Seufert's Cannery, which would receive the catch from the wheels and many other fishers. The string in his left hand tugged much less often, and less often still was it tugged by chinook. But neither he nor Dr. Stone, nor President Roosevelt, when he made his angry remarks in 1908, knew that the gravest challenge to the Pacific salmon was yet to come.

Reworking the Habitat

Thus far, we have seen the salmon and steelhead runs jeopardized by the idea that the runs were invincible. This belief was acted on by people who depended on and, in their own way, revered the big fish—the canners and the fishers themselves. A second lord of yesterday also was at work in California, Idaho, Oregon, and Washington—an attitude that ranged from indifference to disdain to contempt for salmon and steelhead. These other actors, who had no direct tie to the salmon and steelhead, saw only one use—their use—for the rivers and streams, regardless of how it might impinge on anadromous fish. They took a great many actions that, in concert, inexorably drove down the runs. The result was a steady and dramatic decline in the habitat of the salmon: the outright blockage of more than half of the available stream mileage and the degradation of much of the rest. The legal system played a critical, although passive, role, fortifying these activities by affording no mechanism to counteract them.[26]

During the last part of the nineteenth century and well into the 1930s, salmon habitat was assaulted by uncountable numbers of unrelated actions. Throughout ranch country, smaller tributaries were made impassable by unregulated grazing, as occurred at Camp Creek. Logging took out thousands of miles of salmon spawning beds. In the national forests, Pinchot's high standards for good forest practices could not always be enforced for want of personnel, but conditions were far worse on private lands. Timber operations clear-cut right across creeks and streams, leaving spawning habitat inundated by logs, slash, and mounds of silt. Mining operations also layered rock and soil onto streambeds; as noted, hydraulic mining was the chief offender.[27]

In addition to the wholesale elimination of spawning grounds, the water itself was affected. Logging, ranching, mining, and farming all deposited silt and, sometimes, chemicals into the waters. Heavy industry, free of any regulation until after World War II and unencumbered by strict enforcement until the 1970s, dumped its untreated wastes directly into the rivers.

Further, the quantity of water in the salmon and steelhead streams diminished rapidly. As discussed at length in the next chapter, there were no controls on the amount of water that miners, urban areas, and, particularly, irrigators (who use 90 percent of all water in the Northwest) were allowed to divert from the streams. In some cases, irrigation withdrawals simply dried up spawning streams during the spring and summer. But even if water remained, it was warmed and degraded by return flows laden with silt and agrochemicals.[28]

Each of the major watersheds has a different set of causes for the decline of the salmon and steelhead runs. In the Sacramento River basin, historically the largest problem was hydraulic mining, but today the dominant force is irrigation withdrawals for farming in the rich Sacramento–San Joaquin Valley. In the Klamath River drainage, modern problems trace mainly to irrigation withdrawals and sedimentation caused by a variety of land and water use practices. In the Fraser River, diminished runs are due primarily to urbanization in the lower river around Vancouver and to former blockages whose effects continue. Most notably, in 1913, railway construction in the Fraser River Canyon at Hell's Gate, at river mile 129, completely blocked the runs when huge amounts of rock slid into the river. The blockage was cleared, but then further slides closed it again, and in subsequent years some of the sockeye runs virtually disappeared and commercial catches fell to as little as one-seventh of the pre-1913 level. Rehabilitation beginning in 1944 has led to the construction of the most complex fishways in the world at Hell's Gate. In Southeast Alaska, the primary reason for diminished runs is logging in the Tongass National Forest.[29]

In the Columbia River basin, the dominant cause was different. To be sure, these activities, taken in the aggregate and combined with overfishing, might well have been sufficient, if unchecked, to eliminate nearly all of the salmon and steelhead. But the largest single cause of the declines on the Columbia was yet another factor: dams. They came in many forms, and a great amount of habitat was lost in the early days of development through relatively small but impassable dams for stock ponds, tailings ponds, private irrigation reservoirs, and the like. Irrigation cooperatives, using private capital, built larger facilities that made no allowance for fish passage. In spite of the thousands of stream miles blocked off by these activities, their effects paled in comparison with those of the megalithic dams built throughout the Pacific Northwest for energy development beginning in the 1930s. Today, attempts to reduce the many effects of the big dams remain at the center of attempts to rehabilitate the runs.

The landscape of Washington, Oregon, and Idaho has been thoroughly reworked by hydropower development. Hardly any major stream of the

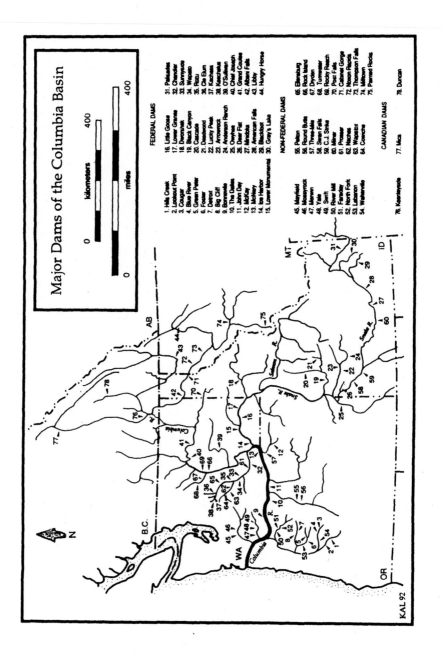

Major Dams of the Columbia Basin

260,000-square-mile Columbia River watershed has been left unaffected. The unobstructed river down which Lewis and Clark drifted in 1805 with only a single portage at Celilo Falls is today a back-to-back series of flat-water reservoirs from Bonneville Dam, at river mile 145, to the Canadian border. Above Bonneville, only 50 miles of the river in the United States remain free flowing. The 1214-mile-long river, which drains an area larger than France and whose annual discharge into the ocean is more than twice that of the Nile, is now a series of placid, computer-regulated lakes.

In September 1932, presidential candidate Franklin D. Roosevelt visited Portland, promising that if elected he would see that the hydropower potential of the Columbia River basin—representing 40 percent of the nation's hydroelectric capacity—was developed. (Hydroelectric capability is high in the Columbia River basin because the river is large and the terrain steep, dropping from 12,000–13,000-foot mountain peaks to sea level. This creates the maximum "head" of water for hydroelectric purposes: basically, the huge rush of falling water can turn big turbines very fast.) As president, Roosevelt took a "gleam in a bureaucrat's eye" and began to forge it into a reality that was complete by the early 1970s. The Columbia River basin became energy rich, as befitting the watershed with the greatest hydroelectric potential on the North American continent: per capita consumption of electrical energy was twice the national average, at half the cost.[30]

With Roosevelt's inauguration in 1933, the era of hydropower began in the Pacific Northwest. That year, the first dam on the main-stem Columbia—the nonfederal Rock Island Dam in central Washington—was completed, and the Bureau of Reclamation and the Army Corps of Engineers began construction of the two federal dams—Bonneville and Grand Coulee—that were to become synonymous in the Northwest with the availability of inexpensive hydropower.

The builders were hardly unaware of the effects of dams on anadromous fish. Early in the planning for development of the river, two contrasting solutions were proposed, and Bonneville and Grand Coulee illustrate well how the proposals actually worked. The first solution was to construct fish ladders, a winding series of gradually elevated pools by which migrating fish could ascend stepwise to the pool behind the dam. The second, and more drastic, solution was applied to dams whose height irreversibly blocked access to or inundated spawning habitat: the displaced wild runs would be relocated or replaced by hatchery production.

The first idea was tried at Bonneville, the first completed component of the federal Columbia River Power System. When finished in 1938, the dam was equipped with a $7.2 million, state-of-the-art engineering marvel for migrating salmon and steelhead, its fish ladders supplemented by an intricate backup system of locks, traps, elevators, and bypass canals. Incredibly, however, the plan originally prepared by the Army Corps of Engineers had no provision at all for a fish bypass system. The chief engineer is said to have replied to a citizen protest, "We do not intend to play nursemaid to fish." The comment has never been fully substantiated, and the Corps denies it. (I am reminded of the remark attributed to President Andrew Jackson after a Supreme Court decision that he disagreed with: "John Marshall has made his law; now let him enforce it." Careful historians have researched the matter and concluded that no proof existed that Jackson ever actually made the comment; historians add, however, that whether or not he actually said it, he almost certainly thought it.) Had the Corps's original design prevailed, the entire watershed of the main-stem Columbia above river mile 145 would have been permanently shut off to salmon and steelhead.[31]

The ladders were experimental; despite the great cost, nobody knew whether they would work, for salmon had never been asked to surmount ladders totaling 65 feet. Many predicted that the fish ladder would be a boondoggle that would doom the upriver salmon runs after all. In June 1938, as the gates were closed, biologists and engineers alike anxiously awaited the spring chinook run. But when the fish returned, they easily negotiated their way up the ladders and into the reservoir behind the dam, as excited cries of "God bless you!" rang out from the fishway's designers.[32]

The apparent success of the Bonneville Dam fishways (then and now the world's highest fish passage facilities) generated widespread optimism. Even today, the glass viewing windows at the Bonneville ladders are a tourist attraction. As a result of that success, hydropower proponents reasoned, if the fish can be so easily detoured around one high dam, why not six, seven, eight, or more? Unfortunately, events of only a few years later would dampen the euphoria.

Grand Coulee Dam—the ultimate symbol of cheap hydropower in the Northwest—was disastrous to fish passage. Hailed as the greatest engineering feat ever undertaken, the dam in north-central Washington was a colossus 343 feet high, with a reservoir that backed up 150 miles, beyond the United States border into British Columbia. It had an impoundment capacity more than sixty times that of Bonneville. The dam was too high for fish ladders to be biologically effective or, it was said, economically feasible. When the gates were closed in 1941, tens of thousands of chinook, sockeye, and steelhead circled helplessly in the river below the dam. They had swum nearly 600 miles up from the ocean but were forever shut out from more than 1100 river miles of salmon habitat. These runs included, of course, the largest and most highly prized specimens in the entire Columbia River basin, the Canadian-born "June hogs," or Royal Chinook. Some of the blockaded fish were trapped and artificially spawned, and the incubated

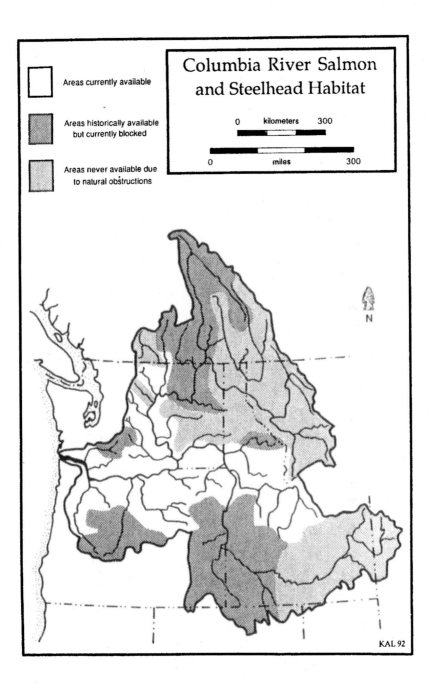

Areas currently available

Areas historically available but currently blocked

Areas never available due to natural obstructions

Columbia River Salmon and Steelhead Habitat

0   kilometers   300

0   miles   300

N

KAL 92

eggs were transported to streams below Grand Coulee. There was some success with this program, although the big upriver chinook runs were completely exterminated. In all, the closing of the gates at Grand Coulee was probably the single most destructive act against the beleaguered Pacific salmon.[33]

Word still traveled fast among the fishing tribes of the basin, and they all knew about Bonneville and Grand Coulee. Feeling powerless to prevent construction of the dams or to alter their design, the Indians' main reaction was to express wonderment at why the white man would do such things. During construction, many of them came to the dam sites and watched stoically from the nearby bluffs. Jim Yahtin was not there—he had passed away in 1924 at the age of 83—but his wife, Yessessi, lived on. Her home was inland, at Simnasho, on the Warm Springs Indian Reservation, but she knew about Grand Coulee and about Bonneville, which had flooded Big Eddy. She told people about the old days and about how sad it was to flood the traditional fishing rocks. But the river still raged at Celilo Falls, and Indian people still came in from all over the basin to fish and to participate in the old ceremonies.

In 1941, the main stem of the Columbia had three dams. Today, it has fourteen. Its principal tributary, the Snake River, has ten. In 1967, the completion of Hells Canyon Dam at river mile 247 of the Snake River did to the upper Snake what Grand Coulee did to the upper Columbia by serving as an impassable barrier to all of the salmon and steelhead runs. In the entire Columbia River watershed, there are now seventy-nine hydroelectric projects with a capacity of 15,000 megawatts or more. Thirty of these are federal dams, which collectively comprise the federal Columbia River Power System. This is just the tip of the iceberg. Throughout the basin, counting dams for irrigation and other purposes, there are more than 450 major dams, many of which have no fish passage facilities. The Columbia and Snake rivers have become the most highly developed river system in the world, supplying more than 80 percent of the Pacific Northwest's electrical energy. In total, the federal dams alone have a storage capacity of 20 million acre-feet of water and produce more than 19,000 megawatts of electricity.[34]

The dams were financed through creative accounting procedures that ensured heavily subsidized electricity to the Northwest's electricity consumers. The United States funded the federal dams. Actual construction of these multipurpose dams was done by the Army Corps of Engineers, when flood control and navigation were primary purposes of a particular dam, and by the Bureau of Reclamation, when irrigation was a major objective. The Bonneville Power Administration (BPA), patterned after the Tennessee Valley Authority, was created in 1937 to market power from the federal dams. The Army Corps of Engineers and the Bureau of Reclamation operate the dams, but they time releases to comport with the needs of the BPA's customers. BPA customer contracts provide for either "firm" power or less expensive, "interruptible" power, in recognition of the fact that in some instances obligations for flood control, navigation, or irrigation must be met first.

The BPA was required to repay the Treasury for the costs of construction of the dams. Repayment would come from customer receipts—from utility companies (which supply homes in urban and rural areas) and direct industrial customers (which receive 30 percent of all federal power). Repayment here, however, is not real repayment. Interest rates are low—3 percent for some dams. In addition, either the repayment schedule is strung out—over forty or fifty years for some dams—or there is no fixed repayment schedule at all, in which case the old, low-interest loans remain in effect indefinitely. In all, the federal government has invested $8 billion in the power system, but the BPA has paid back less than $1 billion. The Office of Management and Budget has called the BPA a "huge drain on the Federal budget." Of course, recognizing the existence of the subsidies does not address whether the subsidies might be justified by the social benefits to the region of below-cost electricity.[35]

And, of course, the falls at Celilo flowed much too stoutly not to be turned into electricity. On a Sunday afternoon in April 1956, tribal people gathered on the stoop-shouldered hills to hold the "first salmon" ceremony for the last time at Celilo. Within the year, Celilo Falls was gone, drowned by the pool behind The Dalles Dam. Tommy Thompson, a full-blooded Sahaptin-speaking Indian, was the longtime leader of the fishermen at Celilo, the person with ultimate authority to enforce all of the law ways. He cried when the water came up, saying: "There goes my life. My people will never be the same." He died in 1959, at the age of ninety. Jim Yahtin's wife, Yessessi, lived right up to the time when her birthplace, Celilo Falls, was about to be inundated. She had seen the whole transformation—of the river, the fish, and her people. She had never revealed her age because, it was thought, she was ashamed at being slightly older than her husband. But a tribal custom was for women to keep a calendar in the form of a long string of hemp. Every year, on the winter solstice, they tied a knot in the hemp. When Yessessi died in late 1955, her family found her calendar, with 114 knots.

The Costs, Indian Treaty Rights, and the Reassessment

The benefits of the power system have been widely heralded, and rightly so. As the Bonneville Power Administration touts it:

In little more than one generation, Man has harnessed the tremendous water power of the Columbia Basin. . . . He has tamed floods, improved navigation, and turned deserts into rich farmland. . . . Production of low-cost electricity has been a major factor in the Pacific Northwest's transition from a regional economy based on agriculture and lumber to a more balanced, widely diversified economic and social structure.[36]

But harnessing the rivers brought costs, costs never reflected in the federal agencies' reports and never much appreciated by the public or taken up in congressional deliberations, until the 1970s.

Hydropower's direct obliteration of spawning habitat by 55 percent only begins to suggest the magnitude of the impact on the salmon runs. At those dams that do allow passage, fish mortality has been exceedingly high. For upstream adult fish, most of the ladders work reasonably well, but there are still sizable losses—about 13 percent for each of the four lower Columbia River dams, less than 5 percent per dam for the others. Flow and spill conditions at the base of dams can confuse migrating salmon, discouraging fish movement in the river or deflecting fish from entrances to fish ladders, particularly when fishway flows are inadequate to attract the fish. Concentrations of fish at the bases of and in the ladders may also increase the incidence of disease.[37]

Perhaps surprisingly, however, downstream migration by juvenile salmon and steelhead has been a far greater cause of mortality than has upstream passage. As fish are forced from the turbine intake through the rotating blades and out a tunnel at the base of the dam, the shearing action of the blades and turbulent water, along with sudden changes in pressure, can kill young fish. Most of the fish that survive passage through the turbines are stunned and disoriented—easy prey for the squawfish and other predatory fish that await them at the base of the dam. During periods of low flow, nearly all of the river's water has been channeled through the turbines at each dam, leaving no alternate route for young, vulnerable fish.

One way to avoid the use of turbines is by "spills," releases of water over the spillway rather than through turbines (of course, spills mean that hydropower generation at the dams must be forgone). Although usually not as lethal or traumatic as passage through turbines, passage by means of spills can result in a sudden drop of a hundred feet or more in turbulent water moving over concrete and can be equally disabling or disorienting to young fish. Until the 1970s, during periods of high river flow, juvenile mortality from spillway passage was compounded by the lethal effects of nitrogen supersaturation in the churning waters at the foot of a dam. Although much alleviated by spill deflectors and dissolved gas monitoring, this "gas-bubble disease" can produce embolisms in young fish, causing them, like deep-sea divers, to die of the "bends."

Further, the reservoirs behind the dams are themselves a cause of juvenile mortality. The reordering—from flowing river to slack pool—affects the delicate timing of the young fish. In the much slower (there is still a trace of current) and warmer waters of the pool behind the dams, some fish lose their migratory urge and die in the reservoir from predation, disease, or thermal shock after failing to complete their journey to the ocean.[38]

During the past decade, as discussed later in this section, these problems have been tackled with real resolve, and significant progress has been made. But in the past—including the recent past—combined mortality from spillway and turbine passage has been estimated at approximately 15 percent *per dam*. During years of acute low flow, as in 1973 and 1977, mortality may have leaped to as much as 35 percent per dam. Some of the inland runs of salmon and steelhead must pass eight dams. Therefore, if there is even a 15 percent mortality at each of the eight dams, 730 fish out of every thousand will perish at the dams. In those low-flow years of 35 percent loss per dam, only thirty fish out of a thousand will survive. Those figures reflect only the young fish that will reach the mouth of the Columbia on their outgoing journey.[39]

The decline in the runs that had begun in the 1880s was accelerated by the dams during the 1940s. By the late 1970s, the runs were in a crisis state. Estimates of the historical annual runs are between 10 and 16 million salmon and steelhead. The runs today average 2.5 million fish per year, a loss of 75 percent to 85 percent. Upriver chinook runs were the hardest hit of all; the chinook were considered for endangered species status as early as the 1970s and all Snake River chinook runs were finally listed as threatened in 1992.[40]

The vaunted cheap electricity of the Pacific Northwest, therefore, is not as cheap as once thought. The financial loss may well be incalculable. As resource consultant Ed Chaney put it, "It would be virtually impossible to accurately estimate the total number of salmon and steelhead lost to northwest fisheries directly as a result of hydroelectric development and operations in the upper Columbia River Basin; only Carl Sagan and his peers could comprehend such a number in any event." Economist Phillip Meyer, however, has not been deterred from attempting an estimate of the economic cost of salmon and steelhead loss caused by operation of the Columbia River Power System. Meyer's calculations found a staggering loss of $372 million annually, with cumulative costs of $6.5 billion between 1960 and 1982 alone. These are direct, tangible costs only. There was no attempt to measure such things as the lost satisfaction to sportfishers, the hundreds of millions of tons of nutrients lost to the animals and the land, or the sense of disorientation and disorder brought upon the Indian people of the Northwest.[41]

After their initial unwillingness to limit catches, or to enforce restrictions that did exist, the state legislatures and wildlife departments gradually began serious efforts to counteract the declining runs. Oregon prohibited gaffs, spears, and foul hooks in 1901, and Washington followed suit. Purse seines were prohibited by both states in 1917. In 1918, the two states entered into the Columbia River Compact, which provided for in-river regulation of commercial fisheries on the Columbia. Oregon barred fish wheels in 1927, and Washington did the same in 1935. In the 1960s, successful citizen petition drives resulted in initiatives outlawing gillnetting of steelhead, which, organized sport groups argued, should be caught only for sport, not as a commercial fish. After 1948, the states also regulated the burgeoning offshore commercial trolling industry, which had the first opportunity to harvest salmon. California and British Columbia took similar steps, while Alaska moved more slowly because its smaller population put less pressure on the fish and their habitat.[42]

Of course, such regulation had significant limits. One was the trenchant matter of the tragedy of the commons. Why should Idaho get tough with its fishers when Oregon's and Washington's fishers, and even Canadian and Alaskan boats, were getting most of the fish? Why should the downriver and ocean jurisdictions crack down when the fish would simply be taken by Idahoans? Why regulate fishers when the even larger issue was the dams and the myriad other actions that had degraded the habitat?

The states had even less success in cutting losses at the dams. They all adopted provisions requiring fishways, but the laws sometimes went unenforced and, in any event, did not get at the problem of mortality of juveniles migrating downstream. Beyond that, the states learned that they had no rights at all as against federal dams. During the 1950s and 1960s, Oregon and Washington both waged campaigns to block federal dams or at least to force design modifications to comport with state laws. The courts held that federal law was supreme and that decisions of federal agencies—the Corps, the BPA, and the Bureau of Reclamation—held sway. In 1978, in *California v. United States*, the states made some inroads on federal authority, but the ruling was too little, too late. The decision seems to apply only to dams built by the Bureau of Reclamation, and in any event, the really big dams had already been completed.[43]

By and large, the citizenry remained impassive until the 1970s. It was a profoundly difficult situation to get a handle on—a combination of dispersed, almost invisible actions that ate up habitat bit by bit combined with the overwhelmingly grandiose plans of the Corps and the BPA, packaged in the glitter of a new and better society for the Northwest. The federal agencies worked effectively both in the shadows (they quietly defused canners' and commercial fishers' opposition to The Dalles Dam by pointing out that the dam would flood out competition for the resource in the form of Indian fishing at Celilo Falls) and in the bright lights of public hearings (presentations by BPA and Corps officials were replete with impressive graphs, charts, and expert assurances that the salmon would be accommodated by their projects). Further, hydroelectric development came on with extraordinary rapidity. As the BPA put it in the quotation given at the beginning of this section, the whole system was accomplished "in little more than one generation." On top of those factors, salmon protection groups did not have the leverage of the Freedom of Information Act or expanded judicial review, both of which trace to the 1970s. Thus, various uprisings by sport and commercial groups were never able to make much headway.[44]

There were exceptions. In the 1960s, objections to a dam that would have flooded lower Hells Canyon on the Snake River led to the area being set aside as a national recreation area. And occasionally, local wrath rose up to thwart the seemingly inevitable march of those who would rework the habitat. In 1910, the Golden Sunbeam Company expanded its mining operations on the Salmon River just below Stanley, Idaho. It put in a dam across the river to generate hydroelectric energy, but the poorly constructed fish ladder virtually eliminated the sockeye runs—the very fish that had given the name to exquisite Redfish Lake, the sockeye's spawning grounds in the Sawtooth Mountains. Finally, in 1934, an anonymous local dynamited the Sunbeam Dam, thereby reviving the runs. A book on the Salmon River, *River of No Return*, included a description of the incident and a postexplosion photograph of the remains of the Sunbeam Dam, along with the following caption, which spoke for more than one frustrated westerner:

> The Sunbeam Dam. It is uncertain at this time who is entitled to an accolade for dynamiting the south abutment. However, there is no limit to what can be accomplished if no one cares who gets the credit.[45]

The events that most directly triggered the beginnings of modern comprehensive reform, however, originated from the most unlikely source of all: the Indian tribes, who nearly everyone had assumed would quietly fade off into oblivion. That was certainly the attitude of state wildlife officials who, during the 1950s and 1960s, were faced with the combination of booming population—especially the droves of sportfishers who took to the rivers in search of the tackle-busting steelhead—and steadily decreasing runs. It became ever more apparent that there were not enough anadromous fish to go around. The states had traditionally recognized, albeit grudgingly, that Indian fishing at the "usual and accustomed" off-reservation sites was not subject to state regulation—seasons, bag limits, and gear restrictions. But fishing conditions had become too tight, and unregulated Indian fishing could no longer be tolerated. It was necessary to crack down on the Indians in order to conserve the resource. In addition, state officers and their commercial and sport constituencies were convinced that Indian fishing was "above the law," smacking of special treatment and privilege.[46]

The tribes had every reason to be dispirited in light of the relentless ways in which their cultures, lands, and natural resources had been assaulted. Certainly, many in the state agencies expected the Indians to submit quietly to regulation, as they had to the dams, but that was not to be the case. To be sure, the tribes were reduced in numbers and in land, and assimilation had played its course in many different ways. Slacks and dresses had replaced buckskin, automobiles had taken the place of horses, alcoholism seemed to have invaded every corner of Indian country, and numbers of tribal members had moved to the cities. In a larger sense, however, the century since the treaties had not changed the essential things for reservation Indians. Subsistence fishing and hunting still provided a significant part of their diet. The old religions still had proponents, and the Indian way—a light, easy-going way of life anchored to the land—still prevailed. A century later, they were still Indians.

They knew all about the treaties, which were epochal events in the histories of their peoples. Treaty time was still vivid to tribal people in the 1960s. From childhood, adults had listened at great length to elders like Jim Yahtin and Yessessi, people who were alive when the agreements were made. Indian people of the 1960s viewed the promises with great respect and expected them to be adhered to. Beyond that, the tribes were outraged at the idea that state, rather than tribal, regulation was somehow needed to conserve the resource. It was clear to them that Indians had never wasted fish. They knew full well that it was the white man's development, not Indian fishing, that had brought down the runs. Indians were on a collision course with the states and their non-Indian constituents.

The barrage of litigation that would produce some of the most far-reaching court cases ever decided in the American West—the Seattle Post-Intelligencer rated the Indian fishing rights controversy the second most important news story in the Pacific Northwest during the 1970s—began with arrests during the 1960s at scattered locations, including Cook's Landing on the Columbia River and Frank's Landing on the Nisqually River in western Washington. Indians took heart at the fiery, articulate speeches of tribal leaders such as Billy Frank. George Dysart, of the Solicitor's Office of the Department of the Interior in Portland, took up the cause. Dysart, a cautious, conservative man with a resolute insistence that law ought to be enforced as written, first defended Indian fishermen in various county courthouses. Then, in 1968, on his recommendation, the United States filed *United States v. Oregon* as a companion case to *Sohappy v. Smith*, initially brought by David Sohappy, a Yakima Indian fisherman, against various Oregon state fish and wildlife officials. The two cases were consolidated for trial.

Dysart's arguments were short and to the point, since there was not much law on the books. The Yakimas' 1855 treaty guaranteed tribal members the right to fish at their "usual and accustomed places." The Supreme Court had ruled just two times on the issue, each time in favor of Indian fishing rights. In 1905, in *United States v. Winans*, the Court upheld access to the traditional off-reservation fishing sites, even if the land had been acquired from the United States by a non-Indian. The unanimous opinion found that before the treaty, the right to fish "was a part of larger rights possessed by the Indians" and that even though the land had been ceded away, fishing rights at the traditional stations had been expressly reserved. Given the situation of the Northwest tribes at treaty time, Justice Joseph McKenna reasoned, the result could not be otherwise: "The right to resort to the fishing places in controversy . . . [was] not much less necessary to the existence of the Indians than the atmosphere they breathed." The other Supreme Court case was *Tulee v. Washington*, handed down in 1942, in which the court relied on *Winans* and held that Washington could not impose a state license fee on Indian fishermen. Finally, Dysart argued, nothing had happened since the treaty to extinguish the tribal rights recognized in the two opinions. When the United States paid the four Columbia River fishing tribes $23 million for the flooding of Celilo Falls, the payment was not intended to buy out all tribal rights but was compensation for a "flowage easement"—that is, the flooding of the old sites. The tribes, Dysart believed, still had a treaty right to fish in the pool behind The Dalles Dam.[47]

The cases were heard before Judge Robert C. Belloni, a federal judge in Portland. Belloni, a tall, slender, white-haired jurist widely respected for his nondoctrinaire views, held for the Indian fishermen on every issue. He also attempted to articulate the quantity of fish to which the tribes were entitled. Judge Belloni did not set a percentage but concluded that the state must conduct its regulatory practices so as to ensure that a "fair and equitable share" of the salmon and steelhead runs would reach Indian fishing sites. *Sohappy v. Smith* did not resolve all of the tough issues—particularly the exact meaning of "fair and equitable"—but it was the first modern decision by a federal judge on Indian treaty rights, and it set a foundation for the more specific rulings to follow.[48]

The legal issues shifted to Puget Sound. In September 1971, the federal government filed *United States v. Washington,* omnibus litigation to determine the treaty fishing rights of fourteen tribes in western Washington. The tribes intervened, and David Getches, director of the Native American Rights Fund, acted as lead counsel in the complex suit. Sit-ins and demonstrations by activists on both sides accelerated. The basic view of the tribes was that the treaty guarantee that they could fish "in common with the citizens of the Territory" meant that they were entitled to an opportunity to take 50 percent of the runs that passed their fishing grounds. The Washington Department of Fisheries (with regulatory authority over commercial fishing, including all salmon fishing) took the position that the tribes were entitled to a "fair share," which might be as high as one-third of the runs on the streams where traditional sites existed. The Washington Department of Game (with jurisdiction over sport fish, including steelhead) argued that the tribes had no special rights at all.

Judge George H. Boldt, an Eisenhower appointee with a tough, law-and-order reputation, was called on to decide these sweeping issues affecting the economy and society of the Pacific Northwest. Pretrial discovery was extensive, and the lengthy trial produced reams of exhibits and expert testimony. On February 12, 1974, the court rendered "the Boldt decision," as it would come to be known as a household word in the region. Judge Boldt ruled for the tribes on all counts. Most importantly, after hearing exhaustive testimony on the treaty negotiations and reviewing a mid-nineteenth-century dictionary definition that "in common" meant "equal," he held that Indian fishers were entitled to the opportunity to take 50 percent of all salmon and steelhead that passed by their off-reservation sites.[49]

A few weeks later, the attorneys returned to the United States Courthouse to hold oral arguments on the state's motion that Judge Boldt reconsider his ruling. They had to work to get through the picket lines of sportfishers and commercial fishers. Judge Boldt was hanging in effigy on the courthouse steps. Once inside, the attorney general of Washington suggested to the court that there might be doubt about the judge's decision. Judge Boldt, diminutive enough that he had to lean forward to see the attorneys directly, stared in his hawk-eyed way at the lawyer and, rendering perhaps his definitive statement on the case that he had lived with for three years and that he would later call the most important event of his long judicial career, said: "Mr. Attorney General, I may be in error, but I am not in doubt."[50]

Litigation and extrajudicial activity continued on numerous fronts. Judge Belloni modified his "fair and equitable share" formulation by adopting Judge Boldt's 50 percent rationale and applying it to the Columbia River. The United States Court of Appeals for the Ninth Circuit affirmed both the Boldt and Belloni decisions, and in 1976 the United States Supreme Court let the Boldt decision stand, refusing to review the case. In the meantime, Washington officials essentially refused to obey the Boldt decision. On several occasions, the state of Washington or private groups took issues to local state courts, who refused to enforce Judge Boldt's rulings in spite of the constitutionally mandated supremacy of federal court orders. These collateral problems, along with the intrinsic difficulty of the litigation—ordering compliance by so many different kinds of fishers and attempting to sort out so many different runs of fish—led Judge Boldt alone to issue literally hundreds of postjudgment orders. West Publishing Company, the nation's largest law book publisher, took the nearly unprecedented step of issuing a special volume collecting all of Judge Boldt's reported decisions in *United States v. Washington.*[51]

Still, the United States Supreme Court had not ruled on the issues. Washington attorney general (and later United States senator) Slade Gorton sought review of one of the many state court rulings refusing to enforce the Boldt decision, arguing that the Court should accept the case because the non-Indian people of Washington could not be expected to adhere to such a sweeping ruling until it had been addressed by the nation's highest court. The Court did take the case, and on July 2, 1979, it substantially affirmed all significant aspects of the Boldt decision. The Court took the occasion to comment on the conduct of the state and its constituency:

> The state's extraordinary machinations in resisting [Judge Boldt's 1974] decree have forced the district court to take over a large share of the management of the state's fishery in order to enforce its decrees. Except for some desegregation cases . . . , the district court has faced the most concerted official and private efforts to frustrate a decree of a federal court witnessed in this century.[52]

Progress and Decline on the Modern Rivers

Almost astonishingly, out of this protracted bitterness was forged an alliance with the capability of building policies with a realistic hope of resuscitating the runs. Initially, such a result seemed impossible. Anthony Netboy, prolific writer on salmon and steelhead, spoke for most organized non-Indian fishers when he said of the 1969 Belloni decision that "[t]his ruling opened a can of worms that has since plagued efforts at administering the fishery in a manner that is 'fair and equitable' to all user groups, and most of all it has inhibited efforts to save a declining resource." But events since have proved such assessments exactly wrong. Today, most knowledgeable observers would agree with this heartfelt assessment, written by sportswriter John de Yonge in a 1984 special issue of the *Seattle Post-Intelligencer* to commemorate the tenth anniversary of the Boldt decision:

Judge George Boldt is dead. In his case the good he did will not be interred with his bones.

Boldt did a lot of good over a tremendously long career as a U.S. District Court judge sitting in Tacoma and elsewhere.

But the good for which [he] is most famous, or infamous, depending on your point of view, is his 1974 decision in United States vs. the State of Washington that the treaty phrase, "in common with" entitled the Indian tribes which had signed the treaties to catch half or more of the salmon and steelhead returning to state waters.

It happens that the decision hurt and angered a lot of people, non-Indian commercial fishermen and sports anglers whose catches up until then were coming out of the Indian's share.

To speak personally, in the short run and perhaps for the rest of my life, Judge Boldt's interpretation of the treaty words has knocked the hell out of my annual catch of salmon and steelhead on my favorite streams, the Skagit River and its tributaries.

The fish were never easy to come by for a fly fisherman like me, especially in the cold rains of winter. A good year would produce a dozen. Now when the Indian gillnets strain the river from shore to shore, my catch has become zero.

At the end of a fishless day, chilled, hungry, tired, feeling the years in my legs, my grumping has been known to have taken Judge Boldt's name in vain—sentiments which during a fishing year issue from the lips of thousands of anglers vainly stumping streams once reputed worldwide for the excellence and abundance of their sea-run fish.

But in rational moments I have praised Judge Boldt for accomplishing two things with his decision.

First, he was fair. To the Indians he restored a right under the law which for a hundred years had been nibbled away by the conscious and unconscious greed of people like me and by the state government's conscious and unconscious mismanagement of its fisheries wealth.

Second, and this is the good that ultimately should profit society in general, Judge Boldt's decision is forcing all of us to take a close look at how we must take care of our fisheries.

We have been poor stewards. Overfishing, dam building, rapacious logging, the sucking up of river flows for irrigation, the dumping of chemical poisons into our waters, the institution of poorly understood hatchery systems—these at the state, national and international levels have so hurt the fish runs that in some cases Indians and others each have a right to take 50 percent of next to nothing. . . .

There is an irony that at the end of a distinguished career as a judge and as a citizen, Boldt found himself being hung in effigy and reviled for his decision on Indian treaty rights to fish.

He refused to be swayed by public opinion. "It is not an essential or even necessarily desirable factor that a conscientious judge should even consider," he said.

True. But if we're brave enough to deal rationally with the effects of his decision, I predict that someday the "Boldt Decision" will be remembered as when this state and its people (Indians included) began, however unwillingly and haltingly, to save the salmon and steelhead runs from oblivion.[53]

It was no mean feat to breathe life into the seemingly self-evident idea that people should work together to improve the runs rather than fight for the right to harvest the last salmon. A cooperative effort to save the Pacific salmon and steelhead presented overwhelming logistical problems. The far-flung array of groups that passionately cared about anadromous fish all saw the situation through their own lenses, whether, to list but a few categories, they were Idaho steelheaders, Indian fishers at the mid-Columbia, sport trollers on the lower Willamette near Portland, gill-netters at the mouth of the Columbia, ocean commercial trollers from Oregon and Washington, or ocean sport boats from both states. Add to them their counterparts in Alaska, California, and British Columbia, all of whom harvested Columbia River salmon and steelhead.

The number of governments with jurisdiction over the salmon harvest was also staggering. In 1983, Dan Conner and I conducted a study of government regulation of Columbia River salmon. We took a hypothetical chinook salmon hatched in the headwaters of the Lochsa River under the Continental Divide in northern Idaho and traced its life journey down the Columbia, up to the Gulf of Alaska, and back home to Idaho. We found that a Lochsa River chinook, in addition to confronting eight dams in each direction, would pass through no fewer than seventeen separate management jurisdictions—international, federal, state, and tribal—during its return journey as an adult fish. Still, the Indian treaty rights controversy served to illuminate the central truth—that all who depend on the salmon ultimately would benefit by focusing on rebuilding the runs rather than on contesting one another for dwindling numbers of fish. Slowly but steadily, cooperative support galvanized for comprehensive efforts to preserve and enhance those magical animals and their habitat.[54]

One foundation for comprehensive management was put in place in 1976. The Fishery Conservation and Management Act (the FCMA, or the Magnuson Act, after Senator Warren Magnuson of Washington) responded to the heavy offshore take by foreign vessels. Before the act, in the band between 3 and 200 miles offshore (states have authority to regulate out to 3 miles), 2700 foreign boats took 2.7 million metric tons of fish (of all species, not just salmon and steelhead), about 70 percent of the total harvest. Under the Magnuson Act, the United States asserted exclusive management authority over the belt from 3 to 200 miles out to sea (with the states retaining jurisdiction out to 3 miles). Foreign boats would be allowed in, but only under federally imposed conditions, including harvest limits. The 1976 act also established eight regional fishery management councils to manage the fish resources under their jurisdictions. On the West Coast, two councils with responsibility for the harvest of Pacific salmon now set policy within the 197-mile belts in their respective jurisdictions. These management plans unify policy for the first time in this key geographic area and serve as the basis for resolving many international and interstate conflicts.[55]

One of the most promising laws for Pacific salmon and steelhead is the Pacific Northwest Power and Conservation Act of 1980. The Northwest Power Act was originally conceived as a comprehensive energy charter for the Northwest. During its deliberations, however, Congress expanded the scope of the legislation and directly took on the issue of the depressed salmon runs, which had reached their historical low at the point when the act was passed. Thus, the 1980 act included strict requirements for energy conservation by directing that, in future Northwest energy development decisions, the highest priority must be given to conservation measures. In other words, Congress directly recognized that energy conservation by existing users can, just as much as yet another dam, be a source of "new" energy. The act also took the historic step of equating anadromous fish as a "co-equal partner" with energy production: the express statutory goal was "to protect, mitigate, and enhance" Pacific salmon and steelhead.[56]

To fulfill its mandate to develop new energy policies while protecting the salmon, the 1980 act created the Northwest Power Planning Council. In doing so, the drafters threw away the book and came up with a new kind of administrative entity. The council was created by Congress, but it is not a federal agency. Rather, as a statement by the federal government that the Pacific Northwest as a region ought to have major responsibility, the membership of the eight-person body is appointed by the governors of the four affected states—two members each from Washington, Oregon, Idaho, and Montana. Two important provisions of federal law do apply: the council must abide by the Freedom of Information Act, and judicial review of council decisions rests in federal, not state, courts. Funding for the council, for both its full-time members and its extensive staff, is to come from the BPA's receipts from marketing of hydroelectric energy: therefore, the costs of protecting and restoring the salmon fishery will be treated as a cost of doing business, borne by the consumers of electrical power rather than being externalized.[57]

The act mandated the Northwest Power Planning Council to develop programs, to be completed within tight statutory deadlines, for governing federal energy development and enhancing the salmon runs. To underscore its emphasis on salmon, Congress directed the council to complete its fish and wildlife program before its energy program.

The act thus places basic planning authority in the council and removes it from the four agencies with an institutional bias in favor of power production: the Army Corps of Engineers, the Bonneville Power Administration, the Bureau of Reclamation, and the Federal Energy Regulatory Commission. The council is to set the course and the agencies are to implement it, subject to council oversight. The 1980 act does not make the council's programs absolutely binding on the four old-line agencies. Rather, they must take the council's programs into account "to the fullest extent practicable," thus giving ample wiggle room to the energy production agencies and the utility companies. One can easily imagine that the time will come when, for example, a general in the Army Corps of Engineers will refuse to comply, citing policy reasons for the record but muttering under his breath something about not being willing to "play nursemaid to fish." Nevertheless, as of the early 1990s, the agencies have carried out the council's ambitious programs in most respects—due in large part, one suspects, to the care with which the council programs have been developed and to the evident broad base of public support for the council's work.[58]

The Northwest Power Planning Council, then, was given a mission to develop a new approach toward energy and salmon in the Northwest. True, the idea of "coequal partners" was far easier to legislate than to achieve: the salmon runs were badly beaten down, and the utility companies and federal development agencies were firmly in control of the river. Still, the new law sent a strong signal for change. The passage of the statute was a historic moment for the region, and the excitement in the air drew generally outstanding council members. The first chairman was Dan Evans, former Republican governor of Washington and subsequently United States senator. Other influential political leaders from both parties received appointments. Intellectual leadership also came from Dr. Kai N. Lee, a professor from the University of Washington. The nature of the challenge made it easy to attract a strong, interdisciplinary staff.

The council's fish and wildlife program, first released in 1982 and revised in 1987, had a number of major provisions, but the following are worth special emphasis. First, the council developed an innovative "water budget." This is a process whereby a fixed quantity of water is budgeted for release at peak times of migration by juvenile fish. The added flow is thus available to help carry the young fish downstream, alleviating a major cause of mortality. The amount of water is substantial: the total amount in the 1987 revised plan was 4.64 million acre-feet (MAF), with 3.45 MAF budgeted for release at Priest Rapids Dam on the main-stem Columbia River and 1.19 MAF budgeted for release at Lower Granite Dam on the Snake River. The timing of the releases is set by tribal and state fish biologists, working cooperatively. Second, the council dealt extensively with fish bypass at the dams. The program called for the agencies to develop comprehensive fish passage plans that will provide at least a 90 percent survival rate at each dam for 80 percent of the runs. Eventually, the agencies will be directed to install submersible traveling screens to deflect fish from the turbines and channel them safely to the area below the dam (an alternative, and less satisfactory, option is to collect the juvenile fish and transport them by truck or barge around the dams). In the interim, the agencies are directed to send the fish over spillways rather than through turbines.[59]

The council has underscored the importance of preserving the dwindling wild runs, which have a number of genetic advantages over hatchery fish. On the other hand, the program recognizes the existence of a substantial hatchery effort to restore salmon runs and has called for experimentation with hatchery methods more compatible with preserving wild runs. The program also has provisions on upstream migration, harvest management, and improved data collection and includes a special section on the critical situation in the Yakima watershed. Expectations are that the council's energy plan will facilitate conservation of energy in the Pacific Northwest, thereby reducing pressure on the salmon and steelhead.[60]

The council's fish and wildlife program sets its directives in the context of an ambitious goal: doubling of the salmon and steelhead runs, from the current level of 2.5 million fish to 5 million fish. The council established a fact-finding process to determine whether and how the goal could be attained, with the understanding that any expanded hatchery effort must be consistent with maintaining the biological integrity of the wild stocks. The doubling goal is an interim objective, with the issue to be revisited if and when it is achieved.[61]

Another key aspect of the council's program is its "protected areas" initiative. The idea is that so much wildlife habitat in the basin has been dammed for hydroelectric production that substantial parts of the remaining free-flowing rivers should be set aside as wildlife habitat. In 1988, the council acted, designating roughly 40,000 miles of stream as protected areas. This is about 20 percent of the stream miles in the Northwest and would affect 202 of 327 pending proposals for hydroelectric development. It is the Federal Energy Regulatory Commission, however, that actually issues hydroelectric licenses, and although FERC staff has expressed support for the protected areas concept, FERC has let it be known that it does not necessarily consider itself bound by the program. In any event, the protected areas idea seems to have taken hold, and a substantial majority of all permits and applications for projects in protected areas have been withdrawn since the council's 1988 action.[62]

The Northwest Power Planning Council, itself a new kind of entity, has been joined by another new breed, the Columbia River Inter-Tribal Fish Commission. The CRITFC was formed in 1977 by the four major Columbia River fishing tribes: the Warm Springs and Umatilla of Oregon, the Yakima of Washington, and the Nez Perce of Idaho. The board is composed of representatives from each tribe. Funding comes from the tribes and the federal government.

The CRITFC, with offices in Portland, has consolidated tribal resources and created clout that could never have been achieved had the tribes acted separately. Using staff biologists, hydrologists, economists, and computer technicians, the organization has developed expertise that is literally second to none—by common agreement, it is at least as good as that of the state and federal agencies. Because salmon issues on the Columbia River are so sprawling and complex, whoever controls the numbers has the leg up in controlling policy. The CRITFC complements its command of the data with careful, reliable presentations at hearings and other public meetings. It made an impact during the passage of the Northwest Power Act of 1980 and since then has increasingly assumed a leadership role in salmon management in the Northwest.

Tim Wapato, a tribal member from the Colville Tribe in northeastern Washington, has been especially influential. Formerly a policeman from Los Angeles (he had the second highest score out of 2700 on the entrance exam), Wapato joined the CRITFC in 1979 and became its director in 1982. Wapato's grasp of the facts, collegial manner, and mastery of the issues, along with the leverage of the 1979 Supreme Court decision, quickly earned him a place in the inner circles of decision making.[63]

The CRITFC and Wapato were players in most decisions regarding the Columbia River during the early 1980s, but perhaps their overriding accomplishment was the negotiation of the United States–Canada Salmon Interception Treaty of 1985. They were joined by the Northwest Indian Fisheries Commission, a consortium of twenty Washington tribes that deals with Washington fisheries issues much as the CRITFC does with Columbia River matters.

A United States–Canada treaty was a necessity. The groundwork laid by the 1976 Magnuson Act and the 1980 Northwest Power Act had failed to solve the familiar tragedy-of-the-commons problem of Columbia River chinook being harvested off Canada and British Columbia. A full 50 percent of all Columbia River upriver bright chinooks, the most prized stocks in the system, were taken by Canadians, and more than 25 percent were harvested by Alaska. But sauce for the goose was sauce for the gander: some Fraser River salmon came down from Canada and into the United States, most of them swimming through the Strait of Juan de Fuca before turning north, while others traveled as far south as the Oregon-

California border. Why should Canada go light on Columbia River brights when the United States takes huge numbers of Fraser River sockeye? Why should the United States hold back even a whit on fish bound for Canada when Canadians load up on the big Columbia River fish? The pattern is familiar by now.

The two countries had negotiated for two decades and were still at loggerheads. Finally, the breakthrough came in 1984, and the treaty was signed in 1985. For an exasperated Bill Wilkerson, director of the Washington Department of Fisheries, there was no alternative, or the advances of the past ten years would go for naught: "We couldn't make sense out of management if we didn't get our act together and negotiate a treaty." The treaty sets limits on the take of Columbia River salmon in Canadian and Alaskan waters and on the harvest of Fraser River salmon in United States waters. It also sets in place mechanisms for both countries to increase their enhancement efforts, which will be mutually beneficial. Indian representatives were at the table during the extended negotiations, and President Reagan appointed Tim Wapato to the four-member United States delegation to the international commission that implements the treaty; Wapato later served as head of the United States delegation.[64]

By 1988, the legal structure erected during the previous decade and a half—the Magnuson Act, the Indian treaty decisions, the Northwest Power Act, the water budget, the protected areas program, and the 1985 treaty with Canada—had created cautious but widespread optimism. There was the promise of rivers in ascendancy for the first time since the Hume brothers and Arthur Hapgood set up their cannery in 1867. Representatives of the utilities, the BPA, and the Army Corps of Engineers were beginning to say in private that the problems with the runs had been solved and that we could begin to think about scaling back the protection programs.

Then in 1989, the bottom fell out. It was a dry year, preceded by three straight years of below-average runoff. With low flows throughout the Northwest, especially in the Snake River, the runs of returning adult fish plummeted. A loud alarm went off on March 21, 1990, when the Shoshone-Bannock Tribe of Idaho filed a petition to list the Snake River sockeye under the Endangered Species Act. At about the same time, three scientists, all members of the Endangered Species Committee of the American Fisheries Society, were completing work on a scholarly paper titled "Pacific Salmon at the Crossroads: Stocks at Risk from California, Oregon, Idaho, and Washington." The paper's authors, Willa Nehlsen, Jack E. Williams, and James A. Lichatowich, showed that the magnitude of the problem was far greater than nearly anyone had realized, extending to nearly all the salmon and steelhead rivers of the Pacific coast. The authors gathered information on hundreds of Pacific salmon stocks—that is, fish populations that originate from specific watersheds and generally return in a particular season to spawn. "It is," they wrote, "at the stock level that conservation and rehabilitation, if it is to be successful, will take place." The scientists named 214 native stocks in all, 101 at high risk of extinction, fifty-eight at moderate risk of extinction, fifty-four of special concern, and one—the Sacramento River chinook—already classified as threatened (three more species of salmon were listed as threatened or endangered soon thereafter). This was scientific work both careful and courageous, cousin to Wayne Elmore's range science at Camp Creek and Jack Ward Thomas's spotted owl biology on the westside ancient forests.[65]

The Northwest Power Planning Council was the logical entity to bring the parties together to build a strategy for combating the crisis—a dozen other endangered species petitions followed the Shoshone-Bannock Tribe's—but the council was paralyzed by the scale of the problem and by dissension among its members. Mark Hatfield, Oregon's senior senator, stepped into the breach. He had always had solid support from industry and the tribes but lukewarm backing at best from the environmental community. He believed that endangered species designation for animals with such a broad geographic range would far eclipse even the spotted owl controversy—he called the results of possible listings "an economic and social tidal wave." Environmentalists, however, were salved by Hatfield's palpable anger at the Army Corps of Engineers, which had taken a go-slow approach toward salmon recovery, including the installation of bypass screens at dams: "I'm really bothered that we've had to push these bypasses on you." No one doubted Hatfield's abilities or his commitment to forge some progress and put his prestige behind a consensus agreement to save the salmon runs.[66]

The "salmon summit" was convened by Hatfield in October 1990 with the blessings of all four governors and most members of the congressional delegations. There were thirty people seated at the table and plenty of apprehension and suspicion to go around. The Wasco chief from the Warm Springs Indian Reservation, the gentle but forceful Nelson Wallulatum, saw the current events with bitter irony: the tribes had finally won their case in the Supreme Court, but now their treaty rights might be destroyed by the Endangered Species Act, imposed as a result of other people's dams. Bill Bakke, the stoic representative of Oregon Trout, was a quiet but intense and firm advocate for wild fish. The brilliant Ed Chaney had come to speak for the fish, rivers, and people of Idaho, at the wrong end of the long gauntlet that the salmon and steelhead had to run. Knowledgeable, effective, and colorful Al Wright was there for the Pacific Northwest utilities, to protect the pocketbooks of the rate payers from what could be tens of millions of dollars of additional annual charges. The Bonneville Power Administration was represented by Jim Jura, tall, lanky, reasonable, and determined to safeguard the electrical power produced by the BPA, for him a regional treasure that had done so much for the Pacific Northwest. The scene was inauspicious because of the deep divisions, auspicious because all the players were present and because the palpable sense of urgency demanded some progress. The governors of Washington, Oregon, Idaho, and Montana all sent top staffers, and all four governors had pledged to take a hands-on approach to the meetings.

Six months later, the salmon summit had produced some movement at a time when movement was essential. The thirty negotiators were unwilling to sign off formally on an agreement, but on May 1, 1991, the four governors jointly wrote Hatfield, reporting that the summit had produced agreement on a short-term plan. It was, the governors said, a "less-complete recovery plan . . . than we had hoped for," but it was "creative thinking by the diverse public and private interests who have a stake in this issue." The heart of the approach was to alter the complex system of water uses and reservoir releases in the Snake River to provide higher water releases for depleted downstream and upstream migrations. It worked in its first year. Although 1991 was dry, the Snake River water budget was fully met; the water release was three times that achieved during dry years in the 1980s.[67]

The Northwest Power Planning Council had participated in the Hatfield meetings but had taken a largely passive role. After the salmon summit had created some momentum, the council seemed resolved to reassert itself and earn its keep. From May through December 1991, the council went through an intensive rule-making process, which included public hearings. The results plainly had spine. The council almost doubled the Columbia River arm of the water budget, hiking it from 3.45 million acre-feet to about 6.5 MAF. The council also budgeted a higher water flow for the Snake River in the short term. In the longer term, it called for at least another million acre-feet in dry years. There would be new programs to improve fish habitat. The council also decided to implement, in 1995, the pet project of Idaho governor Cecil Andrus to draw down four large reservoirs so that the water flow would be much faster through smaller, narrower impoundments. The initial costs of the council's 1991 programs were steep: lost hydroelectric power would amount to about $20 million annually in wet years and as much as $200 million in dry years, translating into a 4 percent wholesale rate increase. The long-term costs are unknown. Environmentalists feared that the plan would be strong enough to stave off the Endangered Species Act but weak enough that it would fail to save the fish. Yet the plan had gained some grudging respect, and it underscored the necessity of having the Northwest Power Planning Council in an active, constructive posture.[68]

Fulfilling Duties to the Ages

During modern times, the rivers of the Pacific Northwest have been the scene of one of the most ambitious conservation efforts ever undertaken. The knowledge and institutions are incomparably superior to those at any time in the past, and legitimately bold and creative initiatives have been put in place. All such progress has been made in the face of immense geographic scale, economic stakes, and biological complexity. Yet the development pressures on the rivers and the fish are themselves extraordinary, and the likelihood is that even if the runs manage to survive and at times prosper, all progress will always be temporary, all advances fragile. There will probably never again be room for confidence. For proof of that, we need look no farther than Idaho's magnificent Redfish Lake, at the top of the Salmon River watershed, set tight against the jagged, granite Sawtooths. Beneath the lake's surface, there is little or none of the life that gave the lake its name. The wild red fish—the endangered Salmon River sockeye that once swarmed and filled the lake and its outlet streams with mad energy—barely come back at all. Sixteen returning adults were counted in 1987, four in 1988, one in 1989, none in 1990, and four in 1991.[69]

In the upcoming years, fish recovery will have to compete with increasing demands on the power system. During the early and mid-1980s, the Pacific Northwest was in a recession, but no more: there is growth aplenty in the 1990s, and it will want electricity.

The Snake River, which produces fully a third of the Columbia's salmon and steelhead, including those wild fish bound for the Salmon River country, remains on the disabled list. Power generation still drastically alters seasonal flow patterns. Irrigation withdrawals are so great that in dry years, even though the flows in the main-stem Columbia may be adequate, there simply is not enough water in the Snake to allow for the water budget as well as energy and agriculture at their current levels. The salmon summit proposals worked in the short term, but they are not a permanent solution. Conservation on the farms and at the switch boxes is one logical way to reduce the stress on the Snake; but we still have not developed a significantly rigorous conservation ethic for energy, or, as will be explored more fully in the next chapter, for water.[70]

There is also the matter of the future of wild fish. Most salmon and steelhead in the Columbia River basin—more than 70 percent of returning adults—are of hatchery origin. Hatchery fish are often incompatible with the wild runs because they compete for feed. There are pressures to move toward increasing the percentage of hatchery fish. Wild salmon and steelhead require relatively pristine habitat for spawning. Hatcheries make habitat policy easier because the cement-lined "habitat" of a single hatchery can substitute for hundreds of miles of natural stream habitat.

Yet wild fish have qualities that hatchery fish do not. Wild runs constitute unique genetic resources that, over eons, have adapted to an extraordinary range of conditions. In most cases, the genetics are so complex that
fish biologists have only begun to understand them. The diversity of these
gene pools contrasts with the monocultures produced in hatcheries, which
can be eliminated by one epidemic. Further, wild fish, precisely because
they have had to survive in the wild, are stronger fish, a factor that weighs
mightily with sportfishers. The wild upriver bright chinooks and Idaho-
bound steelhead also taste better and carry brighter, more vivid colors. And
there are intangibles of wonder, and duties to the ages, that hit home when
a person sees and feels a run of wild fish coursing up through a mountain
current toward spawning grounds that have served for millennia. All of the
choices of economics, development, and energy come to bear, in one form
or another, on these wild animals.[71]

The basic decision to continue to revive the runs, with many of the costs
(about 3 percent to 6 percent of the BPA's budget) being borne by the rate
payers, is the right approach for many reasons, and we should hold firm to
it. The economic returns are widespread. Fishing towns along the Oregon
and Washington coasts are depressed and need a boost in the commercial
fishing economy. The benefits for commercial fishers also reach inland to
the Indian sites and up the coast to Canada and Alaska. The dollars
generated from sportfishing seem to be at least as great, with charter boat
fishing in the ocean and the larger rivers and with fishing from small boats
and by waders on hundreds of inland rivers all the way to the River of No
Return country in the interior of Idaho. Sportfishers are a key element in
the West's recreational economy, creating revenue for motels, gas stations,
restaurants, and many other businesses.

There are still other reasons for reviving the salmon and steelhead runs.
Expenditures for fish are justified to fulfill treaty obligations to Indian
tribes and to Canada. Even such a thing as the nutrients that the dying fish
leave for other animals and for the ground itself has come to matter, as it
ought to. We have even begun to acknowledge that we ought to care, and
care quite a bit, about the bold but vulnerable magnificence of the wild
Pacific salmon and steelhead. Last, it is not sentimentality but rather a
sense of social equity and an appreciation of the validity of the long view
that causes us to keep in mind the images of Wunn-o-ah-chi, Jim Yahtin,
and Yessessi, perhaps the one person who bore witness to the whole
extraordinary sweep of events. They, and what they saw and did and
believed, are fit reminders of the many different people and values that
must be taken into account before a society can make decisions that will
endure the scrutiny of the many other societies that will follow.

Chapter Six

Harvesting the April Rivers

About a mile north of Dulce, in the low mountains of northwestern New Mexico, the west-running Navajo River pushes down into a deep canyon. In some places, the walls are sheer rimrock faces; in others, the canyon sides are covered by steeply canted stands of spruce and fir studded with rocky outcrops. Tall, strong ponderosa pines rise up from benches and knolls. Toward the end of many days, a visitor in the flat bottom is likely to look west and see a red-purple iridescence light up the undersides of low stratocumulus clouds above the far "V" of the canyon.

Yet there is a disquieting aspect to the Navajo River Canyon. The river itself is neat and tidy, small and steady, all year long. Green grasses, almost lawns, come right up to the quiet river's edge. But it could not always have been this way, for the Navajo River had once done a great deal of work to carve its way through these rocks. Even today, you can see an old 200-foot-high gash in the canyon wall on the outside of an oxbow where raging springtime floods gouged out tons of earth, rocks, and trees and caused a massive landslide.

That was another river, not this one. Some people, however, remember the old river. Apaches do, because the canyon is on the ancestral homeland of the Jicarilla Apache Tribe. The Navajo River is the only year-round stream on the entire 750,000-acre reservation. An old man, with the dark skin and high cheekbones distinctive of his people, told me, "If you'd seen the river the way it used to be, it'd look way different."

This river is different because western rivers are not neat and tidy. Whereas rivers east of the 100th meridian are fed by reliable springs and rainfall, nearly all rivers in the arid West depend mainly on the melting of the

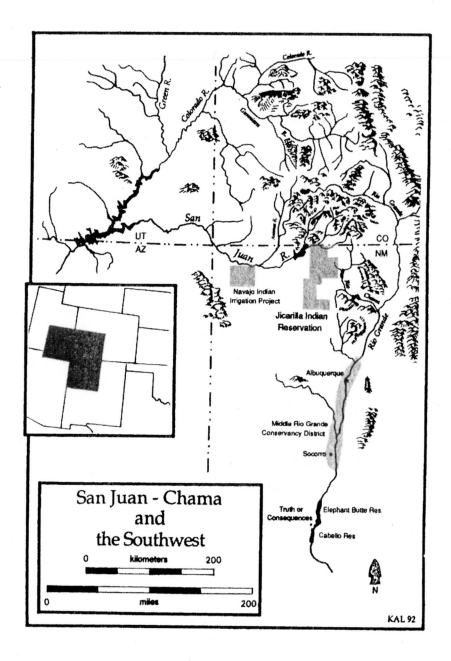

San Juan - Chama
and
the Southwest

0	kilometers	200

0	miles	200

KAL 92

N

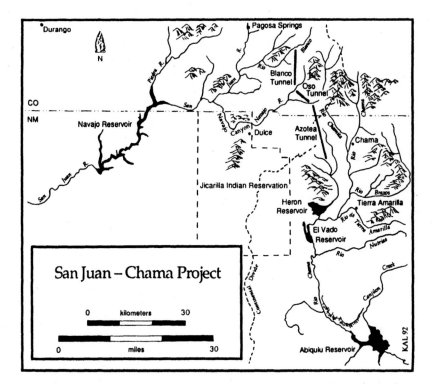

Durango

Pagosa Springs

N

CO
NM

Blanco
Tunnel

Oso
Tunnel

Navajo Reservoir

Chama

Dulce

Azotea
Tunnel

Jicarilla Indian Reservation

Heron
Reservoir

Tierra Amarilla

El Vado
Reservoir

Continental Divide

San Juan – Chama Project

0	kilometers	30

| 0 | miles | 30 |

Abiquiu Reservoir

KAL 92

mountain snowpacks. Most of their flow comes in a rush during the runoff of April, May, and June. In addition, the annual snowfalls fluctuate, often dramatically. The result is that western rivers are wildly inconstant, both month to month and year to year. The small creeks at the tops of watersheds—Camp Creek in central Oregon, for example—can be contained by their willows, sedges, and other vegetation. But not the large rivers that collect all of the feeder creeks. They rage in the spring, bringing down rocks, logs, and other debris, jumping to new channels and leaving sandbars in their wake. Grass does not get the chance to grow right up to the river, as it does in this canyon.

The reason for the tameness of the Navajo River lies higher up in the watershed, about 20 miles upstream. There, under Chama Peak and Banded Peak and other summits of the San Juan Mountains, which form part of the Continental Divide, concrete dams and collection facilities divert into tunnels most of the floodwaters from the Navajo River and its major tributary, the Little Navajo. Those waters join most of the flow of the Blanco River, which has been carried 14 miles from the north by a tunnel 8½ feet in diameter, constructed under the high country pine forests. The diverted waters from the three streams—which otherwise would flow west into the San Juan River and the Colorado River—are then combined and sent south and east into the Azotea Tunnel.

This deep, concrete-lined tunnel, a full 11 feet in diameter and bored 13 miles through the mountains, transports water under the Colorado–New Mexico border, under the Continental Divide itself, to Azotea Creek, a tributary of the Rio Chama in the Rio Grande watershed. The water is then dumped into the Heron Reservoir. Depending on release schedules, some water is released from Heron and stored in Abiquiu Reservoir on the Rio Chama and in Elephant Butte Reservoir far to the south on the mainstem Rio Grande. This operation, the San Juan–Chama Project, sends as much as 110,000 acre-feet of water each year from the San Juan watershed, which ultimately empties into the Pacific Ocean, to the Rio Grande, which eventually reaches the Gulf of Mexico in the Atlantic Ocean.

The San Juan–Chama Project, which has been in operation since 1972, is an engineering *tour de force*, and the miraculous accomplishments of the engineers are a big part of the seductive quality of this and other western water projects. To be sure, the San Juan–Chama Project has run into significant problems in its construction and operation. Two men died cutting the tunnels through the mountains, and many were seriously injured; at least two live on, more than twenty years later, paralyzed from their accidents. The diversion points have suffered from severe, unanticipated siltation and debris buildup; draglines and tractors work regularly, at a cost of $100,000 each year, to keep the system relatively free of sediment, rocks, and logs.

Still and all, this elaborate system of 27 miles of tunnels, each much taller than a person and bored through rugged terrain, almost defies comprehension. In the winter, when no water is run through the tunnels, a well-conditioned hiker would need two days to walk this subterranean route from the Pacific watershed to the Atlantic. The system is fully automated: the tunnel gates all raise and lower automatically according to the flow level in the streams. The full head of water that blasts out of the southeastern portal of Azotea Tunnel and engorges Azotea Creek is a thing to behold.

Last, leave no doubt about it, this state-of-the-art project moves a lot of water. An acre-foot of water covers an acre—roughly the area of a football field—to a depth of 1 foot, about 325,000 gallons in all. The annual flow of 110,000 acre-feet of water that San Juan–Chama can send through Azotea Tunnel is enough to put 50,000 acres of arid land into full crop production, enough to supply a city of 250,000 people or more, enough (if containing walls could somehow be built) to fill a football field to an elevation of 20 miles or to flood a full square mile of land to the height of a fifteen-story office building. From a technical standpoint, the San Juan–Chama Project is a marvel.[1]

The San Juan–Chama Project, however, has deep and abiding drawbacks. The project, like much western water development—including Derby Dam, discussed in chapter 1, which diverted water away from Pyramid Lake and the band of Paiute Indians—is an unsettling story that speaks directly to the limits of technical expertise, the treacherous allure of the grandiose solution, and the consequences that can unfold when the government opens its checkbook and closes its regulation manual.

Once across the Divide, most of the water literally evaporates. The city of Albuquerque, which holds the largest share of San Juan–Chama water, with 48,200 acre-feet, and five other municipalities possess water rights to a total of 56,000 acre-feet annually. But the cities have no current use for it. Albuquerque, for example, will not begin using San Juan–Chama water until 1995 at the earliest and will not employ its full allotment until 2020 or 2030. In the meantime, the water steams off the tops of reservoirs in the hot New Mexico sun.

New Mexico had two reasons for undertaking the San Juan–Chama Project, the bulk of which was subsidized by the federal government. The state wanted to ensure steady future supplies of water for the Rio Grande Valley, where 90 percent of the state's population resides. It is also clear that New Mexico was motivated by the "use it or lose it" mentality that has always driven western water developers to extract as much water as possible as quickly as possible lest it be appropriated by someone else. As Tom

Olson, former general counsel for the New Mexico Interstate Stream Commission, explained in an interview, "We did not want to fall victim under the 'rocking chair theory'—which happens when you sit on your front porch in a rocking chair and just watch the river flow away." The city of Albuquerque made this rush to drain the rivers explicit in 1971, the year before San Juan water was first transported under the Divide, when it invoked the specter of "wasting" water by letting it run downhill to Arizona or, worse yet, California: "Under no circumstances should the city's water be allowed to flow down the Colorado to be used in other states."[2]

New Mexico's insistence on transporting water from the San Juan River affects people other than federal taxpayers and anonymous water users in Phoenix, Tucson, and southern California. This surely includes the members of the Jicarilla Apache Tribe, an Athabascan people who came to what is now northern New Mexico and southern Colorado between 1300 and 1500 A.D. They were superb hunters and followed game, living in seasonal villages over a large landscape. After the United States acquired the area from Mexico in 1848 by the Treaty of Guadalupe Hidalgo, the fiercely independent tribe began a forty-year period of military skirmishes and land negotiations with the United States. In every case, the local citizenry opposed permanent reservations for the Jicarilla Apaches and lobbied to overturn negotiated agreements between the tribe and federal representatives. Treaties were signed in 1851 and 1853, but the Senate never ratified them. Substantial reservations were created by presidential executive orders in 1874 and 1880, but the orders were rescinded. For a time during the 1880s, the Jicarilla Apaches were forced to settle on the reservation of the Mescalero Apaches, a situation acceptable to neither tribe.

Then, on February 11, 1887, President Grover Cleveland signed an executive order affirming an agreement between tribal leaders and local federal officials that recognized the high country reservation that the Jicarilla Apaches own and occupy today. As the tribe's historian observed, the Jicarilla Apaches "had finally found a permanent home where the government could reasonably assure them of noninterference from the whites."[3]

In the century since the executive order, the Jicarilla Apaches have been battered by various aspects of federal Indian policy but have managed a remarkable balancing act. Due to their geographic remoteness and traditional sense of independence, they have kept much of their culture intact. They also are an adaptive people and, since the 1960s, have engaged in substantial economic development to improve conditions on the reservation. The Jicarillas have successfully worked their oil and gas reserves and built a shopping center and two motels. The tribe also established the Jicarilla Game and Fish Department to manage its wildlife for recreation purposes. The hunting is outstanding—elk, mule deer, wild turkey, and bear abound in the mountains and canyons on the northern half of the reservation. Visiting hunters pay hefty license fees to the tribe, stay in tribal motels, and generally contribute to the reservation economy.

Tribal development requiring water is another matter. There are several mountain lakes for fishing, but as noted, the Navajo River is the only perennial river on the reservation. On paper, there was no problem. The Jicarilla Apaches had an unimpeachable legal right, superior to that of Albuquerque or any other participant in the San Juan–Chama Project, to Navajo River water. Further, the tribe already had been making good use of the water before the San Juan–Chama Project ever went on line—the Jicarilla Apaches had developed a prosperous recreational fishery in the scenic Navajo River Canyon for native cutthroat and rainbow trout. After the project started up, the river was too low and warm to support a viable fishery. Of course, the tribe also had lost the diverted 110,000 acre-feet of water for irrigation to grow crops.

The Jicarilla Apaches took their case to federal court and obtained a seemingly historic decision. In 1981, a federal appeals court ruled that Albuquerque was illegally wasting San Juan–Chama water by simply letting it evaporate. The judges also found that the city's asserted use of the interbasin water for recreational purposes in Rio Chama and Rio Grande reservoirs was not an authorized "beneficial use" of water.

The Jicarilla Apache Tribe's hopes of keeping the water on its side of the Divide were quickly dashed. Within five months, the "iron triangle" — made up of western state water agencies; well-placed western members of Congress; and the building agencies, the Bureau of Reclamation and the Army Corps of Engineers—had gone to work. By December 1981, Congress had agreed to pass a law overriding the court opinion and approving the operation of the San Juan–Chama Project.[4]

The San Juan–Chama Project is tied to the tangled history of water development in the whole Colorado River basin, the region where extractive water use has been most keenly and bitterly contested. The basin includes parts of seven states and encompasses one-twelfth of the continental United States. Its water is distributed in an even broader sphere, far outside of the basin: to Los Angeles and San Diego; to Salt Lake City; to Denver and to Colorado's irrigated farmlands on the South Platte River, 200 miles northeast of Denver; and, as we have seen, to Albuquerque and Elephant Butte Reservoir far to the south.

Even before the turn of the century, it had become apparent that Los Angeles's crusade for water, coupled with the demands of big agriculture, might tie up the Colorado River. Smaller states were determined to protect themselves. In 1922, the states of the Colorado River basin signed an interstate compact, duly ratified by Congress. The Colorado River Compact did not allocate water to any specific state, but it did guarantee a supply of water to the slower-growing upper basin states—Wyoming, Utah, Colorado, and New Mexico (New Mexico is considered an upper basin state because almost all of its Colorado River water comes from the San Juan, which empties into the main-stem Colorado above Lee's Ferry, fixed by the 1922 compact as the demarcation point between the upper and lower basins). The idea was to divide the river equally between the upper and lower basins, putting a cap on extractions by Nevada, Arizona, and, especially, California.

Knowledge gained since the 1922 compact has shown that the upper basin states had been inadvertently snookered in one respect. During the compact talks, the negotiators assumed that the watershed produced at least 15 million acre-feet of water each year. The Colorado River Compact, however, had been negotiated during a wet cycle. We have since learned from the flows of later low-water years, plus the evidence of hundreds of years of flows established by sophisticated tests based on tree-ring analyses, that the average annual flow is more like 13 million acre-feet. The 1922 compact, however, had not actually been written in terms of guaranteeing each basin an equal quantity of water. Rather, the agreement (looking to the presumed 15 million acre-feet each year) required the upper basin to deliver, based on a ten-year average, 7.5 million acre-feet annually. Given the actual flows, this left the upper states with less than 6 million acre-feet. In spite of this shortfall, the upper basin states had acquired needed certainty, a congressionally approved share of the river.[5]

A quarter of a century later, the upper basin states divided among themselves the waters due to them under the Colorado River Compact. By the Upper Basin Compact of 1948, Colorado (whose mountain snowpacks produce most of the flow) received 51.75 percent, while Utah and Wyoming were allocated shares of 23 percent and 14 percent, respectively. New Mexico's entitlement was 11.25 percent. Using scaled-down estimates of 5.8 million acre-feet for the total upper basin allocation, New Mexico's share amounted to 647,000 acre-feet annually. Congress ratified the compact in 1949.

New Mexico promptly went to work on obtaining water projects to realize its share of the Colorado River. State officials knew well that the Jicarilla and Navajo tribes had powerful legal and equitable claims to the lion's share of the San Juan. In 1947, during the negotiation of the Upper Basin Compact, the federal representative had made it clear that the Navajos and Jicarilla Apaches had huge, legally supportable claims under the 1908 *Winters* case to the waters of the Colorado and the San Juan, estimating that irrigation projects for the two tribes would require a diversion of

959,000 acre-feet annually, with a consumptive loss to the stream of 367,000 acre-feet each year (much irrigation water returns to the stream by seepage after diversion, so consumptive use is considerably less than the actual diversion). This amount was more than half of New Mexico's share of the Colorado. New Mexico's leaders, like other advocates of water development in the West, saw the tribes as adversaries rather than state citizens, even though the Navajo Tribe, easily the nation's largest tribe in both population and land, had a significant part of its reservation in New Mexico, and the entire Jicarilla Indian Reservation was within the state.[6]

The Bureau of Indian Affairs began studies for a Navajo Indian Irrigation Project (NIIP) on the San Juan as soon as Congress approved the Upper Basin Compact in 1949. In 1950, the agency recommended that it be built. New Mexico responded that it would not support the NIIP, even though all of the land was in New Mexico, unless the San Juan–Chama Project were included as part of the package.

By the mid-1950s, the NIIP and the San Juan–Chama Project had been caught up in basinwide development plans. Fueled by both the increased stability furnished by the 1948 compact and the post–World War II boom in the West, developers pushed to finalize long-proposed major dams and reservoirs in the upper basin to provide water storage for irrigation, power generation, and urban development. The billion-dollar Colorado River Water Storage Project Act, passed in 1956, authorized four major storage units: Glen Canyon Dam on the main-stem Colorado, Flaming Gorge Reservoir on the Green River, the Wayne N. Aspinall Storage Unit (consisting of three dams) on the Gunnison River, and Navajo Dam on the San Juan River. In addition to these megaprojects, which can store 34 million acre-feet of water, more than two and a half times the annual flow of the Colorado River, the 1956 act also authorized eleven participating projects. Although it was expected that some water from Navajo Dam would be targeted for Navajo irrigation lands, the NIIP and San Juan–Chama were not authorized as participating projects in 1956. Nevertheless, New Mexico had obtained a good deal of mileage from the needs of the Navajos by using the obligation to the Indians as a main justification for New Mexico projects. As of 1956, the massive Navajo Dam had been authorized, and both the NIIP and the San Juan–Chama Project had been designated as priority projects.[7]

Construction of Navajo Dam in the rugged upper reaches of the San Juan River moved quickly. The reservoir site, which took in 23 miles of river, would inundate the traditional Hispanic farming and ranching communities of Rosa, Arboles, Rio de los Pinos, and Los Martinez. Community life was shattered, and there was no attempt to relocate the communities as socioeconomic units. The government paid $125 per acre for irrigated lands, but the Hispanic people soon found that prices for comparable lands in the area had gone up to $600 per acre. Nevertheless, Navajo Dam was built and the river plugged, and water began to back up inexorably into the old communities. There were no choices. As Frances Swadesh has explained:

> The final exodus took years, beginning at Los Martinez and the ranches on the Rio de los Pinos, continuing upriver until Rosa and Arboles were finally emptied of their population in 1962. By 1960, only one-third of the population of Rosa on both sides of the river remained in residence. Most who remained were aged people and a few families that sought to fight the low rate of compensation for their condemned homes and lands.[8]

The San Juan–Chama Project and the NIIP were authorized by Congress in 1962. The trans-Divide project moved swiftly. San Juan River water began to flow into Rio Chama in 1972, and the entire project, including diversion works in one basin and reservoir facilities in the other, was completed in 1976. The Navajos, however, learned that congressional authorization of a project is one thing and appropriation of funds to build it is another.

The Navajo Indian Irrigation Project was squeezed in a number of ways. The NIIP was originally authorized for a diversion of 508,000 acre-feet to water 110,000 acres. In the late 1960s, however, the Bureau of Reclamation concluded that the diversion could be reduced to 370,000 acre-feet by conserving water through the use of modern sprinkler systems and that the total water consumed could be lowered from 252,000 to 226,000 acre-feet. Perhaps the savings of water would be achieved, but as historian Ira Clark observed of a theme that has played throughout western water development, the calculation was "a numbers game" in which "there was no reliable evidence to support this conclusion."[9]

Even more fundamentally, the NIIP moved much more slowly than its companion project. Wayne Aspinall, chairman of the House Interior Committee when the NIIP was authorized in 1966, had even less truck with Indian water projects than he did with water projects from states other than his native Colorado. Although, as Congressman John Kyl of Iowa observed, the San Juan–Chama Project could never have passed "without the glamorizing" effect of the NIIP, Aspinall succeeded in separating the two projects for appropriations purposes, scheduling San Juan–Chama for the powerhouse Bureau of Reclamation and funding the NIIP through the Bureau of Indian Affairs, the weak sister agency in the Interior Department.

The NIIP inched along from the beginning. By the time the San Juan–

Chama Project was fully operational in 1976, the NIIP was just one-tenth completed. Today, only 50 percent of potential NIIP acres have been brought under irrigation. In 1988, an Interior Department study recommended that the NIIP be terminated at 60,000 acres, just more than half of its intended size. Although the recommendation was not adopted *per se*, the department has set up a process to set a "termination point" for the NIIP.[10]

The NIIP has been plagued by financial difficulties. Some of this is due to a lack of management expertise in the tribe, especially during the formative years of the late 1960s and the 1970s. Management problems were compounded by the Interior Department's decision to employ high-head sprinkler irrigation; this necessitated a change from a project composed of family plots, as originally contemplated, to a full-scale agribusiness enterprise. The shift to a corporate operation in turn caused cultural dislocation as non-Indians moved into positions of responsibility and as small-plot Navajo farmers were moved farther from the land. The San Juan River projects all passed Congress because they had been wrapped in the Indian blanket, but the Navajos were left with an ill-fitting suit of clothes.[11]

The Jicarilla Apaches remained completely on the outside. During the complex negotiations over the division of San Juan water, the tribe was given assurances of a small irrigation project, but the Bureau of Reclamation later turned the project down as lacking economic feasibility. As to San Juan–Chama, the Apaches objected as early as 1958 but to no avail: two-thirds of the water of the Navajo River, once used by the tribe for its recreation-based fishery in the canyon and coveted also by the Jicarillas for farming, is sent under the mountains, much of it "used" for evaporation.[12]

Perhaps the ultimate irony of the San Juan–Chama Project is not just that Albuquerque and the other cities have yet to use the imported water. More than that, they may not need it in the foreseeable future. Albuquerque's municipal water conservation program is rudimentary at best, and its low prices encourage wasteful water use. Further, the time will soon come when western states will turn, in a serious way, to the many ramifications of the fact that 90 percent of all western water is still used for irrigated agriculture. So much water is used inefficiently in agriculture that minimal waste reduction on the farms can free up substantial supplies for the cities.[13]

One example is especially telling. As shown in the map on page 220, Albuquerque is located within the boundaries of the Middle Rio Grande Conservancy District, a sprawling irrigation district that extends along the Rio Grande for 150 river miles. Almost all farming in the MRGCD is done by flood irrigation (simply releasing water from the ditches onto the fields) rather than by more efficient systems such as sprinkler irrigation. The crudeness of flood irrigation is compounded by the refusal of irrigators in the MRGCD to take precautions to save water in other respects. One Bureau of Reclamation employee said in an interview that "they will run a full ditch whether they need it or not." Irrigators apply so much excess water that farmlands in the district, located in hot, arid country, have begun to suffer from "waterlogging."

Wasteful uses in the MRGCD are directly related to Albuquerque, the San Juan–Chama Project, the Jicarilla Apaches, and other water uses across the Divide. In 1987, a study by Morrison-Knudsen Engineers, Inc., a private consulting firm hired by the Bureau of Reclamation, found that a 5 percent increase in efficiency would eliminate the waterlogging, thus providing important benefits to the irrigators. The savings would be great, and the sacrifice would be modest: according to the Morrison-Knudsen report, "an improvement of five percent in system efficiency would salvage up to 70,000 acre-feet annually. The costs associated with attaining this efficiency improvement should be minimal." This annual savings of 70,000 acre-feet is far more than Albuquerque receives from the San Juan–Chama Project; more, in fact, than all current usage of water within the city of Albuquerque. But the improvements have not been made within the MRGCD, so the saved water cannot be made available to the city. Instead, the MRGCD, Albuquerque, and the Bureau of Reclamation continue to demand that that "urgently needed" water be tunneled under the Continental Divide.[14]

It is not my point to attempt to prove whether the big development projects in the San Juan watershed were actually needed. But these episodes are fundamentally unsettling, for there may well have been other ways, better paths never explored. There was a lack of sharpness, a failure to look precisely at all of the costs, financial, social, and environmental. And all the while, the waters of the Navajo River, once bound for the canyon on the Jicarilla Indian Reservation, rise from the surface of the Heron, Abiquiu, and Elephant Butte reservoirs at the rate of 4 feet per year.

Water development in the American West, as with the San Juan–Chama Project, bears the bright and ironic imprint of the prodigal waste of an assertedly precious resource. The San Juan–Chama Project also demonstrates the other elements of the essential pattern: the single-minded pressure to develop water for extractive uses; the competition among states over interstate rivers; extensive federal subsidies for private users; far-reaching environmental impacts; the subversion of established Indian rights; the raids by cities on rural areas; the blunting of normal market incentives; and the inexorable drive toward bigger and grander projects. As with the other lords of yesterday, the story of the dominant ideas is a story of good law gone bad, of rules developed for common people—for Gifford Pinchot's "little man"—being co-opted by big business and big government, with a consequent destruction of the ideals behind the original ideas. In the case of water, the original ideas belonged to unnamed miners and farmers and to two national figures, John Wesley Powell and Elwood Mead.

"A Universal Sense of Necessity and Propriety"

Western water development has proceeded on two different levels. The first, highly visible, involved the big, mostly federally subsidized dams and transbasin diversion systems, such as the San Juan–Chama Project. The second, much less visible but of the same magnitude in the aggregate, has been the millions of small dams, stream diversions, and groundwater pumps of individual miners, farmers, agricultural districts, corporations, towns, and cities under the no-holds-barred water policies of the western states. The two strains share the same origins, complement each other, and, taken together, have amounted to perhaps the most far-flung natural resource development program the nation has ever undertaken.

Early western water law was symbiotic with hardrock mining law. This was natural, since from 1848 on water was the engine for the mining camps. The early-arriving miners used mining pans to work placer deposits, in which the gold was found in loose soil and gravel. The gold-bearing ore was heavier than the sand and gravel in which it was found. A skillful miner could fill the pan with water and potential pay dirt, swirl the pan in a circular fashion, and slosh the water and gravel over the sloped sides of the pan. The heavier gold would remain in the bottom of the pan. The miner would then rework the discarded material, hoping to recover traces of gold.

The same principles were used for increasingly larger operations. Long Toms and other forms of sluices, some of them hundreds of feet long, were sloped wooden chutes with cleats in the bottom. Gravel was shoveled into the upper end and forced down the sluice by water. With luck, pieces of gold would be caught in the cleats and the dirt and sand would be washed out. By the late 1850s and the 1860s, the size and efficiency of the operations multiplied many times over as hydraulic mining moved into the gold country. A head of water pressure was built up and forced into large fire-fighting hoses. A stream of water from the hoses, which had enough power to kill a man, was then trained on a hillside. The process was so effective that in a matter of minutes, the force of the water could literally tear out tons of earth, which would then be worked through sluices. These were the same hydraulic mining operations that California finally banned in the 1880s because countless thousands of tons of rocks and soil had cascaded down into the rivers and laid waste to the salmon runs in the Sacramento River system. In the meantime, however, the big hoses served the mining industry's ends beautifully. As mining became ever more industrial, milling operations required large amounts of water.

Many mining camps were located in rugged country far from any watercourse. They all had need for water and required the elaborate, serpentine ditch systems that even today wind their way through the foothills and mountains of western states. These ingenious conduits wrapped around hillsides, moving from one watershed to another, often seeming to run uphill to serve high-elevation camps. In reality, of course, amateur engineers, predecessors to the professionals who would remake the West, played the law of gravity to a T.

The miners, just as they did with the mining laws, developed their own water laws before any state or federal court or legislature spoke. As might be expected, the rules for water looked a lot like the rules for minerals.

The miners used a simple, primitive rule of capture for water: "first in time, first in right." Some scholars believe that the idea was borrowed from Mexico, where many of the earlier miners had previously labored, but it is at least as likely that they used their own inventiveness and common sense—reinforced, no doubt, by the equity and inevitability in the cold-eyed glare of a bearded, pistoled miner who was already hard at work.

This rule of priority based on time amounted to a direct rejection of riparian water law, which applied in England and the eastern United States. Riparianism requires the sharing of a watercourse by all of the landowners bordering it, regardless of whether a water user had ever put water to work previously. That made no sense at all to these miners. If two men, or companies, came in and diverted a whole stream, so be it. If just one took the whole stream, so be it. They needed it; they depended on it; they had rights to it. In one sense: absolute anarchy. In another, one that made much better logic in those days: absolute order. In a mining society, how could a person operate without being able to rely on a stable possession of the claim and the water necessary to operate it?

The rules paralleled those for mining in other respects. The due diligence rule that required a miner actively to work a claim operated with equal force as to water; otherwise, the water right was abandoned. (This applied only to the seasons when the water was actually diverted, so abandonment did not run, for example, during winter months, when mining, and water use, was impractical.) In the meantime, as with hardrock minerals, water users had the right—a vested property right, like title to land—to keep using the water. Of course, the water, like the minerals, was free for the taking. In real terms, to whom would payment be made in those frontier times? After the initial appropriation, however, the water right, like a mining claim, could be leased or sold. It was property—from the very moment it was first put to use. First in time, first in right.

The water laws of the mining camps first reached the courts for a definitive opinion in the famous California Supreme Court case *Irwin v. Phillips*, handed down in 1855. The case arose on the South Fork of Poor Man's Creek, in the California gold country not far from James Marshall's initial discovery. Matthew Irwin had arrived first, in 1851, and had appropriated water both for his own diggings and for sale to other miners. Robert Phillips and his colleagues arrived several months later, only to learn that they had, as the court opinion delicately put it, "selected the bank of a stream from which the water had been already turned." That is, Irwin already had taken the entire stream out of its bed and into his diversion canal.[15]

The California Supreme Court had a tough case in some respects. Most notably, one of the state of California's first statutes, adopted in 1850, strongly suggested that the English rule of riparian water law, not prior appropriation, should be the law of California. It provided: "The Common Law of England, so far as it is not repugnant to or inconsistent with the Constitution of the United States, or the Constitution or laws of the State of California, shall be the rule of decision in all the Courts of this State." To be sure, there was no square fit with riparianism because the common-law rule recognized water rights only in owners of lands along watercourses, and Phillips (like nearly all miners in the early days) was attempting to mine on public lands owned by the United States. Nevertheless, no state or federal law had yet been enacted on the question of water rights, and in the abstract, a court might have been expected to grant the latecomer Phillips some amount of water by analogizing his location on the creek to ownership of the land.[16]

But not the highest court in a new state that had become a state precisely because of its gold and the water necessary to process the mineral. The justices knew full well the rules of the camps:

> Among these the most important are the rights of miners to be protected in the possession of their selected localities, and the rights of those who, by prior appropriation, have taken the waters from their natural beds, and by costly artificial works have conducted them for miles over mountains and ravines, to supply the necessities of gold diggers.

One imagines that Matthew Irwin and other miners might have gagged at the court's use of the Latin phrase *qui prior est in tempore potior est in jure* to describe what inhabitants of the gold fields simply called "first in time, first in right." Still, miners of the 1850s, and we latter-day observers as well, can surely appreciate the inexorable social, economic, equitable, and pragmatic forces that drove this 1855 court to approve the miners' own doctrine of prior appropriation. It was, as the opinion put it, a matter of "a universal sense of necessity and propriety."[17]

Prior appropriation swept across the West. The newly arriving farmers and ranchers, like the miners, depended on it. As in California, courts in other states followed actual usage on the ground. The leading decision to bring the doctrine into the courts of the Rocky Mountain states was *Coffin v. Left Hand Ditch Company*, decided by the Colorado Supreme Court in 1882, six years after statehood. Two irrigators had squared off (George Coffin had "torn out" part of Left Hand Ditch Company's dam and diversion works), and Coffin, the junior appropriator, had perhaps an even stronger argument than Robert Phillips in seeking to bring riparian law to the West. Coffin owned farmland on the lower reaches of South Saint Vrain Creek, and Left Hand, the senior water user, had diverted the water out of the upper reaches of South Saint Vrain and transported it by canal into the Boulder Creek watershed. Thus, this was the first reported case to rule on the legality of an out-of-watershed diversion, a practice common in the West but roundly rejected by riparian law. Further, Coffin could point to Colorado statutes in force at the time of the dispute (although later repealed) that seemed flatly to ratify riparian rights.[18]

But Left Hand was senior, and Coffin was junior. The court spoke at length about the adoption of prior appropriation by the settlers of the arid West, twice using the phrase "imperative necessity" to describe the "first in time" rule. Prior appropriation was the law of the courts because it had already become the law of the miners and farmers.

Later developments in the prior appropriation doctrine added other provisions that were inherent in, or consistent with, the intensely utilitarian objectives of the mining camps. To obtain a water right, an appropriator had to "divert" the water—physically take it out of a watercourse, which included running it through turbines to generate electrical power. In addition, water had to be put to a "beneficial use." Beneficial use, as defined first by courts and later by state legislatures, merely ratified the customary rules of western water users and was not nearly as broad as it might sound. To rise to the level of being beneficial, a use had to be consumptive, usually extractive. The list was limited to mining, agriculture, industrial, municipal, domestic, stock-raising, and hydropower. Among other things, these rules meant that in-stream uses could not qualify as appropriations. They were not diversions. Nor did using water—a stream, a lake, or a waterfall—to protect wildlife, to swim in or boat on, or to enjoy for its beauty make for a beneficial use. In-stream uses were doubly disqualified.

Early on, the rubric of beneficial use also came to encompass the idea that water, once validly diverted and put to use, could not be wasted. But the language decrying waste was mostly theoretical. It was always difficult to police waste, and in some cases to define it, so the prohibition against waste, although an announced principle in the cases and statutes of every western state, has been enforced sporadically at best.

This was the classic prior appropriation doctrine, and it was adopted nearly wholesale in every western state. As late as the mid-1970s, water law and policy were essentially monolithic throughout the region. To be sure, there were variations. Following the lead of Elwood Mead and Wyoming, discussed in the following section, states set up agencies to administer prior appropriation rights, except Colorado, which granted its water rights through the courts. As we shall see, however, these procedural changes did little to affect the traditional workings of prior appropriation. Beginning in 1915, Oregon had withdrawn from appropriation the streams above some of its scenic waterfalls. California, Washington, Oregon, and the states along the 100th meridian recognized some riparian rights along with appropriation rights before abolishing or sharply limiting these vestiges of riparianism. There were other differences. But in the larger scheme, such exceptions were wrinkles at best. The classic prior appropriation doctrine governed nearly all water usage in the West.

Prior appropriation had numerous premises, corollaries, and consequences that went well beyond the catchword "first in time, first in right." Only certain uses were allowed, and only the states could grant water rights. State laws not only defined the preferred water rights but also actively promoted and subsidized them—and they successfully enlisted the federal government in the cause. All state constitutions or statutes declared water to be public, but nearly all water was appropriated for private gain. Even superficially public uses had heavy private overtones. The crusades of Los Angeles, Denver, Phoenix, and Albuquerque for water in fact have been mainly the crusades of forward-looking land developers who had staked out subdivisions on the plains and deserts and who needed ample and reliable municipal water supplies to complete their ventures. In all cases, water developers had free call on the resource. Colorado announced it in its constitution, but all states practiced it: "The right to divert . . . shall never be denied." Nearly all western water was zoned for preferred consumptive uses.[19]

Prior appropriation made entirely good sense in the context in which it arose. Irwin and the Left Hand Ditch Company both should have prevailed, as they did. But the law made by them and their colleagues in the mines was tailor-made to be pushed into wholly different contexts and distorted. Western water was there—free for the taking but property once taken—for those who could find a way to get to it first.

"The Soil Is Our Salvation"

The early two-party court decisions laid the foundation, legal and intellectual, for western water development, but most of the work still lay ahead. The last twenty-five years of the nineteenth century and the first decade of the twentieth century was a time of intense, bright-eyed idealism, driven by the Jeffersonian ideal of filling up the "empty" western half of the nation. By the end of this era, which spawned the reclamation movement, the structure of one of the largest public works programs ever accomplished had been put firmly in place. The two dominant figures were John Wesley Powell and Elwood Mead, who initially shared a common vision for the future of the West. In time, Powell's urgings would largely be rejected while Mead altered his practices, if not his whole dream, to oversee a federal reclamation department that operated on a scale and ideology that all but obliterated the spirit that had initially infused the reclamation movement.

Major John Wesley Powell captured the public imagination with his daring expedition down the Colorado River in 1869, the first such adventure in recorded history. In 1875, the bearded, one-armed Powell, by then in charge of the Geographical and Geological Survey for the Rocky Mountain region, published a colorful, widely read account of his river journey and achieved considerable national prominence. But it is his "Report on the Lands of the Arid Region of the United States," released in 1878, that has caused Powell's name to be linked regularly with words like "visionary" and "prophetic."[20]

Powell's government-sponsored report on the West was released at a time of heightened intensity. The California gold rush was still fresh in the public memory, and the great Homestead Act had been passed in 1862. United States citizens, indeed people the world over, saw the West as the place of places for free land and a new, better chance. So that the nation could meet the call of the westward expansion, Powell urged reforms in the public land laws to permit an orderly settlement based on realistic expectations. His reasoning was both imbued with a desire to see a flourishing agrarian society and leavened with a practicality rooted in his knowledge of the region. Wallace Stegner, author of the classic, Pulitzer Prize–winning biography *Beyond the Hundredth Meridian: John Wesley Powell and the Second Opening of the West*, assessed Powell's philosophy in the 1878 report in these terms:

> Almost alone among his contemporaries, Powell recognized the opportunity that lay there to be seized, but already pulling away,

already beginning to vanish. Almost alone among his contemporaries he looked at the Arid Region and saw neither desert nor garden. What he saw was the single compelling unity that the region possessed: except in local islanded areas its rainfall was less than twenty inches a year, and twenty inches he took . . . to be the minimum needed to support agriculture without irrigation. . . .

He saw also the variety, caused by altitude, latitude, topography, climate, soil, that characterized the West in contrast to the essential unity of the Middle West and East. A state like Iowa, nearly one hundred per cent arable, was one thing; a state like Utah, where the arable land was probably less than three per cent of the total area, was another. Land in Utah lay at altitudes varying from three thousand to over thirteen thousand feet. Much of it was too high for crops, much of it too stony, almost all of it too dry. For Utah, and for the whole arid region of which it provided the type, it was essential to differentiate the uses to which land could be put. For several years he had had his crews designating lands they surveyed as mineral, coal, timber, pasturage, or irrigable lands, and he knew that each of these would require different laws and perhaps different kinds of survey.[21]

Powell expounded, in commonsense terms, on the laws and policies that would be required. Much of his work focused on farming and water. The statutory size of the basic homestead unit, 160 acres (640 acres for some designated desert lands), was absolutely wrong. For irrigated areas, a 160-acre homestead was too large. A family could thrive on 80 acres and could not realistically farm any larger unit. For areas lacking irrigation, 160 acres was too small, woefully inadequate. Settlers should be allowed 4 sections—4 square miles, totaling 2560 acres—to have a fair chance at ranching.

Opening the West for stable agrarian societies would be, Powell warned, no easy task. It must be planned out. And it must be supported by government—the federal government, since the states lacked the resources. Many large reservoirs were needed, and they should be low-elevation reservoirs, close to the more valuable low valley lands with the best soils and mildest climates. Powell also concluded that the box-shaped subdivisions of the rectangular survey system did not fit the West, which could best be reorganized by watersheds. Square-edged state boundaries were arbitrary and should be redrawn. Otherwise, lengthy battles among states over shared watercourses were inevitable.

Powell also saw irrigation in social terms and believed that steps should be taken to prevent water monopolies. He proposed two things. The government should sponsor local cooperative unions of farmers. Also, water rights should be attached to the land and should not be made available for sale independent of land title. These safeguards would keep water in the hands of small farmers and their families.

To use terms that would soon come into vogue, the report was populist. It also was progressive. Powell had pre-Pinchoted Gifford Pinchot. Although the Reclamation Act of 1902 would ultimately be played out in ways foreign to Powell's vision, the act was born in 1878 when Interior Secretary Carl Shurz ordered the Government Printing Office to print John Wesley Powell's "Arid Lands" report.

Elwood Mead grew up in Indiana, gained degrees in engineering and agriculture, and in 1883 moved west to join the faculty at Colorado Agricultural College in Fort Collins. Mead, who had been influenced by Powell's report, saw the human side of the agrarian movement. He met regularly with the Grangers and other farmers' rights advocates and saw a big British-controlled ditch company cut off water from small Colorado farmers when they objected to the high fees. Mead also worked for the state engineer, walking irrigation ditches and gauging water flows. Among other things, he found little correlation between the actual capacity of the ditches and the water rights in the court decrees; the official records, approved by the courts in perfunctory hearings based on testimony of the water users themselves, showed much higher quantities of water than the ditches could actually carry. Mead became a staunch opponent of monopolies and a staunch advocate of the need for expert administrative staffing at the state level to oversee water use.[22]

Mead, who had been appointed to a professorship in irrigation engineering, apparently the first such position in the country, became increasingly involved in water policy in Colorado but grew frustrated with the state's refusal to accept his proposals for state administration of water rights. At the invitation of Wyoming's governor, Mead moved to Laramie in 1888, just before statehood, to serve as the first territorial engineer. Mead was an important figure in the Wyoming constitutional convention and was the principal author of the document's provisions on water. Most notably, the new constitution denominated water a public resource, stating, "The water of all natural streams, springs, lakes or other collections of still water, within the boundaries of the state, are hereby declared to be the property of the state." The 1890 constitution also mandated the creation of a Board of Control and a state engineer.[23]

Mead saw that the constitutionally declared public interest in water was incorporated into the Wyoming statutes. He drafted detailed laws to implement the idea that water was the property of the state. No longer could a user acquire a water right simply by diverting water. Wyoming became the first state to declare that appropriators could obtain rights only through a permit issued by the state engineer (the first, of course, being Elwood

Mead). The new code also contained detailed procedures for monitoring and enforcement by the state engineer of all water rights in the state. To ensure comprehensive judicial rulings rather than the existing mélange of random two-party lawsuits, which could and did lead to wildly inconsistent rulings, Mead invented the general stream adjudication. The Board of Control would give notice to all water users in a basin, call them in to an administrative hearing, and establish a complete schedule of rights in the basin—complete with priority dates, user, type of use, and, it was assumed, water quantities that comported, more or less, with the size of the ditch. The final ruling would be appealable to the courts.

Not only that, Mead's new legal structure inaugurated another feature designed to limit the absolute control of private users over Wyoming's waters. Water rights permits would not be issued as a matter of course on a "first in time" basis. Rather, the state engineer could deny requested permits if they were "detrimental to the public welfare." This revolutionary provision would, in theory, place the public interest squarely between water developers and the public's water. The Mead system would protect the small, common farmer and prevent any corporate takeover of Wyoming water:

I believe that any system which puts the values of a farm at the mercy of a corporation, whether its headquarters be in London or at home, is certain to work hardships and injustice, and because under no circumstances should an article, which belongs to all alike, and comes as a gift from the bounty of Nature, be made a subject of barter and sale.[24]

The Wyoming idea spread. Nebraska adopted an administrative system in 1895. Then there was a rash of new systems just after the turn of the century. Nevada, Utah, and Idaho adopted Wyoming-style administrative systems. In 1905, Washington considered a closely related model drafted by Morris Bien, although reform legislation was not enacted until 1917. The New Mexico Territory adopted a "Bien code" in 1907, and nearly all states on or west of the 100th meridian had acted by 1919, when Arizona adopted its code.[25]

It is worthwhile to put this drive toward administrative control of water in perspective. Then, as now, westerners were conservative, especially when it came to establishing bureaucracies. All of the western states were young. The six northern states (Washington, Idaho, Montana, Wyoming, and the Dakotas) all had to wait until either 1889 or 1890 to achieve statehood, and Utah joined the Union in 1896. Arizona and New Mexico remained in territorial status until 1912. The states were also small—the rule of thumb for admission during most of the late nineteenth century was a population of 60,000 citizens. Even at the federal level, administrative processes were in their infancy. It bears remembering that the 1887 creation of the Interstate Commerce Commission, the oldest of the "big seven" agencies, is considered the dawn of the modern federal bureaucracy. But the Federal Trade Commission was not chartered until 1914, and the remaining "big seven" agencies were not established until the New Deal. In the West, the move toward administrative agencies of any size had not even begun to emerge at the turn of the twentieth century.

Not so for water, which was deemed important enough to require its own administrative structure. But western water agencies were unique and, by today's lights, curious institutions. At the outset, the nature of the laws that the offices were charged to uphold cause a person to wonder exactly how a regulatory agency would fit in. The "first in time, first in right" rule of capture at the core of classic prior appropriation was *laissez-faire* policy in the extreme; public resources were thrown open to virtually unfettered private exploitation. Substantive water law embodied much of the social Darwinism in vogue during the late nineteenth century.

Accordingly, this government overlay was in no remote sense a regulatory system. The statutes setting up the water agencies made essentially no change in the underlying body of law. The new agencies existed solely for the purposes of issuing water rights according to the established *laissez-faire* doctrine and, after issuance, for enforcing the rights of record. Despite statutory protestations against waste, state engineers left the use of water to the rights holders, so long as the water was put to one of the prescribed beneficial uses. Despite code provisions allowing the state engineer to deny applications on the basis of the public interest (or the "public welfare," as Mead's code termed it), state engineers in fact simply rubber-stamped all appropriations. They did not even bother to define the public interest. They did not have to. The public interest was met whenever someone diverted water and put it to a beneficial use. What if the stream were already fully appropriated? Grant the permit anyway; give the junior a "paper right." The juniors will not get any wet water, except in an unusually high year, but they need priority status in case they get together and have a dam built.[26]

Thus, the mission of the water agencies was to serve the bidding of the rights holders: to record their rights, to make them official by administrative and court adjudications, to enforce them by shutting junior headgates when the flows were low, and, informally but not incidentally, to lobby—hard—for new projects, regardless of the costs to the public. Mead's veneration for the public interest and active government water management never took: government was enlisted purely to solidify private rights to a public resource. These were captured agencies in the most extreme sense. Consider, for example, this description of captured agencies and apply it to western water agencies:

"Traditional" regulation . . . , e.g., the alphabet federal independent regulatory commissions, involves controls directed by a public regulator on the private sector. Criticism of regulatory performance has often included the observation that, *in practice*, the direction of interference or control is opposite . . . ; regulatory outputs tend to correspond to the interests of the regulated party rather than those specified in the formal regulatory . . . legislation. Thus such "capture" could be understood as a kind of reverse regulation.[27]

The private interests favored by western water policy pushed laws through the state legislatures that created still another unique institution to tighten their hammerlock on western rivers and the public fisc. Starting in the late nineteenth century, and accelerating with the passage of the 1902 Reclamation Act, irrigators formed special districts as corporate-administrative bodies to hold and distribute water. The special districts quickly became extraordinary mechanisms that received additional subsidies for water development projects. Most of these districts (the Middle Rio Grande Conservancy District is one), which number nearly 1000 in the eleven western states, have the authority to issue tax-exempt bonds and to tax all land within their boundaries, even land that does not receive benefits from the districts. Their revenue-raising authority amounts to taxation without representation, for voting rights and other aspects of participation in district activities are typically based on acreage (one acre, one vote, rather than one person, one vote), even when the special districts encompass urban areas.[28]

These organizations build war chests by using their tax authority and ability to encourage investment through the use of tax-exempt bonds. The districts, with the ability to obligate all persons within their boundaries, then promote and fund water projects, and lobby the state and federal legislatures on water issues generally, on behalf of the irrigation interests that benefit from the district's activities. John Leshy has made the following observation:

> [T]he basic rationale underlying the governmental status accorded special water districts has quietly shifted in many cases from an internal institutional need for enforced participation and cooperation by affected landowners to a desire for the financial benefits of tax-exempt status. It is little wonder, then, that one special water district attorney rhapsodized in these terms: "There can be no doubt that the discovery of the legal formula for these organizations was of infinitely greater value to California than the discovery of gold a generation before."[29]

Another major source of subsidies for water development interests is little mentioned but has been in place since the first diversions in the gold country in the 1840s. Water developers have the right to use public water without charge. This is nearly unique in public resource law and policy. To take just a few examples, users must pay some fee for using federal or state timber, grazing land, energy minerals, and even wildlife. The only parallel to water in this respect is with hardrock minerals on federal lands, for which the General Mining Law of 1872 requires no payment of royalties to the United States—a statute, by no mean coincidence, that arose out of the same mining camps that produced western water law and policy.

Let me make my point plain. I understand that water development involves costs, often extraordinary costs, especially when major dams or transmountain diversions are involved. Further, a customer of a water supply company must pay a monthly charge. The developer, however, makes no payment to any government for use of the water. With the exception of the provisions of the Hardrock Act, all extractive users of public resources must pay both the development costs and some charge to the government for use of the resource: timber companies must build their roads and haul their logs and also pay a stumpage fee; ranchers must put up fences and construct stock ponds and also pay a grazing fee; oil and gas companies must pay for their drilling rigs and roads and also pay a royalty. But there is no charge for water.

As the 1800s drew to a close, then, western water users, working through the states, had put into place most parts—and were developing others—of a system that gave them wholesale power over the rivers of the West. The unfettered right to extract free water—first come, first served. A state office, publicly funded, to lend protection to the rights. Special districts, publicly supported, to administer projects. With the weight of the state boosting and subsidizing private water development, one point of the iron triangle was firmly in place. But more—much more—would be needed before the arid country west of the 100th meridian could be made to bloom.

Ever since the Homestead Act of 1862, westerners had been trying to pound a round peg into a square hole or, perhaps more accurately, trying to sprout alfalfa from a dry hole. It was relatively easy for the first wave of settlers to make the river-bottom lands green. The alluvial soil was rich, and the aridity did not matter—the land was close to the water. In some areas, it was not even necessary to dig a ditch; in the spring, the natural overflow would spread out into the bottomlands.

But it was a different matter for later arrivals to the potentially good land and for any arrivals to the sandy soils far from the rivers, groups that constituted most of the settlers. Junior users in the rich bottomlands had problems; the land was there, but flows of water during the irrigation season had been reduced to trickles by senior rights holders. Remote lands had the same problem of physical supply, plus the distance factor.

Dams were the answer. The senior rights holders had a call on the rivers only during the time when they actually diverted the water (in most places, the irrigation season is a three-and-a-half- to four-month period from roughly mid-May through mid-September). Juniors could use winter flows and the high spring runoff. They could build a dam upstream and impound water from, say, January through mid-May, store it in the reservoir behind the dam, and then release the water during the irrigation season. The hydrology of most western rivers lends itself to this; 40 percent or more of their annual flow comes during the spring snowmelt in April, May, and early June, most of it before the irrigation season. The summer and early fall flow of a developed river with a substantial dam and reservoir, then, might consist of 100 cubic feet per second (cfs) of natural flow augmented by 400 cfs or more of released storage water. Dams create water. As an inscription on the rotunda of the Colorado statehouse in Denver puts it, "And Men Shall Fashion Glaciers Into Greenness and Harvest April Rivers In The Autumn."

Dams, and long-distance canal systems to deliver the newly created water, were the key to opening the West, but progress had become stalled by the late 1800s. No individual could take on an impoundment of any size, and cooperative associations of farmers were unable to muster significant amounts of up-front capital. The governments of the small western states and territories had similar limits. For-profit private investment companies tended to shy away from dam and reservoir projects, which were seen as risky, capital-intensive ventures. Of those private efforts that were undertaken, several involved companies that overpromised the benefits to farmers or constructed shoddy projects. Gradually, a consensus built up in the West around Powell's notion that the federal government should fund large-scale reclamation projects.[30]

The reclamation movement—the most powerful force in water policy, and in the West generally, at the turn of the century—was characterized by a rare high-mindedness and emotionalism. Its truest adherents, after all, were working on behalf of no less an exalted figure than Mr. Jefferson's yeoman farmer. Reclamation would make fallow land productive. Reclamation would prevent monopolies. Reclamation would democratize the West by peopling it with farm families and farm communities. Reclamation would fulfill the birthright of every American wanting a fresh, equal start. And it had even more mystical overtones, for the storied era of cowboys and prospectors would not pass away but rather would continue on, right alongside the newly arrived agrarian settlers:

> [T]his realm of romance, of courage, and of a rude physical life, is not going to disappear. The sedentary dweller in the rich and populous irrigated valleys will always be brought into close contact with the bold rider, the daring hunter, and the venturesome seeker for gold and silver.

Truly, as the byword went, "the soil is our salvation."[31]

The leading figures in the West all weighed in. The most influential journals of the day—*Atlantic, Scribner's, National Geographic, The Forum, Overland Monthly, Sunset,* and many others—all carried pieces extolling reclamation. John Wesley Powell promised that "a vast area of the arid lands will ultimately be reclaimed, and millions of men, women, and children will find happy rural homes in the sunny lands." Gifford Pinchot, who had come to Washington in 1898, encouraged Theodore Roosevelt to support reclamation, which he did with enthusiasm. Elwood Mead was a whirlwind of activity, bending ears and writing up a storm in the public journals in support of the impending legislation: "The result will determine whether Western agriculture will be corporate or cooperative; whether rivers shall become an instrument for creating a great monopoly, as the dominant element of Western society, or be a free gift to those who make a public return for their use."[32]

However pure were the motives of many in the reclamation effort, there was another strain, one of opportunism, led by people who thought big, very big. William Smythe, an Omaha journalist and chairman of the Irrigation Congress, was one of reclamation's most energetic and zealous backers. Smythe might talk about making "homes where the common people shall realize the highest average prosperity," but he was the archetypical western booster. For him, corporate control of agriculture was a desirable thing because it could produce maximum production and growth. And make no mistake about there being people in the West who wanted big growth and who knew that it depended on water and federal subsidies. As the Reclamation Act of 1902 was being finally decided on, down in the boomlet town of Los Angeles Fred Eaton and William Mulholland were in the process of plotting ways to take the water from faraway Owens Valley, across the Sierra Nevada. They would need the help of the Reclamation Service—and the bigger and more powerful the Reclamation Service, the better.[33]

The conflicting motives behind reclamation came out in another issue, the question of who would allocate water from the reclamation projects. Since these would be federally financed, there was pressure from some eastern congressmen for control by the United States. Western developers, however, knew how to allocate water—they knew about "first in time" and beneficial use and how those rules gave them control of the rivers— and the westerners wanted state law to control absolutely.

The cross-forces over federal and local roles came to a head early in the reclamation push, and John Wesley Powell was in the middle of the collision. By 1888, Powell had been named head of both the Geological Survey and the Bureau of Ethnology. Two congressional proponents of water development, Senators "Big Bill" Stewart of Nevada (he of the Hardrock Act of 1872) and Henry M. Teller of Colorado, obtained a congressional resolution directing a comprehensive study, to be conducted by the Geological Survey, of potentially irrigable lands and possible reservoir sites. Powell went to work and, buoyed by the reception accorded his 1878 "Arid Lands" report, decided what ought to be done. All land west of the 101st meridian—half of the country—should be closed to settlement until a detailed irrigation survey had been completed. Then the public domain could gradually be reopened for planned settlement in accordance with the results of the study. In the summer of 1889, Powell presented his proposal to William Stone, acting commissioner of the General Land Office, who promptly issued the most sweeping withdrawal in public-lands history, closing to entry all federal land west of the 101st meridian. The closure was effective, no less, back to October 2, 1888, the date of the original Stewart-Teller resolution. Wallace Stegner describes the reaction:

> Instantly there was consternation. What? Close all the land offices? Invalidate claims? Refuse the American yeoman his right to free land? . . .
> Consternation approached apoplexy in Stewart and others who, having in mind a quick federal look-see at irrigation problems and a quick reservation of the obvious sites, now found that by their own act they had instituted federal planning on an enormous scale, put one man in almost absolute charge of it, and totally fouled up the local water and land interests to whom they were all bound to give a polite if not an obedient ear. What Powell aimed to do, it now became clear, would take years, and while he carried out his plans he had despotic powers over the public domain. . . . Now [he was], so far as the development of the West went, the most powerful man in the United States. . . . He could all but command the sun to stand still in the West until he told it to go on.[34]

Bill Stewart was not one to allow such a state of affairs to remain so for long. John Wesley Powell—distinguished administrator, author, scientist, explorer, visionary, prophet, whatever—could be damned. By August 1890, Congress had rescinded both the 1889 withdrawal and the 1888 resolution. The irrigation survey conceived by Powell would in time produce much: its careful stream gauging, mapping, and researching of dam sites amounted to a blueprint for the reclamation movement. But the issue of state and federal authority had crystalized. The federal government was welcome, indeed morally obliged, to fund reclamation in the West. Control over water, however, would remain with the western states. Bernard DeVoto described the unreconstructed, states-rights sentiment that would guide western attitudes toward the federal government, water, and reclamation during the twentieth century: "Get out and give us more money."[35]

The reclamation movement took off for good after the Stewart-Powell fiasco. The necessity of having large amounts of water in storage was underscored by the droughts of the late 1880s, which had been the scourge of both farming and, as described in chapter 3, the ranch cattle industry. Smythe founded his evangelical journal, *Irrigation Age*, in 1890. The first Irrigation Congress was held in Salt Lake City in 1891, and annual gatherings followed. The most noteworthy, in Los Angeles in 1893, featured a confrontation between Powell and Smythe and his backers, who were outraged at Powell's advice that their population projections were overblown and that there simply was not enough water to fulfill all of their plans. The boosters won out, and by 1894 Powell was forced to resign, being replaced by his deputy, Frederick H. Newell. Stegner says this of Powell's departure, at a time when he was deep into work on the irrigation plan:

> But they hadn't given him time. They had beaten him when he was within a year of introducing an utterly revolutionary—or evolutionary—set of institutions into the arid West, and when he was within a few months of saving that West from another half century of exploitation and waste. It was the West itself that beat him, the Big Bill Stewarts and Gideon Moodys, the land and cattle and water barons, the plain homesteaders, the locally patriotic, the ambitious, the venal, the acquisitive, the myth-bound West which insisted on running into the future like a streetcar on a gravel road.[36]

Senator Francis Newlands of Nevada, who soon would christen Derby Dam on the Truckee River above Pyramid Lake and the Paiutes' reservation, introduced the first reclamation bill in 1901. It failed to pass that year, but the reclamation movement gained the support of the most important backer of all. In his first message to Congress, President Roosevelt, in words written by Pinchot, urged that reclamation legislation be passed:

> The forests alone cannot, however, fully regulate and conserve the waters of the arid region. Great storage works are necessary to equalize the flow of streams and to save the flood waters. Their construction has been conclusively shown to be an undertaking too vast for private effort. Nor can it be best accomplished by the individual States acting alone. . . .
> The Government should construct and maintain these reservoirs as it does other public works.[37]

On June 17, 1902, Congress signed off on one of the landmark actions in the history of the American West. The words of the Reclamation Act, or Newlands Act, as it also is called, faithfully reflect the Powell-Mead tradition that formed the genesis of the reclamation movement. The whole West would participate: sixteen states on or west of the 100th meridian (Texas was added in 1906) were eligible for reclamation projects. Reclamation would proceed in an orderly way: the Department of the Interior would withdraw dam and reservoir sites along with adjacent lands, then sell off the land, complete with irrigation water, to homesteaders. The act would benefit only farm families: water would be supplied exclusively to *bona fide* residents living on or near the land. These must be small farms: an acreage limitation required the Reclamation Service to provide project water to parcels ranging in size from a 40-acre minimum to a 160-acre maximum, unless smaller parcels would be "sufficient for the support of a family [upon the] lands." The act would deter speculation and promote agrarian communities: the *bona fide* resident and 160-acre maximum would prevent the use of reclamation water by corporations or absentee landlords. Reclamation projects would involve some federal subsidies, but they would mostly pay for themselves: construction and maintenance costs would be supported by a newly created reclamation fund, generated by proceeds from the sales of federal lands, with the reclamation fund being renewed on a revolving basis by payments from participating farmers, who would repay project costs, within ten years, through "charges [that] . . . shall be determined with a view of returning to the reclamation fund the estimated cost of construction of the project." Water would be distributed according to state law: Section 8 of the original Reclamation Act proclaimed, "Nothing in this Act shall be construed as affecting or intended to affect or to in any way interfere with the [water] laws of any State or Territory."[38]

John Wesley Powell died in September 1902, less than three months after the act was passed. A person could read the statute and see that Powell's vision had been realized, from top to bottom.

But it was not to be. Reclamation would not be the child of John Wesley Powell, nor even of Elwood Mead. Whatever words Congress approved in 1902, the actual workings of the reclamation program and its diverse offshoots would be controlled by lords of yesterday set in place generations earlier that would come to their glory through reclamation and its many consequences.

The Second Gold Rush

Reclamation accomplished many worthy things. Although homesteading is commonly associated with the nineteenth century, in fact the greatest flood of homestead patents occurred between about 1900 and 1920. The high water mark was reached in 1910, when 23 million acres were patented. The 1902 act was a main impetus for this. Reclamation directly irrigated 9.2 million acres of arid land, about 21 percent of all irrigated acres in the seventeen western states, and thus effectively opened them for settlement. In the eleven western states, reclamation water is applied to 8.2 million acres of about 28.4 million irrigated acres, approximately 28 percent of all irrigated lands.[39]

The impact of this irrigated land went far beyond the actual acres watered. Hundreds of acres of alfalfa can provide winter feed for thousands of acres of cattle operations. Farms create jobs in farm employment and in the equipment businesses that supply farms. Whole communities then grow up around the agricultural base. The rhetoric of reclamation has always been overblown, and just as its proponents claimed more than they could deliver during the 1890s, so too have its adherents since claimed more than they in fact delivered. Still, you can see the good that came out of reclamation in many solid farming and ranching communities across the West, whether it be on the Snake River plain, in the lower Yellowstone River valley, or in the Gunnison River valley.

But reclamation brought with it deep, profound problems. The program sank into a morass of fiscal problems. Reclamation, supposedly the epitome of antimonopoly populism, proved to be a tool for agribusiness. Indians and Hispanics were resolutely dealt out. Reclamation projects traditionally were designed with no thought to environmental impacts, which have proved to be of extraordinary dimensions. Further, reclamation, as administered, set the essential context for the out-of-control development of the West. The 1902 act spawned the Bureau of Reclamation (until 1923 called the Reclamation Service); it and the Army Corps of Engineers became a pair of sprawling, high-powered technocracies (and rivals) with the desire, and ability, to build big and bigger projects far beyond the point at which any more big projects were needed. Development interests seized on this apparatus, invoking farming's good name to build megalithic water and energy projects. The 1902 act, by deferring to western state water law, ensured that there would be no limits and allowed the agricultural-urban-industrial alliance to feed on the rudimentary rule of capture set in place in 1855. And although the Bureau of Reclamation is now in eclipse, the program of the Bureau and the alliance it helped build rule western rivers and canyons yet.

The idea of having farmers repay the costs of reclamation projects was in trouble from the beginning. Many farms were marginal operations, and financial difficulties were aggravated for many projects because they had been built for land with sandy soil, excessive salts, or steep or rocky terrain. The farmers, the Reclamation Service, and the state water agencies all pushed hard to keep the program afloat. With most project beneficiaries in arrears, Congress acceded and extended the repayment period. The original reclamation law required beneficiaries of federal water to pay off their debt within ten years. The repayment period was pushed out to twenty years in 1914 and, finally, to forty years in 1926. Other adjustments were made to lighten the repayment obligation.[40]

The repayment obligation had already been light, however, in another respect. The 1902 act had made no explicit reference as to whether farmers were required to pay interest on their repayment obligation for the costs of constructing projects. The Reclamation Service, always avid to keep its constituents viable (among other things, farm failures would jeopardize funding for the many projects on the books), took the position that only the principal need be paid, not interest. By 1926, therefore, project beneficiaries were making repayment by means of forty-year no-interest loans. Further, in 1939, the Reclamation Project Act provided that irrigators would be required to repay reimbursable costs only up to their "ability to pay," a standard that the Bureau calculated generously in favor of the irrigators. Even then, repayment still lagged behind. In many districts, large amounts remain unpaid today.[41]

The most recent analysis of the total subsidy for reimbursable costs has been conducted by Richard Wahl, an economist in the Office of Policy Analysis of the Interior Department. After comparing reclamation repayment with historical borrowing rates of the federal government, Wahl concluded, consistent with earlier studies, that the subsidy for reimbursable construction costs from 1902 to 1986, in 1986 dollars, was between $19 billion and $19.7 billion. This means that 86 percent of the total reimbursable construction costs have not been and will not be repaid.[42]

Wahl's analysis deals with subsidization of "reimbursable" costs—that is, those costs of a multipurpose project that are officially allocated to irrigation. In fact, however, the colorful mathematics of western water policy has always favored irrigation when it came to calculating reclamation's share of a particular project. First, some costs are not reimbursable at all. These include the public benefits of a dam and reservoir, such as recreation, fish and wildlife habitat, and flood control. These values regularly have been inflated and borne by the federal government off the top. Second, some reimbursable costs have been disproportionately allocated to other accounts, notably hydropower, which means that electrical rate payers bear the added expense. This pattern of fixing the books to increase an already massive subsidy to irrigation has been criticized from many fronts, including the National Water Commission in its 1973 report to Congress.[43]

As discussed in the opening chapter, under the right circumstances subsidies can be one appropriate aspect of government policy. Subsidies to assist small family farms are an example of subsidies that many Americans, under the right circumstances, might consider acceptable. But both the text and the spirit of the Reclamation Act were widely abused, and many of its main beneficiaries bear little resemblance to Jefferson's yeoman farmer.

The lure of cheap reclamation water drew corporate farming interests, especially in the most profitable agricultural areas. The 1902 act contained no prohibitions against leasing, so one corporation could control large blocks of irrigated land through leases with individual 160-acre owners. This pattern was accentuated by a loophole that allowed parents to homestead land on behalf of their children and receive reclamation water; the act, although it surely intended "family" farms to be subject to a cap of 160 acres, did not expressly prohibit multiple ownerships within one family, even by minors. This allowed one family to operate irrigated land several times in excess of the 160-acre limitation—necessarily a corporate operation—or to lease all or part of the block to a corporation. Speculators employed a number of other ruses to subvert the act, including the use of dummy homesteaders to obtain a patent and then transfer the land to the speculator.[44]

The most thorough study to date, completed in 1981 by the Bureau of Reclamation, surveyed 126,000 reclamation ownerships. About 90 percent of these parcels met the statutory requirement by being 160 acres or less. These parcels, however, comprised only about 52 percent of all acres; 48 percent of all reclamation acres were held by owners of 160 acres or more. Further, really big ownerships, of more than 960 acres, held 13 percent of all surveyed acreage, about 1.5 million acres.[45]

Even more revealing is an examination of "farm operations," the actual working farms that often combine several individual land ownerships, usually by leasing. The 1981 Bureau of Reclamation study found that the 126,000 ownerships did business in about 48,000 farm operations. Seventy-five percent of these operations were 160 acres or less, but the 25 percent of the operations in excess of 160 acres worked 77 percent of all land. The big operations—more than 960 acres—controlled 2.6 million acres, 26 percent of all acreage.

The westwide impact is even greater than these figures would suggest. Lobbyists for several of the biggest Bureau of Reclamation projects, including the Colorado–Big Thompson Project in Colorado and the Imperial Irrigation Project in southeastern California (the largest single user of Colorado River water), managed to exempt those lands entirely from the 1902 act's acreage limitation and residency requirement. In addition, the 1902 act does not apply to projects built by the Army Corps of Engineers, which provides subsidized water in the same manner as the Bureau of Reclamation does for its projects. The Corps operates several of the biggest dams and reservoirs in California's Central Valley Project.[46]

The bypassing of the 1902 act's requirements has had direct social impacts. Although most areas of the West have been affected to some degree, the consequences have been most extreme in the Imperial and Central valleys of California, two places where the excess land provisions of the Reclamation Act have been most widely circumvented.

One person who saw the pattern up close was Ben Yellen, a medical doctor in the rich farmland of the Imperial Valley. Yellen treated migrant Hispanics working for low wages and without decent living conditions. The situation was the same in the Central Valley—one of the world's great agricultural regions, flat, fertile, stretching 300 miles from south of Bakersfield to north of Sacramento, ranging from 50–100 miles wide. Like Yellen, Paul Taylor, professor of economics emeritus at the University of California, Berkeley, was repelled by the social costs of the economic subsidies and the violations of the acreage limitation and residency requirements. Both men perceived that the reclamation program as it actually worked in many parts of the Imperial and Central valleys was worlds away from Jefferson's—and reclamation's—ideal of creating vital farming communities. In 1975, Taylor wrote this:

> A generation ago a government study in California's Central Valley compared two rural communities: one, Arvin, was surrounded by large-scale farms and the other, Dinuba, was surrounded by smaller family-size farms. Proportionately, Dinuba had twice as many business, professional, and white collar workers; three times as many farm operators; slightly more skilled, semi-skilled, and service laborers; and fewer than half as many agricultural laborers. Per dollar of agricultural production, the family-size farms of Dinuba supported a larger number of persons in the local community at a higher average living standard than did the large-scale farms of Arvin. Similar contrasts were found between the two communities in the quality of civic life—Dinuba had more parks, schools, churches, recreational opportunities, local newspapers, etc.[47]

The large landowners receiving subsidized federal water have, in the main, been able to stave off reform. The Omnibus Adjustment Act of 1926 required landholders to sign "recordable contracts" agreeing to sell off excess land after a grace period of ten years. The Bureau of Reclamation enforced the excess lands provisions halfheartedly or not at all. The agency went even further, turning the 1926 act's attempted reforms on their head by arguing that the statute's failure to refer to the residency requirement had amounted to a repeal of the requirement. In fact, there was no need for Congress to make any such reference, since it was set out in the original 1902 act, which was not repealed in 1926. The Bureau's interpretation, however, brought to an end even paper efforts to enforce residency. Today, after a minor reform effort in 1982, large, absentee farm operators, many of them corporations, continue to control large blocks of reclamation land.⁴⁸

As much as agribusiness piggybacked on the Reclamation Act, originally designed for the small family farm, land developers in the cities did at least as well in riding on the sturdy shoulders of Jefferson's yeoman farmer. Ironically, urban real estate interests became part and parcel of the reclamation program as a result of a pivotal episode in California that never led to a reclamation project.

By the turn of the century, it was apparent that Los Angeles would be a dynamic force in the West. Its population was doubling or tripling each decade. The booming city, however, had an Achilles' heel—its lack of a local water supply. The Los Angeles River was a modest stream, and there was precious little other fresh water near this arid plain bounded by the Pacific. Over time, Los Angeles would reach out to the Colorado River, on California's eastern border; to the Trinity River, 650 miles away at the northern end of the state; and to other locales. The first long-range endeavor involved the Owens Valley.⁴⁹

As of 1904, it was apparent to Fred Eaton and William Mulholland, the two boosters who headed the Los Angeles Department of Water and Power, that the city's surging growth could not be maintained by its existing water supplies. For the desired expansion, Eaton and Mulholland settled on the flow of the Owens River, 200 miles away to the north and east on the other side of the Sierra Nevada. The water could be sent south by aqueduct and pumped over a low divide down to the city. Secrecy and speed were critical. The residents of the Owens Valley had in mind their own project under the new Reclamation Act, and like all westerners, they knew about the race to the rivers that was built into the "first in time, first in right" rule. The locals could tie things up if they got there first.

Joseph Lippincott was a respected official in the Reclamation Service. He began scouting around the Owens Valley, evaluating different dam and storage sites. People in the valley assumed—knew—that he was working on a reclamation project to make their lands bloom. What they did not know was that this loyal proponent of farm communities was moonlighting for Los Angeles at the rate of $2500 per year, more than half of his federal salary.

California had a complicated hybrid system of water rights that recognized both prior appropriation and riparianism. To be safe, in order to take over the entire Owens River, Los Angeles had to appropriate water and, as well, buy up all land along the river that might be the basis for riparian rights. Los Angeles also wanted to be sure that it owned the site that would later become the reservoir. Eaton began buying up parcels at top dollar. He alleviated suspicions by holding out the impression that he was acting on behalf of Lippincott—that is, on behalf of the Reclamation Service. Eventually, Los Angeles bought up 300,000 acres of land in Inyo and Mono counties, about 95 percent of all farmland in the valley and 85 percent of land in the towns. Even today, Los Angeles is, next to the federal government, the largest landowner in Inyo County.[50]

The subterfuge eventually was exposed, and the conflict between local residents and Los Angeles came out into the open. Sylvester Smith, the local congressman, proposed a compromise that would allow the reclamation project to proceed; the valley would be able to irrigate less land and Los Angeles would receive less than the whole river, but both sides would be accommodated. Among other things, this proposal led to a 1906 statute that allowed reclamation water to be used for municipal purposes, thus building the cities into the reclamation program.[51]

Los Angeles temporized on Smith's proposal. This gave the city the opportunity to allow the heavy hitters to weigh in. Construction plans showed that the water would go to Los Angeles by way of the San Fernando Valley, just north of the city. The water would be injected into the aquifer there for efficient storage; there would be no evaporation, and the water would work its way underground down to Los Angeles. The water could also be used by developers in the San Fernando Valley. All of these plans were confidential, but as Marc Reisner put it, "Anyone who knew this, and bought land in the San Fernando Valley while it was still dirt-cheap, stood to become very, very rich." There were people who came to know; they included Harrison Gray Otis of the *Los Angeles Times*; Harry Chandler, Otis's son-in-law; Moses Sherman, who had made millions in transportation (and who sat on the Los Angeles Board of Water Commissioners); Edward Harriman, of the Union Pacific Railroad; and other southern California magnates.[52]

The San Fernando land syndicate and Los Angeles city officials killed Congressman Smith's compromise. Teddy Roosevelt, looking to Pinchot, now at the peak of his power, rather than Lippincott's reclamation-oriented superiors in the Interior Department, came down on the side of Los Angeles's dreams (which, of course, included no reference to the San Fernando Valley) and dashed those of the Owens Valley. The reclamation project was officially abandoned. What to do with the hundreds of thousands of acres that the Reclamation Service had withdrawn for the project? Pinchot and Mulholland had the perfect answer for the land, which was mostly treeless: include it in the Inyo National Forest. That way, the National Forest System would be expanded (Pinchot's motive) and the land would be withdrawn from homesteading, thus preventing any further growth in Owens Valley, now Los Angeles's distant suzerainty (Mulholland's motive). The way was cleared for the construction of the

Los Angeles Aqueduct, which carries the entire Owens River 200 miles south.

The most enduring lessons of Owens Valley are perhaps not the most dramatic that might be drawn from this epic episode. Outright official corruption at the federal level in water policy has been rare. Lippincott (who technically violated no federal criminal statutes but who plainly breached any reasonable ethical standards expected of public officials) apparently acted alone. Pinchot, who seems never to have known of the San Fernando land syndicate, was, typically for him, heavy-handed, not dishonest.

Rather, the lasting lessons from Owens Valley, still the most powerful symbol of the struggles between western cities and the rural West, involve forces that resolutely hammer out a steel-framed system that fosters, shelters, and legitimizes the exercise of broad and unexamined power. One legacy is a state law structure that not only allows water developers to reach hundreds of miles into other communities and remove their sustenance but even encourages such forays by the manic "use it or lose it" rule of capture, while not requiring the developers to show any conservation program for their existing or proposed uses. We have also inherited state and local water agencies bound and determined to serve the building programs of their constituents; a federal bureau that fought off its own crushing financial pressures by taking the any-project-is-a-good-project, conquer-nature mentality to a new level; and private opportunists ready to pounce on any available acre of arid land near the next water project. And caught up in the middle of it all—just like the Pyramid Lake Paiutes on the Truckee and the Hispanics in Rosa and Arboles on the San Juan—were those who had come, or might have come, with their hopes and dreams to the high, dry, crystalline air of the Sierra Nevada valley memorialized in Mary Austin's poignant novel *The Land of Little Rain*.[53]

During the first quarter of the century, the Bureau of Reclamation began to come of age. The projects were not being repaid, and the speculators (Mead called them "vampires") hovered over the program, but the Bureau still managed to back up a lot of water behind a lot of dams. The agency's projects, budget, and influence were all expanding. In the words of one observer, "by 1928, the Bureau was the world's foremost builder of water storage, diversion, and transmission structures." Nevertheless, the really big projects lay ahead.[54]

The turning point was Hoover Dam, begun in 1931 and completed in 1935, at Black Canyon on the lower Colorado River. Mulholland had wanted a mammoth dam on the Colorado for Los Angeles ever since tying up the Owens River. The big farmers of the sprawling Imperial Irrigation District on the Mexican border in southern California had their needs:

reliable storage on the fickle Colorado; an end to the rampaging floods that could and did blast out their diversion works on the river; and an "all-American" canal to replace its existing transportation system, which dipped down into Mexico (American water developers should not—ever—be made subject to the vagaries of Mexican politics). Arthur Powell Davis, commissioner of reclamation and the nephew of John Wesley Powell, came upon the idea of using hydroelectric facilities at the dam as a "cash register" to subsidize the irrigation components of the project, thus finding a way, on a whole-project basis, anyway, to balance Hoover Dam's books. And it was depression time. The nation needed jobs.

As always, actors were waiting in the wings. The construction contract for the dam was obtained by the so-called Six Companies. This consortium, which included Bechtel, Kaiser, and Utah International, and which received financing from the young Bank of America, was the launching pad for what would become some of the world's largest corporations. As Peter Wiley and Robert Gottlieb show in their book *Empires in the Sun: The Rise of the New American West*, Hoover Dam marked the beginning of the modern industrial West.[55]

Hoover Dam was impressive by more than western standards. It was world-class, one of the greatest construction ventures ever undertaken. At 726 feet—the height of a sixty-story office building—Hoover Dam was the world's highest dam. It used 66 million tons of concrete. The reservoir behind the dam stored 28 million acre-feet of water, twice the annual flow of the Colorado River.[56]

Today, still larger dams—Grand Coulee on the Columbia, the Aswan in Egypt, and a few others—have been built, relying in good measure on the engineering know-how and confidence generated by Hoover. Still, given that, given even the knowledge that 110 workers died from falls, explosions, landslides, and heat prostration, the modern visitor will feel a sense of awe at Hoover's long, graceful arch, the white cement playing off against the sheer black-rock canyon walls and restraining the wild Colorado River. This is a place where the human race met nature square on and humans prevailed.

Hoover Dam was named after the engineer-president whose administration began the project. To whom should the 108-mile-long reservoir be dedicated? The answer was easy: Elwood Mead, commissioner of reclamation from 1924 through 1936. But Lake Mead symbolized a very different spirit from that of the idealistic young man who tried to see that Wyoming water law would be permeated with the public interest, who saw the future of the West as symbiotic with the tillers of the soil, who railed against "that pulpy individuality called a corporation" that would subvert the agrarian ideal.[57]

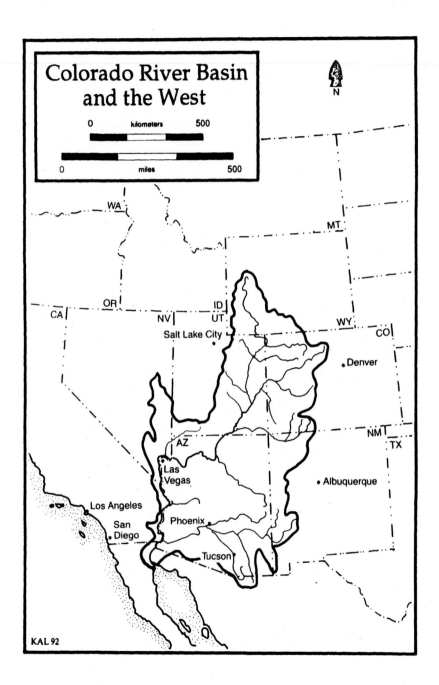

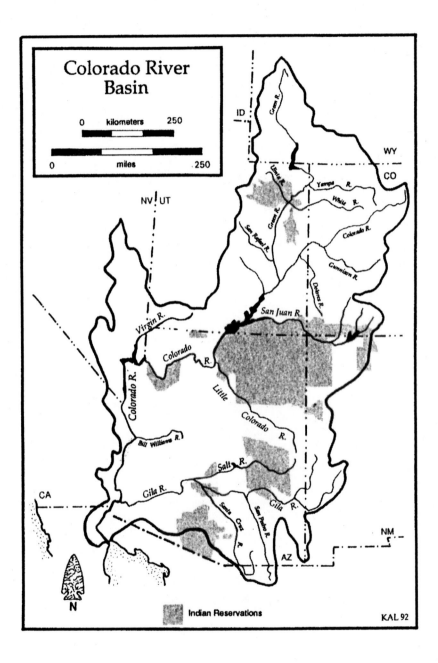

Colorado River Basin

ID

WY

CO

NV · UT

Green R.

Uinta R.

Yampa R.

White R.

Green R.

San Rafael R.

Colorado R.

Gunnison R.

Dolores R.

San Juan R.

Virgin R.

Colorado R.

Colorado R.

Little Colorado R.

Bill Williams R.

Salt R.

Gila R.

Santa Cruz R.

San Pedro R.

Gila R.

CA

NM

AZ

0   kilometers   250

0   miles   250

N

Indian Reservations

KAL 92

No, the Elwood Mead who ran the Bureau of Reclamation during these critical years might mouth the old devotion to the family farm—running the intensity and fervor of the original reclamation ideal up the flagpole remained a key ingredient in the recipe for a still bigger bureau budget—but this Elwood Mead was subservient to the agency's new constituency, big agriculture, big cities (read: big real estate developers), and big industry. Perhaps Elwood Mead's heart still lay with the family farm, but in these waning days of his career, Mead became first and foremost a builder. As Interior Secretary Harold Ickes wrote in one memorandum, "Commissioner Mead, of course, is always in favor of any new reclamation project." This attitude meshed well with the plans of the Franklin Roosevelt administration, determined to spend its way out of the depression. Mead died in office in 1934—FDR eulogized him as "a builder with vision"—but he was succeeded by other zealous and able builders who served as reclamation commissioners, most notably Michael Straus, commissioner from 1945 until 1953, and Floyd Dominy, who held the office from 1959 through 1969.[58]

The dam-building movement from the 1920s through the 1970s remade the face of the West. It was led by the Bureau of Reclamation but was also fueled by the Army Corps of Engineers, the Bonneville Power Administration, cities and towns, the state engineer's offices, and various irrigation districts and other special water districts. Private irrigators, energy companies, and developers of all sorts either participated in the publicly funded efforts or went their own ways. The era bred hundreds of major projects, tens of thousands of smaller ones. Dams, reservoirs, and diversions reworked virtually every river in the region.

We have seen how the Columbia River, all the way from Bonneville Dam near Portland, Oregon, to the Canadian border, is almost all reservoir—just a few short stretches of free-flowing river remain. On the Colorado River, Hoover Dam set off a rush to develop that reached throughout the basin. The other gargantuan structure, every bit the equal of Hoover, is Glen Canyon Dam. Seven hundred and ten feet tall, the dam created the 27-million-acre-foot Lake Powell, at 186 miles the longest reservoir in the world. Lakes Mead and Powell together hold almost exactly four years' flow of the Colorado River. Dozens of other major dams, lesser than the two Goliaths but giants nonetheless, plug up the Colorado and its tributaries. Massive canal and pipeline systems transport water hundreds of miles away from the river—the Colorado River Aqueduct to the Los Angeles–San Diego area, the $4 billion Central Arizona Project to Phoenix and Tucson, the San Juan–Chama Project to Albuquerque, and no fewer than nine major tunnels bored under the Continental Divide to export water from Colorado's Western Slope to the East Slope cities and suburbs of Denver and Colorado Springs and irrigation projects on the South Platte and Arkansas rivers. Every other western river basin—the upper Missouri, draining large parts of Montana, Wyoming, Colorado, and the Dakotas; the Sacramento–San Joaquin system of California; the Klamath of California and Oregon; the Rio Grande of Colorado, New Mexico, and Texas; and many smaller ones—saw project after project, diversion after diversion.

From the 1920s through the 1960s, reservoir capacity in the West mushroomed, expanding at the rate of 80 percent per decade. The dams of the Colorado River watershed hold back 72 million acre-feet of water in storage—nearly six times the annual flow of the river. Missouri River impoundments dam up 85 million acre-feet. In the Pacific Northwest, reservoirs capture 55 million acre-feet; in California, the figure is 39 million acre-feet. On the much smaller Rio Grande, 7.8 million acre-feet of water are held each year, more than twice the annual runoff of the river. The Bureau of Reclamation alone has built 355 storage reservoirs and 16,000 miles of canals, 1500 miles of pipelines, and 278 miles of tunnels. Apparently no one has tried to count the total number of miles (though they surely exceed 100,000) of canals that divert the flows of western rivers and deliver water to irrigators and other water users. Westwide, more than a million artificial reservoirs, lakes, and ponds store 294 million acre-feet. This is the equivalent of twenty-two Colorado Rivers backed up behind dams and over former canyons. It is enough to put Montana, Wyoming, Colorado, and New Mexico—an entire tier of states, from Canada to Mexico—under a foot of water.[59]

The Costs of the Harvest

A great deal of good has come from this Herculean engineering effort. The Missouri, for example, was a killer river in its natural state, carrying whole trees down from the Rockies and blasting out of its banks in Montana, the Dakotas, Nebraska, and Iowa. Dams on that river and others have saved human lives and uncountable hundreds of millions of dollars in property damage. Almost 50 million acres of farmland are in irrigation. Cities and towns have been allowed to rise up and grow through domestic water supplies and hydroelectric, fossil fuel, and nuclear power facilities, which all depend on substantial water supplies. Westerners achieved the multibillion-dollar, job-producing building boom they so avidly sought. Some of the reservoirs afford fishing, boating, and other flat-water recreation opportunities. Some dams, while inundating miles of trout streams, actually improve the fishing on rivers below the dams by cutting the high runoffs in the early spring and releasing flows of cool water during the dog days of July and August.

Yet nearly a century and a half of unrestrained water development has brought relentless difficulties to the American West. The pattern witnessed at Pyramid Lake and with the San Juan–Chama Project has played out across the region.

One pervasive problem is the waste of water. The combination of overbuilt water supplies, heavy subsidies, and a hands-off attitude toward individual water use has created a situation in which the arid American West has some of the worst water conservation practices in the world. Per capita water consumption in the West is three times greater than in the eastern states. Much of this is accounted for by irrigation, but even in the cities, westerners use 45 percent more water than their eastern counterparts. The disparity is even larger when comparisons are made with foreign countries. In the United States, nonagricultural per capita use, at 180 gallons per day (gpd), is several times that of other nations, including developed countries such as Germany (37 gpd), France (30 gpd), Sweden (54 gpd), and England (53 gpd). Major losses occur before water is even diverted due to evaporation from reservoirs. In the East, this is not a problem: precipitation often exceeds evaporation into the humid air. In the dry, hot West, however, annual evaporative losses from surfaces of reservoirs range from 2 feet in the Pacific Northwest to nearly 10 feet in some parts of the Southwest, where so much San Juan–Chama water goes up into the atmosphere. The estimated regional total of reservoir evaporation is 14.6 million acre-feet, more than the annual flow of the entire Colorado River.[60]

Still greater losses occur elsewhere. In western cities, the high water use is attributable mainly to lush lawns and golf courses (both of which give rise to large evaporative losses in the arid climate when water is overapplied) and to excessive use inside homes and businesses. The greatest losses of all, however, take place in irrigation, due to inefficiencies in transportation from stream or reservoir to the fields and on-field application in agriculture.

The Truckee-Carson Irrigation District (or Newlands Project), which receives water bound for Pyramid Lake, and the Middle Rio Grande Conservancy District, which uses water from the other side of the Continental Divide, are typical of many irrigation operations across the West. The TCID and the MRGCD are old-style operations that work mostly on unlined, earthen irrigation canals and ditches. These leaky earthen conveyance systems allow extensive carriage loss through seepage. They also permit phreatophytes—noncrop, water-sucking plants such as cottonwood trees and tamarisk—to extend their roots into the conveyance systems. The phreatophytes then discharge the water into the atmosphere through evapotranspiration.

In addition to incurring carriage losses, the TCID, the MRGCD, and most other western irrigation districts follow wasteful practices in the fields. When fields are not leveled, water collects in pools—causing loss by evaporation—or runs off the fields without reaching the root systems of the crops. Profligate amounts of water are dumped on the fields by flood irrigation, causing huge losses by evaporation and seepage. As one progressive water official said in frustration, "[W]e're just trying to get them to stop irrigating up to the third strand of barbed wire."[61]

By and large, the states allow the irrigators—who, remember, use 80 percent to 90 percent of all water in every western state—to continue their traditional practices. In a few cases, perhaps most notably in the Central Valley of California and the fields in the Phoenix-Tucson area, irrigators have begun to adopt conservation measures such as leveling fields by laser systems and installing cement-lined canals; drip and trickle irrigation, based on the use of corrugated pipes run down furrows between rows of crops; and sprinkler systems, which, due to precise application, use much less water than does flood irrigation.

Much more typically, however, state officials simply abdicate to the irrigators. The most common administrative approach, traditionally accepted by the courts, is for the state to defer to "local custom" in a particular area. Neighboring farms thus set the standard, if any, for water conservation. Elwood Mead's original prohibition against waste, put into Wyoming law in 1890 and adopted in every other state, has never much been enforced. The slogans are that water is precious, that waste of water is prohibited, and that the states regulate water use, but the reality is that conservation and waste of public water are decided by the irrigators themselves.[62]

There are disagreements over the exact definition of water waste. Farmers cannot be expected to find a way for crops to consume every drop of water—to inject water into the plants by hypodermic needle. Still, by any standard, western irrigation is extraordinarily inefficient. Westwide, only 41 percent of diverted water is consumed by crops, while 46 percent returns to the streams as return flows and 13 percent is lost to the system through evaporation, consumption by phreatophytes, or seepage into impervious underground formations. The 13 percent of diverted water lost to the system may sound insignificant, but due to the huge quantity of agricultural diversions, it is not; according to a Soil Conservation Service study, on a westwide basis it amounts to 24 million acre-feet per year, nearly twice the annual flow of the Colorado River. The Department of Interior, the Department of Agriculture, and the Environmental Protection

Agency reached a similar conclusion, finding a westwide loss of 21.1 million acre-feet.[63]

Private interests often attempt to explain away inefficient practices by arguing that much of the unused diverted water is not "wasted" but rather becomes return flow by trickling back into the stream on the surface or by seeping underground and rejoining the stream. The late Colorado water lawyer Glenn Saunders was fond of saying: "My farmers never waste a drop. They reuse a molecule up to 12 times." The argument is factually wrong in part, because of the estimated 13 percent of diversions that are wholly lost to the streams, but it also fails to account for contemporary knowledge about whole river systems.[64]

When excess water is diverted from a stream, the return flow will usually cause stream temperatures to rise, producing negative effects on fish life. Further, return flows are laden both with natural salts and soils and, often, with agricultural chemicals. Doris Ostrander Dawdy has correctly written: "To read the history of irrigation is to read the story of salt." The most severe problems are in the Colorado River basin, where the combination of return flows and out-of-basin diversions, which concentrate salts in the remaining flows, has begun to force farmland out of production. The salty water simply kills off the crops. In order to meet the United States's obligation to deliver water to Mexico (presumably usable water, although federal officials debated the point for decades), the federal government has been required to build one of the world's largest desalinization facilities at Yuma, on the lower Colorado River.[65]

When excess water carries off salts, it also carries off the soil itself. Sediment is one of the major polluting agents of water: "In terms of volume, it exceeds all other sources of pollution combined." Soil movement has a threefold adverse effect, with total national costs estimated by the Council on Environmental Quality at $3.2 billion each year. First, on the fields, soil erosion depletes the growing capacity of the farmlands from which the soil is lost. Second, once it enters the rivers, sediment causes injury in transit through increased costs of water treatment and decreased water quality for wildlife and other in-stream uses. Finally, when sediment comes to rest at a site of deposition, the buildups diminish the capacity of reservoirs and eventually may eliminate water storage altogether, as at silted-up Severance Reservoir at Camp Creek. In the West, the amount of soil loss from agricultural operations exceeds even the erosion from grazing.[66]

Soil loss is gradual, and for most citizens, the damage is hard to detect. Yet soil is eroding at the rate of 4 billion tons per year. In-stream costs are already extravagant, and drops in agricultural production due to elimination of the soil base are expected in the first or second decade of the twenty-first century. Aldo Leopold, saying that "soil is the fundamental resource, and its loss the most serious of all losses," called soil erosion "a leprosy of the land."[67]

Agricultural runoff has caused still other problems, and unlike the slow sapping of the vitality of the land, some are visible, and dramatically so. During the 1980s, investigations began to turn up new and macabre problems. Selenium, a nonmetallic, sulfuric chemical found in soils, is beneficial to humans in very small quantities and is used in some medications, but heavy concentrations are highly toxic to animals and humans. In the early 1980s, the U.S. Fish and Wildlife Service observed rapidly increasing numbers of deaths and deformities of aquatic birds in Kesterson National Wildlife Refuge in California's Central Valley. The cause was pinned to wastewater with high concentrations of selenium leached from the soils in the Westlands Water District. Federal biologists later determined that selenium poisoning had also been detected in Utah, Wyoming, and Nevada. The Nevada killings, already related in chapter 1, occurred at the Stillwater National Wildlife Refuge, which received runoff from the Newlands Project near Pyramid Lake.[68]

The final returns on selenium—and the other chemicals, including arsenic, boron, and mercury, that it associates with to cause magnified effects—are not in yet. Areas near at least fifteen other water projects are known to contain concentrations of selenium at least as high as those at Kesterson. In total, forty-three areas, some with multiple sites, in fifteen western states are under investigation. There may well also be effects on livestock from selenium-laced water and grain. Reporter Tom Harris found that hundreds of cattle, sheep, horses, and swine in five western states had died from selenium poisoning. Human deaths due to selenium are difficult to diagnose, but there have been numerous cases over the years of serious illness and death due to "alkali poisoning," as deaths due to selenium, arsenic, or both have traditionally been called. Research is continuing, as are most of the irrigation discharges.[69]

Water law in the western states traditionally dealt only with water quantity, not quality. Those who built the system had an intense interest in a supply of water but virtually none in pollution controls. The tacit understanding that controls of any kind were to be avoided kept pollution matters, especially as to mining and agriculture, out of the statute books. When the federal government began to get serious about water pollution with the passage of the Clean Water Act of 1973, irrigators managed to lobby through an exemption from the "nonpoint source" provisions of the act. Thus, the Clean Water Act dealt with point source pollution (from discrete sources, such as industrial pipes) and with most forms of nonpoint sources (diffuse surface runoff, including soil erosion, such as from logging, grazing, and road building or other construction activity). The agribusiness lobby, however, had worked hard, and a conspicuous exception from the 1973 act was runoff from agriculture, the largest source of soil loss.[70]

The 1973 act has been a resounding success for point source pollution: industrial discharges and other such pollution have been sharply reduced. But virtually no progress was made on nonpoint source pollution. The problem of nonpoint source pollution is more difficult to attack because of its diffuse nature and, politically, because farmers, ranchers, and timber companies have been able to stave off any significant alterations in their manner of operation. In 1987, Congress came up with a new nonpoint source program, this time including irrigated agriculture, but the effort mainly involves a handoff to the states, which are required, in general terms, to come up with programs to combat nonpoint source pollution. To date, the state efforts, especially among the western states, have had few teeth. In the West, the controlling idea about water pollution, as about other areas of western water law, is still that irrigators ought to have sway over the rivers.[71]

Another product of the large diversions of water, especially for irrigation, involves depletion of the flows of western river systems, often with drastic results. We have seen how the San Juan–Chama Project has taken most of the water from streams once bound for the Navajo River Canyon on the Jicarilla Indian Reservation and how the Truckee-Carson Irrigation District has plagued the Truckee River, its rare fish species, Pyramid Lake, and the Paiutes. In most years, the Colorado River is literally dry at its mouth; no water at all reaches the once-verdant delta of the Gulf of California. In Arizona, the middle and lower Gila no longer run. In the Pacific Northwest, the main-stem Columbia River has plenty of water, but its largest tributary, the Snake, and dozens of smaller tributaries are drawn way down; they drain the arid lands of the interior east of the Cascades, and their precarious state has endangered the salmon runs and recreational use.

Senior irrigation water rights hold a hammer over the streams in the Missouri River system of the northern Rockies and Great Plains. In normal years, the rivers run low during the summer but the fisheries survive. Low-water and drought years, however, bring real chaos. In the dry year of 1988, blue-ribbon trout streams throughout Montana and Wyoming—famous rivers like the Madison, Gallatin, Beaverhead, Bitterroot, Bighorn, and Big Hole—ran low and warm in some stretches, dead dry in others. There were fish kills by the thousands; state fish biologists estimated that five to eight years of normal precipitation would be required to bring the fisheries back. In California, irrigation withdrawals have reduced the San Joaquin River to such an extent that the freshwater flow into San Francisco

Bay is no longer sufficient to hold back the ocean's tidal action; saltwater intrusion into the delta is ruining prime fish and nesting habitat.[72]

Countless other streams still run but, like the Navajo River in the canyon on the Jicarilla Indian Reservation, are rivers only in a superficial sense. The Rio Blanco is another stream that has been reworked by the San Juan–Chama Project's system of tunnels, and the Forest Service has performed detailed stream surveys below the diversion point. With the flows drawn down, there is insufficient water power to move the silt out: "Sediment deposits were high ... with 74–80% of the sand/silt occurring in riffles. This is an indication that the system is unable to transport the sediment load out of the system." As the sediment has collected, the bottom of the Rio Blanco has risen, the channel has become "overwide," and the hot sun has raised the temperature of the slower, wider, and shallower stream. Due to these forces and others detailed in its report, the Forest Service concluded that "[f]ish habitat is poor throughout the surveyed reaches." The Rio Blanco, too, has been tamed and lost.[73]

No one has made a formal count, but there are many hundreds of dry rivers across the West and many hundreds more that are wet but not much more.

Diversions can and do destroy wetland areas as well as rivers. At Camp Creek, the many different values of the riparian zone—water storage, sediment filtering, flood control, wildlife habitat—were all devastated by poor grazing practices. Dewatering of rivers and streams also ruins the green ribbons of vegetation that accompany streams as well as other wetland areas, including swamps, marshes, estuaries, and riparian forests. Vast expanses of wetland areas have also been filled to create farmlands or residential areas. Like the Camp Creek riparian zone, these wetlands—long treated as nuisances—are highly productive systems. In 1989, President Bush approved the general policy goal of "no net loss of wetlands"—that is, there would be a presumption against any project destroying wetlands. However, if the benefits of destroying wetlands are shown to outweigh the costs, the project can go ahead but the developer must mitigate the losses and provide for compensatory wetlands (by restoring degraded wetlands elsewhere or by creating wetlands, usually by flooding) for those wetlands that are lost to new development. This unglued industry, which formed a group, calling itself The Natural Wetlands Coalition. The Bush administration was listening and, among other things, floated a proposed redefinition of wetlands that would have cut in half the total area of wetlands protected by federal law. Obviously, the "no net loss" policy, as a meaningful basis for decision making, has a long way to go. So does the longer-term objective of creating a net gain by rehabilitating wetlands. We have already lost more than 50 percent of our wetlands, and the destruction is proceeding apace. As explained by Ralph Morgenweck of the U.S. Fish and Wildlife Service:

> If you consider wetland conservation in terms of a ledger-sheet account, our annual losses, or outlays, are running at 300,000–450,000 acres while our gains, or income, range from 20,000–25,000 acres. This means that we have a deficit of as much as 425,000 acres annually.[74]

We also are depleting water resources deep underground. The nation's groundwater aquifers—formations of saturated sand, soil, or porous rock—hold an estimated 180 billion acre-feet of water. This dwarfs the 1 billion acre-feet in all of the nation's rivers and 27 billion acre-feet in all of the freshwater lakes in North America. There is a lot of groundwater, but four qualifications must be considered. First, most of it is too deep to be pumped economically with existing technology. Second, most groundwater aquifers renew themselves to some extent, but they are not renewable resources in the sense that surface waters are; total annual recharge to the aquifers is just 1 billion acre-feet, about one-half of 1 percent. Third, groundwater is disproportionately located in the East; the arid West has less groundwater. Fourth, groundwater use may be limited by contamination.[75]

Groundwater use was initially minimal as westerners turned first to the more accessible streams and rivers. In the 1930s, western groundwater pumping—agriculture, of course, was far and away the largest user—began to increase as surface supplies grew increasingly tight and as new high-lift pumps were put into use. After World War II, rural electrification brought a power supply to the irrigation fields, and groundwater pumping boomed. Today, it amounts to about 26 percent of all water use in the West, and its share continues to grow.[76]

Groundwater law in the West developed separately from prior appropriation. The more complex body of rules, however, reflected many of the same traditions: senior water users are usually protected on a "first in time, first in right" basis, and the states worked from the premise that they had little business regulating senior irrigators or other groundwater users. The law encouraged a race to the pump house, and numerous aquifers have taken precipitous drops. Some farms have begun to go out of production (usually not because the water has literally all been sucked out but because the aquifers have been pumped down below the point at which drilling and power costs make extraction economically unfeasible). Nine of the seventeen western states are pumping groundwater in excess of annual recharge; in those states, 45 percent of all groundwater use is from declining groundwater aquifers. As with surface water, groundwater use is plagued by widespread waste. The situation is most acute in California, Arizona, New Mexico, and the lands overlying the vast Ogallala Aquifer (parts of South Dakota, Nebraska, Kansas, Oklahoma, Texas, Wyoming, and Colorado).[77]

Unregulated water development also has threatened whole societies. The victims have been land-based societies like the Hispanic town of Rosa and the Jicarilla Apache Tribe, both victims of the San Juan–Chama Project, and the Pyramid Lake Band of Paiutes, whose water was taken by the Truckee-Carson Irrigation Project. Another affected group has been rural communities burdened by metropolitan water projects, a dynamic witnessed with the Owens Valley and Los Angeles and with the upper end of the San Juan watershed and the San Juan–Chama water diverted under the Continental Divide to Albuquerque.

The most extensive impacts have involved American Indians, whose established water rights have been expropriated in every corner of the American West. Tribal water priorities were set by the United States Supreme Court in *Winters v. United States* in 1908. The famous case arose on the Milk River in northern Montana near the Canadian border. Henry Winter (the "s" was added to the end of his name in the official court proceedings because the Bureau of Indian Affairs misspelled his name) and other settlers began diverting Milk River water in the early 1890s. In 1898, the Fort Belknap Tribe, which was downstream of the homesteaders, put in a small irrigation project. In the dry year of 1905, there was not enough water to go around, and a courageous United States Attorney, on behalf of the tribe, sued the homesteaders in federal court to require them to close their headgates and let water flow down to the reservation. Of course, under Montana law, the outcome was clear. Winter and the others had actually diverted water out of the stream before the tribe. First in time, first in right.[78]

But the federal judge in Montana held for the tribe, and so did a unanimous Supreme Court. The reasoning was the same as in *United States v. Winans*, the Indian fishing rights case handed down three years earlier, in 1905. There, as discussed in chapter 5, the Supreme Court reasoned that the tribes possessed sovereignty and real property rights in their aboriginal territory long before any treaties with the United States; at treaty time, they reserved—kept—the right to take salmon and steelhead at their traditional sites in the Pacific Northwest. The right to fish was "not much less necessary . . . than the [air] they breathed."

So, too, with water in *Winters*. The Assiniboine and Gros Ventre tribes of the Fort Belknap Indian Reservation had inhabited the Milk River country for centuries before any contact with white people. As the *Winters*

Court put it, "The Indians had command of the lands and the waters—command of all their beneficial use, whether kept for hunting, 'and grazing roving herds of stock,' or turned to agriculture and the arts of civilization." The tribes had ceded land in 1874 and in 1888, when the Fort Belknap Indian Reservation was slashed in half to allow homesteading by non-Indians. But the Court asked rhetorically: "Did they give up all this? Did they reduce the area of their occupation and give up the waters that made it valuable or adequate?" The answer was no; otherwise, the tribes would be left, in the Court's words, with a "barren waste." The tribes at Fort Belknap possessed reserved water rights, under federal law, dating to the establishment of the reservation. These Indian rights were superior to any rights under Montana law or, for that matter, under the law of any state.[79]

Coming from the nation's high court or not, the *Winters* doctrine has provided few benefits to the tribes. *Winters* was common knowledge, but it was ignored, subverted, and circumvented. Water developers detested any rules outside of their tightly controlled state systems. Taking the cue, state officials effectively read *Winters* out of existence through a business-as-usual approach of granting state water rights and allowing diversions that directly conflicted with Indian rights. Federal officials, supposedly bound to act as trustees for Indian rights, were, if anything, worse. They pushed for federal subsidies for non-Indian projects on Indian rivers and ignored potential Indian projects. There were almost no exceptions. The Navajo Indian Irrigation Project (NIIP) on the San Juan River was one of a handful of Indian water projects, and it went forward only because of the conjunction of two forces: Indian equities were necessary cover for the marginal-at-best San Juan–Chama Project; and the dry, 16-million-acre Navajo reservation (an area as large as West Virginia) and its *Winters* rights were simply too big, too visible, to ignore. Even then, the NIIP was poorly planned, underfunded, and, finally, radically downsized as the shiny San Juan–Chama Project went full steam ahead.[80]

The pattern was essentially the same everywhere, but the upper Missouri River basin, where the Milk River is located and the *Winters* case was litigated, serves as another example. Before the New Deal, the upper Missouri had seen only small water projects (one was a federal dam on the Milk River, built shortly after *Winters* was handed down, to guarantee water to Henry Winter and the other settlers who had been found to be junior in the *Winters* case). The situation on the Missouri was complicated because the Missouri is "two rivers": above Sioux City, Iowa, it drains arid western land, where irrigation is the dominant use; below Sioux City, the river moves east of the 100th and 98th meridians into wetter country, where in-river flows are needed for river traffic and flood control.

The Bureau of Reclamation (irrigation) and the Army Corps of Engineers (channels, levees, and locks and dams for transportation) were competitors for the Missouri. They had never been able to get together and agree on a mutually acceptable plan for the river. As World War II drew to a close, the promise of huge federal appropriations for construction created a shotgun wedding. On October 16 and 17, 1944, Colonel Lewis A. Pick and William Glenn Sloan met at the Great Northern Hotel in Billings and reached agreement. The Pick-Sloan Plan, enacted by Congress later that year, called for 316 projects, including 112 dams. Yet the eleven tribes of the upper Missouri—all poor, all suffering from massive unemployment—received almost nothing from Pick-Sloan. Nothing, that is, except flooded lands under reservoirs sending out irrigation water and electricity to non-Indians. Don Snow, executive director of the Northern Lights Institute, explains:

> Vast areas of the Indians' best bottomlands—the only farmable or forested zones on several reservations—were inundated, with extraordinarily heavy costs to long-established cultures and econom[ies]. The Garrison Dam in North Dakota, for example, flooded the best lands of the Three Affiliated Tribes on the Ft. Berthold Reservation: Arikara, Hidatsa, and Mandan Indians, whose agricultural economy and culture had been granted a permanent homeland along the Missouri by the Ft. Laramie Treaty of 1851. Not only were the Indians forced to move up out of the rich, protected river bottoms onto high, windy, sterile, and treeless ground, but the rising reservoirs [flooded low bridges over the Missouri River and] cut off much of their social intercourse, splitting closely-knit tribal groups into isolated pockets. The Pick-Sloan dams were the most recent of the many injuries brought to the peaceable River People by white commerce and settlement.[81]

As I say, this was not just the Missouri, Truckee, and San Juan basins. In a comprehensive, carefully worded paragraph, the National Water Commission set out this conclusion in its 1973 report:

> Following *Winters*, more than 50 years elapsed before the Supreme Court again discussed significant aspects of Indian water rights. During most of this 50-year period, the United States was pursuing a policy of encouraging the settlement of the West and the creation of family-sized farms on its arid lands. In retrospect, it can be seen that this policy was pursued with little or no regard for Indian water rights and the *Winters* doctrine. With the encouragement, or at least the cooperation, of the Secretary of the Interior—the very office entrusted with protection of all Indian rights—many large irrigation projects were constructed on streams that flowed through or bordered Indian Reservations, sometimes above and more often below the Reservations. With few exceptions the projects were planned and built by the Federal Government

without any attempt to define, let alone protect, prior rights that Indian tribes might have had in the waters used for the projects. . . . In the history of the United States Government's treatment of Indian tribes, its failure to protect Indian water rights for use on the Reservations it set aside for them is one of the sorrier chapters.[82]

The impacts on Hispanic culture have been more localized—mostly in the Southwest—and in some respects more subtle, but they too have been severe. The greatest effects have occurred in the Rio Grande valley, which begins in southern Colorado, runs the entire length of New Mexico, and encompasses the region around El Paso in west Texas. In the late sixteenth and early seventeenth centuries, Spaniards moved north from Mexico and settled in San Gabriel (near the modern town of Espanola) in 1598, founded Santa Fe in 1610, and moved into the El Paso area around 1650. Over time, Hispanic towns grew up in nearly all sectors of the valley.

The Spanish and Mexican settlers brought with them their time-honored water traditions and institutions, ones very different from the system that would develop hundreds of years later, when the area was annexed to the United States in 1848 by the Treaty of Guadalupe Hidalgo. The heart of the Spanish water system was the *acequia*, an association of citizens in each community. In contrast to prior appropriation, the emphasis was on cooperation rather than individual rights. Through the *acequias*, members irrigated the agricultural plots and provided for domestic water. They maintained the ditch system, consisting of the "mother ditch," which diverted water directly from the river, and various laterals running off the mother ditch. The *mayordomo*, or ditch boss, held a key position in these communities, where water was so important, and by tradition the *mayordomo*'s orders were always obeyed. All members of the *acequia* worked together to keep the ditch system in repair; the spring cleaning of the ditches was a major community event. (This celebratory ditch-cleaning time also was laborious—people called it *la Fatiga*.) Spanish and Mexican law recognized individual ownership in water, and water uses could be, and regularly were, transferred within the community. Each town, as a community, also held collective water rights, in many respects superior to those of any individual; these public rights were held in trust for the good of the whole community.[83]

Anglo water development and prior appropriation have taken a heavy toll on Hispanic land, water, and culture. In 1916, when the Bureau of Reclamation completed the giant Elephant Butte Reservoir in southern New Mexico, where some San Juan–Chama water is stored (and evaporated) today, it meant an end to the small, stable Hispanic farming societies that populated the area below the dam.

A remarkable 1936 government study by Hugh G. Calkins, regional conservator of the U.S. Soil Conservation Service, has chronicled in detail the effects of Elephant Butte and other water projects in the Rio Grande valley. In 1910, before construction of Elephant Butte began, there were about 1400 farms in the area, with a population of 6000 and about 50,000 acres in crops; a large majority of these operations were individually owned by Hispanic farmers. Calkins's painstakingly documented work shows how the traditional, longtime Hispanic farmers were unable to pay the operation and maintenance charges necessary to support the expensive dam and conveyance systems needed to open up an additional 100,000 acres that were mostly dedicated to large corporate farming. After Elephant Butte went in, the Hispanic farmers were left with no choice but to forsake their small subsistence farms and become laborers on the new operations, soon to be joined by large numbers of migrant workers from Mexico. Calkins's clinical analysis lays bare the essential irony of how the classic reclamation project, heavily subsidized but still burdensome to the small farmer, can displace these family farms—supposedly the reclamation ideal—with agribusiness:

> This area, thirty years ago, supported a small, native Spanish-American population, largely self-sufficient and secure. . . . Through the construction of a costly irrigation project, three principal things were accomplished: 1) an additional land area of 100,000 acres was made available for agricultural use; 2) the native population unable to meet the new high cash costs was in large measure displaced from 50,000 acres it had owned; 3) the new owners of the land were obliged, by virtue of the new high cash costs, to institute a highly commercial and intensive type of land use.
> The land speculation which was rife during the construction of the project and after its completion drove the cost of land so high that the annual cost of carrying the indebtedness incurred in the purchase of land, plus the high cost of water, made the choice of a crop bringing high cash returns inevitable. Cotton brought these high returns for a time; it also brought the insecurity attendant upon dependence on a crop subject to wide variation in price, and it brought the need for a large labor supply. The result, at the present time, is that the area contains a large but highly stratified population directly dependent upon the land resources, either as farm operators or farm laborers. . . . The great majority of the resident population is supported at a permanently low income level and a high insecurity level.[84]

Western water law and policy worked much the same results further up the Rio Grande Valley. The Middle Rio Grande Conservancy District (MRGCD) was formed in the Albuquerque area in 1925, just eleven years before Calkins's 1936 report, but the returns were already beginning to come in. Calkins reported:

> The Spanish-American population of the Middle Rio Grande Valley persisted in their older economy for many years after American occupation. They neither sold nor mortgaged their land but only their labor. Even at present, no more than six or seven per cent of the farms are mortgaged, whereas for the nation as a whole, the percentage is well over forty.

But then the MRGCD was formed by a small group of businessmen who wanted to improve the local economy and enhance the value of their investments by providing a regular water supply and opening new lands. The Hispanic farmers were interested in neither objective: they already had their land, and they were already senior users under state law. The traditional Hispanics tried to fight the MRGCD by filing court protests against the district's formation and by physically resisting construction. As one study recounted:

> [T]he construction crews of the District attempted to cross the Los Chavez community ditch, angering the irrigators served by that ditch, and resulting in the [MRGCD] board members (who were present to mitigate the difficulties) scurrying up the boom of a dragline as an avenue of escape from the angry residents.[85]

The legal authority of the MRGCD, small though the number of organizers may have been, overrode all objections. Calkins explained:

> Overnight, there occurred what for centuries the Spanish-American and Indian populations had contrived to escape. Every piece of land in the Conservancy District was assessed. The annual charges for construction, operation, and maintenance constituted a levy both for interest and principal on a total assessment which is, in effect, a mortgage secured by land.

There were approximately seventy functioning *acequias*, but they were all collapsed into the MRGCD. The old community ditches were shut down and replaced by the newly built reclamation canals. With the *acequias*— the center of village life—gone, the traditional communities began to fade. Today, one can drive north from Albuquerque, beyond the boundaries of the MRGCD, and pass through many traditional Hispanic villages. South of the city, within the MRGCD, only remnants of the villages remain. This loss of community, along with the assessments (including those for the San Juan–Chama Project), is the legacy of projects that Hispanic farmers had neither requested nor needed.[86]

State law has resulted in loss of Hispanic water rights in ways other than
assessments by state-authorized special districts such as the MRGCD.
There is a water market in the Rio Grande valley, and many Hispanic
farmers have sold out; these sales have often been opposed by neighbors,
who see such sales as threatening the community's viability, but the firm,
rights-based rules of state law make no allowance for cultural concerns.
The protection of water rights often requires recourse to Byzantine court
and administrative hearings, and poor Hispanic farmers typically lack the
wherewithal to pay attorneys' fees. In some cases, traditional Hispanics are
simply unaware of, or confused by, high-powered court proceedings and
fail to appear. This can lead to a complete loss of water rights—the basis
for the epic conflict in John Nichols's novel *The Milagro Beanfield War*.[87]

Even more subtly, the instability identified in Hugh Calkins's government survey can adversely affect relationships with Anglo neighbors. As
one example, after the San Juan–Chama Project began bringing water into
the Rio Grande basin, the state of New Mexico filed suit to adjudicate all
water rights in the upper Rio Grande basin. This was necessary, at least in
the state engineer's view, to sort out the ramifications of having more than
100,000 new acre-feet of San Juan–Chama water—physically indis-
tinguishable, of course, from native Rio Chama and Rio Grande acre-
feet—in the river each year. The case, *New Mexico v. Aamodt*, joined
thousands of parties—municipalities, irrigation districts, individual users,
corporations, Indian tribes and pueblos, and *acequia* associations. Lucy
Moore, water expert with Western Network, puts *Aamodt* and numerous
other conflicts in this context:

> Prior appropriation is a newfangled idea forced on a system that already
> worked. It does not fit into New Mexico's web of land-based peoples—
> mostly Hispanics and Indians. The current process of stream adjudica-
> tions has broken down the social fabric that has existed for generations.
> The old system's spirit of cooperation has been replaced by competition.
> Old friends are now enemies.[88]

Almost incredibly, the Hispanic land-based culture continues to perse-
vere in many quarters. The old Hispanic system—*acequias, mayordomos,
la Fatiga*, the idea of a powerful community value in water—continues to
exist today. Hundreds of *acequia* associations still operate in New Mexico
and southern Colorado. Hispanics have organized in recent years and have
achieved a new level of awareness about Anglo water law and policy. But
much has been lost and the pressures are great, and one fears for Hispanic
water and traditions if significant adjustments to prior appropriation's
relentless machinery are not made.

Social implications are also part and parcel of the raids that urban areas continue to make on rural water supplies. The Central Utah Project is nearing completion, its giant plumbing system designed to bring water from eastern Utah across the Wasatch Range to Salt Lake City. Phoenix, Tucson, Scottsdale, and other central Arizona cities are aggressively buying up land in counties hundreds of miles away to pump off the groundwater. Las Vegas has filed claims for 60,000 acre-feet of Virgin River water and for 800,000 acre-feet of water in twenty-six northerly valleys as far as 250 miles away. The battle cry in the outlying areas is "Remember the Owens Valley!"[89]

The demands of Colorado real estate developers in Front Range cities such as Denver, Colorado Springs, and Aurora continue. So does their insistence on transporting the water from Western Slope streams. Total transmountain diversions from the Western Slope already exceed 650,000 acre-feet annually (most of this water goes to the Colorado East Slope, but the 110,000 acre-feet of San Juan–Chama water from Colorado's Western Slope is transported to New Mexico). As of the early 1990s, there are numerous proposed projects, including the Two Forks Project, a 550-foot dam that would flood 22 miles of river and canyon in the popular South Platte Canyon; Homestake II, which would dry up four streams and associated wetlands areas in the Holy Cross Wilderness Area; and the $446 million Union Park Dam, which would send Gunnison River water east. The Colorado Front Range also has designs on the Rio Grande valley. American Water Development, Inc. wants to pump as much as 200,000 acre-feet of groundwater under the San Luis Valley, ship it out of the valley by pipeline, and sell it for urban development. "Owens Valley" is muttered regularly in rural Colorado, too.[90]

In every instance, the rural areas make political arguments and can raise various legal objections. Indeed, each of the proposed Colorado projects just mentioned has been held up by some administrative or judicial decision. Ultimately, however, state law sides mightily with the urban development interests. There are still few restrictions on water developers who want to reach out into distant watersheds. First in time, first in right.[91]

Reforming the Water Lords

Since about the mid-1970s, there have been stepped-up efforts to ameliorate western water law and policy's social, economic, and environmental impacts. For the first time, citizens and public officials have begun to take a hard look at the basic question of whether the traditional ways of dealing with western water make sense. These efforts are just preliminary, for as of the early 1990s there has not yet been fundamental structural reform. In water, the lords of yesterday remain well entrenched. At the same time, the work of the past generation has been a necessary and constructive forerunner for a deeper reform movement that seems to lie ahead.

The first flash of appreciation that the established way of doing business often led to destructive results took place in the early 1950s, a full century after Matthew Irwin and Robert Phillips engaged in their gold country dispute that ended up in the California Supreme Court. To be sure, John Muir had taken on San Francisco and Gifford Pinchot in the 1910s in Muir's holy war to block the plugging up and flooding of Hetch Hetchy, the sister valley of Yosemite to the north. But Pinchot won out, and Muir's spirited defense of rivers and canyons played essentially no role in water policy for nearly forty years.[92]

The setting was the Colorado River, where the construction of Hoover Dam in the 1930s had marked the beginning of the rise of the modern industrial West. After the end of World War II, the developers turned in earnest to their proposal for a second gargantuan dam higher up in the Colorado watershed. It would be built in the state of Colorado, on the main stem of the Green River just below its confluence with the Yampa River. This original proposal would have flooded Dinosaur National Monument.

The effort to protect Dinosaur helped found the modern environmental movement. David Brower, then executive director of the Sierra Club, discharged the full weight of his charismatic and energetic personality into the fray. Wallace Stegner, who had just completed his biography of John Wesley Powell, *Beyond the Hundredth Meridian*, put together an evocative collection of essays and photography, published by Knopf, that detailed the glories of Dinosaur. In 1955, the book, *This is Dinosaur: Echo Park and Its Magic Rivers*, was placed on the desk of each senator and House member.

The unprecedented effort was successful in that Dinosaur was spared. But progress had to proceed, and in a compromise that Brower rues to this day, the project was moved downstream, just below the Utah-Arizona border. When construction began in 1956 and the waters began to back up behind Glen Canyon Dam to create Lake Powell, they slowly entombed huge expanses of some of the world's most mystical red rock country: most of Forbidding Canyon; Bridge Canyon up beyond Rainbow Bridge, the world's tallest natural arch and the wondrous centerpiece of Rainbow Bridge National Monument, leaving the base of the arch in a pool of water; numerous other named and unnamed side canyons; and Glen Canyon itself, a full 160 miles of glory.

Glen Canyon was so remote that few had ever seen it. Although Powell had floated through it in 1869 and Stegner had gone down in 1947, only a handful of people had visited it before Congress authorized the dam in 1956. But many people visited Glen Canyon just before and during its gradual inundation in the 1960s. Rage grew and spread, but it was too late, much too late. One visitor, Ed Abbey, wrote his best-selling novel and environmental anthem, *The Monkey Wrench Gang*, around the idea of dynamiting Glen Canyon Dam. But most telling was the Sierra Club's book-obituary on the area. It is titled *The Place No One Knew*.[93]

After the flooding, people did begin to know what Glen Canyon had been, and out of the episode emerged the idea that the dam-building rush of the 1930s through the 1960s ought to be reexamined. The awareness went far beyond the new environmentalist movement *per se*, to the general public. Glen Canyon did seem to have been an extraordinary place. Some dams had been, and probably still were, necessary. But perhaps the developers ought not to have their choice of the West's rivers and canyons.

One early example arose in the Paradise Valley on the upper reaches of the Yellowstone River in Montana. This valley is not lightly named. The Yellowstone, one of the last major free-flowing, undammed rivers in the world, pushes north out of Yellowstone National Park near the town of Gardiner. About 10 miles downstream, the river spills into the valley, 35 miles long, up to 12 miles wide, and bounded on the west by the Gallatin Range and on the east by the upthrusting, snowbound peaks of the Absaroka Range. The fine, pastoral bottomlands support ranch and farm operations and several small communities that have built up around them. The Yellowstone, which spreads out to as much as 600 feet here, winds gently down the center of the valley. But for the vagaries of gold discoveries, homesteading, and the necessity of drawing boundary lines at some ultimately arbitrary point, the region might well have been included in the Yellowstone Park Act of 1872 or one of the subsequent additions to the first national park. Still, as it is today, the Paradise Valley is as inspiring a working valley as a person can find.

To the water developer's eye, however, such a valley is a perfect tub, ready to become a reservoir if it can just be plugged. And Paradise Valley can be plugged, for at its northern end, just above the city of Livingston, the landscape narrows. The gap is named after an old railroad siding called Allenspur. The Yellowstone is already a big river here (the river, which produces an average of 9.8 million acre-feet when it reaches the Missouri near the Montana–North Dakota line, flows at about 2.7 million acre-feet at Livingston), and by laying in a 380-foot-high, ½-mile-long dam at Allenspur, a project could flood nearly the whole valley, create a pool 31 miles long and up to 4 miles wide, and store as much as 4 million acre-feet of water.[94]

A dam at Allenspur was proposed as early as August 1902, just as the Reclamation Act was being passed. The project received regular attention over the years, with justifications ranging, as politically convenient, from irrigation to flood protection to hydropower to recreation to coal development. The Allenspur issue came to a head in 1972 and 1973, when the Bureau of Reclamation, which for years had opposed wild and scenic river designation for the upper Yellowstone because such status would bar any dams, issued studies assessing potential water development in the upper Missouri River basin and featuring Allenspur.[95]

Local ranchers, conservationists, and businesspeople organized in late 1973, forming the Allenspur Committee to Save the Upper Yellowstone. They included Dan Bailey, Livingston's "first citizen," the quiet, world-famous fisherman and fly-fishing store owner; Urana Clarke, tiny, reserved, and elderly, who had a hand in everything in Livingston; and Sandy Sargent and her husband, Leonard, a rancher whose white-maned intensity in defense of the Paradise Valley inspired support in numerous quarters. Bill Hornby, a Montana native and executive editor of the *Denver Post*, gave an elegant speech to the Miles City Chamber of Commerce, later reprinted in the *Livingston Enterprise*. As Hornby, who generally favored water development, put it, Montanans need to find "composers for a Yellowstone Concerto." The Allenspur gang need not apply: "[W]e must move [government] away from petty, nickel-and-dime personality politics which feeds on divisions and dogmas and ignores the unique things that Montanans have in common and the very grave new problems they can only face in concert." Jim Posewitz, scientist-activist with the Montana Department of Fish, Wildlife, and Parks, picked up on the idea and put together a film called *Yellowstone Concerto*.[96]

The locals, with support from the Northern Rockies Action Group and the Montana Environmental Information Center, met regularly. They commissioned a detailed, straightforward historical and factual analysis, written by Bob Anderson, a licensed engineer and doctoral candidate in environmental engineering. Armed with Anderson's study, the opponents laid bare the illogic of Allenspur. Flood control benefits, a main justification for the dam, would in fact be meager because downstream damage from past flooding had not been great. The benefits from irrigating new areas of land on the downriver plains also were illusory because they would come at the expense of flooding the existing farm and ranch operations in the Paradise Valley. Land acquisition costs would be high because so much private land would be inundated and because prices in the valley had begun to skyrocket. Road relocation costs for Highway 89, the main arterial to the north out of Yellowstone Park, would also be extravagant. Because of these and other factors, Allenspur Dam had little to recommend it economically.

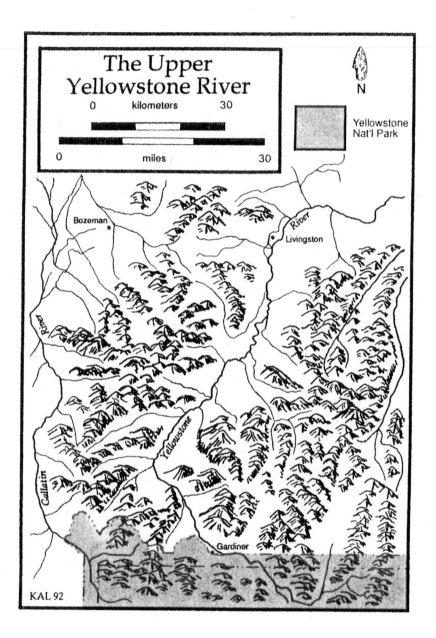

The Upper Yellowstone River

0   kilometers   30

0   miles   30

N

Yellowstone
Nat'l Park

Bozeman

Livingston

River

River

Gallatin

Yellowstone

Gardiner

KAL 92

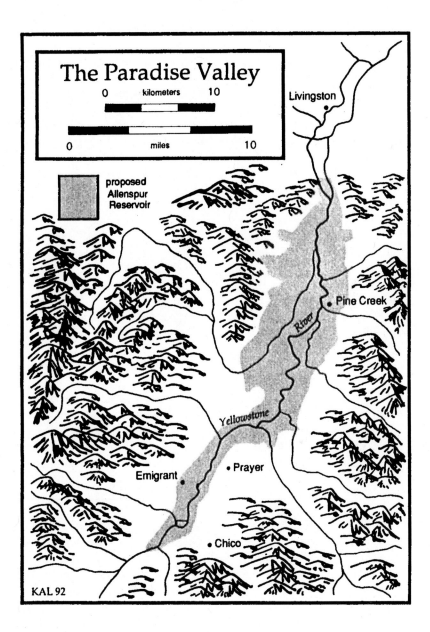

The Paradise Valley

0　　kilometers　　10

0　　miles　　10

proposed Allenspur Reservoir

Livingston

Pine Creek

River

Yellowstone

Emigrant

Prayer

Chico

KAL 92

The low benefit-cost ratio of 1.42 (which was, in any event, surely inflated) was similar to that of the marginal San Juan–Chama Project.[97]

There were many other problems with Allenspur. Thirty-one miles of some of the country's best trout water and popular floating runs would be lost. Miles of silt-laden reservoir bottom at the upper end of the project would be exposed when the water level was drawn down, leaving unsightly mud flats and creating a serious dust problem. The proposed earthen dam, to be built in a potential landslide area, presented safety risks and water quality problems. The Paradise Valley had been used by Indian people for thousands of years, and archaeological sites would be lost.

The Bureau of Reclamation finally backed away from its plans to build Allenspur. The upper Yellowstone, however, has never been included in the Wild and Scenic Rivers System. The project is still on the books, inactive but not disavowed.[98]

Allenspur played a role, along with numerous other proposed water projects that dotted the West during the 1970s and 1980s, in building a popular constituency for a much tougher scrutiny of big water projects. The would-be dam at Paradise Valley also serves to illuminate the difficulties that the big projects face today. Most of the "easy," "good" dam sites have already been used. U.S. Geological Survey studies show the precipitous decline in reservoir efficiency. Dams built before 1930 created 10.4 acre-feet of reservoir capacity per cubic foot of dam volume. By the 1930s, the figure had fallen to 2.1 acre-feet, and in the 1960s a cubic foot of dam stored just 0.29 acre-foot. And society has taken a broader view of what a river is. Thus, nearly all projects face a triple whammy. They are less efficient and more expensive in traditional benefit-cost terms; and they must cope with many new kinds of costs, not always readily quantifiable. Lost days of trout fishing and river rafting. Mud flats and blowing dust. The loss of homes. The drowning of long-abandoned prehistoric Indian communities and graveyards. The destruction of deep western canyons— formerly storage basins, now rare places of beauty, mystery, and solitude.[99]

The Carter and Reagan administrations responded with go-slow approaches toward western water development. In 1977, Carter issued his (take your choice) famous or infamous "hit list," in which he ordered the withdrawal of requests for appropriations for nineteen western water projects. Howls resounded from Nebraska to California and the Dakotas to New Mexico, and Carter eventually restored a few of the projects with reduced funding, but the hit list signaled a new era. Reagan did not share Carter's environmental concerns, but he was every bit as resolute on the ledger-sheet issues. Bound to his western constituencies or no, Reagan opposed nearly every new start.

The general suspicion of still more dams spread to those projects in which the federal government was to make no financial contribution. In Colorado, Denver and other metropolitan water providers had pushed for the Two Forks Dam, which would flood 22 miles of canyon and prime trout and elk habitat. The effects would have been felt from Colorado's Western Slope (some of the water would be transported under the Continental Divide from the Blue River) to Nebraska (whooping crane habitat on the Platte River would be partially dewatered). The Environmental Protection Agency in both the Reagan and Bush administrations, in actions that have been challenged by the project proponents, vetoed Two Forks on the grounds of excessive environmental destruction. This was not a case of a federal agency failing to look beyond the Beltway: the EPA had its eyes on the polls, which showed that a majority of Coloradans opposed the project on the basis of its high costs and environmental impacts.[100]

The gradually heightening public awareness also manifested itself in a movement to reform existing reclamation projects. During the 1960s, westerners of a different stripe began to participate in reclamation policy— people like Ben Yellen, the California physician who lived near the sprawling Imperial Irrigation District and saw the waste of water, the subsidies, and the big absentee agribusiness interests who held sway in spite of the requirement that reclamation water users be residents and in spite of the 160-acre acreage limit, both designed to promote the family farm. Paul Taylor, the eminent economist from the University of California, wrote up a storm in both the academic journals and the popular press. Hispanic leaders weighed in, objecting to working conditions and the lack of basic community facilities. National Land for People and the Mexican-American Legal Defense and Education Fund took excess land and residency to the courts in the 1970s, but the results were mixed.[101]

The issues all ended up in Congress in the early 1980s. A main assertion by irrigation interests was that farm production is stultified by the 160-acre maximum; the provision, they protested, is simply economically irrational in some regions. Reformers countered by arguing that the limit may indeed be unreasonable in some instances, but the answer is for agribusiness to relinquish subsidized federal water. As author Marc Reisner put it, "The Central Valley Project was without question the most magnificent gift any group of American farmers had ever received; they couldn't have dreamed of building it themselves, and the cheap power and interest exemption constituted a subsidy . . . worth billions over the years."[102]

The debates were marked by a pitch shrill even for western land and water conflicts. Principal orators turned to various European political philosophies for support. The administration of reclamation, by the lights of reform-minded California congressman George Miller, amounted to "socialism for the rich." For Idaho senator James McClure, the proposals of the reformers (which mainly consisted of eliminating subsidies and enforcing the provisions of the 1902 act) were "part of the dogma of Marxism." In the packed committee hearing rooms, you could feel all the weight of all the accumulated years of law, policy, and political power.[103]

In the end, the old forces prevailed when the loosely titled Reclamation Reform Act of 1982 became law. Congress abolished the residency requirement. It loosened the acreage limitations by setting, for most operations, a new ceiling of 960 acres (1½ square miles) for lands receiving project water. But excess landholders (now those in excess of 960, not 160, acres) could still get federal water: the 1982 act directed that holders of excess lands could receive project water for five years (twenty-five years for perennial crops) if they signed contracts to dispose of the excess lands within five years. Excess landholders had another option, but this provision was not to their liking: rather than agreeing to sell off the excess lands, they could keep the lands and pay "full cost" (defined in the act in a manner advantageous to landholders), rather than the subsidized rate, for water to irrigate their excess land. In a last bow to agribusiness, Congress overturned contrary court decisions and entirely exempted from the reclamation laws all projects, including several in California's Central Valley, constructed by the Army Corps of Engineers. Subsequently, as with past laws, the Bureau of Reclamation bent this legislation toward the interests of the big irrigators. The impact of the 1982 act has been to ratify most existing operations. Meanwhile, a decade later, as the Central Valley continues to boom, in four rural counties a shadow society of 86,000 households, most of them Hispanic and most of them farm workers, lives below the poverty line. Hunger gnaws at them every day, and many of the children are already preparing for the underside of big reclamation—they, too, are working in the fields.[104]

The federal government has taken other, more successful, actions to address long-standing water needs in the West. Congress has added segments of rivers to the Wild and Scenic Rivers System. One stretch, on the Rio Chama above Abiquiu Reservoir, where water from the San Juan–Chama Project flows, includes the sublime Chama Canyon, one of the Southwest's most scenic and popular white-water rafting areas, its cliffs striped horizontally with grey-purple, mustard, chalk, and brick red. But in some years, the Army Corps of Engineers had stored additional water in the reservoir, backing the pool up into the lower reaches of the canyon and leaving mud flats slathered on the canyon floor in 3- and 4-foot layers. The Corps and the New Mexico state engineer opposed wild and scenic designation because it would prohibit the Corps from expanding the pool into the canyon. There was no justification to use the canyon for still more water storage because San Juan–Chama water was already going unused and there was no foreseeable need for the water; the objections to wild and scenic status for the river in Chama Canyon reflected only the continuing desire of the building agencies, the state engineers, and their constituencies to keep their hold on the rivers. In 1990, Congress finally gave protection to the river and the canyon.[105]

Congress also has begun to take on the long-neglected issue of Indian water rights. During the 1980s and early 1990s, more than a dozen statutes resolved Indian water claims. Most of those settlements provided for construction funds for storage projects; the projects allowed tribes to divert water while not adversely affecting existing non-Indian users under state law. As discussed in chapter 1, one of these settlements provided relief to the Pyramid Lake Paiute Tribe; this comprehensive legislation calls for a number of programs that may reduce diversions from the Truckee River so that more water can flow to Pyramid Lake. Further, the Jicarilla Apache Tribe in New Mexico was able to reach a tentative settlement. If the settlement is finally approved, the tribe will establish rights to 40,000 acre-feet of water annually. This will do little to lessen the impacts of the San Juan–Chama Project on the tribe—of the tribe's total share of water, 6500 acre-feet will come from the San Juan–Chama Project, only 6 percent of the project's total diversion—but such an agreement will still bring some measure of justice to the Jicarilla Apaches. Nevertheless, scores of tribes remain unserved, ground under to varying degrees by the cost and complexity of achieving major federal legislation in the context of the megapolitics of western water.[106]

A fast-emerging matter of federal law involves the Endangered Species Act. We have already seen how the impending listing of stocks of Pacific salmon prompted Senator Hatfield's "salmon summit" and may help reshape river policy in the Pacific Northwest. The tiny delta smelt is being considered for listing in the Sacramento River Delta, and a recovery plan could mean significant adjustments for agribusiness in California's Central Valley. In the Southwest, the Colorado River squawfish has been listed as endangered; protecting this species in the San Juan River watershed may block construction of Colorado's Animas–La Plata Project. Another leading example involves Pyramid Lake in Nevada. After pressure from the tribe, the Bureau of Reclamation agreed to time water releases from Stampede Reservoir, on a tributary to the Truckee River, so that high flows would coincide with the migration patterns of the cui-ui. The Endangered Species Act has only begun to play out on western rivers. It may not come to much. The last-resort statute for wildlife may, however, prove to be a sturdy hammer for dislodging long-established extractive water uses that have worked over so many western watersheds and drained them of much of their vitality.[107]

The states have shown some movement in western water law and policy.

In the courts, one potentially major development has involved the public trust doctrine, the rule deriving from Roman and English law that the public has overriding rights on major rivers and lakes that cannot be granted away to any single segment of the population. The trust has been employed in one dramatic instance. After draining the Owens River and Owens Lake in the early 1900s, Los Angeles water development interests moved even farther north, along the eastern side of the Sierra Nevada to Mono Lake. By 1940, Los Angeles began diverting water from four of the five streams that feed the lake. The lake level dropped precipitously, killing off the brine shrimp in the saline lake and, in the process, depleting the food supply for the diverse and extensive bird population at the lake.

In 1983, the California Supreme Court held that the interest of the whole public in Mono Lake was protected by the public trust doctrine and that Los Angeles could not appropriate this lake, 250 miles away, for itself. Rights under prior appropriation must be balanced against the public interest. In the early 1990s, Los Angeles and public interest groups representing Mono Lake were close to a settlement based on a lesser appropriation by Los Angeles that would stabilize Mono Lake at its current level, much lower than the natural level but sufficient to maintain a substantial wildlife population.[108]

The public trust doctrine has the potential to be a significant leavening force against the single-mindedness of prior appropriation. It is noteworthy that the doctrine has been employed against such a large and powerful user as Los Angeles. To date, however, although the doctrine has been alluded to in court opinions in several other states, the public trust has yet to play an important role outside of California.[109]

The state legislatures—by rhetoric, at least, the ultimate seat of authority over western water—have also taken some actions. Almost everywhere, state-mandated reform programs are still in their infancy, but real strides have been made in a few instances.

The issue of water conservation first came to a head in a major way in Arizona, where heavy and steadily increasing pumping since World War II had been causing a rapid decline of groundwater tables. By the late 1970s, Arizona confronted the daunting fact that it had become the first state to consume more water than entered its borders each year. Secretary of the Interior Cecil Andrus sharpened the issues (prodded, one may surmise, by Arizona governor Bruce Babbitt, who wanted long-term groundwater reform). Andrus announced that Arizona would not receive a drop of its hard-won Colorado River water—the state had achieved a Supreme Court victory in 1963, after combatting California since the 1930s—until the state addressed its excessive groundwater pumping. Unless groundwater reform came, Andrus flatly stated, the United States would refuse to divert any water from the Colorado into the 200-mile-long aqueduct system, well under construction with billions of federal dollars, that would bring water to the Phoenix and Tucson areas. Maybe Andrus was bluffing, but he had a federal statute on his side. Crises a generation away are one thing—Arizona pumps would start going dry about 2010—but holding the family's most precious possession hostage at gunpoint is another.

The Arizona water establishment blinked. In 1980, under Babbitt's leadership, the state adopted and began to implement a truly comprehensive groundwater code. The Arizona Groundwater Management Act of 1980 required cutbacks by groundwater users on a progressive basis and mandated increased efficiency every ten years. New agricultural areas may not be opened up in the so-called active management areas. To encourage water conservation and to fund administration of the new program, the Arizona legislature required "groundwater withdrawal fees"—a polite term for a pump tax.[110]

There have been other encouraging signs on the water conservation front. Tucson reduced its per capita consumption by 14 percent during the 1980s. Denver announced a conservation plan in 1989, shortly after it became apparent that new supplies might not be forthcoming from the Two Forks Project, and then began to implement a mandatory water-metering program. The city of Casper, Wyoming, financed canal lining and other conservation measures in the Alcova Irrigation District, then applied the salvaged water to municipal uses. In southern California, the Metropolitan Water District will put to urban use water saved through conservation measures in the Imperial Irrigation District. The district is the largest single user of Colorado River water, with a "right" to 2.9 million acre-feet, almost as much as the entire Rio Grande: "Enough water is being transferred this way to meet the needs of 800,000 Californians, yet no cropland is being taken out of production." Dry years in the late 1980s and early 1990s have prompted real soul-searching among California cities, especially in the southern part of the state, and innovative and increasingly rigorous urban water conservation plans are in the works.[111]

A number of other issues have been addressed at the state level. Most western states have adopted programs for in-stream flow rights to protect fish, wildlife, and recreation. The programs are progressive and have made a difference on some streams and rivers. The in-stream rights, however, are junior, with modern priority dates, and have no effect on established uses. States also have increased their regulation of groundwater. Most states have upgraded their procedures for allowing water marketing; this allows existing, often inefficient, uses to be transferred to new uses and can obviate the need for construction of a water project. In some states, notably in California and Washington, officials have begun to enforce the "public interest" provisions that Elwood Mead first invented in Wyoming in 1890. This can mean that new rights, instead of being automatically granted, may be conditional or denied altogether if they are contrary to the public interest, usually in the form of recreation or wildlife.[112]

Private organizations have started to play new roles. The Nature Conservancy, an environmental organization that employs market techniques, has been especially active in buying up senior rights and then transferring them to state in-stream flow programs so that the water can remain in the rivers rather than being diverted. The Nature Conservancy also has been able to assist the federal government. At Nevada's Stillwater National Wildlife Refuge near Pyramid Lake, the environmental organization has already spent $1 million to buy up rights to 2700 acre-feet of water from local farmers. The fresh water will be applied directly to the wildlife refuge, thereby flushing out toxins, diluting them, and rejuvenating the ecosystem.[113]

But in spite of its creativity, the reform movement in western water is young and has achieved reform only around the edges. Almost all of the reform is limited in scope and, even when it applies, usually affects only the granting of new rights. The huge mass of rights granted during the long tenure of pure, monolithic prior appropriation has been little disturbed. A minimum stream flow to protect wildlife with a priority date of 1980 gets the public nothing on those many western streams for which a priority date of 1920, or even 1880, is needed to get wet water. "First in time, first in right." On the other hand, even an ancient priority can be insufficient to guarantee social equity. An Indian water right, like that of the Jicarilla Apaches, with an 1887 priority date, gets a tribe little or nothing when there is a competing project on the same river, built and subsidized for non-Indians under the 1902 Reclamation Act. Even after a long decade of reexamination and some impressive paper laws, most wet water is still allocated to the beneficiaries of the classic prior appropriation doctrine. It is still mostly business as usual.

Carrying What We Can Lift

Setting water policy right in a relatively short time is a realistic objective, and it can be done without taking draconian measures. Ironically, one of the greatest aids in correcting the excesses of western water development is those excesses themselves. The West is so extravagantly overbuilt—so much water has been developed, and so many water users are so wasteful—that the water supplies in the present system, if used sensibly, can meet most or all future needs for the foreseeable future without investment in more structural alternatives, such as substantial dams and stream diversions. The San Juan–Chama Project, and urban and agricultural waste in the Rio Grande watershed, stand as just one prototype both of the overbuilding and of how uses might be adjusted to meet future demands in both the Rio Grande and San Juan watersheds, whether they be from the city of Albuquerque, the Jicarilla Apache Tribe, Hispanic *acequias* or Indian pueblos in the Rio Grande valley, or new water users.

The starting point, then, is that the current situation affords an extraordinary amount of flexibility, a powerful ability to create new supplies of water from existing supplies. The importance and potential of more efficient water management were underscored by the influential 1986 report "Western Water: Tuning the System," released by a task force of the Western Governors' Association. As water analysts Steven Shupe, Gary Weatherford, and Elizabeth Checchio have explained it, the West has completed a long era of water allocation. The region is now entering an era of reallocation to accommodate both new uses and those uses that were ignored during the first era.[114]

The possibilities of reallocation without undue hardship are so great in part because the waste and excessive use are so great. The technology is available to save huge quantities of water in both urban and agricultural settings. In the cities, low-flush toilets and water-saving, or xeriscape, landscaping in new homes can be used. On the farms, water can be conserved with ditch lining; low-energy precision sprinklers, which "spoon-feed" water under low pressure to crops through hoses that drop from elevated pipes; laser-leveling of fields, which prevents pooling, seepage, and runoff; or drip or trickle irrigation, which applies water to the root systems of crops through pipes placed in furrows.[115]

Water conservation in the West, however, has barely begun. Even though, as noted, there have been some advances and even though the benefits are undeniable—one study concludes that the modest objective of a 7 percent reduction in agricultural use would support a 100 percent increase in all other uses—resistance is deep and profound. Some of the objections deserve respect. Lining a canal system with cement or installing a precision-application sprinkler system requires a large capital expenditure. In addition, leaky earthen canals sometimes support cottonwood trees and other vegetation; lining the canals to prevent water loss may reduce or eliminate wildlife habitat for small animals. Economic and environmental concerns, therefore, require a selective approach to conservation. The deeper problem, however, lies with the old attitudes, the idea that the water developers control the rivers: "It's their water, and they'll do with it as they please." They get the support of silence from the state engineers' offices and the state legislatures. The silence translates into inaction and the preservation of the *status quo*. As one Bureau of Reclamation official said of water users in the Middle Rio Grande Conservancy District, "Flood irrigation is the old-time practice and irrigators are not about to change it."[116]

Yet changes are in the wind, enough movement to make a person believe that the West is entering a period of transition for western water. Perhaps we are nearing the point when we will heed the call of Wallace Stegner, who has understood the West and its aridity better than anyone since John Wesley Powell:

> [W]here is the democratic, Jeffersonian, agrarian society the West hoped to become and once approximated? Every one of them, to establish and keep control of the waters of life, became an oligarchy. That is what the West is now, an elite of landowners and water experts on the top, an army of migrant aliens, most of them illegals, on the bottom. . . .
>   The West cannot carry what it has lifted. . . .
>   We need a Redeemer. We need a Congress that will say no to any more water boondoggles in the West. We need a moratorium on boosters and developers and raiders who can't or won't see the consequences of their acts. We need to scale down our expectations and advise a lot of hopeful immigrants that what they seek is not here.
>   For in creating the modern West we have gone a long way toward ruining this magnificent and fragile habitat. And as Marcus Aurelius said a long time ago, what is bad for the beehive cannot be good for the bee.[117]

The outlines of a program to answer Stegner's call are not hard to sketch. First and foremost, states should adopt phased-in conservation programs to require reduced consumption and diversion of water. Over time, the current high level of waste can be significantly reduced through installing affordable and available technology that would permit more efficient use of the water resources.

The conservation effort should emphasize the pricing of water. Water pricing should be applied in two situations: the first, already used by some municipal water suppliers, would replace the flat rates now employed with a graduated price structure that requires a higher per-unit cost for high-volume users. Commentators draw a direct connection between the current rate structures in western cities, which are too low and are based on a flat rate, and the high per capita water use in the urban West.[118]

Pricing should also be applied in another, even more fundamental, setting. From the beginning, as one manifestation of their control over the rivers, water users have enjoyed the perquisite of free water—they have never paid any fee to the state or federal government for the right to use water.

Governments ought to receive revenues when public water is put to private use, just as they do when other public resources are used for extractive purposes. The charge, which should be levied on every water developer for every acre-foot diverted, should be nominal at first but should gradually be increased to a higher, but still reasonable, level. Such a charge at the front end would encourage conservation at all levels. Further, since all elements of a conservation policy must be acutely sensitive to the needs of individual water users, especially struggling farm and rural communities, all or part of this charge for water diversions could be placed in a conservation fund to assist in paying for conservation measures—a recognition that today conservation means saving water, not building more water projects.

A new approach toward western water also should respond to the existing public consensus and incorporate a heavy, near-absolute presumption against new dams and other structural alternatives. The West is currently so overbuilt that few, if any, new dams are necessary. The current antipathy against dams has begun to inspire some conservation efforts; the stronger and more absolute the official declaration that dams are not needed, the quicker and stronger will be the response of looking to nonstructural alternatives. We have already harvested enough April rivers. Now we need to put those April rivers to much more efficient use.

Again, these approaches will not be draconian. They will be phased in and will come easily and naturally. Remember, the lords of yesterday provide ironic assistance: the West has slipped into such a profligate use of water that a relatively small percentage of savings will free up large amounts of water.

Nor is there an argument—although senior water rights holders attempt it loudly, in order to fend off reform measures—that a conservation program such as proposed here would infringe on the property rights of appropriators. Water users do plainly possess vested property rights, but they are limited to beneficial use—that is, efficient use without unreasonable waste. This means that states can squeeze current usage to reduce inefficient practices.

Take, for example, an irrigator who irrigates 1000 acres with 4000 acre-feet of water. By installing an efficient sprinkler system, however, the irrigator could economically grow the same crop with 2500 acre-feet. If the state adopts a requirement that this irrigator can divert only 2500 acre-feet, thus forcing the adoption of conservation measures, there has been no taking of any vested property right. The amount in excess of the water needed to grow the crop is not beneficial use and never was within the vested property right. This is true even if custom and practice in a watershed allow the higher diversion. As a federal court of appeals has explained, water use can change as the needs of society change: "[B]eneficial use expresses a dynamic concept, which is a 'variable according to conditions,' and therefore [is variable] over time." Professor Eric Freyfogle has made exactly the right comparison—of regulation of water to regulation of land:

> Takings jurisprudence now clearly supports a government's power to limit the bundle of rights that a property owner possesses. Water should be no more sacred than land. Courts should require a water owner, like a landowner, to comply with property use restraints so long as the restraints permit some reasonable property uses and amortize nonconforming uses fairly.[119]

Conservation programs will accomplish little if they are not complemented by programs to allocate the conserved water. If nineteenth-century prior appropriation is simply allowed to run its course, as it still does on most western rivers, the saved water will simply be captured by whichever private interest is next in line. It will still be mostly business as usual.

The basic approach should be to put teeth in Elwood Mead's old Wyoming idea that appropriations should be allowed only if they are in the public interest. This means that we should make provision for river use just as we have become accustomed to doing for land use. Future water uses (including uses of conserved water) should be allowed only if consistent with a state or local government plan that defines the public interest.

Oregon is one state that has begun to do this by providing for a reasoned reallocation of senior rights that are no longer being put to a beneficial use. Its 1988 water conservation statute encourages conservation of water by allowing appropriators to sell part of the conserved water. Twenty-five percent of the saved water, however, goes back to the state as an in-stream flow for fish, wildlife, and recreational purposes. Thus, if an appropriator with an 1880 priority date conserves 100 acre-feet of water, 25 acre-feet will normally be held by the state as an in-stream water right—with an 1880 priority date. Of course, there are numerous variations. The percentage to the state could be higher. Saved water could also be made available not just to in-stream flows but also to other uses ignored by traditional prior appropriation, including uses by Indian tribes. The idea could be expanded to include abandonment of water. Under prior appropriation, when a water right is abandoned, junior consumptive users simply move up a notch in the priority system. The Oregon concept would allow abandoned water rights to revert to the state, with part or all being applied to in-stream flows. Again, this state in-stream flow right would be the original priority—1880 in the example just used.[120]

There are other necessary parts of an effective reform movement. The legacy of Owens Valley ought to be the adoption of laws protecting basins of origin, usually rural river valleys, from water projects that benefit water users, usually urban land developers in other regions. The heart of the laws should be the requirement that no out-of-basin use can even be considered unless the water developer in the other basin has put in place a comprehensive water conservation program. This would prevent unnecessary raids on other communities, of which the San Juan–Chama Project is just one example.

Last, water decision making needs to be opened up. Western water has long been the province of "experts," mostly engineers and lawyers. Professionals from many other disciplines—economists, historians, biologists, sociologists, political scientists, and ecologists are just a few—have much to offer to water policy. So, too, does the generalist, the conscientious citizen, have much to offer in this field, where a fresh look is so critical. These changes should be made at two levels. State water policy boards with citizen members should be created, and in those few states that already have them, their membership should be further diversified. The same approach should be taken for personnel in the state administrative offices. Policy in the national forests went wrong in part because the Forest Service is dominated by foresters. The engineering mentality has been one factor in making water policy one-sided in favor of building and extractive uses. It is now clear that there is more in our rivers than we are allowed to see through the lens with which our policies view them.

Wallace Stegner has been able to change the lenses, to achieve clarity. Raised in the upper Great Plains just after the turn of the century, he saw the West when it was, by any definition, still a frontier. He was personally confronted with the old ideas there and, over the course of his life, in Utah, Washington, and California, and, in one way or another, in virtually every cranny of the region west of the 100th meridian.

Stegner did more, for he merged his life's experiences with his work and with his straightforward, unerring pen. He steeped himself in the literature of the West, its waters, its aridity, and its peculiar institutions. He forced his mind back to the very beginning of the westward expansion and put himself with the earnest first Mormon irrigators in the fields of the Great Salt Valley, next to the first dreamers of the great irrigation projects of the Boise Valley, side by side with the Montanans who settled the Milk River valley and other valleys of open, flat, eastern Montana. He rode down the Colorado River in the 1940s, when it was still mostly its original self, and during that journey managed to put himself in Powell's boat in 1869. He wrote his epic, Pulitzer Prize–winning book about Powell. Then, in the 1950s, when it came time to put a life of living and reading and learning on the line, he came down in favor of Dinosaur National Monument and Glen Canyon, and against still more big dams and still more control over the rivers by the big interests.

Stegner always has seen through the cries of complexity that have been the last refuge of the vested interests. No engineer or lawyer, just an English professor, a self-taught historian, an exquisite writer, and, perhaps most of all, a tough-minded westerner who knew his region, Stegner showed that "expertise" in the traditional sense is no prerequisite. The West, as he put it, cannot carry what it has lifted. When that basic message finally burns in, all the policies and institutions will finally begin to conform to the modern West, and to the West's rivers themselves, instead of to the notions of another time.

Chapter Seven

Crossing the
Next Meridian

Writing this book has been a long journey, an adventure, and the lasting joy for me has been in the learning. Some has come from reading and thinking, much more of it from visiting places and meeting the people whom those places have ignited.

I remember vividly my summer's-day meeting in 1988 with Delbert Frank, the Warm Springs Indian who told me the story of the Columbia River gorge and his grandparents, Jim Yahtin and Yessessi, and great-grandfather, Wunn-o-ah-chi. Delbert and I have had many conversations over the years, but this subject required a full and all-consuming day that left me exhausted, wrung out. Delbert is a very precise person, and he was determined to tell the history of his people, family, and place with complete precision. Often, this required him to use his own Sahaptin language, and many of the terms were so rich and complex that it took him ten or fifteen minutes of speaking in English to flesh out the full meaning of just one Sahaptin phrase.

Delbert felt history in a way that I had never before encountered. The fishing day at Big Eddy in 1848 was utterly real and tangible to him. He was not born until nearly eighty years later, but the oral tradition was so refined—there had been so much telling and retelling—that he could recreate every last detail of that long-ago time. This also was true with the fishing and living days of 1803 when, unbeknownst to the Sahaptins, a man in a powdered wig signed a purchase document, launching the expedition that made the opening of the West—for Delbert, the closing of it—inevitable.

Over in the shaded flats of Tygh Valley, near the old family home, and on the banks of the Deschutes River near Sherars Bridge, Delbert furrowed his brow and clenched his fist over and over again and tried to take me with him back to those days. I only partly made it, but part way was good enough for the moment. I saw and felt Delbert's palpable sense of morality about time and about salmon and the rivers and about the people and communities who depend on them.

I learned other lessons—of the same kind, ultimately—through my work at Camp Creek, in central Oregon. On two bright days on this ordinary little watershed, Wayne Elmore in his genial but concerted way gave me instruction as precious as any formal education I have ever had. Grounded in the things he knows best—range science and the Camp Creek system—he showed me poor land health, the history that made it that way, and how we can—we *must*—both restore the land health and preserve the communities that depend on the land. Community. It has always stuck with me that Wayne served several years on the local school board. Wayne is not given to moralizing, and never articulated it this way, but his beliefs and conduct shouted it out: we have high duties—good lands and good waters, and good schools in good towns.

Wayne is a scientist, and one of the unexpected revelations from my work on this book has been the role of the scientific community in causing change. Modern American natural resource policy began about 1970, the year when Earth Day was first celebrated and when the National Environmental Policy Act became law. Lawyers dominated the field in the 1970s, through their lawsuits and the comprehensive statutes marked by detailed hearings and appeal procedures and by reasonably extensive regulatory regimes. During the 1980s, economists came to the fore. Various proposals for deregulation, free market transfer systems, and incentives were made; many were adopted. In recent years, we have increasingly looked to the physical sciences, and my sense is that the work of the scientific community will continue to grow in importance in the making of public policy.

We have seen scientific contributions of sweeping significance and, in many cases, of extraordinarily principled, almost heroic, proportions. Wayne Elmore is one example. Another is Jack Ward Thomas, the Forest Service biologist who knows species diversity and who, despite the pressure to tell it otherwise, told it straight about the impacts of high-yield timber cutting on *Strix occidentalis caurina* and its ancient-forest habitat. Still another involves Pacific salmon and steelhead. By the late 1980s, there was a growing sense that the runs were down—way down—but the magnitude of the problem never hit home until drafts of the careful work of Willa Nehlsen and her colleagues began to be circulated, showing more than 200 separate stocks in severe distress. Nehlsen was an employee of the Northwest Power Planning Council, but she did all of the painstaking research on her own time.

The accumulated scientific evidence has aided us in trying to understand the current state of the land and waters of the West. Those species officially listed under the Endangered Species Act are only the tip of the iceberg, but the endangered and threatened species alone tell a chilling tale. Further, we now realize that these imperiled animal populations speak not only for their own existence but also for land and water health throughout their range.

Several of these species speak for vast geographic areas. The beleaguered spotted owl is the harbinger for the unique and irreplaceable ancient forests of northern California and western Oregon and Washington, 87 percent of which have been logged out. The reach of the salmon and steelhead extends all the way into the saw-toothed ridges of deep Idaho, and we have learned from these voyagers that the river and land systems have been battered too much. These fish have shown us that we can learn more from their health than from our maps. As we drive up into the Columbia River gorge above Bonneville Dam, we use road maps solemnly telling us of the "Columbia River." The maps are wrong; the name is just a euphemism. Above Bonneville, there is no longer a Columbia River. All the way to Canada, nearly 600 river miles, there is virtually no river, just a succession of reservoirs backed flush up against one another, leaving only 50 miles of open river in a few chopped-up segments. How could we have killed off nearly the whole River of the West within our borders in the finger-snap-short time of just twenty-five years?

John Muir—born just a few years before Delbert Frank's grandfather, Jim Yahtin—stepped off the boat onto the wharf at San Francisco in March 1868 and immediately asked which was the quickest way out of town. When the perplexed passer-by understandably inquired where the young man intended to go, Muir responded, "To any place that is wild." With directions in hand, he lit out for the mountains. Muir soon came to Pacheco Pass and looked across at the great sierra that he called the Range of Light. He was equally absorbed by what lay between him and the mountains that would hold his destiny: "At my feet lay the Great Central Valley of California, level and flowery, like a lake of pure sunshine, forty or fifty miles wide, five hundred miles long, one rich furred garden of yellow compositae."[1]

Today? The sprawling San Joaquin wetlands that Muir looked down on, even extending as far south as Tulare Lake, are gone. Their life sources, the spring overflows from the mountains, have been funneled into diversion ditches for the big farms and cities. The Central Valley has been transformed. In Muir's time, the Sacramento River Delta, the meeting place of all of the waters of the valley, was a green land of twisting, labyrinthine water passages, teeming with wildlife. Yet now the delta is in steep decline. As we have seen, so little good water reaches the delta, where the delta smelt lives, that the hardy little fish is being considered for listing as a threatened species. Although any of us can sense it by a visit to the Central Valley, the tenuous existence of the delta smelt, unlikely messenger though it might be, has told us in plain terms that the health of this land and water system, nearly as large as West Virginia, is poor.

The same message has been called out in the Rockies. The San Juan–Chama Project and its many siblings have drawn down the Colorado River system, which drains about one-fourth of the entire West, to the breaking point. One of the pending projects is the Animas–La Plata Project, which would take 150,000 acre-feet out of the Animas River just below Durango, Colorado. This is enough water to fill a football field with containing walls to a height of 30 miles each year. The Colorado River squawfish is on the edge of extinction, and some of the fish inhabit the San Juan River, into which the Animas flows. U.S. Fish and Wildlife Service biologists believe that the Animas–La Plata Project might tip the precarious balance for the squawfish: the scientists think that the project (compounded by the San Juan–Chama Project and scores of other diversions) would render the San Juan unable to do its work as a river, leaving the water so low and the channels so braided that the fish could not make it up to their spawning grounds to reproduce.

The Colorado River squawfish, like the delta smelt, is not an animal to which Americans have traditionally given much deference—indeed, as recently as the 1960s, the same U.S. Fish and Wildlife Service viewed them as trash fish and tried to poison them out of existence. Still, today the squawfish, like the others, has a message. It is the same message as Philip Fradkin's, who gave his book on the Colorado River such a straightforward title: *A River No More*. The Columbia and the Colorado, rivers no more.[2]

In the big open country of the northern Rockies, where soils are sturdier and population pressure is less, overall land and water health is probably better. Still, hard questions go unanswered. Where is the call of the wolf, extinct in most of the country and hanging on as an endangered species in a few scattered pockets? Can the great bear make it back from the edge? And what is the future of the Greater Yellowstone Ecosystem, magical site for citizens the world over but burdened with too many loving visitors, shot through with logging and mining roads, and raked by too high a timber cut, especially in the Targhee National Forest, where the waves of irresponsible clear-cuts butt right up against the park itself?

The state of the West is far worse than I thought when I first began to imagine this book in 1984. A person trying to write a principled account wants to avoid overstatement, to skirt being shrill. But I am satisfied that the far greater danger is in the other direction. I remember driving back to Boulder from one of my first interviews for this book with Ed Marston in Paonia on Colorado's Western Slope. It was September; the skies were clear, the slopes flecked with gold. I barely resisted my urge to shake my son Philip, who was just five then, from his nap of exhaustion so that he could take it all in with me. It seemed that we had the whole Western Slope to ourselves and that the land was so vigorous, indomitable.

The problem, of course, is that you cannot judge land health from a car window. The bad timber cuts are assiduously tucked away from view. Destruction from grazing takes a practiced eye to comprehend. Low, even dry, streams have become expected parts of the landscape. Acid mine drainage and the other poisons usually work in secret. There are no road signs to advise that a forest or stream is missing vital cogs. Far better truths than we can observe from car windows have come from the scientists and from the endangered species and the land and water systems they represent. We cannot cross the next meridian until we understand and heed those truths.

Another part of the crossing involves eliminating the lords of yesterday and replacing them with approaches that are sensible in light of the needs of today and the foreseeable future. Each of these areas has its own traditions and policies, and different policies need to be tailored for each. I have made suggestions in that spirit over the course of this book.

More is required, however, than dealing with the specifics of these policies. We also need to redefine the overarching ideas that create the context for our whole treatment of the land and waters of the American West. The lords of yesterday arose in an age when the controlling ideas were that the West should be thrown open to unfettered development and, extraordinarily, that the force of this extreme *laissez-faire* approach should be multiplied several times over by an unparalleled program of subsidies. Those ideas, compelling though they may have been in their time, are surely no longer valid. A number of replacement ideas have already emerged; I have listed some of them in chapter 1. In particular, during my work on this book I have come to realize that one unifying principle, which embodies the values of Delbert Frank, Wayne Elmore, and many of the other people who have enlightened me, underlies all wise resource use by human beings.

Good science, good laws, good economics, and good communities come together in the idea of sustainability. At its core are the responsibilities lodged in intergenerational equity, which Edith Brown Weiss describes as the principle that "[e]very generation receives a natural and cultural legacy in trust from its ancestors and holds it in trust for its descendants." Development cannot wear the lands and waters down but rather must maintain their vigor. A working policy of sustainability encompasses a practical and phased-in, but still rigorous and comprehensive, program of conservation so that consumption can be reduced. But the obligation to provide for the next generations also includes the duty to maintain a vital economy. Sustainability, then, affirmatively recognizes the need for development. Indeed, a program of sustainability ought to include the knowledge, technology, and planning needed to increase the productivity of the land.[3]

Sustainability is still largely untried in the United States. It thus brings with it the frustrations—a dearth of specifics, an abundance of abstract and sometimes unrealistic proposals—that usually accompany young ideas that exist mainly on paper. Installing it would bring changes to many parts of our lives, for it requires not just a simple adjustment in focus but rather a fundamental change in concept and approach. Still, the future lies with sustainability: the cumulative effects of the lords of yesterday have become so evident and so unacceptable that reform and the search for new approaches are already well under way. My guess is that in not so many years hence, western states and communities will be deeply into the process of wrestling with, and gradually implementing, the ideas embodied in sustainable development.

The first step in approaching sustainability is to identify exactly what must be sustained—the "natural and cultural legacy" that we have received and must pass on. Traditional extractive development in the West has focused only on the specific resources being extracted. Water projects, for example, were designed to meet only the demand for water, by which was meant water as a commodity—for mining, farming and ranching, energy development, and industrial, municipal, and domestic use. Any other benefits, such as the blue-ribbon trout stream below Navajo Dam on the San Juan River, were purely secondary and often accidental. Avoidance of negative effects, such as loss of the salmon runs, was largely a matter of luck, as when the Army Corps of Engineers' fish ladder at Bonneville Dam on the Columbia actually turned out to be workable. The overriding goal was to create commodity benefits, which were viewed as being nearly infinitely sustainable in those simpler times.

I saw this at work in a recent conversation with an engineer. He was frustrated because extravagant proposals, taken seriously a generation ago, were no longer much discussed. They included the construction of a water pipeline from the Yukon River to the lower 48 states and the towing of icebergs from the Arctic to southern California for melting. Another proposal involved transferring Montana water to San Diego. "It was so easy," he said, shrugging his shoulders. "All you had to do was build a pipeline under Yellowstone National Park, divert some of the Yellowstone River—not all of it—and shoot the water into the Green River."

His unspoken premises about this long-distance, trans–Continental Divide project are revealing. To him, this *was* sustainable development because his training taught him that this project could go on forever: the snowpack would renew the supply each year, and there was not even a dam to silt up.

What he did not see, but what modern conditions force us to take into account, is that the Yellowstone River must sustain much more than just the extraction of water for commodity purposes. Fish and wildlife. The falls in the world's first national park. The magic of Paradise Valley, which Dan Bailey, Len Sargent, and others worked so hard to protect from the Allenspur Dam in the 1970s. The ranching, farming, mining, and recreation economy from Gardiner to Livingston and even farther down the Yellowstone River. Depending on the amount of water diverted, the Yellowstone–San Diego Project might not have sustained these other benefits.

National forest management is another example. The high-yield timber harvest that has held sway since the mid-1960s is entirely sustainable in the traditional sense in which the term "sustained yield" has been used in American forestry since Pinchot's days. The Forest Service will cut the mature trees and stock the slopes with seedlings, and the stand will regenerate.

But our thinking has evolved; in many national forests, a broader view of sustainability is not being achieved. Only the specific resource being extracted—commercial timber—is being renewed. Other parts of the forests, which must be taken into account to achieve true sustainability, are in jeopardy. The health of certain fish and wildlife populations. Soil on steep slopes. The recreation economy. Species diversity. The ancient forests. Views. Beauty. Glory. Awe. Sustainability is measured not by board feet but by the whole forest.

Sustainability involves cultural as well as natural and economic factors. In chapter 6, I recounted the effects of Garrison Dam on the Fort Berthold Indian Reservation, where rich tribal bottomlands along the Missouri River were flooded and bridges connecting tribal communities were inundated. Fort Berthold, like Pyramid Lake, Celilo Falls, and the Hispanic settlements near Elephant Butte and Navajo Dam, is just one of a great many examples of our neglect of cultural sustainability. A friend, at once a traditional and modern Standing Rock Sioux tribal member, took me to a place similar to Fort Berthold, downstream on the Missouri at the Standing Rock Indian Reservation. We stood on a bluff looking at spartan replacement houses on a windswept ridge. Below, the reservoir had been drawn down, and we could see mud flats that had caked over bottomlands that once knew farms and sheltered homes. We could see, too, the white skeletons of trees that had been drowned by the reservoir. The Indian people had not even been allowed to cut the trees for firewood before the flooding.

Sustainable use, though rigorous, is not impractical. Companies can cut timber, lots of it. Developers can divert water, build dams, and flood land. At first blush, mineral development might not seem to fit with a literal application of sustainability, since the minerals cannot be replaced within a time period imaginable to humans. But mining is necessary, and the idea of sustainability can easily be adapted to mineral development through attention to the duration of the mining activity. Carefully paced mineral development lasting, say, as long as forty or fifty years, depending on the circumstances, can be considered sustainable. Clearly, mining can satisfy other elements of sustainability, such as community and economic fulfillment, and it need not be inconsistent with environmental and societal goals.

How, then, might sustainable use work in the West? After identifying all economic, environmental, cultural, and abstract—call them spiritual—elements that need to be sustained, it seems to me inevitable that westerners increasingly will turn to various forms of planning. When I say planning, I mean it in the broadest sense: the process of a community coming together; identifying problems; setting goals—a vision—for a time period such as twenty or forty years; adopting a program to fulfill those goals; and modifying the program as conditions change. Some developers, imbued with the traditional *carte blanche* attitude so evident in the lords of yesterday, try to paint any form of planning as a straitjacket. But sensible yet visionary planning is the opposite: it can open our minds to the possibilities for our communities—our neighborhoods, schools, businesses, environment, and culture—so that we can build flexible arrangements for trying to achieve and sustain those possibilities. All across the West, stresses have built to the point where it is hard to imagine a sustainable future without some form of planning.

Some of this has already come to pass, and it is interesting to see how "communities" have been defined for particular purposes. The California Coastal Commission has worked to preserve substantial stretches of open space, so vital to coastal residents and visitors alike. The cleanup of Oregon's Willamette River was a gargantuan accomplishment that could have been achieved only by a concerted, forward-looking effort. Also in Oregon, an acclaimed land use planning system has been put in place by innovative legislation premised on broad state-mandated goals, with specific plans being drawn by county and local governments. Nevada and California created the Tahoe Regional Planning Agency, which has adopted stringent restrictions on development of private land in order to preserve Lake Tahoe's fabled blue clarity, to protect wetlands, to improve air quality in the Tahoe basin, and to limit automobile congestion. At the local level, cities and towns are making increased use of zoning and other land use planning devices. All of these efforts have been imperfect; all have received their share of criticism from many, if not most, directions; but all represent substantial advances in the face of severe challenges.[4]

We have seen two planning efforts that have been even more expansive. Forest Service planning has brought some improvement to most national forests. The effort, however, has been deeply flawed in two ways. As implemented, it has been too expensive and bureaucratic. Even more fundamentally, planning at the national forest level has been largely emasculated because the key determinant—the timber cut—has been set from above. There is every likelihood, if and when the cut comes down, that the hard work expended in forest planning will pay large dividends.

In the Pacific Northwest, the Northwest Power Planning Council struck off on the most difficult course of all. The effort to rescue the salmon and steelhead, whose habitat reaches from Idaho to Alaska, is probably the most ambitious attempt at sustainability ever undertaken in the United States, perhaps anywhere. The results seemed truly impressive—until the runs collapsed in 1989. The effort has been intensified since then, but everyone has their fingers crossed. One thing seems certain. If we are to sustain salmon and steelhead, we will have to have a strong and effective Northwest Power Planning Council, or some comprehensive intergovernmental planning effort very much like it.

I well understand that it is a long way from the printed page to an actual working sustainability. The West has never been characterized by community decision making. The people have been footloose and on the move due to a regional economy, dependent on fast-paced extraction, that has traditionally been erratic. Although there is well-grounded optimism about a new western economy based on recreation, light industry, and more stable natural resource development, the returns are not yet in. Since the 1960s, sharp hostilities between industry and environmentalists have created separate armed camps. Everyone cares deeply about the land—most westerners, when pressed, are comfortable with a word like "sacred"—but the distrust and instability run so deep that people are leery about committing to consensus solutions. We are working on it, and making some progress, but we have not yet overcome the fact that it is hard for western communities to act like communities.

There is also a sense of helplessness bred of the perception that decisions in the West are made from the outside and that western communities have never been able to control their own destinies. The poor health of the

West's lands and waters, and of its economy, has often been attributed to forces outside of the West. Bernard DeVoto called the West a "plundered province." In *The Angry West*, Richard Lamm and Michael McCarthy argue that the West has been a "colony" and has been exploited accordingly. The fine historian K. Ross Toole has made a similar point about his native Montana. Carey McWilliams refined the colony idea by identifying the mountain West as a colony of both the East and California.[5]

I ascribed to those views when I began work on this book, but I see it somewhat differently now. In the case of fossil fuel energy production, which is the focus of much of the work of Toole and Lamm and McCarthy, the colony idea plays out quite well: although western urban centers (notably Phoenix, Tucson, Albuquerque, El Paso, Denver, and Salt Lake City) outside of California have taken an increasing share in recent years, it is true that much western oil, gas, and coal has been transported out of the region. With many other areas of development, however, the colony metaphor is much less compelling.

From the beginning, westerners have exerted rock-solid control over water development, hardrock mining, and grazing on public lands. Federal activity has been mainly in the form of subsidies. A "federal" law like the Hardrock Mining Law was in fact just a pass-through, a congressional imprimatur on the practices that the western mining industry was already following. Until the past few years, there were no significant federal water laws. Even the state laws were pass-throughs, ratifying the no-holds-barred approach favored by western water users. Gifford Pinchot and the Taylor Grazing Act notwithstanding, the public rangeland remains the province of western ranchers. DeVoto said it of water, as we saw in chapter 6, but his sharp-tongued adage about the attitudes of westerners toward the federal government applies fairly in all of these areas: "Get out and give us more money."

Nor is federal timber or Northwest energy much different. To be sure, Pinchot was the eastern born-and-bred *enfant terrible* in his day, but his building of the National Forest System, staffed by foresters, played perfectly into the hands of the western timber industry by the 1950s. The hydroelectric system of the Pacific Northwest was funded mainly through federal initiatives, but its "cheap" electricity is used, coveted, and promoted by numerous interests in the region.

The question of who has developed the West, and who has benefited, is a complicated matter, and I am not trying to settle it here. I understand that untold billions of dollars in profits have left the region and that there are a great many major outside players, including the federal landlord, multinational corporations located on both coasts, the military, and foreign investors. The global market has come on strong in the West as elsewhere, and that trend seems likely to continue. Still, untold billions of dollars in profits have also stayed in the region. All of the key congressional committees and federal agencies have long been controlled by westerners, beholden to the region. It is hard to avoid the conclusion that westerners themselves have made or controlled a great many, probably most, of the key societal decisions west of the 100th meridian. At a minimum, westerners should feel confident in their ability to chart the main directions of the region's course for the future.

They had better feel such confidence, and exercise it wisely, for there is a great deal at stake in the late twentieth and early twenty-first centuries. As just one illustration of this, let me return to Phoenix, where I began this book and my love affair with the West. In 1945, at the end of World War II, Phoenix was a town of about 80,000. By 1965, when I first went there, it had boomed to a city of 500,000. In 1985, Phoenix had become a metropolis, with a population of 875,000 within its city limits and nearly 2 million within the metropolitan area. Within just two generations: from a town to a city to a metropolis. And can there be any doubt that by the year 2000 Phoenix will be a megalopolis?

We can make roughly the same observations about Denver, Tucson, Salt Lake City, and Seattle. In California, Los Angeles and San Francisco were already cities by the end of World War II, but they too have transformed themselves in a short time, and so have their metropolitan areas. San Jose and San Diego have followed Phoenix's pattern, and all manner of other, somewhat smaller, municipalities in California have taken off.

The cities of the West are not somehow the enemy. Yet we cannot ignore the effects of the cities on the intermountain West. The urban centers—Los Angeles, San Diego, Las Vegas, Phoenix, Tucson, Albuquerque, Salt Lake City, and Denver—take a large and growing share of Colorado River water. Phoenix, joined by a consortium of municipalities stretching from San Diego to El Paso, has installed the power plants and mines that have stripped out the coal, water, and fabulously clean air of the red rock Colorado Plateau—the Four Corners country. Again, these are just examples: all of the cities have reached deep into the mountain West. This is true even of the Pacific Northwest. There is no need for those urban centers to import water from rural areas, traditionally the impetus for urban conquest of the mountain West, because the Northwest gets rain and because the big cities are on the same side of the mountains as the rivers. But is it not the energy demands of Seattle and Portland that have killed off the salmon and steelhead runs in the River of No Return country in the deep Rockies?

So, too, is the mountain West itself building up. Aspen, Telluride, and Summit County, just over the Divide from Denver, have all made themselves over in twenty years or less. So have Taos, Sun Valley, and Coeur d'Alene. Others are on the way.

So short. The time has been so short. We can realize now that the post—

World War II boom has been a rush of the same dimension as the great migration triggered in 1848. Spread out over more years, yes; lacking the electric clarity of Marshall's find, yes; but just as historic, just as transforming.

The unpleasant fact, as unpleasant for this writer as for any reader, is that we must come to grips with population growth. Our real choice comes down to this: Western communities can either take charge of the future by adopting some form of conscious management and direction, based on full and brightly etched visions of the future, and sustain the West's lands, waters, and way of life; or western communities can continue to abdicate—by allowing developers to charge ahead with few restraints—and surrender the distinctive qualities of the West within a very few decades. This is not something I fully understood when I began this journey, but when one takes the time to work through the current state of the West, it becomes self-evident.

Take the Truckee River watershed in Nevada and its terminus, Pyramid Lake. As discussed in chapter 1, in 1990 Congress approved a bipartisan settlement, agreed to by most interest groups in the Reno area, to save the cui-ui and Lahontan cutthroat trout of Pyramid Lake and the white pelicans, grebes, and other waterfowl of Stillwater National Wildlife Refuge. The settlement may still founder—many details still must be negotiated and implemented—but it is a superb arrangement: it shouts out sustainability. Reno will conserve water, and so will the irrigators. The Sierra Pacific Power Company will adjust its flow regime. The Pyramid Lake Pauite Tribe, also seeking out a middle ground, has put several lawsuits on hold. Wildlife biologists have struggled to define with precision the varying habitat needs of the many species of fish and birds.

But how long can this carefully drawn, principled accommodation last? The Reno-Sparks area, which has a growth curve like Phoenix's, now houses a population of nearly 300,000 people. What will happen to Pyramid Lake, the tribe, the river, Stillwater, the fish, and the birds in twenty-five years, when the population reaches 500,000? Were not Powell and Stegner right, after all, about their central point—that the aridity and terrain dictate a finiteness beyond the 100th meridian? Is not the finite in view?

This is an area in which it is even harder to move from words on paper to hard results. Growth control is difficult to achieve in an equitable way. Some property owners may bear a disproportionate burden from zoning that slows new development. Poor people and racial minorities may be forced out when rental prices accelerate in a tight housing market. It takes determination, sensitivity, innovation, and a cautious pace of change to prevent these kinds of injuries. Further, political opposition runs deep.

"You can't stop growth" is not just a truism in the West; it is a dictate not even worthy of serious discussion.

Still, not so long ago, "first in time, first in right" also seemed set in stone, yet today we have begun the process of putting aside that maxim. It may be that western communities are now ready to address growth based on an ethic emanating from the seriousness of the threat, a final commitment to protecting the values of the lands and waters and places, and an understanding that population growth in no way equates with economic growth or prosperity and may impede them.

There are many different ways to approach growth control. In combination, they breed flexibility and may make it unnecessary to approach the matter by adopting fixed, and perhaps arbitrary, limits on growth. Some population control comes voluntarily, when an area simply becomes so congested that people choose to settle elsewhere. Another part of the growth issue involves channeling development, as by setting urban growth boundaries and requiring the building of low- and middle-income housing. Economic policy plays a role by discouraging growth through programs ensuring that developers and their customers—all of us—must absorb the true costs of development. A key part can be resolved by hewing to the standards that will flow from a working policy of sustainability, as when an aquifer can take no more pumps because it already is producing its maximum safe yield. If we decide to listen, our lands and waters will tell us what our population can be.[6]

But no matter how difficult the process may be, we can no longer escape the fact that we are close up against our inevitable confrontation with the matter of stabilizing the population. There is a long list of people who have already made that point. This journey has taught me that I must add myself to that list.

Crossing the next meridian, then, requires more than abolishing the lords of yesterday—the various policies and laws governing hardrock mining, the public range, the national forests, the salmon and steelhead runs, and the region's rivers. It will require abolishing the philosophical ideas that fueled them and replacing those ideas with new ones. They include sustainability, which in turn directly implicates the level of population. The crossing also will require westerners to accept personal responsibility for the impacts on the lands, waters, and communities in a way that has not occurred before. Although I hope that this book will be of use in suggesting the magnitude of the problem and some of the paths toward resolution, I will not attempt here to catalogue all of the specific ways in which those ideas might be instilled. That will require another journey.

But I do believe that we must act now, at this meridian, or we will be too late. Not too late, perhaps, to preserve a West that mostly passes a car-window test but too late to preserve as living places the vast and sacred habitats that the dying-off animals speak for. It would be painful—even, Delbert Frank and Wayne Elmore might suggest, immoral—to pass by the opportunity to act now, because it should not be so hard to mesh the needs of the lands and the waters and the people. They ought to be the same. In the last analysis, they are the same.

Notes

CHAPTER ONE

1. Some of the facts here are taken from Forest Service documents in the court records for *Thomas v. Peterson*, 753 F.2d 754 (9th Cir. 1985). In that case, the United States Court of Appeals for the Ninth Circuit enjoined construction of the Jersey-Jack road and ordered the Forest Service to conduct further studies of the environmental impacts of the project, in light of the requirements of the National Environmental Policy Act and the Endangered Species Act. Subsequently, environmental impact statements were completed, and the Forest Service plans to go ahead with what is substantially the same project, now called the Cove/Mallard Timber Sales. *See* U.S. Department of Agriculture, Forest Service, Nez Perce National Forest, "Final Environmental Impact Statement: Cove Timber Sales" (Washington, DC: U.S. Government Printing Office, Dec. 1990); U.S. Department of Agriculture, Forest Service, Nez Perce National Forest, "Final Environmental Impact Statement: Mallard Timber Sales" (Washington, DC: U.S. Government Printing Office, Dec. 1990). For information on TJ International, see TJ International, *Annual Report: 1990* (Boise, ID: TJ International, Feb. 1991). I also traveled to Dixie, Idaho, and the surrounding area on October 4 and 5, 1986, to conduct interviews and view the area. In addition, my research assistant Valerie Russo conducted follow-up telephone interviews with Emmett Smith on January 13 and 27, 1992.

Finally, I benefited greatly from communications with Tom Kovalicky, former forest supervisor of the Nez Perce National Forest, letter to author, May 11, 1992; Neal "Pete" Parsell, technical publication editor for biological sciences, Nez Perce National Forest, memo, May 4, 1992, and telephone conversation with research assistant Ellen Kohler, May 22, 1992; Ron Mitchell, Idaho Sportsmen's Coalition, telephone conversations with author and research assistant Ellen Kohler, May 20–21, 1992.

2. U.S. Department of Agriculture, Forest Service, Intermountain Forest and Range Experiment Station, Donald H. Gray and Walter F. Megahan,

"Forest Vegetation Removal and Slope Stability in the Idaho Batholith,"
p. 22 (Washington, DC: U.S. Government Printing Office, 1981).

3. On Pacific salmon and steelhead, see generally *infra* chapter 5 and the
authorities cited therein. On wildlife management generally, see Aldo
Leopold, *Game Management* (New York: Charles Scribner's Sons, 1933).

4. The chinook salmon in the Snake River system, which includes the Salmon
River, have been declared a threatened species. *See* Paul Koberstein, "Chinook Put on Endangered List," *Oregonian*, p. A1 (Apr. 18, 1992).

5. Donald Jackson and Mary Lee Spence, eds., *The Expeditions of John
Charles Frémont: Travels from 1838 to 1844*, vol. 1, pp. 604–7 (Urbana:
University of Illinois Press, 1970).

6. The standard history of the Pyramid Lake tribe, and of many of the events
recounted here, is Martha Knack and Omer Stewart, *As Long as the River
Shall Run: An Ethnohistory of Pyramid Lake Indian Reservation*
(Berkeley: University of California Press, 1984). The book contains complete bibliographical notes.

7. *See* Jackson and Spence, *supra* note 5, at p. 609.

8. The Reclamation Act of 1902 can be found at 43 U.S.C. § 371 *et seq.*
(1988). On the irrigation program, see *infra* chapter 6, notes 30–38.

9. On the current and historical status of the Truckee River watershed, see
generally State of California, Department of Water Resources, *Truckee
River Atlas* (Sacramento, CA: Department of Water Resources, 1991) and
the authorities cited therein. The facts concerning the lake and the fish
species are set out in U.S. Department of the Interior, Fish and Wildlife Service, Cui-ui Recovery Team, "Technical Agency Draft Cui-ui
Recovery Plan," 2d rev. (Reno, NV: U.S. Fish and Wildlife Service, July
1991). *See also Carson-Truckee Water Conservancy District v. Clark*, 741
F.2d 257 (9th Cir. 1984), *cert. denied sub nom. Nevada v. Hodel*, 470 U.S.
1083 (1985). The litigation upheld the Department of the Interior's decision to allocate all of the storage water in Stampede Reservoir to protect
the two fish species in order to fulfill the department's obligations under
the Endangered Species Act.

10. The quotation is from Tom Harris, "Scientists Try to Find Out What Is
Wiping Out Life at Carson Sink," *Fresno Bee*, p. A1 (Feb. 15, 1987). On
the Stillwater National Wildlife Refuge, see also Tom Harris, "Getting Off
on the Wrong Foot," *High Country News*, p. 8 (Nov. 20, 1989); Don
Vetter, "Researchers Eye Geology as Possible Culprit for Stillwater Toxic
Problems," *Reno Gazette Journal*, p. 1A (Mar. 26, 1989). I also benefited
from a site visit and interview with Ron Anglin, refuge manager of the
Stillwater National Wildlife Refuge, on Mar. 24, 1992.

11. Water conservation issues are discussed *infra*, in chapter 6. As for litigation by the tribe, the largest setback was *Nevada v. United States*, 463 U.S.
110 (1983), in which the Supreme Court ruled that the tribe's claim to a
reserved water right, even if valid, was barred by the doctrine of *res
judicata* because the United States failed to raise the tribal right in litigation begun in 1913.

12. On the economy in the modern West, see generally Ed Marston, ed., *Reopening the Western Frontier* (Washington, DC: Island Press, 1989). On Colorado tourism, see Colorado Legislative Council Staff Report, Dr. Nancy J. McCallin, "Focus Colorado: Economic and Revenue Forecast, 1992–93," p. 30 (Denver: Colorado Legislative Council, Dec. 1991). The quotation concerning the Wyoming economy was taken from Wyoming Futures Project Executive Summary, *Building a Stronger Wyoming: Opportunities in a Troubled Economy*, p. 8 (Menlo Park, CA: Stanford Research Institute International, Oct. 1985). *See also* Thomas M. Power, "Thinking about the Wyoming Economy: Extraction, Environmental Protection, and Economic Development," paper presented at Wyoming Outdoor Council's 1990 annual meeting, Sheridan, WY (Sept. 29, 1990). The "three-legged stool" quotation is from Ed Marston, "The West Braces for a Welcome Onslaught," *High Country News*, p. 2 (May 26, 1986).
13. *See* Gretel Ehrlich, *The Solace of Open Spaces* (New York: Viking Penguin, 1985).
14. Walter Prescott Webb, "Ended: Four Hundred Year Boom. Reflections on the Age of the Frontier," vol. 203 *Harper's Magazine*, p. 26 (Oct. 1951).
15. *See generally* Patricia Nelson Limerick, *The Legacy of Conquest: The Unbroken Past of the American West* (New York: W. W. Norton & Company, 1987); T. H. Watkins and Charles S. Watson, Jr., *The Lands No One Knows* (San Francisco: Sierra Club Books, 1975). For the "Great Barbecue" phrase, see *id.* at p. 46.
16. For total land transfers to citizens and corporations, see generally Paul W. Gates, *History of Public Land Law Development* (Washington, DC: U.S. Government Printing Office, 1968). On dispositions to railroads, see Samuel T. Dana and Sally K. Fairfax, *Forest and Range Policy: Its Development in the United States*, 2d ed., p. 20 (New York: McGraw-Hill Book Company, 1980).
17. U.S. Congress, Joint Economic Committee, "Subsidy and Subsidy-Effect Programs of the U.S. Government," 89th Congress, 1st Session, p. 1 (Washington, DC: U.S. Government Printing Office, 1965).
18. On the economics of guides and packers in Idaho, see James M. Lansche, "Industry Report on the 1983–84 Through 1986–87 Idaho Outfitting Seasons" (Nov. 20, 1987) (copies available from Idaho Outfitters and Guides Association, P.O. Box 95, Boise, ID 83701). The $60 million revenue estimate calculation was provided by Grant Simonds, executive director of the Idaho Outfitters and Guides Association, in a telephone interview conducted by my research assistant Valerie Russo, Jan. 24, 1992.
19. Proceedings honoring Roscoe Pound, Roscoe Pound, "The Causes of Popular Dissatisfaction with the Administration of Justice," vol. 35 *Federal Rules Decisions*, pp. 241, 273, 277 (1964) (reprint of address originally delivered by Dean Pound in 1906).
20. The 1985 court decision and the subsequent environmental impact statements are cited *supra* note 1.

21. The legislation is the Fallon Paiute Shoshone Indian Tribes Water Rights Settlement Act of 1990, 104 Stat. 3289; Title II of this act is the Truckee-Carson-Pyramid Lake Water Settlement. *See* David Yardas, "Restoring Endangered Ecosystems: The Truckee-Carson Water Rights Settlement," *Resource Law Notes*, p. 5 (Boulder: University of Colorado School of Law, Natural Resources Law Center, Jan. 1992). On conservation efforts and The Nature Conservancy's program, see John Lancaster, "Buying Peace in Western Water War," *Washington Post*, p. A3 (June 10, 1990). *See generally* State of California, Department of Water Resources, *supra* note 9.

CHAPTER TWO

1. On Goldstrike and American Barrick, see U.S. Department of the Interior, Bureau of Land Management, Elko District Office, "Final Environmental Impact Statement: Betze Project, Barrick Goldstrike Mines Inc." (June 1991); American Barrick Resources Corporation, Annual Report, 1991; Michael Satchell, "The New Gold Rush," vol. 111 *U.S. News & World Report*, p. 44 (Oct. 28, 1991); John Seabrook, "A Reporter at Large: Invisible Gold," *New Yorker*, p. 45 (Apr. 24, 1989); Philip Hocker and Stewart Udall, "What's Mined Is Theirs," *Sierra*, p. 20 (Sept.–Oct. 1989); Briefing Paper, "Who Owns the Gold Mines? Corporate Ownership of the Twenty-Five Leading Gold-Producing Mines in the United States" (Washington, DC: Mineral Policy Center, June 1991); American Barrick Resources Corporation, Form 10-K (Washington, DC: U.S. Securities and Exchange Commission, Mar. 1991). I visited the site and met with John McDonough and other employees on Mar. 20, 1992. The Dutton quote is from Walter Sullivan, *Landprints*, p. 95 (New York: Times Books, 1984).
2. The quotation is from "Final Environmental Impact Statement," *supra* note 1, at pp. 5–7.
3. This quotation is from an interview with Professor Glenn Miller on Mar. 23, 1992. Mining pollution is discussed in more detail in the text accompanying notes 43–44, 79, *infra*. On the Superfund National Priority List and mining sites, see generally Van E. Housman and Stephen Hoffman, "Mining Sites on Superfund's National Priorities List: Past and Current Mining Practices," paper to be presented at the Society of Mining Engineer's Conference, St. Louis, MO (Oct. 1992).
4. John McPhee, *Coming into the Country*, pp. 429–30 (New York: Farrar, Straus & Giroux, 1977).
5. Jeff Jones, U.S. Department of Agriculture, Forest Service, Sawtooth National Recreation Area, interview with author, Sept. 9, 1985.
6. For statistics on mining claims, see U.S. Department of the Interior, Bureau of Land Management, "Public Land Statistics: 1990," p. 89 (Washington, DC: U.S. Government Printing Office, 1991).
7. McPhee, *supra* note 4, at p. 410.
8. On the California gold rush, see generally Rodman Paul, *California Gold:*

The Beginning of Mining in the Far West (Cambridge: Harvard University Press, 1947); J. S. Holliday, *The World Rushed In: The California Gold Rush Experience* (New York: Simon & Schuster, 1981). On acquisition of land from foreign nations, see Paul W. Gates, *History of Public Land Law Development*, pp. 75–86 (Washington, DC: U.S. Government Printing Office, 1968); Treaty of Guadalupe Hidalgo, 9 Stat. 922.

9. See Paul, *supra* note 8, at p. 25.
10. For the quotation on the Feather River find, see Plumas County Historical Society, Publication no. 29, *Plumas Memories*, p. 2 (Sattley, CA: Sierra Reproduction, July 14, 1968). Shortly thereafter, "Dame Shirley" arrived at Rich Bar and wrote her famous account of life in "Gold Country." *See* Carl I. Wheat, ed., *The Shirley Letters* (New York: Alfred A. Knopf, 1949). For the J. Ross Browne quotation, see U.S. House of Representatives, Executive Document no. 202, "Mineral Resources of the States and Territories West of the Rocky Mountains," 40th Congress, 2d Session, p. 605 (Washington, DC: U.S. Government Printing Office, Mar. 5, 1868).
11. On California Indians during this era, see generally Francis Paul Prucha, *The Great Father: The United States Government and the American Indians*, vol. 1, pp. 381–92 (Lincoln: University of Nebraska Press, 1984). On aboriginal Indian landownership before treaties, see Felix S. Cohen, *Cohen's Handbook of Federal Indian Law*, rev. ed., pp. 486–93 (Charlottesville, VA: Michie Company/Bobbs-Merrill Law Publishing, 1982).
12. *United States v. Sioux Nation of Indians*, 448 U.S. 371, 377 (1980).
13. *Id.* at p. 383, quoting Frank B. Fiske, *The Taming of the Sioux*, p. 132 (Bismarck, ND: Bismarck Tribune Press, 1917).
14. *See* Browne, *supra* note 10, at p. 613. *See generally* Paul, *supra* note 8, at pp. 240–62.
15. The Union District Code is sporadically on display in the law library at the University of Colorado School of Law.
16. For the placer mining regulations of the North San Juan District in California, see U.S. House of Representatives, Executive Document no. 29, "A Report upon the Mineral Resources of the States and Territories West of the Rocky Mountains," 39th Congress, 2d Session, p. 240 (Washington, DC: U.S. Government Printing Office, Jan. 8, 1867).
17. *Morton v. Solambo Copper Mining Co.*, 26 Cal. 527, 532–33 (1864).
18. See the chapter on mining laws written by Robert W. Swenson in Gates, *supra* note 8, at pp. 702–6; Loren L. Mall, *Public Land and Mining Law*, 3d ed., pp. 169–70 (Seattle: Butterworth Legal Publishers, 1981).
19. *Hicks v. Bell*, 3 Cal. 219 (1853). On trespassers on public lands, see Cheryl Outerbridge, Rocky Mountain Mineral Law Foundation, eds., *American Law of Mining*, 2d ed., vol. 6, pp. 203-2 to 203-3 (New York: Matthew Bender & Company, 1991).
20. Abraham Lincoln, "Message from the President of the United States to the Two Houses of Congress," 38th Congress, 2d Session, p. 10 (Washington, DC: U.S. Government Printing Office, 1864).

21. For authorities on the New Almaden incident and a discussion of this era generally, see Swenson, in Gates, *supra* note 8, at pp. 714–15.

22. John S. Hittell, *The Resources of California Comprising Agriculture, Mining, Geography, Climate, Commerce, etc., and the Past and Future Development of the State*, 4th ed., pp. 438–44 (San Francisco: A. Roman & Company, 1868).

23. Stewart's oft-humorous personal account of his life (Mark Twain was once his secretary) is published. *See* George R. Brown, ed., *Reminiscences of Senator William M. Stewart of Nevada* (New York: Neale Publishing Company, 1908).

24. On the 1866 act, see Swenson, in Gates, *supra* note 8, at pp. 714–21.

25. *Congressional Globe*, 39th Congress, 1st Session, p. 3226 (Washington, DC: Congressional Globe Office, 1866).

26. The Mining Act of 1866 can be found at 14 Stat. 251. For the Martz quote, see Swenson, in Gates, *supra* note 8, at p. 719; The Rocky Mountain Mineral Law Foundation, eds., *The American Law of Mining*, vol. 1, p. 41 (New York: Matthew Bender & Company, 1983).

27. The Mining Act of 1870 can be found at 16 Stat. 217. For Congressman Sargent's comment, see *Congressional Globe*, 42d Congress, 2d Session, p. 534 (Washington, DC: Congressional Globe Office, 1872). For the quotation comparing English and American mining, see William J. Trimble, "The Mining Advance into the Inland Empire," vol. 3 *Bulletin of the University of Wisconsin*, pp. 382–83 (1914).

28. For an outstanding full-length treatment of hardrock mining, see John D. Leshy, *The Mining Law: A Study in Perpetual Motion* (Washington, DC: Resources for the Future, 1987). *See also* George Cameron Coggins and Charles F. Wilkinson, *Federal Public Land and Resources Law*, 2d ed., pp. 420–507 (Westbury, NY: Foundation Press, 1987).

29. The quotations in this and the preceding two paragraphs are from 30 U.S.C. § 22 (1988).

30. *Hanson v. Craig*, 170 F. 62, 65 (9th Cir. 1909), quoting Geo. P. Costigan, Jr., *Handbook on American Mining Law*, p. 156 (St. Paul, MN: West Publishing Company, 1908).

31. The two statutory quotations are from 30 U.S.C. § 28 (1988) and 30 U.S.C. § 23 (1988), respectively.

32. 30 U.S.C. §§ 23, 35–36 (1988).

33. For the statutory quotation, see 30 U.S.C. § 26 (1988). The court quotation is from *United States v. Etcheverry*, 230 F.2d 193, 195 (10th Cir. 1956).

34. *See generally* Coggins and Wilkinson, *supra* note 28, at pp. 432–39; U.S. Congress, General Accounting Office, "Federal Land Management: Unauthorized Activities Occurring on Hardrock Mining Claims" (Washington, DC: General Accounting Office, Aug. 1990). *See also* the Surface Resources Act of 1955, 30 U.S.C. § 612(a) (1988).

35. The "prudent person" test is set out in *Castle v. Womble*, 19 Pub. Lands Dec. 455, 457 (1894).

36. *United States v. Coleman*, 390 U.S. 599, 600 (1968). For the "very high-handed" quote, see Coggins and Wilkinson, *supra* note 28, at p. 437.
37. For statistics on mining claims, see U.S. Department of the Interior, Bureau of Land Management, *supra* note 6, at p. 89.
38. On annual assessment work, see 30 U.S.C. §28 (1988). On the 1976 filing requirements, see 43 U.S.C. § 1744 (1988). The claim must be staked, and documents filed with the county, within sixty to ninety days, depending on each state's requirements.
39. The statutory quote is from 30 U.S.C. § 28 (1988).
40. Jones, *supra* note 5.
41. 30 U.S.C. §§ 29, 42 (1988).
42. For total patents issued, see U.S. Congress, General Accounting Office, "Federal Land Management: The Mining Law of 1872 Needs Revision," p. 10 (Washington, DC: General Accounting Office, Mar. 1989). For 1990 statistics, see U.S. Department of the Interior, Bureau of Land Management, *supra* note 6, at p. 88.
43. On the total waste and affected areas of rivers and lakes, see Robert L. P. Kleinmann, "Acid Mine Drainage in the United States," *Proceedings: First Midwestern Region Reclamation Conference*, p. 1–1 (Carbondale: Southern Illinois University, Coal Research Center, June 1990). On stream mileage in Colorado, see Western Interstate Energy Board, *Inactive and Abandoned Noncoal Mines: A Scoping Study*, vol. 1, p. 26 (Denver: Western Governors' Association Mine Waste Task Force, Aug. 1991). On the Clark Fork River basin, see, for example, Peter Nielsen, "Arsenic and Old Wastes," *Northern Lights*, p. 6 (Jan. 1989). *See generally* Duane A. Smith, *Mining America: The Industry and the Environment, 1800–1980* (Lawrence: University Press of Kansas, 1987); Johnnie N. Moore and Samuel N. Luoma, "Mining's Hazardous Waste," vol. 24 *Environmental Science & Technology*, p. 1278 (1990).
44. On acid mine drainage, see generally Kleinmann, *supra* note 43; Moore and Luoma, *supra* note 43. The quotation is from University of California, Berkeley, Mining Waste Study Team, "Mining Waste Study: Final Report," p. xix (Berkeley: University of California, July 1988).
45. *See* Coal Act of 1864, 13 Stat. 343; Coal Lands Act of 1873, 17 Stat. 607; Oil Placer Act of 1897, 29 Stat. 526.
46. American Mining Congress, "Report of Proceedings of the American Mining Congress, Sixteenth Annual Session," p. 157 (Denver: American Mining Congress, 1914). On the demand for oil at the turn of the century, see generally Daniel Yergin, *The Prize: The Epic Quest for Oil, Money, and Power*, pp. 71–95 (New York: Simon & Schuster, 1991).
47. *See generally* Samuel P. Hays, *Conservation and the Gospel of Efficiency: The Progressive Conservation Movement, 1890–1920* (Cambridge: Harvard University Press, 1959).
48. Robert H. Nelson, *The Making of Federal Coal Policy*, pp. 15–16 (Durham, NC: Duke University Press, 1983).

49. The director's quotation is from *United States v. Midwest Oil Co.*, 236 U.S. 459, 466–67 (1915).
50. American Mining Congress, "Report of Proceedings of the American Mining Congress, Fourteenth Annual Session," pp. 141–42 (Denver: American Mining Congress, 1911).
51. On Congress's power over the federal lands, see U.S. Const. art. IV, § 3, cl. 2. For the paraphrased maxim quotation, see *United States v. Midwest Oil Co., supra* note 49, at p. 472. On the question of whether federal or state law governs a particular problem on federal lands, see generally *Kleppe v. New Mexico*, 426 U.S. 529 (1976).
52. 30 U.S.C. §§ 181–287 (1988). The first quotation is from American Mining Congress, *supra* note 46, at p. 175; the second quotation is from vol. 58 *Congressional Record*, 66th Congress, 1st Session, p. 4250 (Washington, DC: U.S. Government Printing Office, 1919).
53. For a more specific discussion of mineral leasing, see Coggins and Wilkinson, *supra* note 28, at pp. 503–97, and the authorities cited therein.
54. *See* Trimble, *supra* note 27.
55. Yellowstone Park Act of 1872, 17 Stat. 32.
56. On withdrawal law and policy, see David H. Getches, "Managing the Public Lands: The Authority of the Executive to Withdraw Lands," vol. 22 *Natural Resources Journal*, p. 279 (1982). On the Pelican Island withdrawal, including the "stark raving mad" quotation, see Coggins and Wilkinson, *supra* note 28, at pp. 779–80. The Antiquities Act of 1906 can be found at 16 U.S.C. § 431 (1988). For the acreage figures, see Coggins and Wilkinson, *supra* note 28, at pp. 255–56.
57. The National Park Service Organic Act of 1916 can be found at 16 U.S.C. § 1 (1988).
58. 16 U.S.C. §§ 1131–36 (1988); 16 U.S.C. §§ 3101–3233 (1988). The statistics on wilderness were obtained from Richard Hoppe, assistant director of public affairs, The Wilderness Society, by telephone interview with my research assistant Ellen Kohler, Mar. 9, 1992.
59. The 1976 provision for a secretarial review of withdrawals can be found at 43 U.S.C. § 1714(e) (1988). *See generally* Getches, *supra* note 56.
60. The "overdrawn account" quotation is from Gary Bennethum and Courtland Lee, "Is Our Account Overdrawn?" vol. 61 *American Mining Congress Journal*, p. 33 (1975); the "Progress Keep Out!" quotation is from J. Allen Overton, "A Mining Industry Viewpoint," p. 194, paper presented at the Rocky Mountain Energy-Minerals Conference, Billings, MT (Oct. 1975).
61. U.S. Congress, Office of Technology Assessment, "Management of Fuel and Nonfuel Minerals in Federal Land: Current Status and Issues," pp. 215–20 (Washington, DC: U.S. Government Printing Office, 1979).
    There have been other inroads on the right of free access. Although most national forest lands remain subject to the 1872 act, Congress mandated in the Acquired Lands Act of 1947 that all minerals would be

subject to leasing on acquired lands—those lands (most of which are in eastern national forests) that the United States had transferred out to private or state ownership but has since reacquired. Another method of minerals disposal was established by the Material Disposal Act of 1947 and the Common Varieties Act of 1955. Those laws depart from the Hardrock Act's free-entry system and provide for sale of common varieties of gravel, sand, stone, cinders, and other designated materials. The Acquired Lands Act of 1947 can be found at 30 U.S.C. §§ 351–59 (1988); the Material Disposal Act of 1947 can be found at 30 U.S.C. §§ 601–4 (1988); the Common Varieties Act can be found at 30 U.S.C. § 611 (1988).

62. The Surface Resources Act can be found at 30 U.S.C. §§ 612–15 (1988). Both quotes are from U.S. House of Representatives, Report no. 730, "Amending the Act of July 31, 1947 (61 Stat. 681), and the Mining Laws to Provide for Multiple Use of the Surface of the Same Tracts of the Public Lands," 84th Congress, 1st Session, p. 6 (Washington, DC: U.S. Government Printing Office, 1955).

63. *See* 43 U.S.C. § 1782(c) (1988) (roadless areas); 43 U.S.C. § 1744 (1988) (recordation). The quotation is from *Topaz Beryllium Co. v. United States,* 649 F.2d 775, 778 (10th Cir. 1981). *See generally United States v. Locke,* 471 U.S. 84 (1985).

64. The quotations are from 16 U.S.C. § 551 (1988) and 30 U.S.C. § 22 (1988), respectively.

65. The codified regulations can be found at 36 C.F.R. § 228 (1990).

66. On agency mining regulations, see Leshy, *supra* note 28, at pp. 196–99; 36 C.F.R. §228 (1990) (Forest Service regulations); 43 C.F.R. § 3800 (1991) (BLM regulations).

67. *See* Leshy, *supra* note 28, at p. 79. Both Cameron and Zweifel inspired litigation that memorializes their episodes. *See Cameron v. United States,* 252 U.S. 450 (1920); *United States v. Zweifel,* 508 F.2d 1150 (10th Cir. 1975).

68. The information about the schoolteacher near Stanley was obtained from an interview with Jeff Jones, cited *supra* note 5. On the cabin in Belden, see Victoria Metcalf, "USFS Burns Home," *Plumas County Bulletin,* pp. 1, 10 (Apr. 13, 1983). On Galice Creek, see Bruce Bartley, "Government Agencies and Mine Claimants Battle Over Rent-Free Land in West," *Washington Post,* p. A3 (Dec. 30, 1979).

69. Information on the Yucca Mountain nuisance claims was obtained from Kevin Rohrer, information specialist, Yucca Mountain Project, by telephone interview with my research assistant Ellen Kohler, Mar. 10, 1992. For the quoted report, see House Committee on Interstate and Foreign Commerce, Subcommittee on Oversight and Investigations, "Uranium Lode Mining Claims on Federal Lands," 95th Congress, 2d Session, p. III (Washington, DC: U.S. Government Printing Office, 1978).

70. 43 U.S.C. § 299 (1988). The issues are discussed comprehensively in *Watt v. Western Nuclear, Inc.,* 462 U.S. 36 (1983).

71. The information on Fort Robinson State Park is from "Park Workers Pull Up Mining Stakes" and "Claims Staked at Fort Rob: Mining Companies Ordered Off State Park's Lands," *Scottsbluff-Gering Star Herald*, p. 1 (Feb. 15, 1981). The quotation is from Willis V. Carpenter, "Severed Minerals as a Deterrent to Land Development," vol. 51 *Denver Law Journal*, pp. 1, 24–25 (1974). On the Silver City, New Mexico, incident, see "Company Pulling Up Stakes from Property in Subdivision," *Silver City Daily Press*, p. 1 (Dec. 9, 1991); Glenn Griffin of television station KRWG-TV was kind enough to send his script on the subject from the Dec. 6, 1991 broadcast.

72. The Wild and Scenic Rivers Act can be found at 16 U.S.C. § 1280 (1988). The Mining in the Parks Act can be found at 16 U.S.C. §§ 1901–12 (1988). The information on unpatented claims in the parks was provided by Sid Covington, mineral examiner, National Park Service, by telephone interview with my research assistant Ellen Kohler, Mar. 3, 1992.

73. The Wilderness Act of 1964 can be found at 16 U.S.C. §§ 1131–36 (1988). For the Brower quote, see Coggins and Wilkinson, *supra* note 28, at p. 988.

74. 16 U.S.C. § 1133(d)(3) (1988).

75. On Conundrum Creek, see Kit Miniclier, "Marble to Be Retrieved Near Maroon Bells," *Denver Post*, p. 3B (Sept. 25, 1987). On the Cabinet Mountains, see Bruce Farling, "Mining May Come to a Wilderness," *High Country News*, p. 1 (May 13, 1985). *See generally* Kathryn Toffenetti, "Valid Mining Rights and Wilderness Areas," vol. 20 *Land & Water Law Review*, p. 31 (1985). On Three Sisters, see Dennis H. Elliott and L. Craig Metcalf, Comment, "Closing the Mining Loophole in the 1964 Wilderness Act," vol. 6 *Environmental Law*, p. 469 (Winter 1976); Sierra Club, Many Rivers Group, "Rock Mesa Saved from Mining," vol. 21 *The Runoff*, p. 2 (Jan. 1983).

76. *See, e.g., Geomet Exploration, Ltd. v. Lucky Mc Uranium Corp.*, 601 P.2d 1339 (Ariz. 1979), *cert. granted*, 447 U.S. 920 (1980), *cert. dismissed*, 448 U.S. 917 (1980).

77. Lawrence MacDonnell, "Public Policy for Hard-Rock Minerals Access on Federal Lands: A Legal-Economic Analysis," vol. 71 *Quarterly of the Colorado School of Mines*, pp. 1, 37–38 (1976).

78. On the decrease in acid mine drainage, see Kleinmann, *supra* note 43, at pp. 1-1 to 1-2. On mercury and asbestos, see University of California, Berkeley, Mining Waste Study Team, *supra* note 44, at pp. xxi–xxii.

79. On the effectiveness of modern waste management practices, see U.S. Environmental Protection Agency, Office of Solid Waste & Emergency Response, "Report to Congress: Wastes from the Extraction and Beneficiation of Metallic Ores, Phosphate Rock, Asbestos, Overburden from Uranium Mining, and Oil Shale" (Washington, DC: Environmental Protection Agency, Dec. 1985). On heap-leaching and the effects of cyanide, see Philip M. Hocker, "Cyanide Spring: Heaps of Gold, Pools of Poison,"

Clementine, p. 6 (Autumn 1989) (*Clementine* is the quarterly publication of the Mineral Policy Center, in Washington, DC); Dirk Van Zyl, ed., *Cyanide and the Environment*, vol. 1, proceedings of Conference on Cyanide and the Environment in Tucson, AZ, Dec. 11–14, 1984 (Fort Collins: Colorado State University, Department of Civil Engineering, Geotechnical Engineering Program, 1985).

80. *See* Raymond E. Krauss, "Homestake's Success," *Clementine*, p. 10 (Winter 1989); Robert T. Richins, "Coeur d'Alene Leads," *Clementine*, p. 1 (Winter 1991). The information on the Mineral Hill Mine was taken from a letter to the author by John Hoak, administrative superintendent, Mineral Hill Mine, Apr. 16, 1982; in personal interviews with John Hoak, L. R. (Len) Sargent, Sandy Sargent, and Lill Erickson conducted on Mar. 27–30, 1989; and during a site visit to the mine on Mar. 29, 1989. *See also* Todd Wilkinson, "Mining with a Light Touch: Mineral Hill Mine Strives for Balance with Environment," Idaho Falls *Post Register*, p. A1 (Mar. 24, 1992).

81. The quotation is from U.S. Environmental Protection Agency, Office of Solid Waste & Emergency Response, *supra* note 79, at p. ES-18. On the importance of mine location and environmental hazards, see Dr. Glenn Miller's testimony before the House Committee on Energy and Natural Resources, Subcommittee on Mineral Resources Development and Production, "Hard Rock Mining," 101st Congress, 2d Session, pp. 113, 124–25 (Apr. 19, 1990); Western Governors' Association, Mine Waste Task Force, *Recommendations for a Mine Waste Regulatory Program under Subtitle D of the Resource Conservation & Recovery Act*, pp. 37–43 (Denver: Western Governors' Association Mine Waste Task Force, Apr. 1990); Robert E. Walline, "A Perspectiye on the Environmental Regulation of Cyanide," paper presented at Conference on Cyanide and the Environment, *supra* note 79, at p. 14; Leshy, *supra* note 28, at pp. 183–90, 220–28, 328–30.

82. For overviews of regulatory authority over mining, see Jerry Marcus, "Mining Environment: Regulatory Control of Mining at the Federal Level, Part One," *Engineering and Mining Journal*, p. 16U (June 1990); James S. Burling, "Local Control of Mining Activities on Federal Lands," vol. 21 *Land & Water Law Review*, p. 33 (1986). On the ability of states to regulate hardrock mining on federal lands more restrictively than the federal agencies, see *California Coastal Commission v. Granite Rock Co.*, 480 U.S. 572 (1987).

83. *United States v. Weiss*, 642 F.2d 296 (9th Cir. 1981).

84. The preamble can be found at 39 Fed. Reg. 31317 (1974). The quotes from Chief McGuire and the district ranger are both from Council on Environmental Quality, "Hard Rock Mining on the Public Land," p. 18 (Washington, DC: U.S. Government Printing Office, 1977).

85. *See generally* U.S. Congress, General Accounting Office, "Federal Land Management: Limited Action Taken to Reclaim Hardrock Mine Sites"

(Washington, DC: General Accounting Office, Oct. 1987). For the "loosely regulated" quotation, see U.S. Congress, General Accounting Office, "Change in Approach Needed to Improve the Bureau of Land Management's Oversight of Public Lands," p. 4 (Washington, DC: General Accounting Office, Apr. 1989). *See also* Leshy, *supra* note 28, at pp. 195–212. *Sierra Club v. Penfold*, 857 F.2d 1307 (9th Cir. 1988), describes the BLM's very limited regulation of mining in Alaska.

86. There is no clear statement by the courts on Forest Service or BLM authority. The United States Court of Appeals for the Ninth Circuit, for example, has said that "the power to prohibit initiation or continuation of mining in national forest for failure to abide by applicable and environmental requirements lies with the Forest Service," but the case went to the Supreme Court, which reversed the appeals court's decision on other grounds and failed to address the issue. *Granite Rock Co. v. California Coastal Commission*, 768 F.2d 1077, 1081 (9th Cir. 1985), *rev'd on other grounds*, 480 U.S. 572 (1987). *See generally* George Cameron Coggins, *Public Natural Resources Law*, vol. 2, pp. 25-31 to 25-49 (Deerfield, IL: Clark Boardman Callaghan Press, 1992). The basic reason why the courts have not ruled on these critical questions under the 1974 and 1984 Forest Service and BLM regulations, respectively, is that both agencies have been reluctant to exercise their authority, thus ensuring that the questions will rarely come to court.

87. In the early twentieth century, when the public interest was still viewed as synonymous with the interest of the industry, miners agitated for amendments to the 1872 act. In the 1910s and 1920s, various proposals were floated to strengthen prediscovery rights, to promote diligence after discovery, to impose antimonopoly provisions by limiting the acreage any one entity might control, and to simplify various technical requirements. This program, offered up by large mining companies, was beaten back by small prospectors fearful of any encroachment on the right of free access.

In the 1930s, Harold Ickes, Franklin Roosevelt's activist secretary of the interior, argued for a leasing system, but miners united against the idea. The Hoover Commission of 1947 called mainly for changes that would assist serious miners during prospecting. The Paley Commission of 1951 recommended a mixed system of location and leasing. In 1970, the Public Land Law Review Commission voted, with three dissenting members, to retain many aspects of the location system but to institute a program of prospecting permits during the prediscovery stages and to require royalty payments. On early reforms, see MacDonnell, *supra* note 77. On modern reform proposals, see John D. Leshy, "Reforming the Mining Law: Problems and Prospects," vol. 9 *Public Land Law Review*, pp. 1, 4–10 (1988). The Udall remark was supplied by Philip Hocker, director of the Mineral Policy Center, Washington, DC, in a personal letter to the author, p. 3, Feb. 19, 1992.

88. On events leading up to reform, see Leshy, *supra* note 28, at pp. 5–10. For the Udall quotation, see Letter from Stewart Udall, Secretary of the

Interior, to the Chairman and Members of the Public Land Law Review Commission (Jan. 15, 1969).

89. On oil shale, see generally Harry K. Savage, *The Rock That Burns* (Boulder, CO: Pruett Publishing Company, 1967); Andrew Gulliford, *Boomtown Blues: Colorado Oil Shale, 1885–1985* (Niwot: University Press of Colorado, 1990).

90. *See Andrus v. Shell Oil Co.*, 466 U.S. 657 (1980); *Tosco Corp. v. Hodel*, 611 F. Supp. 1130 (D. Colo. 1985).

91. *See generally* Senate Committee on Energy and Natural Resources, Subcommittee on Mineral Resources Development and Production, "Oil Shale Mining Claims," 100th Congress, 1st Session (1987). *See also* Bob Silbernagel, "Shift of Shale Claims Moves Ahead," *Grand Junction Daily Sentinel*, p. 1 (Dec. 13, 1988) (status of pending claims); Bob Silbernagel, "Campbell's Shale Bill Fuels Debate," *Grand Junction Daily Sentinel*, p. 1A (July 6, 1987) ($37 million sale); Sue Lindsay, "Plan for Oil-Shale Land Riles Ranchers," *Rocky Mountain News*, p. 10 (July 27, 1986) (local reactions); Jim King, attorney, telephone interview with my research assistant Ellen Kohler, June 3, 1992; House Committee on Interior and Insular Affairs, Subcommittee on Mining and Natural Resources, "Oil Shale Claims," 101st Congress, 1st Session, testimony of Ronald W. Cattany, Colorado Department of Natural Resources, pp. 134, 136 (1989).

92. On reform proposals, see "1872 Mining Law Reform Legislation Examined: Side by Side," *Clementine*, p. 4 (Spring 1991); Philip M. Hocker, "D.C. Dallies," *Clementine*, p. 12 (Winter 1991).

93. Clifton J. Hansen, "Why a Location System for Hard Minerals?" vol. 13 *Rocky Mountain Mineral Law Institute*, pp. 1, 17 (1967).

94. On industrial hardrock mining in the nineteenth century, see Richard E. Lingenfelter, *The Hardrock Miners: A History of the Mining Labor Movement in the American West, 1863–1893* (Berkeley: University of California Press, 1974). On the Zortman-Landusky Mine, see Canada Mineral Resources, *American Mines Handbook, 1991–92*, p. 144 (Don Mills, ON: Southam Business Communications, 1991).

95. Council on Environmental Quality, Anthony Payne, "Nevada Mineral Exploration and Mine Development, 1950–1972," pp. 13, 72 (Springfield, VA: National Technical Information Service, 1976).

96. MacDonnell, *supra* note 77, at p. 99.

97. The quotation is from Don H. Sherwood, "Mining Law at the Crossroads," vol. 6 *Land & Water Law Review*, pp. 161, 183 (1970).

98. In thinking through reform proposals, I benefited enormously from my telephone conversations with Philip M. Hocker of the Mineral Policy Center, in Washington, DC, and from his thoughtful essay, "Red, White, 'n' 1872: Mining Law Reform Will Benefit Everyone," *Clementine*, p. 6 (Winter 1989).

99. *See* interview with Jones, *supra* note 5.

100. The quotation is from *Freese v. United States*, 639 F.2d 754, 758 (Ct. Cl. 1981). *See generally United States v. Locke*, 471 U.S. 84 (1985).

CHAPTER THREE

1. Peter Skene Ogden, *Snake Country Journals*, pp. 106, 107, 110 (London: The Hudson's Bay Record Society, 1950); U.S. Department of the Interior, Bureau of Land Management, Prineville District, "Camp Creek Watershed: Revised Activity Plan," p. 10 (June 1985); Vanison Gesner, deputy surveyor, "Field Notes of the Survey of the Subdivisional lines of Township 8 South of Range 21-East Willamette Meridian in the State of Oregon," pp. 103–65 (June 1875).

2. U.S. Department of the Interior, Geological Survey, Bulletin no. 252, Israel C. Russell, "Preliminary Report on the Geology and Water Resources of Central Oregon," pp. 62–63 (Washington, DC: U.S. Government Printing Office, 1905).

3. On rangeland hydrology, see generally Farrel A. Branson, et al., *Rangeland Hydrology*, 2d ed. (Dubuque, IA: Kendall/Hunt Publishing Company, 1981); John R. Wunder, ed., *Working the Range: Essays on the History of Western Land Management and the Environment* (Westport, CT: Greenwood Press, 1985).

4. The information on Camp Creek is based in part on several technical journals and reports. *See, e.g.*, Harold H. Winegar, "Camp Creek Channel Fencing: Plant, Wildlife, Soil, and Water Response," vol. 4 *Rangeman's Journal*, p. 10 (Feb. 1977); U.S. Department of the Interior, Bureau of Land Management, *supra* note 1; BLM memorandum by Angela G. Evenden, "Camp Creek Vegetation Study: 1985"; undated BLM memorandum titled "Camp Creek Watershed Facts." In addition, I benefited enormously from two full-day inspections of the watershed with Wayne Elmore, rangeland specialist, Prineville District of the BLM, on Sept. 5, 1986, and Apr. 3, 1987, and from several lengthy discussions with, and slide presentations by, Elmore. *See generally* Richard H. Braun, "Emerging Limits on Federal Land Management Discretion: Livestock, Riparian Ecosystems, and Clean Water Law," vol. 17 *Environmental Law*, p. 43 (1986).

5. The quotation is from Hugh Hammond Bennett, *Elements of Soil Conservation*, p. 55 (New York: McGraw-Hill Book Company, 1947). A leading study in desertification is Harold Dregne, "Desertification of Arid Lands," vol. 53 *Economic Geography*, p. 322 (Oct. 1977). The estimate of storage capacity in Prineville Reservoir due to sedimentation was made by Harold H. Winegar, a wildlife biologist with the Oregon Department of Fish and Wildlife in Prineville. Mr. Winegar, though recently retired, has studied the region since the 1960s. *See* Winegar, *supra* note 4. My research assistant Ellen Kohler discussed the issue of sedimentation with Mr. Winegar in a telephone conversation on Apr. 16, 1992. The Bureau of Reclamation has conducted no official calculations on the reservoir's current storage capacity (Don Stelma, geologist, Bureau of Reclamation, Prineville District, Apr. 22, 1992).

6. The percentages were calculated from information contained in Lynn

Jacobs, "Amazing Graze: How the Livestock Industry Is Ruining the American West," *The Animals' Agenda*, p. 15 (Jan.–Feb. 1988); U.S. Department of Agriculture, National Agricultural Statistics Service, "Livestock Slaughter: 1991 Summary" (Washington, DC: National Agricultural Statistics Service, 1992). For the information on current fees, see "U.S. Raises Grazing Fees in Western States," *Los Angeles Times*, p. 3D (Jan. 17, 1991); "Congress Threatens to Cut 'Cowboy Welfare,' " *Denver Post*, pp. 12A, 13A (July 7, 1991).

7. Edward Abbey, "The Ungulate Jungle: Something About Mac, Cows, Poker, Ranchers, Cowboys, Sex and Power ... and Almost Nothing About American Lit," vol. 1 *Northern Lights*, p. 12 (July–Aug. 1985) (emphasis is in the original).

8. On the history of the western range, see generally Walter Prescott Webb, *The Great Plains* (Lincoln: University of Nebraska Press, 1931); T. H. Watkins and Charles S. Watson, Jr., *The Lands No One Knows: America and the Public Domain* (San Francisco: Sierra Club Books, 1975). *See also* William Voigt, Jr., *Public Grazing Lands: Use and Misuse by Industry and Government* (New Brunswick, NJ: Rutgers University Press, 1976).

9. On homesteading, see generally Paul W. Gates, *History of Public Land Law Development*, pp. 393–413, 512–23 (Washington, DC: U.S. Government Printing Office, 1968); Samuel T. Dana and Sally K. Fairfax, *Forest and Range Policy: Its Development in the United States*, 2d ed., pp. 21–24, 103–4 (New York: McGraw-Hill Book Company, 1980). The General Homestead Act of 1862 can be found at 43 U.S.C. §§ 161–284 (portions repealed 1976).

10. G. Weis, *Stock Raising in the Northwest, 1884*, pp. 3–4 (Evanston, IL: Branding Iron Press, 1951).

11. 25 U.S.C. § 331 (1988). *See generally* Frederick E. Hoxie, *A Final Promise: The Campaign to Assimilate the Indians, 1880–1920* (Lincoln: University of Nebraska Press, 1984).

12. On the railroads, see generally Dana and Fairfax, *supra* note 9, at pp. 12–20; Robert S. Henry, "The Railroad Land Grant Legend in American History Texts," vol. 32 *Mississippi Valley History Review*, p. 171 (1945); Robert E. Reigel, "Comment on 'The Railroad Land Grant Legend in American History Texts,' " vol. 32 *Mississippi Valley History Review*, p. 565 (1946).

13. *See supra* notes 8, 9.

14. Paul H. Roberts, *Hoof Prints on Forest Ranges*, pp. 22–23 (San Antonio: Naylor Company, 1963).

15. The quotation is from Velma Linford, *Wyoming: Frontier State*, p. 338 (Denver: Old West Publishing Company, 1947). *See also* T. A. Larson, *Wyoming: A Bicentennial History*, pp. 128–31 (New York: W. W. Norton & Company, 1977). *See generally* Harry S. Drago, *The Great Range Wars: Violence on the Grasslands* (Lincoln: University of Nebraska Press, 1970).

16. *See* Unlawful Inclosures Act of 1885, 43 U.S.C. § 1061 (1988); *Camfield v. United States,* 167 U.S. 518 (1897).
17. These and other nineteenth-century laws and customs relating to the cattle industry are discussed in an excellent fashion in Valerie Weeks Scott, "The Range Cattle Industry: Its Effect on Western Land Law," vol. 28 *Montana Law Review,* p. 155 (Spring 1967).
18. *Omaechevarria v. Idaho,* 246 U.S. 343 (1918).
19. *See e.g., Red Canyon Sheep Co. v. Ickes,* 98 F.2d 308 (D.C. Cir. 1938).
20. *Buford v. Houtz,* 133 U.S. 320, 326–28 (1890).
21. Gates, *supra* note 9, at pp. 482–83.
22. Webb, *supra* note 8, at p. 206. References to the rancher's code are common. *See, e.g.,* Phillip O. Foss, *The Battle of Soldier Creek,* p. 9 (Tuscaloosa: University of Alabama Press, 1961).
23. Webb, *supra* note 8, at p. 224.
24. Theodore Roosevelt, *Ranch Life and the Hunting-Trail* (illustrated by Frederic Remington), pp. 21–22 (New York: Century Company, 1888).
25. The quotations are from, respectively, Richard Goff and Robert H. McCaffree, *Century in the Saddle,* pp. 144–45 (Denver: Colorado Cattlemen's Centennial Commission, 1967); Denzel Ferguson and Nancy Ferguson, *Sacred Cows at the Public Trough,* p. 17 (Bend, OR: Maverick Publications, 1983); Voigt, *supra* note 8, at p. 29.
26. Quoted in Edward A. Ross, *Foundations of Sociology,* 2d ed., p. 388 (New York: Macmillan Company, 1905).
27. Gifford Pinchot, *The Fight for Conservation,* pp. 4, 20 (Seattle: University of Washington Press, 1910). The Transfer Act of 1905 is codified at 16 U.S.C. § 472 (1988).
28. On the 1906 grazing regulatory program, see Voigt, *supra* note 8, at pp. 45–50; Dana and Fairfax, *supra* note 9, at pp. 86–89.
29. The "occupancy and use" provision can be found at 16 U.S.C. § 551 (1988). The quotation is from Roberts, *supra* note 14, at p. 81.
30. *Light v. United States,* 220 U.S. 523 (1911) (the quotations can be found at pp. 535, 537, and 536, respectively); *United States v. Grimaud,* 220 U.S. 506 (1911).
31. The Taylor Grazing Act can be found at 43 U.S.C. §§ 315–315r (1988). On the Dust Bowl and the Taylor Grazing Act, see generally Louise E. Peffer, *The Closing of the Public Domain: Disposal and Reservation Policies, 1900–50* (Stanford, CA: Stanford University Press, 1951); Voigt, *supra* note 8, at pp. 249–62; Dana and Fairfax, *supra* note 9, at pp. 158–65.
32. Watkins and Watson, *supra* note 8, at p. 142. Professor George Cameron Coggins tellingly concludes that the Taylor Act amounted to only a modest inroad on the ranchers' traditional prerogatives:

> The Taylor Grazing Act represented a considerable advance over the legal void at the federal level that preceded it. The BLM could not overcome the contradictions inherent in the Act, however, and

the agency never achieved one of the Act's major goals. The Taylor Act's preference permits, advisory boards, and lack of emphasis on other resources guaranteed continuing tension between industry desires and management control for range improvement. Congress has long mistreated the BLM and its predecessors, but those agencies contributed to their own impotence and near destruction by unwavering decentralization, undue deference to the major users, and unwillingness to apply either law or management expertise rigorously. Consequently, the BLM acquiesced in the creation of de facto private rights in the public rangelands while neglecting to improve range condition.

George Cameron Coggins and Margaret Lindberg-Johnson, "The Law of Public Rangeland Management II: The Commons and the Taylor Act," vol. 13 *Environmental Law*, pp. 100–101 (1982).

33. The essays are collected in Bernard DeVoto, *The Easy Chair* (Cambridge, MA: Riverside Press, 1955). The quotation is found on pp. 254–55. For a biography, see Wallace Stegner, *The Uneasy Chair: A Biography of Bernard DeVoto* (Garden City, NY: Doubleday & Company, 1974).

34. NEPA can be found at 42 U.S.C. §§ 4321–70a (1988). The quoted language is from 42 U.S.C. § 4331(b) (1988).

35. The quoted language can be found at 42 U.S.C. § 4332(C) (1988).

36. On the device of the citizens' suit, see generally Joseph L. Sax, *Defending the Environment* (New York: Alfred A. Knopf, 1971). The judicial review provisions of the Administrative Procedure Act can be found at 5 U.S.C. §§ 702–6 (1988). The leading "hard look" case is *Citizens to Preserve Overton Park v. Volpe*, 401 U.S. 402 (1971). "Hard look" review was leavened somewhat by cases such as *Vermont Yankee Nuclear Power Corp. v. Natural Resources Defense Council, Inc.*, 435 U.S. 519 (1978), but federal review unquestionably remains far more adventuresome than in pre–*Citizens to Preserve* days. The major liberal standing case, *Sierra Club v. Morton*, 405 U.S. 727 (1972), has been narrowed by *Lujan v. National Wildlife Federation*, 110 S. Ct. 3177 (1990). Nevertheless, although later cases have somewhat restricted (and confused) standing law, it is rare when citizens actually using an area cannot get into court to raise objections against federal officials or developers. The waiver of sovereign immunity is set out in 5 U.S.C. § 702 (1988). *See generally* Charles F. Wilkinson, "The Field of Public Land Law: Some Connecting Threads and Future Directions," vol. 1 *Public Land Law Review*, p. 1 (1980). For developments in environmental law since 1970, see generally Symposium, "NEPA at Twenty: The Past, Present and Future of the National Environmental Policy Act," vol. 20 *Environmental Law*, p. 447 (1990).

37. *Natural Resources Defense Council, Inc. v. Morton*, 388 F. Supp. 829, 840 (D.C. Cir. 1974), *aff'd per curiam*, 527 F.2d 1386 (D.C. Cir. 1976), *cert. denied sub nom., Pacific Legal Foundation v. Natural Resources Defense Council, Inc.*, 427 U.S. 913 (1976).

38. *See* George Cameron Coggins, Parthenia Blessing Evans, and Margaret Lindberg-Johnson, "The Law of Public Rangeland Management I: The Extent and Distribution of Federal Power," vol. 12 *Environmental Law,* pp. 535, 554 (1982).

39. FLPMA can be found at 43 U.S.C. §§ 1701–84 (1988). The quoted language is from 43 U.S.C. § 1701(a)(1) (1988). On FLPMA, see generally Symposium, "The Federal Land Policy and Management Act of 1976," vol. 21 *Arizona Law Review,* p. 267 (1979).

40. FLPMA's grazing provisions can be found at 43 U.S.C. §§ 1751–53 (1988).

41. PRIA is codified at 43 U.S.C. §§ 1901–8 (1988). The quoted language was enacted in 1978 as section 1908(a) of PRIA but is codified as an amendment to the grazing provisions of FLPMA. *See* 43 U.S.C. § 1752(d) (1988). On PRIA, see generally George Cameron Coggins, "The Law of Public Rangeland Management IV: FLPMA, PRIA, and the Multiple Use Mandate," vol. 14 *Environmental Law,* pp. 1, 109–22 (1983).

42. The McClure Amendment of 1979 can be found at 93 Stat. 954, 956.

43. *Nevada ex rel. Nevada State Board of Agriculture v. United States,* 512 F. Supp. 166 (D. Nev. 1981), *aff'd on other grounds,* 699 F.2d 486 (9th Cir. 1983).

44. *Natural Resources Defense Council, Inc. v. Hodel,* 618 F. Supp. 848, 853 (E.D. Cal. 1985).

45. *Natural Resources Defense Council, Inc. v. Hodel,* 624 F. Supp. 1045, 1062 (D. Nev. 1985), *aff'd,* 819 F.2d 927 (9th Cir. 1987).

46. Vol. 9 *Public Lands Institute Newsletter,* p. 1 (Mar. 1986).

47. *See* U.S. House of Representatives, Report no. 99-593, "Federal Grazing Program: All Is Not Well on the Range," 99th Congress, 2d Session, p. 61 (1986). The italics in the quotation by Congressman Synar are in the original.

48. Phillip A. Davis, "The Senator's Western Stalwarts," vol. 49 *Congressional Quarterly,* p. 2150 (Aug. 3, 1991). Synar's 1990 reforms were attached as amendments to the Department of the Interior's appropriations bill. The text of the amendments can be found at vol. 136 *Congressional Record,* 101st Congress, 2d Session, pp. 9662–63 (Washington, DC: U.S. Government Printing Office, Oct. 16, 1990). The 1991 reforms were written into a reauthorization bill for the Bureau of Land Management, H.R. 944, "Fair Market Grazing for Public Rangelands Act of 1991," 102d Congress, 1st Session (introduced Feb. 6, 1991).

49. For authorities on Camp Creek, see *supra* note 4.

50. *See* "Bucking Tradition: Moving Toward Sustainable Ranching," *High Country News,* special issue (Mar. 12, 1990); Lisa Jones, "Overgrazing: Feds Move to End It," *High Country News,* p. 1 (Apr. 8, 1991); Jon Christensen, "High Noon in Nevada: Forest Service Goes Head-to-Head with an Angry Rancher," *High Country News,* p. 1 (Sept. 9, 1991). The GAO quotation is from U.S. Congress, General Accounting Office, Report

no. RCED-88-105, "Public Rangelands: Some Riparian Areas Restored but Widespread Improvement Will Be Slow," p. 3 (Washington, DC: General Accounting Office, June 1988).

51. Allan Savory, "The Ungulate Jungle: Saving the Brittle Lands: Holism and the Health of the Commons," vol. 1 *Northern Lights*, p. 18 (July–Aug. 1985).

52. On Savory's approach, including his view that better grazing practices often can allow greater numbers of stock, see "Rangeland Revolutionary: An Interview with Allan Savory," vol. 39 *Journal of Soil and Water Conservation*, p. 235 (July–Aug. 1984); Mark Cherrington, "Stopping Deserts: Allan Savory's Radical Approach Restores Rangelands," *Earthwatch*, p. 11 (Dec. 1988).

53. *See generally* Allan Savory, *Holistic Resource Management* (Washington, DC: Island Press, 1988). Although the HRM approach has been applied mainly to ranching (Savory's letterhead once read "Holistic Ranch Management"), the model applies to the management of any land system and thus can be a useful framework for farming, timber harvesting, and other resource-intensive endeavors.

54. For scholarly criticism of Savory's approach, see Lee E. Hughes, "A Drought and 2 Grazing Systems," vol. 13 *Rangelands*, p. 229 (Oct. 1991); Thomas L. Thurow, et al., "Some Vegetation Responses to Selected Livestock Grazing Strategies, Edwards Plateau, Texas," vol. 41 *Journal of Range Management*, p. 108 (Mar. 1988); Michael H. Ralphs, et al., "Vegetation Response to Increased Stocking Rates in Short-duration Grazing," vol. 43 *Journal of Range Management*, p. 104 (Mar. 1990); Steven D. Warren, et al., "The Influence of Livestock Trampling under Intensive Rotation Grazing on Soil Hydrologic Characteristics," vol. 39 *Journal of Range Management*, p. 491 (Nov. 1986).

55. For research papers prepared by leading specialists on the effects of grazing intensity and specialized grazing systems on rangeland, see National Research Council, National Academy of Sciences, *Developing Strategies for Rangeland Management: A Report Prepared by the Committee on Developing Strategies for Rangeland Management*, pp. 867–1166 (Boulder, CO: Westview Press, 1984).

56. Heather Smith Thomas, "Guest Essay: A Rancher Argues Cattle Grazing Helps Everyone," *High Country News*, p. 14 (Dec. 23, 1985).

57. On the notion that federal AUMs are capitalized into the value of ranches, see generally Philip O. Foss, *Politics and Grass: The Administration of Grazing on the Public Domain* (Westport, CT: Greenwood Press, 1960).

58. Charles Callison, director of the Public Lands Institute, Natural Resources Defense Council, interview with author, May 12, 1986.

59. The use of manipulative range improvements is treated comprehensively in National Research Council, National Academy of Sciences, *supra* note 55, at pp. 1167–1426. For an article putting range improvements in the context of grazing subsidies generally, see George Wuerthner, "The Price

Is Wrong," vol. 75 *Sierra*, p. 38 (Sept.–Oct. 1990). As noted in the text, disputes continue in both the literature and the field over just how intensive management ought to be—for example, the extent to which the use of specialized grazing systems ought to be supplemented by practices such as burning and chaining junipers and using chemicals to eradicate undesirable plant species. These controversies tend to be much more acute in upland areas, which do not rejuvenate as quickly as riparian zones. My sense is that the mood is gradually moving toward a general dissatisfaction with drastic manipulative practices and toward a greater acceptance of the use of specialized grazing systems coupled with natural regeneration. But this can differ according to locale and individual specialist and is the kind of detailed matter that is difficult to resolve by merely applying general principles. In any event, disagreement on particulars does not change the clear consensus that substantially increased management is badly needed on federal grazing lands.

60. *See* "The Grazing Guru: Two Views of Allan Savory," *High Country News*, pp. 1, 10–13, 16 (Apr. 27, 1987).
61. Author's conversation with Med Bennett, Wyoming rancher, June 28, 1987, and information sent by Gregg Simonds, general manager, Deseret Land and Livestock, May 8, 1992.
62. A number of case studies on riparian zones are reported in U.S. Department of Agriculture, Forest Service, First North American Riparian Conference, Report no. RM-120, "Riparian Ecosystems and Their Management: Reconciling Conflicting Uses," pp. 276–309 (1985). The quotation is from Steve Gallizioli, "Outdoors Issues and Answers," vol. 3 *Arizona Hunter & Angler*, p. 21 (Feb. 1986).
63. Ed Marston, "The Public Range Begins to Green Up," *High Country News*, p. 1 (May 7, 1990).
64. U.S. Congress, General Accounting Office, "Rangeland Management: More Emphasis Needed on Declining and Overstocked Grazing Allotments," p. 22 (Washington, DC: General Accounting Office, June 1988); Johanna Wald and David Alberswerth, *Ailing! Condition Report—1989* (San Francisco: National Wildlife Federation and Natural Resources Defense Council, 1989).
65. Cynthia Lenhart, "Appendix J: Federal Fish and Wildlife Program Budgets," in William J. Chandler, ed., *Audubon Wildlife Report 1988/1989*, pp. 775–76, 781–82 (San Diego: Academic Press, 1988). *See also* House Committee on Interior and Insular Affairs, Subcommittee on National Parks and Public Lands, "Change in Approach Needed to Improve the Bureau of Land Management's Oversight of Public Lands," testimony of James Duffus III, director, natural resources management issues, U.S. Congress, General Accounting Office (Washington, DC: General Accounting Office, 1989).
66. On citizen involvement, see generally Joseph M. Feller, "Grazing Management on the Public Lands: Opening the Process to Public Participation," vol. 26 *Land & Water Law Review*, p. 571 (1991).

67. I was particularly struck by a letter I received from William DeBuys, who is knowledgeable on these issues and is the author of the fine book *Enchantment and Exploitation: The Life and Hard Times of a New Mexico Mountain Range* (Albuquerque: University of New Mexico Press, 1985). He wrote: "The increases [Congressman Synar] has sought, in my view, are not corrective, but punitive. They would put my neighbors in El Valle and Trampas, for instance, out of business." William DeBuys, letter to author, p. 1 (Jan. 15, 1992).
68. 43 U.S.C. § 1752(g) (1988).
69. 43 U.S.C. § 1752(a) (1988).

CHAPTER FOUR

1. The quotations are from, respectively, "Forest Service out on a Limb on Timber Sales," *Denver Post*, p. 2C (Sept. 23, 1984); "Quality Water for the Future," *Idaho Statesman*, p. 2F (Jan. 4, 1987).
2. The "coon and turkey hunters" quotation is from a personal communication with the author on June 8, 1987. Jeff Sher, "Roads to Ruin," vol. 91 *American Forests*, p. 17 (Apr. 1985).
3. On opposition by ranchers and farmers, see *infra* text at note 48 (the Bitterroot controversy); *Big Hole Ranchers' Association, Inc. v. U.S. Forest Service*, 686 F. Supp. 256 (D. Mont. 1988). On local opposition, see, for example, Daniel P. Jones, "Logging Plan Could Wipe Out Ranch Owner," *Denver Post*, p. 12A (Dec. 23, 1984). The quotation is from "West Rebelling against Forest Service Plans," *Arizona Daily Star*, p. 1E (Feb. 12, 1984), which discusses state government opposition. One of the most notable pieces of litigation is *California v. Block*, 690 F.2d 753 (9th Cir. 1982), in which the state of California and Trinity County obtained an injunction against timber harvesting in wilderness study areas (lands being evaluated for their wilderness potential) until valid environmental impact statements had been completed.
4. *See* U.S. Department of Agriculture, Forest Service, "Land Areas of the National Forest System," pp. 14–31 (1990); U.S. Department of Commerce, Economics and Statistics Administration, *Statistical Abstract of the United States 1991*, pp. 203–4 (Washington, DC: U.S. Government Printing Office, 1991).
5. For sources of the statistics discussed in this paragraph, see Charles F. Wilkinson and H. Michael Anderson, *Land and Resource Planning in the National Forests*, pp. 8–9 (Washington, DC: Island Press, 1987), which I have drawn upon freely in preparing this chapter.
6. On national park law and policy, see Joseph Sax, "Helpless Giants: The National Parks and the Regulation of Private Lands," vol. 75 *Michigan Law Review*, p. 239 (1976); Robert B. Keiter, "On Protecting the National Parks from the External Threats Dilemma," vol. 20 *Land & Water Law Review*, p. 355 (1985).
7. On wildlife refuges, see Michael Bean, Environmental Defense Fund, *The Evolution of National Wildlife Law*, 2d ed., pp. 119–36 (New York: Praeger Publishers. 1983).

8. On federal land acquisition from foreign nations, see Paul W. Gates, *History of Public Land Law Development*, pp. 75–86 (Washington, DC: U.S. Government Printing Office, 1968).

9. The 1831 law can be found at 4 Stat. 472. Policy during these early years is discussed in Wilkinson and Anderson, *supra* note 5, at pp. 130–33.

10. For a summary of timber fraud, see Gates, *supra* note 8, at pp. 463–94; Samuel T. Dana and Sally K. Fairfax, *Forest and Range Policy: Its Development in the United States*, 2d ed., pp. 50–69 (New York: McGraw-Hill Book Company, 1980); Stephen A. Douglas Puter, *Looters of the Public Domain* (Portland, OR: The Portland Printing House, 1908).

11. U.S. Department of Agriculture, Forest Service, Franklin B. Hough, "Report on Forestry," p. 196 (Washington, DC: U.S. Government Printing Office, 1882); U.S. Department of Agriculture, Forest Service, Nathaniel H. Egleston, "Report on Forestry," vol. 4, pp. 183–84 (Washington, DC: U.S. Government Printing Office, 1884).

12. U.S. House of Representatives, vol. 1 *Executive Documents*, no. 1, part 5, "Report of the Secretary of the Interior," 45th Congress, 2d Session, p. XVI (1877).

13. Act of March 3, 1891, 26 Stat. 1095, 1103; repealed by 90 Stat. 2792 (1976).

14. For the Fernow quotation, see U.S. Department of Agriculture, Forest Service, "Report of the Chief of the Division of Forestry," p. 223 (Washington, DC: U.S. Government Printing Office, 1892).

15. For the Seattle Chamber of Commerce quotation, see Harold K. Steen, *The U.S. Forest Service: A History*, p. 33 (Seattle: University of Washington Press, 1976). The second quotation can be found in "Forest Reserves," *Plumas National-Bulletin* (undated, 1902), in the collection of the Plumas County Museum, Quincy, CA.

16. The quotations are from vol. 25 *Congressional Record*, 53d Congress, 1st Session, pp. 2431–32 (1893). On the events leading up to the 1897 act, see John Ise, *The United States Forest Policy*, pp. 128–41 (New Haven, CT: Yale University Press, 1920); Steen, *supra* note 15, at pp. 30–36; Wilkinson and Anderson, *supra* note 5, at pp. 46–52.

17. 30 Stat. 35 (1897).

18. The funding and management authority is from 16 U.S.C. § 551 (1988); the original language permitting sale of timber was in 16 U.S.C. § 476 (repealed 1976); the jurisdiction, water, and mining provisions are located in 16 U.S.C. §§ 480, 481, and 482 (1988), respectively; the presidential authority is located in 16 U.S.C. § 475 (1988).

19. The Udall quote is from Stewart L. Udall, *The Quiet Crisis and the Next Generation*, p. 104 (Salt Lake City, UT: Peregrine Smith, 1988). *See also* M. Nelson McGeary, *Gifford Pinchot: Forester-Politician*, p. 66 (Princeton, NJ: Princeton University Press, 1960).

20. The Pinchot quotation is from Charles F. Wilkinson, " 'The Greatest Good for the Greatest Number in the Long Run': The National Forests in the Next Generation," p. 4, paper presented as the keynote address for the

1985 Natural Resources Days at Colorado State University, College of Forestry and Natural Resources, Fort Collins, CO. For the leading biography on Pinchot, see McGeary, *supra* note 19. All of the standard sources on the Forest Service and the national forests contain discussions of Pinchot's career.

21. The Bell quotation is from Gifford Pinchot, *Breaking New Ground*, p. 199 (New York: Harcourt, Brace and Company, 1947). For the Steen quotation, see Steen, *supra* note 15, at p. 99. On grazing regulations, see chapter 3, *supra* notes 28–29 and the accompanying text; Harold T. Pinkett, *Gifford Pinchot: Private and Public Forester*, pp. 76–78 (Urbana: University of Illinois Press, 1970).

22. Theodore Roosevelt, *An Autobiography*, pp. 404–5 (New York: Charles Scribner's Sons, 1924). *See generally* Steen, *supra* note 15, at pp. 84–86.

23. All standard sources on the Forest Service discuss Pinchot's dismissal. For the fullest treatment, see James Penick, Jr., *Progressive Politics and Conservation: The Ballinger-Pinchot Affair* (Chicago: University of Chicago Press, 1968).

24. The Pinchot Letter quotation is from U.S. Department of Agriculture, Forest Service, "The Principal Laws Relating to the Establishment and Administration of the National Forests and Other Forest Service Activities," p. 67 (1964). On the Pinchot Letter as the genesis of the 1960 act, see Edward C. Crafts, "Saga of a Law, Part I," vol. 76 *American Forests*, p. 12 (June 1970). On the Pinchot Letter's influence on agency regulations, see, for example, 47 Fed. Reg. 43,026 (1982) (codified at 36 C.F.R. part 219).

25. The "first duty of the human race" quotation is from Gifford Pinchot, *The Fight for Conservation*, p. 45 (New York: Doubleday, Page & Company, 1910). The "government controlled" quotation is from Gifford Pinchot, "The Public Good Comes First," vol. 39 *Journal of Forestry*, pp. 208, 211 (1941).

26. The two quotations are, respectively, from Pinchot, *Breaking New Ground, supra* note 21, at p. 32, and *id.* at p. 31. On Pinchot's philosophy, see his two major books, cited *supra* note 21 and *supra* note 25. The leading work on the conservation movement is Samuel P. Hays, *Conservation and the Gospel of Efficiency* (New York: Atheneum Publishers, 1980). *See also* Glen O. Robinson, *The Forest Service: A Study in Public Land Management*, pp. 258–59 (Baltimore: Johns Hopkins University Press, 1975); Richard M. Alston, *The Individual vs. the Public Interest: Political Ideology and National Forest Policy*, pp. 11–23 (Boulder, CO: Westview Press, 1983).

27. Pinchot, *Breaking New Ground, supra* note 21, at pp. 44, 98, 99, respectively.

28. The quotation about the Adirondack Forest Reserve is from Roderick Nash, *Wilderness and the American Mind*, 3d ed., pp. 108, 116–21 (New Haven, CT: Yale University Press, 1982). On forest homesteads, see Steen,

supra note 15, at p. 79, n. 27. On national parks, see Hays, _supra_ note 26, at pp. 195–96. On Pinchot's use of the terms "forest reserves" and "national forests," see Pinchot, _Breaking New Ground, supra_ note 21, at pp. 116–22. Hetch Hetchy is treated in all of the standard sources. _See, e.g._, Stephen Fox, _John Muir and His Legacy: The American Conservation Movement_, pp. 139–47 (Boston: Little, Brown & Company, 1981).

29. Robinson, _supra_ note 26, at p. 258.

30. The "public welfare" quote is from Pinchot, _The Fight for Conservation, supra_ note 25, at p. 60. _See also id._ at pp. 60–64.

31. Wilkinson and Anderson, _supra_ note 5, at pp. 133–36.

32. _See, e.g._, Wilkinson and Anderson, _supra_ note 5, at pp. 135–36 (timber sales to local communities); _id._ at pp. 202–6 (watershed protection); _id._ at pp. 313–16 (recreation); _id._ at pp. 336–41 (wilderness). The Chief Graves quote is from U.S. Department of Agriculture, Forest Service, _Report of the Chief_, p. 194 (1919).

33. On the fires of 1910, see Michael Frome, _Whose Woods These Are: The Story of the National Forests_, pp. 207–11 (Garden City, NY: Doubleday & Company, 1962); the "chickens" quotation is from Jane Reed Benson, _Thirty-Two Years in the Mule Business_, p. 2 (Seattle: Pacific Northwest Parks and Forest Association, 1987).

34. Benson, _supra_ note 33, at p. 3. Forest Service research during this era is treated in Steen, _supra_ note 15, at pp. 135–39. The invention of the Pulaski is discussed in Frome, _supra_ note 33, at pp. 208–9.

35. Kreutzer's charge is noted in a letter from Gifford Pinchot in the foreword to Len Shoemaker, _Saga of a Forest Ranger: A Biography of William R. Kreutzer, Forest Ranger No. 1, and a Historical Account of the U.S. Forest Service in Colorado_, p. vi (Boulder: University of Colorado Press, 1958). The beetle story is found _id._ at p. 206.

36. The quotation about the old Land Office custom is from Pinchot, _Breaking New Ground, supra_ note 21, at p. 267. On the Fritz Olmstead examination, see _id._ at p. 281. The Bill Bell story is recounted in Norman Maclean, _A River Runs Through It and Other Stories_, p. 126 (Chicago: University of Chicago Press, 1976).

37. U.S. Department of Agriculture, Forest Service, "Report of the Chief of the Forest Service," p. 3 (Washington, DC: U.S. Government Printing Office, 1942).

38. The Colonel Sherrill quote is from Dana and Fairfax, _supra_ note 10, at p. 175. For a fine discussion of the war's impact on the Forest Service, see Steen, _supra_ note 15, at pp. 246–55. _See also_ Wilkinson and Anderson, _supra_ note 5, at pp. 136–37.

39. _See_ Steen, _supra_ note 15, at pp. 253–55.

40. On "one-shot forestry," see Leon S. Minckler, "The Tragedy of One-Shot Forestry," vol. 63 _Sierra_, p. 38 (July–Aug. 1978) (applying the term to the national forests rather than to private timberlands).

41. On the impact of logging practices on private lands, see Steen, _supra_ note 15, at p. 257; Dana and Fairfax, _supra_ note 10, at p. 175.

42. Wilkinson and Anderson, *supra* note 5, at pp. 137–38.

43. *Id.* at p. 138. For a study of timber domination in the Forest Service, see David A. Clary, *Timber and the Forest Service* (Lawrence: University Press of Kansas, 1986).

44. On the recreation boom, see generally United States Outdoor Recreation Resources Review Commission, "Outdoor Recreation for America" (1962). On increased recreation visitor days and ski areas, see Charles F. Wilkinson, "The Forest Service: A Call for a Return to First Principles," vol. 5 *Public Land Law Review*, pp. 1, 12–13 (1984).

45. The Multiple-Use Sustained-Yield Act of 1960 can be found at 16 U.S.C. §§ 528–31 (1988). On its passage, see Crafts, *supra* note 24, at pp. 12, 18–19, 52.

46. On wilderness, see generally Nash, *supra* note 28. The Wilderness Act of 1964 can be found at 16 U.S.C. §§ 1131–36 (1988).

47. On the exceptions within the Wilderness Act of 1964 that allow limited mining and grazing, see George C. Coggins and Charles F. Wilkinson, *Federal Public Land and Resources Law*, pp. 986–93 (Westbury, NY: Foundation Press, 1987). *See also* ch. 2, *supra* notes 62–63. The quoted statutory language is from 16 U.S.C. § 1131(c) (1985 & Supp. 1992). *See generally* Wilkinson and Anderson, *supra* note 5, at pp. 341–44.

48. Burk's articles for the *Missoulian* are collected in Dale A. Burk, *The Clearcut Crisis* (Great Falls, MT: Jursnick Printing, 1970). The quotes are from pp. 11, 13, 25–26, and 28.

49. *Id.* at p. 81.

50. The Metcalf quotation is from Wilkinson and Anderson, *supra* note 5, at p. 139, n. 725.

51. The Bolle Report is reprinted at U.S. Senate, Committee on Interior and Insular Affairs, Document no. 115, "A University View of the Forest Service," 91st Congress, 2d Session (1970). The two short quotations are found *id.* at pp. 14, 21. The report is summarized in Burk, *supra* note 48, at pp. 150–52.

52. These events are chronicled in Wilkinson and Anderson, *supra* note 5, at pp. 140–47. The McGee quotation is from U.S. Senate, Committee on Interior and Insular Affairs, Subcommittee on Public Lands, " 'Clear-cutting' Practices on National Timberlands," 92d Congress, 1st Session, p. 3 (1971).

53. Wilkinson and Anderson, *supra* note 5, at pp. 146–47.

54. *West Virginia Division of the Izaak Walton League of America, Inc. v. Butz*, 522 F.2d 945, 954–55 (4th Cir. 1975).

55. *Zieske v. Butz*, 406 F. Supp. 258 (D. Alaska 1975).

56. On the passage of the NFMA, see generally Dennis C. Le Master, *Decade of Change: The Remaking of Forest Service Statutory Authority During the 1970s* (Westport, CT: Greenwood Press, 1984); Wilkinson and Anderson, *supra* note 5, at pp. 40–42, 69–72.

57. The Humphrey quotations are from Wilkinson and Anderson, *supra* note 5, at pp. 69–70.

58. 16 U.S.C. § 1604(g)(3)(F) (1988). *See generally* Wilkinson and Anderson, *supra* note 5, at pp. 186–88.

59. *See* Coggins and Wilkinson, *supra* note 47, at pp. 663–69; Wilkinson and Anderson, *supra* note 5, at pp. 154–200. The NFMA "water conditions" requirements are at 16 U.S.C. § 1604(g)(3)(E)(iii) (1988). The "diversity" requirement is at 16 U.S.C. § 1604(g)(3)(B) (1988). The "nondeclining even flow" requirement is from 16 U.S.C. § 1611(a) (1988).

60. Dan Postrel, "Management Project Is Big, Bold, Bogged Down," *Salem Statesman-Journal*, p. 1G (Jan. 18, 1987).

61. *See* Donald Snow, *Inside the Environmental Movement: Meeting the Leadership Challenge* (Washington, DC: Island Press, 1992).

62. Data were provided by Rebecca Wodder, vice president of public affairs, The Wilderness Society, interview with author, Sept. 15, 1988; Laura Fisher, administrative assistant, letter of Apr. 24, 1992; Tom Watkins, vice president–editor, telephone interview with research assistant Ellen Kohler, June 4, 1992; Stephen Fox, "We Want No Straddlers," *Wilderness*, pp. 5, 16–17 (Winter 1984); The Wilderness Society, "Fact Sheet" (June 1992).

63. James Montieth, executive director, Oregon Natural Resources Council, interview with author, Sept. 15, 1988; Candace Guth, director of administration and finance, Oregon Natural Resources Council, telephone interview with my research assistant Ellen Kohler, Apr. 16, 1992.

64. On Dr. Clawson's testimony, see Wilkinson and Anderson, *supra* note 5, at pp. 163–64. The NFMA's provisions on economic issues are discussed *supra*, notes 5–9, and in the accompanying text.

65. The NRDC quotation is from Natural Resources Defense Council, *Giving Away the National Forests: An Analysis of U.S. Forest Service Timber Sales Below Cost*, p. 29 (June 1980); U.S. Department of Agriculture, Forest Service, "Response to 'Giving Away the National Forests' Issued by the Natural Resources Defense Council" (June 3, 1980).

66. In approaching this set of issues, the most helpful single source, which dissects all of the various reports and issues in a fair-minded way, is William E. Shands and Thomas E. Waddell, *Below-Cost Timber Sales in the Broad Context of National Forest Management* (Washington, DC: The Conservation Foundation, 1988).

67. I have based my calculations (as did Shands and Waddell, *supra* note 66) largely on the figures developed in a study by The Wilderness Society, Resource Planning and Economics Department, "Issue Brief: Below-Cost Timber Sales on the National Forests" (July 1984). Other accounting methods would produce different absolute numbers, but the disparities among the various Forest Service regions would remain roughly the same. *See also* Richard E. Rice, "Taxpayer Losses from National Forest Timber Sales, FY 1990" (Washington, DC: The Wilderness Society, May 1991); U.S. Congress, General Accounting Office, "Forest Service Needs to Improve Efforts to Reduce Below-Cost Timber Sales" (Washington, DC:

General Accounting Office, Apr. 1991); "The Citizens' Guide to the Forest Service Budget," *Forest Watch*, special issue, p. 30 (Apr. 1992).

68. Examples of influential pieces include Chris Maser and James M. Trappe, BLM and Forest Service research scientists, respectively, *The Seen and Unseen World of the Fallen Tree* (Washington, DC: U.S. Government Printing Office, 1984); Larry D. Harris, *The Fragmented Forest: Island Biogeography Theory and the Preservation of Biotic Diversity* (Chicago: University of Chicago Press, 1984); The Wilderness Society, "Conserving Biological Diversity in Our National Forests" (June 1986); Elliott A. Norse, *Ancient Forests of the Pacific Northwest* (Washington, DC: Island Press, 1990); William R. Meehan, ed., "Influences of Forest and Range-land Management on Salmonid Fishes and Their Habitats" (Bethesda, MD: American Fisheries Society, 1991). The 1987 Clean Water Act amendments can be found at 33 U.S.C. § 1254 (1988) and are discussed in Environmental Law Reporter *Clean Water Deskbook*, 2d ed. (Washington, DC: Environmental Law Institute, 1991).

69. The "intelligent tinkering" quote is from Aldo Leopold, *A Sand County Almanac: With Other Essays on Conservation from Round River*, p. 177 (New York: Oxford University Press, 1966). The quotation on biological diversity is from Norse, *supra* note 68, at pp. 64–65.

70. *See generally Inner Voice*, published by the Association of Forest Service Employees for Environmental Ethics, P.O. Box 11615, Eugene, OR 97440.

71. The "supervisors' letters" are printed in *Inner Voice*, p. 11 (Winter 1990).

72. Mumma's testimony is reproduced in full in *High Country News*, p. 12 (Oct. 7, 1991).

73. On regional literature, see Charles F. Wilkinson, *The American West: A Narrative Bibliography and a Study in Regionalism* (Niwot: University Press of Colorado, 1989).

74. The quotation is from p. 8 of the Congressional Research Service report, which is reprinted in House Committee on Interior and Insular Affairs, Committee Print no. 6, "Greater Yellowstone Ecosystem: An Analysis of Data Submitted by Federal and State Agencies," 99th Congress, 2d Session. *See also id.* at pp. 8, 69, 177 (1986). The summary as to recreation creating two-thirds of the total jobs can be found *id.* at p. 177. In using the two-thirds figure, the Congressional Research Service excluded a large phosphate mine at the far southwestern end of the ecosystem, about 100 miles from the park, because it skewed the results (*id.* at p. 68). Employment tables for all activities in national forests within the ecosystem can be found *id.* at p. 69. *See also* Ray Rasker, Norma Tirrell, and Deanne Kloepfer, *The Wealth of Nature: New Economics Realities in the Yellowstone Region* (Washington, DC: The Wilderness Society, Jan. 1992); Cascade Holistic Economic Consultants, "Economic Database for the Greater Yellowstone Forests," Research Paper no. 18 (Eugene, OR: Cascade Holistic Economic Consultants, May 1987). Useful economic data

can also be obtained from the forest plans of the seven national forests in the Greater Yellowstone Ecosystem.

75. On Dubois, see "Women Timber Activists Organized to Fight for, Save Families' Way of Life," *Denver Post*, p. 3C (Mar. 2, 1987).

76. The plans are analyzed in depth in the sources cited *supra* note 74. The quotation is from Congressional Research Service report, *supra* note 74, at p. 8.

77. For the figures on public benefits and budget expenditures, see Cascade Holistic Economic Consultants, *supra* note 74, at pp. 21–22 (budget figures refer to timber, grazing, and recreation budgets only).

78. On remaining old growth, see Douglas E. Booth, "Estimating Prelogging Old-Growth in the Pacific Northwest," *Journal of Forestry*, p. 25 (Oct. 1991); Norse, *supra* note 68, at pp. 247–49.

79. *Id.* at pp. 249–51.

80. On the historical development of the northern spotted owl as an indicator species, see U.S. Department of Agriculture, Forest Service, Pacific Northwest Region, vol. 1 "Final Supplement to the Environmental Impact Statement for an Amendment to the Pacific Northwest Regional Guide: Spotted Owl Guidelines," pp. 1-8 to 1-13 (1988).

81. On the NFMA diversity requirement, see 16 U.S.C. § 1604(g)(3)(B) (1988). On the Forest Service diversity regulations, see 36 C.F.R. § 219.3 (1991). *See generally* Wilkinson and Anderson, *supra* note 5, at pp. 288–96.

82. On biological diversity, see, for example, Harris, *supra* note 68, and the authorities cited therein. The Leopold quotation can be found in Leopold, *supra* note 69, at pp. 177–78.

83. U.S. Department of Agriculture, Forest Service, Pacific Northwest Region, "Final Supplement to the Environmental Impact Statement for an Amendment to the Pacific Northwest Regional Guide: Spotted Owl Guidelines" (1988).

84. U.S. Department of Agriculture, Forest Service, U.S. Department of the Interior, Bureau of Land Management, U.S. Department of the Interior, Fish and Wildlife Service, U.S. Department of the Interior, National Park Service, Interagency Scientific Committee to Address the Conservation of the Northern Spotted Owl, "A Conservation Strategy for the Northern Spotted Owl," p. 57 (Portland, OR: May 1990).

85. *Id.* The 4.2 million to 4.8 million acres reflects the actual area where timber harvesting would be prohibited. The report required protection of 8.1 million acres, of which 2.1 million were already protected as wilderness areas or national parks, and of which an additional 1.2 million to 1.8 million were unsuitable for timber harvest. The Thomas Committee report prescribed limited cutting in an additional 12 million to 15 million acres. 57 Fed. Reg. 1796, 1811 (1992). On the administration's task force and its conclusion, see Dianne Dumanowski, "Environmental Notebook," *Boston Globe*, National/Foreign Section, p. 8 (Aug. 31, 1990); Associated

Press, "Scientists Praise Plan to Save Owl," *Boston Globe*, National/ Foreign Section, p. 13 (Aug. 29, 1990).

86. The original injunction was handed down in an unpublished decision, *Seattle Audubon Society v. Robertson*, no. C89-160 (W.D. Wash. Mar. 24, 1989). The appellate decision is *Seattle Audubon Society v. Robertson*, 914 F.2d 1311 (9th Cir. 1990). Another issue in the *Seattle Audubon* litigation involved the "riders" attached to annual appropriations bills in the late 1980s by Oregon senator Mark Hatfield that took the extraordinary step of prohibiting judicial review of Forest Service and BLM forest management. Judge Dwyer and the appeals court found the riders invalid, but the Supreme Court upheld them. See *Robertson v. Seattle Audubon Society*, 112 S. Ct. 1407 (1992). The timber-harvesting issues in the *Seattle Audubon* case were not affected by the Supreme Court's ruling on the riders because the Forest Service vacated the contested 1988 guidelines in 1990. *See* text accompanying note 87, *infra*. No appropriations riders of this nature have been passed since 1989, so the power recognized in the 1992 decision has yet to bar any lawsuits. On litigation over the spotted owl and old-growth timber in the Pacific Northwest, see generally Michael Blumm, "Ancient Forests, Spotted Owls, and Modern Public Land Law," vol. 18 *Boston College Environmental Affairs Law Review*, p. 605 (1991).

87. On vacating the 1988 plan, see 55 Fed. Reg. 40,412 (1990). On Leonard's statement, see *Seattle Audubon Society v. Evans*, 771 F. Supp. 1081, 1091 (W.D. Wash. 1991). The quoted comments from the opinion can be found *id.* at p. 1090. Testimony from Dr. Eric Forsman, a research wildlife biologist with the Forest Service, indicated that the 1988 plan was inadequate because "there was a considerable—I would emphasize considerable—amount of political pressure to create a plan which was an absolute minimum. That is, which had a very low probability of success and which had a minimum impact on timber harvest." *Id.* at p. 1089. Judge Dwyer justified the injunctions in part on the basis of the Forest Service's failure to comply with a section of the Hatfield riders that required the Forest Service to revise its owl management plans by September 30, 1990. Judge Dwyer wrote: "The problem here has not been any shortcoming in the laws, but simply a refusal of administrative agencies to comply with them. . . . This invokes a public interest of the highest order: the interest in having government officials act in accordance with law." *Id.* at p. 1096. Judge Dwyer's opinion was affirmed by an appellate court in *Seattle Audubon Society v. Evans*, 952 F.2d 297 (9th Cir. 1991).

88. On the internal recommendation for listing and the altering of the report, see *Northern Spotted Owl v. Hodel*, 716 F. Supp. 479, 481 (W.D. Wash. 1988). On the Endangered Species Act, 16 U.S.C. § 1531 (1988), see Kathryn Kohm, ed., *Balancing on the Brink of Extinction* (Washington, DC: Island Press, 1991); Daniel J. Rohlf, *The Endangered Species Act: A Guide to Its Protections and Implementation* (Stanford, CA: Stanford Environmental Law Society, 1989).

89. The two decisions are *Northern Spotted Owl v. Hodel*, 716 F. Supp. 479 (W.D. Wash. 1988), and *Northern Spotted Owl v. Lujan*, 758 F. Supp. 621 (W.D. Wash. 1991). On the U.S. Fish and Wildlife Service's critical habitat designation, see 57 Fed. Reg. 1796, 1810 (1992). The 4.7-million-acre reduction was primarily motivated by economic concerns. Although economic factors cannot be considered during the listing process, they can be considered during a critical habitat designation. *See id.* at p. 1807.

90. On the committee and its authority, see 16 U.S.C. § 1536(e) (1988); George C. Coggins and Irma S. Russell, "Beyond Shooting Snail Darters in Pork Barrels: Endangered Species and Land Use in America," vol. 70 *Georgetown Law Journal*, pp. 1433, 1485–95 (1982). For information on past applications for exemption, see Rohlf, *supra* note 88, at pp. 135–36. Rohlf discusses the "Greyrocks–whooping crane" litigation, in which a project was allowed to go forward conditioned on an additional $13 million for habitat protection. *Nebraska v. REA*, 12 Env't Rep. Cas. (BNA) 1156 (D. Neb. 1978).

91. On the BLM's request for an exemption, see 56 Fed. Reg. 48,548 (1991). On the May 14 exemptions and the Knauss quotation, see Kathie Durbin and Roberta Ulrich, "13 BLM Timber Sales Win OK," *Oregonian*, p. A1 (May 15, 1992).

92. The Carey quotation is from "Special Report: Old Growth," *Eugene Register Guard*, pp. 1B, 10B (Jan. 18, 1987); the second quotation on old growth is from Society of American Foresters, *Scheduling the Harvest of Old Growth*, p. 17 (Washington, DC: Society of American Foresters, 1984).

93. The "no free lunch" quotation is from K. Norman Johnson, et al., "Alternatives for Management of Late-Successional Forests of the Pacific Northwest," a report presented to the Agriculture Committee and the Merchant Marine and Fisheries Committee of the U.S. House of Representatives by the Scientific Panel on Late-Successional Forest Ecosystems, p. 15 (Oct. 8, 1991).

94. The most detailed report from the environmental side is H. Michael Anderson and Jeffrey T. Olson, *Federal Forests and the Economic Base of the Pacific Northwest: A Study of Regional Transitions* (Washington, DC: The Wilderness Society, Sept. 1991). For the industry perspective, see John H. Beuter, "Social and Economic Impacts of Spotted Owl Conservation Strategy" (1990), and Alberto Goetzl and Con Schallau, "Tomorrow's Timber Supply: Is the Nation Ready for the 21st Century?" (1991) (both papers are available from American Forest Resource Alliance, 1250 Connecticut Avenue, NW, Suite 200, Washington, DC 20036). For a joint agency analysis, see U.S. Department of Agriculture, Forest Service, and U.S. Department of the Interior, Bureau of Land Management, "Actions the Administration May Wish to Consider in Implementing a Conservation Strategy for the Northern Spotted Owl" (1990). University of Oregon professor of economics Ed Whitelaw has written "Oregon's Turn: A Blueprint for Economic Growth in the 1990s," *Old Oregon*, p. 22

(Spring–Summer 1990) (published by the University of Oregon). Another useful analysis is in a report by Oregon State University associate professor of forest economics, Brian J. Greber, "An Overview of Forest Resource Industries and the Economy of the Owl Impact Region of the Pacific Northwest," which is discussed in a thoughtful way by Phil Cogswell in "Timber Related Job Calculations Take Work," *Oregonian*, p. B4 (Sept. 1, 1991).

95. On the quotation from the former Weyerhaeuser logging manager, who asked not to be named, see Perri Knize, "The Mismanagement of the National Forests," *Atlantic Monthly*, pp. 98, 100 (Oct. 1991).

96. On the decline in jobs, see Anderson and Olson, *supra* note 94, at pp. 43–45. For Judge Dwyer's quote, see *Seattle Audubon Society v. Evans*, 771 F. Supp. 1081, 1095 (W.D. Wash. 1991). On log exports, see Anderson and Olson, *supra* note 94, at pp. 58–60; 57 Fed. Reg. 1796, 1814 (1992) (exports represent a potential 24,000 direct timber industry jobs in the Pacific Northwest).

97. 57 Fed. Reg. 1796, 1815 (1992) (27,705 jobs will be lost if the Thomas Committee recommendations are implemented, an additional 3311 jobs will be lost as a result of listing the spotted owl, and 1420 jobs will be lost as a result of designating critical habitat); Anderson and Olson, *supra* note 94, at pp. 58–60. The Wilderness Society is quick to point out, though, that even in the worst-case scenario, unmitigated job losses resulting from spotted owl protection would fall to only 5900 by the year 2040 because timber availability is expected to decline regardless of spotted owl protection. *Id.*

98. *See* U.S. Department of Agriculture, Forest Service, and U.S. Department of the Interior, Bureau of Land Management, *supra* note 94. For additional information on the log export ban, see Anderson and Olson, *supra* note 94, at pp. 58–60, 76–77; 57 Fed. Reg. 1796, 1813, 1814, 1818, 1819 (1992). On the administration's initial refusal to release the Forest Service report (apparently to avoid publication of alternatives to making basic changes in the laws), see *Inner Voice*, p. 3 (Summer 1991).

99. For a comparative study of Forest Service performance, see Jeanne Nienaber Clarke and Daniel McCool, *Staking Out the Terrain: Power Differentials Among Natural Resource Management Agencies* (Albany: State University of New York Press, 1985).

100. The numbers on the Forest Service are from U.S. Department of Agriculture, Forest Service, "Work Force Data Book 1990–1991," pp. 28–30 (1991). On the practical effects of having this concentration of foresters in the Forest Service, see Paul J. Culhane, *Public Lands Politics: Interest Group Influence on the Forest Service and the Bureau of Land Management*, p. 68 (Baltimore: Johns Hopkins University Press, 1981).

101. Randal O'Toole, *Reforming the Forest Service* (Washington, DC: Island Press, 1988).

102. *See id.* at pp. 4, 132–33, 135–36. The general funding statute can be found at 16 U.S.C. § 500 (1988).

103. *See, e.g.,* "House, Senate Part on Road Building, Are Close on Timber Sales," *Public Lands News,* pp. 1–2 (Aug. 21, 1987); "Panel Reduces Timber Sale to About 8 bbf; New ESA Bird?" vol. 16 *Public Lands News,* p. 3 (June 27, 1991); "Positions Staked Out over Next Timber Sale, Old Growth," vol. 16 *Public Lands News,* p. 1 (Feb. 28, 1991); Kathie Durbin, "Politics Helped Delay Timber Management Plans," *Oregonian,* p. A12 (Sept. 18, 1990).

104. Data on timber-dependent communities are supplied in U.S. Department of Agriculture, Forest Service, timber management staff, memoranda of Dec. 17, 1976, and Sept. 29, 1987.

105. On the policy of public use, first articulated by former Arizona governor Bruce Babbitt, see Coggins and Wilkinson, *supra* note 47, at pp. 1055–56.

106. Senator Packwood's bill is S. 1156, 102d Congress, 1st Session (1991). Senator Adams's bill is S. 1536, 102d Congress, 1st Session (1991). Congressman Jontz's bill is H.R. 842, 102d Congress, 1st Session (1991).

107. "Final FS Timber Sale Could Be Almost 4 bbf Less Than '90," vol. 16 *Public Lands News,* pp. 6–7 (Nov. 14, 1991).

108. On the cut in the Pacific Northwest, see Johnson, et al., *supra* note 93. The calculation that more than half of all timber is sold below cost is from *Forest Watch, supra* note 67, at p. 31. For additional information on below-cost timber sales, see *supra* notes 66–67 and accompanying text.

109. The quotation is from U.S. Department of Agriculture, Forest Service, "Draft 1990 RPA Program," p. A-19 (Washington, DC: U.S. Department of Agriculture, 1989). For the 500,000 new homes figure, see William Booth, "Study: Logging Cut Needed to Save Northwest Forests," *Washington Post,* p. A3 (July 25, 1991).

110. For a fine comprehensive treatment of dependent communities, *see* Shands and Waddell, *supra* note 66, and the authorities cited therein.

CHAPTER FIVE

1. I thank Delbert Frank of the Warm Springs Tribe of Oregon for patiently spending a full day with me on June 30, 1988, in order to recount in detail his family history of Wunn-o-ah-chi, Jim Yahtin, Yessessi, and others who are referred to throughout this chapter.

2. On the characteristics of Pacific salmon and steelhead, see generally R. J. Childerhose and Marj Trim, *Pacific Salmon and Steelhead Trout* (Seattle: University of Washington Press, 1979); Anthony Netboy, *The Salmon: Their Fight for Survival* (Boston: Houghton Mifflin Company, 1973).

3. The quotation is from Charles Wilkes, *Narrative of the United States Exploring Expedition During the Years 1838, 1839, 1840, 1841, 1842,* vol. 4, pp. 344–45 (Philadelphia: Lea and Blanchard, 1845).

4. On physical deterioration, see, for example, Jacques Cousteau, *The Ocean World,* pp. 20–21 (New York: Harry N. Abrams, 1979). On the effect of delays, see, for example, Robert J. Browning, *Fisheries of the North Pacific: History, Species, Gear & Processes,* rev. ed., p. 50 (Edmonds, WA: Alaska Northwest Publishing Company, 1980).

5. Bruce Brown, *Mountain in the Clouds: A Search for the Wild Salmon*, p. 231 (New York: Simon & Schuster, 1982).

6. David Rains Wallace, *The Klamath Knot: Explorations of Myth and Evolution*, p. 59 (San Francisco: Sierra Club Books, 1983).

7. Clark's "crouded with salmon" quotation is from Reuben Gold Thwaites, ed., vol. 3 *Original Journals of the Lewis and Clark Expedition: 1804–1806*, p. 122 (New York: Arno Press, 1969). The chronicler's comment is from Paul R. Cutright, *Lewis and Clark: Pioneering Naturalists*, p. 225 (Urbana: University of Illinois Press, 1969). Muir's quotation is from John Muir, *Travels in Alaska*, p. 177 (San Francisco: Sierra Club Books, 1988). On the fanciful motif of crossing streams on the backs of fish, see Phillip Johnson, "Wild Rivers, Wild Salmon: New Respect for Nature's Fishery," vol. 16 *Oceans*, p. 67 (Mar.–Apr. 1983).

8. On early Indian fishing and society on the Pacific Coast, see, for example, Philip Drucker, *Indians of the Northwest Coast* (Garden City, NY: Natural History Press, 1963); Courtland L. Smith, *Salmon Fishers of the Columbia* (Corvallis: Oregon State University Press, 1979); Hilary Stewart, *Indian Fishing: Early Methods on the Northwest Coast* (Seattle: University of Washington Press, 1977). The quotation is from Chuck Williams, *Bridge of the Gods, Mountains of Fire: A Return to the Columbia Gorge*, p. 73 (San Francisco: Friends of the Earth, 1980), a fine treatment of aboriginal life in the Columbia River basin.

9. Northwest Power Planning Council, "Compilation of Information on Salmon and Steelhead Losses in the Columbia River Basin," pp. 66–76 (Mar. 1986).

10. For an excellent discussion regarding California natives, see Arthur F. McEvoy, *The Fisherman's Problem: Ecology and Law in the California Fisheries 1850–1980*, pp. 19–40 (Cambridge: Cambridge University Press, 1986). On the signals to other fishermen to cease fishing, see Williams, *supra* note 8, at p. 73. *See generally* Deward E. Walker, *Mutual Cross-Utilization of Economic Resources in the Plateau: An Example from Aboriginal Nez Perce Fishing Practices*, pp. 14–15 (Pullman: Washington State University, Laboratory of Anthropology, 1967). The information on fishing platforms as inherited property rights was confirmed in the author's telephone interview with Professor Deward E. Walker, Mar. 11, 1992.

11. On California Indians, see *supra* chapter 2, note 11.

12. On the nature of aboriginal land title, see Felix S. Cohen, *Cohen's Handbook of Federal Indian Law*, rev. ed., pp. 50–58 (Charlottesville, VA: Michie Company/Bobbs-Merrill Law Publishing, 1982). The leading case recognizing Indian title is *Johnson v. M'Intosh*, 21 U.S. (8 Wheat.) 543 (1823). *See generally* Charles F. Wilkinson, *American Indians, Time, and the Law* (New Haven, CT: Yale University Press, 1987).

13. *See, e.g.*, Alvin M. Josephy, Jr., *The Nez Perce Indians and the Opening of the Northwest*, abridged ed., p. 293 (New Haven, CT: Yale University Press, 1971); Alvin M. Josephy, Jr., *Now That the Buffalo's Gone: A*

Study of Today's American Indians, pp. 181–87 (Norman: University of Oklahoma Press, 1984); Francis Paul Prucha, *The Great Father: The United States Government and the American Indians*, pp. 402–8 (Lincoln: University of Nebraska Press, 1984).

14. On the Stevens treaties, see Cohen, *supra* note 12, at pp. 101–2.

15. On treaty negotiations, see *United States v. State of Washington*, 384 F. Supp. 312, 355–57 (W.D. Wash. 1974), *aff'd*, 520 F.2d 676 (9th Cir. 1975), *cert. denied*, 423 U.S. 1086 (1976). The quoted language is from *id.* at p. 356. See also, for example, the Yakima Treaty of 1855, which can be found at 12 Stat. 951. On subsequent determination of many of these treaty negotiations issues, see *Washington v. Fishing Vessel Association*, 443 U.S. 658 (1979).

16. On early canneries, see Anthony Netboy, *The Columbia River Salmon and Steelhead Trout: Their Fight for Survival*, p. 20 (Seattle: University of Washington Press, 1980); McEvoy, *supra* note 10, at pp. 70–71; Smith, *supra* note 8, at p. 16.

17. The quotation is from Francis Seufert, *Wheels of Fortune*, p. 9 (Portland: Oregon Historical Society, 1980).

18. On the 1883 harvest, see Smith, *supra* note 8, at pp. 20–21. On the aboriginal take, see *supra* note 9. On the decline in chinook harvest after 1883, see Netboy, *supra* note 16, at pp. 22–23.

19. *See generally* Smith, *supra* note 8, at pp. 41–45; Netboy, *supra* note 16, at pp. 20–36.

20. On dynamiting and the Puget Sound incident, see Childerhose and Trim, *supra* note 2, at p. 24.

21. *See* Ivan J. Donaldson and Frederick K. Cramer, *Fishwheels of the Columbia* (Portland, OR: Binfords & Mort, 1971); Seufert, *supra* note 17.

22. *See generally* Smith, *supra* note 8, at pp. 24–30. On chinook as admission to the dance hall, see Stewart Hall Holbrook, *The Columbia*, 2d ed., p. 238 (New York: Rinehart & Company, 1974).

23. McEvoy, *supra* note 10, at p. 72.

24. The Oregon Fish and Game Protector quotation is from Netboy, *supra* note 16, at p. 36. *See* Charles F. Wilkinson and Daniel Keith Conner, "The Law of the Pacific Salmon Fishery: Conservation and Allocation of a Transboundary Common Property Resource," vol. 32 *Kansas Law Review*, pp. 17, 33–34 (1983), and the authorities cited therein; I have drawn liberally upon this article in preparing the historical material in this chapter. Alaska's White Law is discussed in Peter Larkin, "Pacific Salmon: Scenarios for the Future," Washington Sea Grant Publication no. 80-3 (Seattle: University of Washington, 1980). On early hatcheries, see Livingston Stone, "The Artificial Propagation of Salmon on the Pacific Coast of the United States," vol. 16 *Bulletin of the Fish Commission*, pp. 203, 218 (1897).

25. The Roosevelt quotation is from President Theodore Roosevelt, "Special Message to Congress" (Dec. 8, 1908), James D. Richardson, vol. 10

Messages and Papers of the Presidents, p. 7610 (New York: Bureau of National Literature and Art, 1913). For the full text of Dr. Stone's address, see Anthony Netboy, *Salmon: The World's Most Harassed Fish*, p. 213 (London: André Deutsch, 1980).

26. On the total reduction of accessible spawning habitat (a drop from 163,000 square miles to 73,000 square miles), see Northwest Power Planning Council, *Columbia River Basin Fish and Wildlife Program*, p. iii (Nov. 1982).

27. *See generally* Netboy, *supra* note 16, at pp. 55–71.

28. *Id.*

29. *See* Northwest Power Planning Council, Derek Poon and John Garcia, *A Comparative Analysis of Anadromous Salmonid Stocks and Possible Cause[s] for Their Decline*, p. 176, table 24 (June 1982). On the Fraser River episode at Hell's Gate, see Childerhose and Trim, *supra* note 2, at pp. 76–77.

30. Ed Chaney, *Cogeneration of Electrical Energy & Anadromous Salmon & Steelhead in the Upper Columbia River Basin: An Economic Perspective on the Question of Balance*, p. 2 (Northwest Resource Information Center, June 1982).

31. On the "nursemaid" quotation, see Netboy, *supra* note 16, at p. 75. On Jackson's quotation, see Marquis James, *The Life of Andrew Jackson*, pp. 603–4 (New York: Bobbs-Merrill Company, 1938); Charles Warren, vol. 1 *The Supreme Court in United States History*, pp. 759–65 (Boston: Little, Brown & Company, 1928).

32. *See* Netboy, *supra* note 16, at p. 77.

33. *See generally* Netboy, *supra* note 16, at pp. 73–75.

34. *See, e.g.*, U.S. Department of Energy, Bonneville Power Administration, "1979 Annual Report: Federal Columbia River Power System" (1980). For a list of all dams in the Columbia-Snake basin, see Northwest Power Planning Council, *supra* note 9, at appendix C. On the Snake River, an excellent source is Tim Palmer, *The Snake River: Window to the West* (Washington, DC: Island Press, 1991).

35. On BPA marketing and subsidies, see Western Governors' Association, *The Western Hydro System*, pp. 5–9 (1985). The Office of Management and Budget quotation is from Andrew Pollack, "Debate on Bonneville's Future," *New York Times*, p. 29 (Feb. 4, 1986).

36. U.S. Department of Energy, Bonneville Power Administration, "Power and the Pacific Northwest: A History of the Bonneville Power Administration," p. 101 (1976).

37. *See, e.g.*, Northwest Power Planning Council, *supra* note 26, at p. 6-1. On the mortality at dams, I was greatly assisted by an interview with Jim Ruff, staff hydrologist with the Northwest Power Planning Council, Oct. 4, 1988.

38. On passage mortality, see generally Wilkinson and Conner, *supra* note 24, at pp. 63–66, 78, and the authorities cited therein.

Notes to Pages 201–206

39. On percentages of mortality, see Columbia River Fisheries Council, "Columbia River Basin Salmon and Steelhead Management Framework Plan," p. 8 (Mar. 1981). I also relied on Jim Ruff, *supra* note 37.
40. *See* Northwest Power Planning Council, *1987 Columbia River Basin Fish and Wildlife Program*, pp. 3, 36–39 (1987). *See also* Northwest Power Planning Council, *supra* note 26. On Snake River chinook listing, see ch. 1, *supra* note 4; ch. 4, *infra* note 65.
41. The quotation is from Chaney, *supra* note 30, at p. 9. *See* Phillip Meyer, *Fish, Energy and the Columbia River: An Economic Perspective on Fisheries Values Lost and at Risk*, p. 14 (Northwest Resource Information Center, Mar. 1982).
42. *See generally* Wilkinson and Conner, *supra* note 24, at pp. 74–76, and the authorities cited therein; Northwest Power Planning Council, *supra* note 9, at pp. 91–96; McEvoy, *supra* note 10, at pp. 156–84.
43. On state objections being overridden by federal plans, see, for example, *Federal Power Commission v. Oregon*, 349 U.S. 435 (1955); *State of Washington Department of Game v. Federal Power Commmission*, 207 F.2d 391 (9th Cir. 1953), *cert. denied*, 347 U.S. 936 (1954); *City of Tacoma v. Taxpayers of Tacoma*, 357 U.S. 320 (1958); *City of Tacoma v. Taxpayers of Tacoma*, 371 P.2d 938 (1962). For a broader view of state authority under the reclamation laws, see *California v. United States*, 438 U.S. 645 (1978) (construction of New Melones Dam must comply with conditions imposed by the state). States, however, have much more limited authority when federal agencies build under authorizing statutes other than the reclamation laws. *See First Iowa Hydro-Electric Cooperative v. Federal Power Commission*, 328 U.S. 152 (1946); *California v. Federal Energy Regulatory Commission, et al.*, 495 U.S. 490 (1990).
44. *See, e.g.*, Netboy, *supra* note 2, at p. 290; Netboy, *supra* note 16, at pp. 78–97.
45. On citizen objections, see Netboy, *supra* note 16, at pp. 78–97. The quotation is from Johnny Carrey and Cort Conley, *River of No Return*, p. 66 (Cambridge, ID: Backeddy Books, 1978).
46. On the Indian fishing controversy, see American Friends Service Committee, *Uncommon Controversy: Fishing Rights of the Muckleshoot, Puyallup, and Nisqually Indians* (Seattle: University of Washington Press, 1970); Fay G. Cohen, *Treaties on Trial: The Continuing Controversy over Northwest Indian Fishing Rights* (Seattle: University of Washington Press, 1986).
47. The quotation is from *United States v. Winans*, 198 U.S. 371, 381 (1905); *Tulee v. Washington*, 315 U.S. 681 (1942). The "flowage easement" reasoning had been set out in *Whitefoot v. United States*, 293 F.2d 658 (Ct. Cl. 1961), *cert. denied*, 369 U.S. 818 (1962).
48. *Sohappy v. Smith*, 302 F. Supp. 899 (D. Or. 1969), *aff'd*, 529 F.2d 570 (9th Cir. 1976).
49. *United States v. Washington*, 384 F. Supp. 312 (W.D. Wash. 1974), *aff'd*, 520 F.2d 676 (9th Cir. 1975), *cert. denied*, 423 U.S. 1086 (1976).

50. Author's personal interview with David H. Getches, professor of law, University of Colorado School of Law, Boulder, CO, Aug. 24, 1988.
51. The subsequent case histories of the Boldt and Belloni decisions are cited *supra* notes 48–49.
52. *Washington v. Washington State Commercial Passenger Fishing Vessel Association*, 443 U.S. 658, 696 n.36 (1979) (quoting from United States Court of Appeals for the Ninth Circuit decision) (citations omitted).
53. Netboy, *supra* note 16, at p. 126. The quotation is from John de Yonge, "Boldt's Good Deeds Will Live After Him," *Seattle Post-Intelligencer*, p. A11 (Mar. 21, 1984).
54. The study referred to is Wilkinson and Conner, *supra* note 24.
55. For a helpful analysis of the Magnuson Act, see Lee G. Anderson, "Marine Fisheries," in Paul R. Portney, ed., *Current Issues in Natural Resource Policy*, p. 149 (Washington, DC: Resources for the Future, 1982). *See also* Wilkinson and Conner, *supra* note 24, at pp. 48–53. The 1976 act can be found at 16 U.S.C. §§ 1801–82 (1988).
56. The Northwest Power and Conservation Act of 1980 can be found at 16 U.S.C. §§ 839–839h (1988). On its legislative history and provisions, see Michael C. Blumm and Brad L. Johnson, "Promising a Process for Parity: The Pacific Northwest Electric Power Planning and Conservation Act and Anadromous Fish Protection," vol. 11 *Environmental Law*, p. 497 (1981).
57. The act was attacked as an unconstitutional delegation of authority to a nonfederal agency, but the court rejected the argument. *Seattle Master Builders Association v. Pacific Northwest Electric Power*, 786 F.2d 1359 (9th Cir. 1986).
58. The limiting language can be found at 16 U.S.C. § 839b(h)(11)(A) (1988).
59. *See* Northwest Power Planning Council, *supra* note 40, at pp. 51–76.
60. *See generally id.*
61. *Id.* at pp. 35–44; author's personal conversations with council and staff members, June 29 through July 1, 1988.
62. I learned about the positions of the Army Corps of Engineers and the Federal Energy Regulatory Commission at meetings in Welches, OR, on June 29–30, 1988. On the protected areas proposal, see Michael C. Blumm and Andy Simrin, "The Unraveling of the Parity Promise: Hydropower, Salmon, and Endangered Species in the Columbia Basin," vol. 21 *Environmental Law*, pp. 657, 696 (1991). On the dropping of applications for projects since the 1988 protected areas action, I relied on a letter I received from John M. Volkman, Feb. 3, 1992, quoting Peter Paquet, the protected areas coordinator for the Northwest Power Planning Council.
63. On Wapato's personal background, see Northwest Power Planning Council, Dulcy Maher, "Interview with Tim Wapato," *Northwest Energy News* p. 11 (Feb.–Mar. 1987).
64. On the 1985 treaty, see Thomas C. Jensen, "The United States–Canada Pacific Salmon Interception Treaty: An Historical and Legal Overview," vol. 16 *Environmental Law*, p. 363 (1986). The quotation is from a

telephone interview with Bill Wilkerson by my research assistant Brian Kuehl, May 18, 1992.

65. Willa Nehlsen, Jack E. Williams, and James A. Lichatowich, "Pacific Salmon at the Crossroads: Stocks at Risk from California, Oregon, Idaho, and Washington," vol. 16 *Fisheries*, p. 4 (Mar.–Apr. 1991). At the time of this writing, four species of salmon had been officially listed as threatened or endangered: the Sacramento River winter-run chinook salmon, the Snake River sockeye salmon, the Snake River fall chinook salmon, and the Snake River spring/summer chinook salmon (personal communication by my research assistant Brian Kuehl with the U.S. Department of Commerce, National Marine Fisheries Service, May 22, 1992). For a complete list of threatened and endangered species, see 50 C.F.R. § 17.11 (1991).

66. On additional endangered species petitions, see Nehlson, et al., *supra* note 65, at pp. 8–10. On Hatfield's comments, see *Clearing Up*, p. 11 (July 6, 1990).

67. For a fine overview of these developments, see John M. Volkman, "Making Room in the Ark: The Endangered Species Act and the Columbia River Basin," vol. 34 *Environment*, p. 13 (May 1992). The governors' report to Senator Hatfield is set out in a letter dated May 1, 1991, and signed by Barbara Roberts, governor of Oregon; Cecil D. Andrus, governor of Idaho; Booth Gardner, governor of Washington; and Stan Stephens, governor of Montana. There was also a second letter of the same date, with three governors signing, but Governor Stephens refused to approve.

68. On the council's 1991 plan, see Volkman, *supra* note 67. On the costs of the plan, see "Council Adopts Salmon Plan," *Seattle Times*, p. G2 (Dec. 12, 1991). On environmentalists' reactions to the council's planning process, see generally the articles collected in "Salmon: The 'Parity' Promise and Fish Flows," vol. 4 *Transitions* (Oct. 1991) (available from Inland Empire Public Lands Council, P.O. Box 2174, Spokane, WA 99210). For editorial reactions to the plan, see "Salmon-Recovery Plan Is a Balanced Beginning," *Seattle Times*, p. A10 (Dec. 13, 1991); "Power Council's Save-Salmon Plan," *Seattle Post-Intelligencer*, p. A14 (Dec. 17, 1991).

69. For a personal and evocative description of the sockeye at Redfish Lake, see Pat Ford, "The Snake's Imperiled Salmon," *High Country News*, p. 1 (July 1, 1991). The numbers of returning salmon are from a personal communication by my research assistant Brian Kuehl with the U.S. Department of Commerce, National Marine Fisheries Service, June 4, 1992.

70. Information on the water budget on the Snake is from a memorandum to the Northwest Power Planning Council from Rick Applegate, director, Fish and Wildlife Division, and Jim Ruff, staff hydrologist. On proposals to improve fish passage in the Snake River system, see generally direct testimony of James D. Ruff on behalf of applicant, *In the Matter of Applications for Transfer Nos. 3883, 3884 and 3885 in the Name of the United States Bureau of Reclamation*, before the Department of Water Resources of the State of Idaho (Mar. 2, 1992).

71. Wild salmon and steelhead are treated in Brown, *supra* note 5. The Northwest Power Planning Council's policy is set out in section 700 of its 1987 program, *supra* note 40.

CHAPTER SIX

1. On the San Juan–Chama Project, I was fortunate to have interviews and a site visit with Charles Fisher and Isadoro Manzares of the Bureau of Reclamation in Chama, NM, on Aug. 29, 1990. *See also* U.S. Department of the Interior, Bureau of Reclamation, "Factual Data—San Juan–Chama Project—Colorado–New Mexico" (undated map; available from Regional Director, Region 5, Bureau of Reclamation, P.O. Box 1609, Amarillo, TX 79105); U.S. Department of the Interior, Bureau of Reclamation, "Albuquerque Projects: Water Accounting Report to the Rio Grande Compact Commission" (Albuquerque, NM: Bureau of Reclamation, 1988); Colorado Water Conservation Board and U.S. Department of Agriculture, Soil Conservation Service, Economic Research Service, and Forest Service, "Water and Related Land Resources: San Juan River Basin—Arizona, Colorado, New Mexico, and Utah" (Denver: 1974).

2. The Olson quote is from an interview with Tom Olson by my research assistant Roger Flynn, Albuquerque, NM, Aug. 7, 1990. The quotation from the city of Albuquerque can be found in the court opinion in *Jicarilla Apache Tribe v. United States*, 657 F.2d 1126, 1132 (10th Cir. 1981), which contains a useful summary of the history and current operation of the San Juan–Chama Project. *See also* Ira G. Clark, *Water in New Mexico: A History of Its Management and Use*, pp. 503–16, 635–53 (Albuquerque: University of New Mexico Press, 1987); Senate Committee on Energy and Natural Resources, Subcommittee on Public Lands, National Parks and Forests, "Rio Chama River, New Mexico: Hearing on S. 850," 100th Congress, 1st Session (1987).

3. The quotation is from Veronica E. Velarde Tiller, *The Jicarilla Apache Tribe: A History, 1846–1970*, p. 97 (Lincoln: University of Nebraska Press, 1983), which provides a comprehensive history of these events.

4. For the citation of the court opinion, see *Jicarilla Apache Tribe v. United States, supra* note 2. The statute overriding the court opinion is Public Law no. 97-140, §§ 5(a), (b) (Dec. 29, 1981), and can be found at 95 Stat. 1717. The city of Albuquerque and the Army Corps of Engineers had asserted that the water was in fact being put to a beneficial use since the project water, although not being used for municipal purposes, was used by recreationists on the various reservoirs where the water was stored. Although the court rejected the argument, the congressional action explicitly made recreation an authorized beneficial use for San Juan–Chama water. *See also* Clark, *supra* note 2, at pp. 650–51, 686–87.

5. On the history of water issues in the Colorado River watershed, see Gary D. Weatherford and F. Lee Brown, eds., *New Courses for the Colorado River: Major Issues for the Next Century* (Albuquerque: University of

New Mexico Press, 1986); Philip L. Fradkin, *A River No More: The Colorado River and the West* (New York: Alfred A. Knopf, 1981); Charles J. Meyers, "The Colorado River," vol. 19 *Stanford Law Review*, p. 1 (1966); Norris Hundley, Jr., *Water and the West: The Colorado River Compact and the Politics of Water in the American West* (Berkeley: University of California Press, 1975).

6. On the reference to Indian claims during the compact negotiations, see Clark, *supra* note 2, at pp. 635–36; Fradkin, *supra* note 5, at p. 167. Most of the estimated water usage was for a Navajo irrigation project.

7. On the Colorado River Water Storage Project Act of 1956, see generally David H. Getches, "Competing Demands for the Colorado River," vol. 56 *University of Colorado Law Review*, p. 413 (1985), and the authorities cited therein. On New Mexico's citing of the Navajos' needs in lobbying for inclusion of New Mexico water projects within the scope of the 1956 act, see Clark, *supra* note 2, at p. 639.

8. The account of the inundation of Hispanic communities is from Frances Leon Swadesh, *Los Primeros Pobladores: Hispanic Americans of the Ute Frontier*, pp. 117–27 (Notre Dame, IN: University of Notre Dame Press, 1974).

9. For the Bureau of Reclamation's calculations on the use of sprinklers, see Clark, *supra* note 2, at p. 648.

10. On passage of the legislation, see Clark, *supra* note 2, at pp. 641–42, 647–48. On the progress of the NIIP and the San Juan–Chama Project and the 1988 attempt to set a termination point, see Judith Jacobsen, "Sometimes the Feds Do Pinch Pennies," *High Country News*, pp. 6–7 (Aug. 28, 1989); Judith Jacobsen, "A Promise Made: The Navajo Indian Irrigation Project and Water Politics in the American West," NCAR Cooperative Thesis no. 119 (1989).

11. On the NIIP, and the tribal enterprise, Navajo Agricultural Products Industry, see Designwrights Collaborative, *People and Water in New Mexico*, pp. 168–69 (Sante Fe, NM: Designwrights, 1984); Clark, *supra* note 2, at pp. 644–48; Fradkin, *supra* note 5, at pp. 171–72; Jacobsen, "Sometimes the Feds Do Pinch Pennies," *supra* note 10.

12. For a complete account of the Jicarilla Apache situation, see Clark, *supra* note 2, at pp. 650–53, 663. In late 1991, the tribe reached a tentative settlement on its water rights, but the settlement would not substantially lessen the impacts of the San Juan–Chama Project on the tribe. Of the 40,000 acre-feet of water to be awarded to the tribe, about 6500 acre-feet (approximately 6 percent of the amount diverted out of the watershed) would come from the San Juan–Chama Project. *See* Karen Peterson, "Water-Rights Claim Settled for Jicarillas," *Albuquerque Journal*, p. N1 (Jan. 17, 1992).

13. On Albuquerque's water conservation program, see John A. Folk-Williams, Susan C. Fry, and Lucy Hilgendorf, *Water in the West: Western Water Flows to the Cities—A Sourcebook*, vol. 3, p. 136 (Washington,

DC: Island Press, 1985). On Albuquerque's water pricing, see Peter Rogers, "The Future of Water," vol. 252 *Atlantic Monthly*, pp. 80, 86 (July 1983).

14. U.S. Department of the Interior, Bureau of Reclamation, "Inventory and Analysis of High Water Table Areas, Middle Rio Grande Valley, New Mexico," p. v (Denver: Morrison-Knudsen Engineers, Inc., Feb. 1987). My research assistant Roger Flynn obtained information on irrigation practices in the MRGCD in an interview with Robert Grano, Bureau of Reclamation, Albuquerque, NM, Aug. 7, 1990; and in telephone conversations with Subhas Shah, chief engineer of the MRGCD, Aug. 14, 1990, and Larry Walkoviak, Bureau of Reclamation, Aug. 15, 1990. The Bureau of Reclamation describes San Juan–Chama water as "urgently needed" in the Rio Grande Valley in its map and description, *supra* note 1. On water conservation, see *infra* notes 111–115 and the accompanying text.

15. *Irwin v. Phillips*, 5 Cal. 140, 146 (1855). For background on this case, see Douglas R. Littlefield, "Water Rights during the California Gold Rush: Conflicts over Economic Points of View," vol. 14 *Western Historical Quarterly*, p. 415 (1983). On the development of early western water law, see Donald J. Pisani, "Enterprise and Equity: A Critique of Western Water Law in the Nineteenth Century," vol. 18 *Western Historical Quarterly*, p. 15 (1987); Wells A. Hutchins, *Water Rights Law in the Nineteen Western States*, vol. 1, pp. 159–75 (1971).

16. 1850 Cal. Stat. 219.

17. *Id.* at p. 146.

18. *See Coffin v. Left Hand Ditch Co.*, 6 Colo. 443 (1882).

19. *See generally* Hutchins, *supra* note 15. The quote from the Colorado Constitution may be found at Colo. Const. art. xvi, § 6.

20. Powell's life is described in the biography by Wallace Stegner, *Beyond the Hundredth Meridian: John Wesley Powell and the Second Opening of the West* (Boston: Houghton Mifflin Company, 1954).

21. Stegner, *supra* note 20, at pp. 223–24.

22. For a fine history of the development of western water law that emphasizes Mead's contributions, see Robert G. Dunbar, *Forging New Rights in Western Waters* (Lincoln: University of Nebraska Press, 1983). *See also* Paul K. Conkin, "The Vision of Elwood Mead," vol. 34 *Agricultural History*, p. 88 (1960).

23. The quoted language is from Wyoming Const. art. VIII, § 1. *See also* Wyoming Const. art. VIII, §§ 1–5.

24. On the development of Wyoming's water laws, see Hutchins, *supra* note 15, at pp. 298–301. The quoted statutory language may be found at Wyoming Stat. Ann. § 41-4-503 (1977 & Supp. 1991). The Elwood Mead quotation is from "Twenty-sixth Biennial Report of the State Engineer of the State of Wyoming: 1941–42," p. 87 (1942).

25. Montana held out until 1973, when it adopted an administrative permit system. Only Colorado has remained true to its original system of

judicially decreed rights, forswearing any administrative control over the granting of water rights. On the development of water codes in other western states, see Charles J. Meyers, et al., *Water Resource Management: A Casebook in Law and Public Policy*, 3d ed., pp. 399–425 (Westbury, NY: Foundation Press, 1988).

26. On the very limited use of public interest statutes, see Ronald B. Robie, "The Public Interest in Water Rights Administration," vol. 23 *Rocky Mountain Mineral Law Institute*, p. 917 (New York: Matthew Bender & Company, 1977). In recent years, Idaho, Washington, and (especially) California have begun to employ the public interest provisions with considerable force. *See also Shokal v. Dunn*, 109 Idaho 330, 707 P.2d 441 (1985); *Stempel v. Department of Water Resources*, 82 Wash. 2d 109, 508 P.2d 166 (1973).

27. Barry M. Mitnick, *The Political Economy of Regulation*, p. 14 (New York: Columbia University Press, 1980).

28. *See generally* Tim De Young, "Special Districts: The Conflict Between Voting Rights and Property Privileges," vol. 1982 *Arizona State Law Journal*, p. 419 (1982); James N. Corbridge, Jr., ed., *Special Water Districts: Challenge for the Future* (Boulder: University of Colorado School of Law, Natural Resources Law Center, 1985).

29. The quotation is from John D. Leshy, "Special Water Districts: The Historical Background," in Corbridge, *supra* note 28, at p. 22.

The favored treatment given to special water districts has reached many extremes, but perhaps the most notable involves the Salt River Project (SRP) in central Arizona. The SRP is run to benefit 236,000 acres of irrigated land, but the district also includes most of the Phoenix metropolitan area—about 50 percent of the state's population. Voting rights in the SRP are determined by acreage, and the district's hydroelectric facilities were used to supply electricity to Phoenix—at market rates, with proceeds from the sale of electricity being used to subsidize distribution of water to the irrigators. This system was challenged, but the Constitution turned out to be too blunt an instrument for the finely tuned laws benefiting the SRP and other special districts. The United States Supreme Court found that the equal protection clause requirement of "one person, one vote" did not apply since the SRP, under Arizona law, was technically not a government entity. Rather, in spite of the district's sweeping powers, the Court found that the SRP exercises only "narrow functions" not rising to the level of government activity, to which the equal protection clause applies. *Ball v. James*, 451 U.S. 355 (1981). *See generally* De Young, *supra* note 28, at p. 419. The California Supreme Court struck down, on "one person, one vote" grounds, a requirement that directors of the Imperial Irrigation District must be landowners. *Choudhry v. Free*, 17 Cal. 3d 660, 552 P.2d 438, 131 Cal. Rptr. 654 (1976).

30. For a summary, including the role of private investment, see Richard W.

Wahl, *Markets for Federal Water: Subsidies, Property Rights, and the Bureau of Reclamation*, pp. 13–17 (Washington, DC: Resources for the Future, 1989).

31. The "realm of romance" quotation is from E. V. Smalley, "The Future of the Great Arid West," vol. 19 *The Forum*, pp. 466, 475 (June 1895). The "soil is our salvation" quotation is referenced in, among other places, Bill G. Reid, "Agrarian Opposition to Franklin K. Lane's Proposal for Soldier Settlement, 1918–1921," vol. 41 *Agricultural History*, pp. 167, 168 (Apr. 1967).

32. The Powell quotation is from John Wesley Powell, "The Irrigable Lands of the Arid Region," vol. 39 *Century Magazine*, p. 770 (1890); the Mead quotation is from Elwood Mead, "Problems of the Arid Region," vol. 66 *Outlook*, pp. 337, 344 (Oct. 1900). *See also* Elwood Mead, "Irrigation Legislation," vol. 70 *Outlook*, p. 907 (Apr. 1902); Elwood Mead, "Problems of Irrigation Legislation," vol. 32 *The Forum*, p. 573 (1902).

33. The Smythe quotation is from William E. Smythe, "The Progress of Irrigation Thought in the West," vol. 10 *Review of Reviews*, p. 396 (July–Dec. 1894). *See also* William E. Smythe, *The Conquest of Arid America* (New York: Macmillan Company, 1905). For various critiques of Smythe and his motives and methods, see, for example, Walter Prescott Webb, *The Great Plains*, p. 357 (Lincoln: University of Nebraska Press, 1981); Donald Worster, *Rivers of Empire*, pp. 118–24 (New York: Pantheon Books, 1985); Fradkin, *supra* note 5, at pp. 25–26. On Los Angeles and the Owens Valley, see *infra* notes 49–53.

34. Stegner, *supra* note 20, at pp. 319–20.

35. On the irrigation survey, see Dunbar, *supra* note 22, at pp. 47–51; Stegner, *supra* note 20, at pp. 301–43. DeVoto is quoted in Wallace Stegner, *The American West as Living Space*, p. 9 (Ann Arbor: University of Michigan Press, 1987).

36. Stegner, *supra* note 20, at p. 338.

37. Address by President Roosevelt of Dec. 3, 1901, vol. 35 *Congressional Record*, 57th Congress, 1st Session, p. 86 (Washington, DC: U.S. Government Printing Office, 1902).

38. The original residency requirements are located at 43 U.S.C. § 431 (1928 & Supp. 1963). The "sufficiency" exception is found at 43 U.S.C. § 434 (1928 & Supp. 1963). The quotation on the allocation of project costs under the original act is from 43 U.S.C. § 461 (1928 & Supp. 1963). Section 8 of the Reclamation Act of 1902 (with the quoted language still intact in the current statute) can be found at 43 U.S.C. § 383 (1988).

39. For a table displaying state-by-state acreage totals of reclamation projects, see Wahl, *supra* note 30, at p. 24.

40. *See generally* Wahl, *supra* note 30, at pp. 28–33.

41. *Id.* at pp. 33–36.

42. *Id.* at p. 36.

43. National Water Commission, *Water Policies for the Future*, pp. 486–87 (Washington, DC: U.S. Government Printing Office, 1973).

44. *See generally* Meyers, et al., *supra* note 25, at pp. 869–74; Wahl, *supra* note 30, at pp. 71–77.
45. U.S. Department of the Interior, Water and Power Resources Service, "Acreage Limitation: Draft Environmental Impact Statement," pp. 3–11 (1981); Wahl, *supra* note 30, at pp. 72–77.
46. On exemptions involving Army Corps of Engineers projects and other specific projects, see Wahl, *supra* note 30, at pp. 90–91. The Supreme Court found that the Imperial Irrigation District (IID) had been exempted in *Bryant v. Yellen*, 447 U.S. 352 (1980), discussed *infra* note 101.
47. Paul S. Taylor, "California Water Project: Law and Politics," vol. 5 *Ecology Law Quarterly*, pp. 1, 2–3 (1975).
48. On the 1982 act, see *infra* note 104.
49. The leading full-length treatments of the Los Angeles–Owens Valley saga are William L. Kahrl, *Water and Power* (Berkeley: University of California Press, 1982); Remi A. Nadeau, *The Water Seekers* (Garden City, NY: Doubleday & Company, 1950). A shorter account is found in Marc Reisner, *Cadillac Desert*, pp. 54–107 (New York: Penguin Books, 1987).
50. For figures on Los Angeles's landownership in Owens Valley, see Doris Ostrander Dawdy, *Congress in Its Wisdom: The Bureau of Reclamation and the Public Interest*, p. 22 (Boulder, CO: Westview Press, 1989); Reisner, *supra* note 49, at p. 104.
51. The act of June 27, 1906 can be found at 1 Stat. 519 and is discussed in Dawdy, *supra* note 50, at pp. 14–16.
52. The quotation is from Reisner, *supra* note 49, at p. 77.
53. Mary Austin, *The Land of Little Rain* (Boston: Houghton Mifflin Company, 1904).
54. The "foremost builder" quotation is from Michael C. Robinson, *Water for the West: The Bureau of Reclamation, 1902–1977*, p. 48 (Chicago: Public Works Historical Society, 1979).
55. Peter Wiley and Robert Gottlieb, *Empires in the Sun: The Rise of the New American West* (New York: G. P. Putnam's Sons, 1982).
56. On Hoover Dam, see generally William E. Warne, *The Bureau of Reclamation*, pp. 104–22, 242 (New York: Praeger Publishers, 1973); Fradkin, *supra* note 5, at pp. 238–42; Russell Martin, *A Story That Stands Like a Dam: Glen Canyon and the Struggle for the Soul of the West*, pp. 2–4, 35–42 (New York: Henry Holt & Company, 1989).
57. The Elwood Mead quote is cited *supra* note 24, at pp. 83–84.
58. The Ickes quotation is from Reisner, *supra* note 49, at p. 153. The "builder with vision" quotation is from U.S. Department of the Interior, Bureau of Reclamation, vol. 26 *The Reclamation Era*, p. 32 (Feb. 1936).
59. For statistics, see, for example, U.S. Water Resources Council, "The Nation's Water Resources: 1975–2000," vol. 2, pp. 12–13, tables IV-3, IV-4 (1978); U.S. Department of the Interior, Bureau of Reclamation, "1989 Summary Statistics: Water, Land, and Related Data," p. 1 (Denver: Bureau of Reclamation, 1989).

60. On water use, see, for example, U.S. Department of the Interior, Geological Survey, Geological Survey Circular no. 1001, Wayne B. Solley, Edith B. Chase, and William B. Mann, "Estimated Use of Water in the United States in 1980" (Alexandria, VA: U.S. Geological Survey, 1983); Kenneth D. Frederick, *Scarce Water and Institutional Change*, pp. 6–7 (Washington, DC: Resources for the Future, 1986); Rogers, *supra* note 13, at pp. 80, 85. On evaporation, see, for example, U.S. Water Resources Council, *supra* note 59, at pp. 13–14; Wallace Stegner, *The American West as Living Space*, p. 6 (Ann Arbor: University of Michigan Press, 1987).

61. The "barbed wire" quote is from a personal communication with the author on Apr. 9, 1988. Antiquated irrigation systems clearly seem to preponderate in the West, although I have been unable to find a definitive regional survey. Perhaps the most reliable statistics are in a study by the U.S. Department of Agriculture, which finds that 61.6 percent of all farmland in the West is irrigated by "gravity" systems, defined as "gated pipe, ditches with siphon tubes, flooding and subirrigation." The remaining 38.4 percent is watered by more modern sprinkler systems, which include "center pivot, mechanical move, hand move, solid sprinkler, and drip and trickle irrigation." U.S. Department of Agriculture, Bulletin no. 523, John C. Day and Gerald L. Horner, "U.S. Irrigation: Extent and Economic Importance," p. 10, table 6 (Washington, DC: U.S. Government Printing Office, 1987).

62. On conservation, see Steven J. Shupe, "Waste in Western Water Law: A Blueprint for Change," vol. 61 *Oregon Law Review*, p. 483 (1982); Bruce Driver, ed., "Western Water: Tuning the System: Report to the Western Governors' Association from the Water Efficiency Task Force" (Denver: Western Governors' Association, 1986). For authority on the role of local custom, see Shupe, *supra*, at p. 491. For a case on water conservation in the Truckee-Carson Irrigation District in Nevada, see *United States v. Alpine Land & Reservoir Co.*, 697 F.2d 851 (9th Cir.), *cert. denied sub nom. Pyramid Lake Paiute Tribe of Indians v. Truckee-Carson Irrigation District et al.*, 464 U.S. 863 (1983).

63. *See* U.S. Department of Agriculture, Soil Conservation Service, "Crop Consumptive Irrigation Requirements and Irrigation Efficiency Coefficients for the United States," p. 17 (1976); U.S. Department of the Interior, U.S. Department of Agriculture, and U.S. Environmental Protection Agency, "Interagency Task Force Report: Irrigation Water Use and Management," pp. 22–27 (Washington, DC: U.S. Government Printing Office, 1979). Both estimates are for irrecoverable losses to the stream systems.

64. The Saunders quotation is from the Colorado Water Conference in Gunnison on July 27, 1987.

65. The quotation is from Dawdy, *supra* note 50, at p. 135. On salinity in the Colorado River basin, see Norris Hundley, Jr., "The West Against Itself: The Colorado River—An Institutional History," in Weatherford and Brown, *supra* note 5, at pp. 9, 37–39.

66. Donald R. Satterlund, *Wildland Watershed Management*, p. 256 (New York: Ronald Press, 1972).

67. *See* Council on Environmental Quality, "Environmental Quality: Twentieth Annual Report," p. 236 (1990); James L. Arts and William L. Church, "Soil Erosion: The Next Crisis?" vol. 1982 *Wisconsin Law Review*, p. 535 (1982); Kenneth E. Barker, "The New Federalism: Time for States to Pull the Plow in Soil Conservation," vol. 30 *South Dakota Law Review*, p. 546 (1985). For the Leopold quotes, see, respectively, Aldo Leopold, "Erosion as a Menace to the Social and Economic Future of the Southwest," vol. 44 *Journal of Forestry*, pp. 627, 630 (1946); Aldo Leopold, "Conservation Economics," vol. 32 *Journal of Forestry*, pp. 537, 539 (1934).

68. *See generally* Tom Harris, *Death in the Marsh* (Washington, DC: Island Press, 1991). *See also* Dawdy, *supra* note 50, at pp. 97–109, 113–27.

69. On livestock deaths, see Dawdy, *supra* note 50, at p. 99. On the effects on humans, see *id.* at pp. 99–100. For the ongoing investigations, see Tom Harris, "Getting Off on the Wrong Foot," *High Country News*, pp. 8–10 (Nov. 20, 1989).

70. On nonpoint source pollution, see generally John H. Davidson, "The 1987 Nonpoint Source Pollution Amendments and State Progress Under the New Program," in *Water Quality Control: Integrating Beneficial Use and Environmental Protection* (Boulder: University of Colorado School of Law, Natural Resources Law Center, 1988). On point source pollution, see The Conservation Foundation, *State of the Environment: A View toward the Nineties*, p. 87 (Washington, DC: The Conservation Foundation, 1987). On coordinated management of water quality and quantity, see David H. Getches, Lawrence J. MacDonnell, and Teresa A. Rice, *Controlling Water Use: The Unfinished Business of Water Quality Protection* (Boulder: University of Colorado School of Law, Natural Resources Law Center, 1991).

71. On the 1987 act, see Davidson, *supra* note 70.

72. On the Gila River, see Amadeo M. Rea, *Once a River: Bird Life and Habitat Changes on the Middle Gila* (Tucson: University of Arizona Press, 1983). On the Colorado River, see Fradkin, *supra* note 5; Bob Saile, "Drought Causes Variety of Problems," *Denver Post*, p. 8F (Aug. 24, 1988). On Montana, see Bruce Farling, "Drained Rivers Rouse Montana," *High Country News*, p. 16 (Nov. 20, 1989); "Two Groups Fight over Montana Water," *New York Times*, p. A16 (Aug. 18, 1988). On Sacramento River Delta saltwater intrusion, see *United States v. State Water Resources Control Board*, 182 Cal. App. 3d 82, 227 Cal. Rptr. 161 (1986).

73. The quotations are from U.S. Department of Agriculture, Forest Service, "Stream Survey Summary: Rio Blanco 1989," pp. 1–2 (available from U.S. Department of Agriculture, Forest Service, San Juan National Forest, Pagosa Springs Ranger District, Pagosa Springs, CO 81147).

74. The Bush administration policy goal of "no net loss of wetlands" was quoted in "No Easy Choices Will Face 'No Net Loss' Wetlands Panels," *Public Lands News*, p. 5 (June 1, 1989). The Morgenweck quotation may

be found *id.* at p. 6. On the Bush administration proposal to change the definition of wetlands, see "What Is a Jurisdictional Wetland?" vol. 13 *National Wetlands Newsletter,* p. 5 (Sept.–Oct. 1991); Warren E. Leary, "In Wetlands Debate, Acres and Dollars Hinge on Definitions," *New York Times,* p. C4 (Oct. 15, 1991).

75. *See generally* National Water Commission, *supra* note 43, at p. 230.

76. *See generally* William Ashworth, *Nor Any Drop to Drink,* pp. 25–26 (New York: Summit Books, 1982). The percentage figure was extracted from U.S. Department of the Interior, Geological Survey, "National Water Summary 1987: Hydrologic Events and Water Supply and Use," p. 126 (Washington, DC: U.S. Government Printing Office, 1990).

77. Groundwater law is intricate and varies from state to state far more than does surface water law. For a summary, see David H. Getches, *Water Law in a Nutshell,* 2d ed., pp. 235–90 (St. Paul, MN: West Publishing Company, 1990). The literal application of seniority is unworkable: "A senior groundwater appropriator theoretically could demand that no pumping be allowed because virtually any new pumping causes some effect," such as requiring a senior user to sink the pump deeper when a junior user lowers the groundwater table. *Id.* at p. 250. Nevertheless, western states have structured their regulatory systems to protect existing uses. *See generally id.* at pp. 261–70. The two states with the most advanced systems, Colorado and New Mexico, have applied seniority to the groundwater context by adopting conjunctive management, in which surface water and groundwater uses on a river and on connected ("tributary") aquifers are administered in an interlocking fashion based on seniority. *Id.* at pp. 277–85. *See also* Frank J. Trelease, "Conjunctive Use of Groundwater and Surface Water," vol. 27B *Rocky Mountain Mineral Law Institute,* p. 1853 (New York: Matthew Bender & Company, 1982). Regulation of groundwater use by western states is very recent (beginning in the 1960s or later), and in spite of widespread pumping in excess of annual recharge, the laws struggle mightily to allow existing uses to continue (an exception is the Arizona Groundwater Management Act of 1980; see *infra* note 110). These trends are the basis for my statement in the text that states have been reluctant to regulate groundwater users. *See generally* J. David Aiken, "Ground Water Mining Law and Policy," vol. 53 *University of Colorado Law Review,* p. 505 (1982); Natural Resources Law Center, *Groundwater: Allocation, Development and Pollution* (Boulder: University of Colorado School of Law, Natural Resources Law Center, 1983); David H. Getches, "Controlling Groundwater Use and Quality: A Fragmented System," vol. 17 *Natural Resources Lawyer,* p. 623 (1985); The Conservation Foundation, *Groundwater Protection* (Washington, DC: The Conservation Foundation, 1987); Sierra Club Legal Defense Fund, Eric P. Jorgensen, ed., *The Poisoned Well* (Washington, DC: Island Press, 1989). On states pumping in excess of annual recharge, see Day and Horner, *supra* note 61, at p. 12, table 10.

78. 207 U.S. 564 (1908). On the background of the case, see Norris Hundley,

354 Notes to Pages 268–272

"The 'Winters' Decision and Indian Water Rights: A Mystery Reexamined," vol. 13 Western Historical Quarterly, p. 17 (1982).

79. The Winans quotation is from United States v. Winans, 198 U.S. 371, 381 (1905); the Winters quotations are from Winters v. United States, 207 U.S. 564, 576–77 (1908). On the Winters doctrine, see generally Felix S. Cohen, Cohen's Handbook of Federal Indian Law, rev. ed., pp. 578–95 (Charlottesville, VA: Michie Company/Bobbs-Merrill Law Publishing, 1982); Richard B. Collins, "The Future Course of the Winters Doctrine," vol. 56 University of Colorado Law Review, p. 481 (1985).

80. On Indian water development, see generally Daniel McCool, Command of the Waters: Iron Triangles, Federal Water Development, and Indian Water (Berkeley: University of California Press, 1987). On the NIIP, see supra notes 7–12 and the accompanying text.

81. Donald R. Snow in Mark D. O'Keefe et al., Boundaries Carved in Water: An Analysis of River and Water Management in the Upper Missouri Basin, p. 19 (Missoula, MT: Northern Lights Institute, 1986). This resource contains a complete bibliography on water development in the upper Missouri River basin. See also Michael L. Lawson, Dammed Indians: The Pick-Sloan Plan and the Missouri River Sioux, 1944–1980 (Norman: University of Oklahoma Press, 1982).

82. National Water Commission, supra note 43, at pp. 474–75.

83. On the allocation of water between individuals and the community "good," see F. Lee Brown and Helen M. Ingram, Water and Poverty in the Southwest, p. 33 (Tucson: University of Arizona Press, 1987); Michael C. Meyer, Water in the Hispanic Southwest: A Social and Legal History, 1550–1850, pp. 159–61 (Tucson: University of Arizona Press, 1984). As both discussions show, community considerations and individual equities played a major role, in sharp contrast to the hard, fixed individual rights recognized by prior appropriation: "Who had the legal right was no more than one answer to this essential question [of how water was to be divided]. Judicial decision, in effect, came to the aid of custom. Legal rights, whether they be corporate [that is, community] or individual, did not constitute a single, overbearing consideration in the adjudication of water disputes." Meyer, supra at p. 161. On acequias, see Meyer, supra; Brown and Ingram, supra at p. 33; Designwrights Collaborative, supra note 11, at pp. 51–57; Oliver LaFarge, The Mother Ditch (Santa Fe, NM: Sunstone Press, 1983); Stanley Crawford, Mayordomo (Albuquerque: University of New Mexico Press, 1988).

84. See U.S. Department of Agriculture, Soil Conservation Service, Regional Bulletin no. 33, Hugh G. Calkins, "Reconnaissance Survey of Human Dependency on Resources in the Rio Grande Watershed," pp. 126–27 (Albuquerque, NM: U.S. Department of Agriculture, Dec. 1936). Calkins's description of the Mesilla Valley before Elephant Butte can be found id. at pp. 98–101.

85. For the Calkins quotation, see id. at p. 137. The information on the

MRGCD, including the "dragline" quotation, is from M. Brian McDonald, et al., Technical Completion Report, "Case Studies in the Development of New Mexico Water Resources Institutions: The Middle Rio Grande Conservancy District and Urban Water Pricing," pp. 13–25 (Albuquerque: University of New Mexico, Water Resources Research Institute, 1981).

86. For the Calkins quotation, see *supra* note 84, at p. 138. On the seventy *acequias*, see McDonald, et al., *supra* note 85, at p. 18.

87. On the very limited use—certainly not extending to cultural concerns—of the "public interest" and "public welfare" provisions in most western state water codes, see *supra* note 26. In New Mexico, the public interest statute has traditionally had a narrow scope. *See Young & Norton v. Hinderlider*, 15 N.M. 666, 110 P. 1045 (1910) (Hispanic cultural concerns raised in litigation as a bar to a transfer of water from farming to a proposed ski area). *See generally* Charles F. Wilkinson, "Law and the American West: The Search for an Ethic of Place," vol. 59 *University of Colorado Law Review*, pp. 401, 422–23 (1988). The statute was subsequently amended in 1985, and the New Mexico state engineer worked with Hispanic representatives in developing criteria to define "public welfare," the term now used in the amended statute. N.M. STAT. ANN. § 72-5-7 (1985 & Supp. 1991). These new criteria may include cultural concerns, according to Lucy Moore, Western Network, Santa Fe, personal correspondence with the author, Jan. 17, 1992. *See also* John Nichols, *The Milagro Beanfield War* (New York: Ballantine Books, 1974).

88. Author's interview with Lucy Moore, Western Network, Santa Fe, NM, Aug. 8, 1990. On the *Aamodt* case, see Brown and Ingram, *supra* note 83, at pp. 65–72. On sales of water by Hispanics and other aspects of prior appropriation, see Designwrights Collaborative, *supra* note 11, at pp. 5–6.

89. *See* Douglas Towne, "Arizona Digs Deep for Water," *High Country News*, pp. 20–21 (Nov. 20, 1989); Jon Christensen, "Will Las Vegas Drain Rural Nevada?" *High Country News*, p. 1 (May 21, 1990).

90. On total transmountain diversions in Colorado, see League of Women Voters of Colorado, *Colorado Water*, p. 23 (Denver: League of Women Voters of Colorado, 1988). On pending Colorado projects, see Rushworth M. Kidder, "Water Debate Rises in Rockies," *Christian Science Monitor*, p. 12 (Oct. 27, 1989) (Two Forks Dam); Charles F. Wilkinson, "In Depth: Water Rights and Wrongs," vol. 74 *Sierra*, p. 35 (Sept.–Oct. 1989) (Homestake II); Bill McBean, "Project Feeds Gunnison River Dispute," *Denver Post*, p. 1B (Jan. 28, 1990); Patrick O'Driscoll, "Water War Intensifies in Runoff-Blessed [San Luis] Valley," *Denver Post*, p. 1C (July 22, 1990).

91. On current state law protections for the basin of origin against an outside developer, see Lawrence J. MacDonnell and Charles W. Howe, "Area-of-Origin Protection in Transbasin Water Diversions: An Evaluation of

Alternative Approaches," vol. 57 *University of Colorado Law Review*, p. 527 (1986).

92. On Hetch Hetchy, see Stephen Fox, *John Muir and His Legacy: The American Conservation Movement*, pp. 139–47 (Boston: Little, Brown & Company, 1981).

93. The Glen Canyon story is told in full in Martin, *supra* note 56.

94. Two useful sources are Robert Anderson, "The Challenge of Allenspur: A Report on Allenspur Dam," *Livingston Enterprise*, Supplement (Oct. 1974); Gary Williams and Alan Newell, "Yellowstone River Navigability Study," presented to the U.S. Army Corps of Engineers, Omaha District (Aug. 12, 1974).

95. *See generally* Anderson, *supra* note 94.

96. The quotation is from W. H. Hornby, "Our River Needs a 'Yellowstone Concerto,'" *Livingston Enterprise*, p. 6 (Jan. 21, 1974).

97. *See generally* Anderson, *supra* note 94.

98. Telephone interview with Jim Posewitz by my research assistant Brian Kuehl, Mar. 5, 1992.

99. For the figures on reservoir efficiency, see U.S. Department of the Interior, Geological Survey, "National Water Summary 1983: Hydrologic Events and Issues," p. 33 (Washington, DC: U.S. Government Printing Office, 1984).

100. On Two Forks, see Kidder, *supra* note 91.

101. The reformers lost a major case, *Bryant v. Yellen*, 447 U.S. 352 (1980), when the United States Supreme Court held that the requirements did not apply to the Imperial Irrigation District. The Court looked beyond the statutory requirements to a letter obtained by irrigation interests, written by Secretary of the Interior Ray Lyman Wilbur in 1933 during the waning days of the Hoover administration, assuring farmers in the Imperial Valley that the excess land provisions did not apply to them. The results in court were different in the Central Valley, where objecting parties prevailed in a number of cases. Perhaps most notably, National Land for People obtained an injunction directing the Bureau of Reclamation to require that excess lands in the Westlands Water District be sold off in lots no larger than 160 acres to local residents. *National Land for People v. Bureau of Reclamation*, 417 F. Supp. 449 (D.D.C. 1976). *See generally* Mary L. Frampton, "The Enforcement of Federal Reclamation Law in the Westlands Water District: A Broken Promise," vol. 13 *University of California–Davis Law Review*, p. 89 (1979).

102. Reisner, *supra* note 49, at pp. 348–49.

103. The Miller and McClure quotations are from Kathy Koch, "Classic Confrontation: Senate Water-Use Bill Pits Big Firms Against Small Farms," *Congressional Quarterly*, pp. 2121, 2122, 2125 (Sept. 29, 1979).

104. Reclamation Reform Act of 1982, 43 U.S.C. §§ 390aa to 390zz-1 (1988). *See* Wahl, *supra* note 30, at pp. 71–105; Myers, et al., *supra* note 25, at pp. 873–74. For the court opinion refusing to exempt Army Corps of Engi-

neers projects from the reclamation laws, see *United States v. Tulare Lake Canal Co.*, 535 F.2d 1093 (9th Cir. 1976). This holding, however, was later overturned by the 1982 act. On hunger and poverty in the Central Valley in the 1990s, see California Rural Legal Assistance Foundation, *Hunger in the Heartland* (San Francisco: California Rural Legal Assistance Foundation, 1991).

105. For the Rio Chama wild and scenic river designation, see 16 U.S.C. § 1274(a)(108) (1988). For a listing of wild and scenic rivers, see generally 16 U.S.C. §§ 1274–76 (1985 & Supp. 1992), and Sierra Club, *National Wild and Scenic Rivers System* (San Francisco: Sierra Club Books, Apr. 1988; supplemented Jan. 1991).

106. On recent Indian water legislation and pending proposals, see American Indian Resources Institute, *Sourcebook on Indian Water Settlements* (Oakland, CA: American Indian Resources Institute, 1989). On the Pyramid Lake settlement, see *supra* chapter 1, note 10 and accompanying text. On the Jicarilla Apaches, see Peterson, *supra* note 12.

107. On the delta smelt, see Jane Gross, "Bid to Save Delta Smelt Jolts California," *Denver Post*, p. 2A (Oct. 27, 1991). On the Animas–La Plata Project, see Mark Obmascik, "Rare Fish May Alter, Kill Project," *Denver Post*, p. 1B (Feb. 8, 1990); Mark Obmascik, "Water Fight's Tab Placed at $885,000: No End to Dispute in Sight," *Denver Post*, p. 1C (Oct. 6, 1991). On the use of Stampede Reservoir, see *Carson-Truckee Water Conservancy District v. Clark*, 741 F.2d 257 (9th Cir. 1984), *cert. denied sub nom., Nevada v. Hodel*, 470 U.S. 1083 (1985). *See generally* A. Dan Tarlock, "The Endangered Species Act and Western Water Rights," vol. 20 *Land & Water Law Review*, p. 1 (1985).

108. *See National Audubon Society v. Superior Court*, 33 Cal. 3d 419, 189 Cal. Rptr. 346, 658 P.2d 709 (1983), *cert. denied*, 464 U.S. 977 (1983). On recent settlement negotiations, see Connie Koenenn, "The Challenger: Martha Davis' Small but Tenacious Mono Lake Committee Has Taken On the DWP—and May Even Win," *Los Angeles Times*, p. 1E (Aug. 28, 1991).

109. The other leading use of the doctrine by a California court is in *United States v. State Water Resources Control Board*, 182 Cal. App. 3d 82, 227 Cal. Rptr. 161 (1986), in which the California Court of Appeal limited excessive diversions by senior users in the San Joaquin and Sacramento valleys because their depletions had permitted salt water from the San Francisco Bay to push farther into the Sacramento River Delta. *See generally* "Symposium on the Public Trust and the Waters of the American West: Yesterday, Today and Tomorrow," vol. 19 *Environmental Law*, p. 425 (1989).

110. On the Arizona groundwater law, see the Arizona Groundwater Management Act of 1980, ARIZ. REV. STAT. ANN. §§ 45-401 to 45-637 (1987 & Supp. 1991). The act was significantly amended in 1991. *See* Arizona Department of Water Resources, "Summary of Arizona House Bill

2499: Phoenix AMA Groundwater Replenishment District" (Oct. 1991); Rodney T. Smith and Roger Vaughan, eds., "Arizona Rewrites Groundwater Law," vol. 5 *Water Strategist*, p. 1 (July 1991). *See generally* Jon L. Kyl, "The 1980 Arizona Groundwater Management Act: From Inception to Current Constitutional Challenge," vol. 53 *University of Colorado Law Review*, p. 471 (1982); Desmond D. Connall, Jr., "A History of the Arizona Groundwater Act," vol. 1982 *Arizona State Law Journal*, p. 313 (1982).

111. On Tucson, see William E. Martin, et al., *Saving Water in a Desert City* (Washington, DC: Resources for the Future, 1984). On Denver, see Mark Obmascik, "Denver Water Meters Will Be Mandatory," *Denver Post*, p. 1A (Nov. 28, 1990); Denver Water Department, Office of Water Conservation, *Water Conservation Plan of the Denver Water Department* (Denver: Board of Water Commissioners, Summer 1989). On Casper, see Richard W. Wahl and Frank H. Osterhoudt, "Voluntary Transfers of Water in the West," in U.S. Department of the Interior, Geological Survey, "National Water Summary 1985—Hydrologic Events and Surface-Water Resources," p. 113 (Washington, DC: U.S. Government Printing Office, 1985); Lawrence J. MacDonnell, ed., "The Water Transfer Process as a Management Option for Meeting Changing Water Demands," vol. 2, ch. 6, p. 15, U.S. Geological Survey grant award report (May 1990). The quotation on the Metropolitan Water District–Imperial Irrigation District transaction is from Worldwatch Institute, *State of the World 1990: A Worldwatch Institute Report on Progress Toward a Sustainable Society*, p. 50 (New York: W. W. Norton & Company, 1990). For a more detailed discussion of the deal, see Marc Reisner and Sarah Bates, *Overtapped Oasis: Reform or Revolution for Western Water*, pp. 149–66 (Washington, DC: Island Press, 1990). One example of progressive thinking in southern California occurred when the Municipal Water District of Southern California commissioned the Rocky Mountain Institute (Amory Lovins's conservation research organization) to prepare an extensive analysis of "best management practices" that might save large amounts of water in a cost-effective manner. *See* Robert C. Wilkinson, *California BMP Assessment* (Snowmass, CO: Rocky Mountain Institute, 1991). For an especially influential analysis, which spurred the IID-MWD water conservation transaction, see the Environmental Defense Fund, Robert Stavins, *Trading Conservation Investments for Water* (Berkeley, CA: Environmental Defense Fund, 1983).

112. On in-stream flows, see generally Lawrence J. MacDonnell, Teresa A. Rice, and Steven J. Shupe, eds., *Instream Flow Protection in the West* (Boulder: University of Colorado School of Law, Natural Resources Law Center, 1989). On marketing water, see MacDonnell, *supra* note 111; Wahl, *supra* note 30. On the public interest, see David H. Getches, ed., *Water and the American West*, pp. 127–64 (Boulder: University of Colorado School of Law, Natural Resources Law Center, 1988); Natural

Resources Law Center, *Water as a Public Resource: Emerging Rights and Obligations*, proceedings from the eighth annual summer program, June 1–3, 1987 (Boulder: University of Colorado School of Law, Natural Resources Law Center, 1987).

113. *See* Steve Hinchman, "Irrigation Water Revives a Wildlife Refuge in Nevada," *High Country News*, p. 6 (Aug. 27, 1990). For a survey of The Nature Conservancy's water programs, see Ken Wiley, "Untying the Western Water Knot," vol. 40 *The Nature Conservancy Magazine*, p. 5 (Mar.–Apr. 1990).

114. *See* Driver, *supra* note 62; Steven J. Shupe, Gary D. Weatherford, and Elizabeth Checchio, "Western Water Rights: The Era of Reallocation," vol. 29 *Natural Resources Journal*, pp. 413–14 (1989). *See generally* David H. Getches, "Water Use Efficiency: The Value of Water in the West," vol. 8 *Public Land Law Review*, p. 1 (1987); Harrison C. Dunning, "The 'Physical Solution' in Western Water Law," vol. 57 *University of Colorado Law Review*, p. 445 (1986); A. Dan Tarlock, "The Changing Meaning of Water Conservation in the West," vol. 66 *Nebraska Law Review*, p. 145 (1987).

115. *See* Reisner and Bates, *supra* note 111. *See also* Western States Water Council, *Water Conservation and Western Water Resource Management: A Study Prepared for the Western Governors' Association* (May 1984).

116. On the magnitude of the gains from conservation, see Frank Welsh, *How to Create a Water Crisis*, p. 55 (Boulder, CO: Johnson Publishing Company, 1985). The quotation on flood irrigation in the MRGCD is from an interview with Robert Grano, cited *supra* note 14. For a fine analysis of the situation in the late 1980s, see Getches, *supra* note 114.

117. Wallace Stegner, "Water in the West: Growing Beyond Nature's Limits," *Los Angeles Times*, p. 3 (Dec. 29, 1985).

118. *See* Rogers, *supra* note 13, at p. 86; Frederick, *supra* note 60, at p. 6.

119. The court of appeals quotation is from *United States v. Alpine Land & Reservoir Co.*, 697 F.2d 851, 855 (9th Cir. 1983) (citation omitted). The Freyfogle quote is from Eric T. Freyfogle, "Water Justice," vol. 1986 *University of Illinois Law Review*, pp. 481, 518 (1986). For a complete discussion of the nature of vested property rights in water, see Joseph L. Sax, "The Constitution, Property Rights and the Future of Water Law," vol. 61 *University of Colorado Law Review*, p. 257 (1990). For a contrary piece (untenable in my view) suggesting that government regulatory measures may violate vested property rights, see Jan G. Laitos, "Water Rights, Clean Water Act Section 404 Permitting, and the Takings Clause," vol. 60 *University of Colorado Law Review*, p. 901 (1989). *Lucas v. South Carolina Coastal Council*, 60 U.S.L.W. 4842 (1992), which found a taking when all commercial use of a parcel was curtailed, does not seem to cast doubt on the kind of comparatively modest regulatory program suggested in the text. Further, as noted, the

property right in western water has always been defined by beneficial use, not by the total amount of water diverted.

120. On the Oregon program, see Charles F. Wilkinson, "Aldo Leopold and Western Water Law: Thinking Perpendicular to the Prior Appropriation Doctrine," vol. 24 *Land & Water Law Review*, pp. 32–34 (1989), an article in which I earlier set out some of the proposals made here.

CHAPTER SEVEN

1. For Muir's quotation, see Edwin Way Teale, ed., *The Wilderness World of John Muir*, p. 100 (Boston: Houghton Mifflin Company, 1976).

2. On the history of the water regime in the Central Valley, see William L. Kahrl, *The California Water Atlas*, pp. 15–27 (Sacramento: State of California, 1979). Information on the current condition of Tulare Lake and Wetlands was attained from Randy Kelly, fisheries expert, California Fish and Game Department, by telephone interview with my research assistant Ellen Kohler, Apr. 22, 1992. On the Animas–La Plata Project, see Mark Obmascik, "Rare Fish Find May Alter, Kill Project," *Denver Post*, p. 1B (Feb. 8, 1990); U.S. Department of the Interior, Bureau of Reclamation, Upper Colorado Region, *Animas–La Plata Project* (undated pamphlet, available from Projects Manager, Bureau of Reclamation, P.O. Box 640, Durango, CO 81302). On the Colorado River, see Philip L. Fradkin, *A River No More: The Colorado River and the West* (New York: Alfred A. Knopf, 1981).

3. The quotation is from Edith Brown Weiss, "In Fairness to Future Generations," vol. 32 *Environment*, p. 6 (Apr. 1990). On sustainability, see generally World Commission on Environment and Development, *Our Common Future* (Oxford: Oxford University Press, 1987). For accounts on sustainability in the Pacific Northwest, see Kai N. Lee, "The Columbia River Basin: Experimenting with Sustainability," vol. 31 *Environment*, p. 6 (July–Aug. 1989); John M. Volkman, "Making Room in the Ark: The Endangered Species Act and the Columbia River Basin," vol. 34 *Environment*, p. 13 (May 1992). *See also* Charles F. Wilkinson, "Crossing the Next Meridian: Sustaining the Lands, Waters, and Human Spirit in the West," vol. 32 *Environment*, p. 14 (Dec. 1990), based on my work for this book, in which I earlier set out some of these views on sustainability.

4. On the Willamette River, see Oregon Department of Environmental Quality, *Willamette River Basin Study* (Portland, OR: Department of Environmental Quality, Mar. 1992); Joe Uris, "Uncovering Problems in Portland's Sewers," *Oregonian*, pp. B1, B4 (Sept. 1, 1991). On land use planning in Oregon, see Edward C. Rochette, "Statewide Land Use Control: The Oregon Experience," a study contained in Fredric A. Strom, ed., *1981 Zoning and Planning Law Handbook*, pp. 111–25 (New York: Clark Boardman Company, 1981). On the Tahoe Regional Planning Agency, see Richard J. Fink, "Public Land Acquisition for Environmental

Protection: Structuring a Program for the Lake Tahoe Basin," vol. 18 *Ecology Law Quarterly*, pp. 485, 504–11 (1991).

5. *See* Bernard DeVoto, "The West: A Plundered Province," vol. 169 *Harper's Magazine*, p. 355 (Aug. 1934); Richard D. Lamm and Michael McCarthy, *The Angry West: A Vulnerable Land and Its Future* (Boston: Houghton Mifflin Company, 1982); K. Ross Toole, *Twentieth-Century Montana: A State of Extremes* (Norman: University of Oklahoma Press, 1972); K. Ross Toole, *The Rape of the Great Plains: Northwest America, Cattle and Coal* (Boston: Little, Brown & Company, 1976); Carey McWilliams, *California: The Great Exception* (New York: Current Books, 1949). A helpful essay on the subject is William G. Robbins, "The 'Plundered Province' Thesis and the Recent Historiography of the American West," vol. 55 *Pacific Historical Review*, p. 577 (1986).

6. On growth management and economic development, see World Commission on Environment and Development, *supra* note 3; Daniel R. Mandelker and Roger A. Cunningham, *Planning and Control of Land Development*, 2d ed. (Charlottesville, VA: Michie Company/Bobbs-Merrill Law Publishing, 1985); Henry R. Richmond, "Does Oregon's Land Use Program Provide Enough Desirable Land to Attract Needed Industry to Oregon?" vol. 14 *Environmental Law*, p. 693 (1984).

Acknowledgments

My debts run deep on this book, far more than with anything else I have written. I send out my lasting thanks to the great many people who have taken the time to make *Crossing the Next Meridian* possible.

I began with rough ideas. At the very start, John Thorson, Dick Trudell, Alvin Josephy, and Vine Deloria, Jr., helped shape them and gave me encouragement. Then I visited a number of people who know the West and have influenced its directions; I benefited enormously from long, informal discussions with Wallace Stegner, John McGuire, Ted Swem, Ed Marston, Maggie Fox, Len and Sandy Sargent, and Stewart Udall. Because the book draws heavily on the facts of local controversies that I believe stand as metaphors for westwide issues of pressing importance, I traveled to those places, conducted site visits, and held extensive interviews. Each of these ventures was a joy, and I thank all who participated: Emmett and Zona Smith of Dixie, Idaho, and Harold Thomas of Boise; Glorene Gurrero, Paul Wagner, and many others at Pyramid Lake; Ron Anglin and Cliff Creger of the Stillwater National Wildlife Refuge; John McDonough and many employees of the Goldstrike Mine; Glenn Miller of the University of Nevada; Jeff Jones of the Forest Service, stationed at the Sawtooth National Recreation Area; John Hoak of the Mineral Hill Mine in Gardiner, Montana; Lill Erickson of Gardiner; Wayne Elmore of the BLM in Prineville, Oregon; Jamie and Beth McKinney of Pueblo, Colorado; Alan and Diana Kessler of the Orme Ranch in Mayer, Arizona; Tony and Jerri Tipton of the Carter Ranch in Austin, Nevada; Forest Service employees, too many to count, in national forests and ranger districts across the West (whatever may be the agency's problems with timber domination, the Forest Service's professionalism is nowhere more evident than in its employees' willingness to talk through an issue or arrange a site visit to a grazing allotment, roadless area, dam site, timber sale, research natural area, hardrock claim, or vista point); Delbert Frank, Olney Patt, Sr., Nelson Wallulatum, Zane Jackson, and Bernice Mitchell of the Confederated Tribes of the Warm Springs Indian Reservation, and Dennis Karnopp, Jim Noteboom, and Howie Arnett, the lawyers for the Confederated Tribes; and Isadoro Manzanares and Charles Fisher of the Bureau of Reclamation in Chama, New Mexico.

I received help with the manuscript from many people. Several were generous enough to read all of it: Ed Marston, Don Snow, Wally Stegner, Carl Brandt, David Getches, Gary Holthaus, Larry MacDonnell, Sarah Bates, and Patty Limerick. I learned a great deal from their many comments. Phil Hocker, John Leshy, Joe Feller, John Volkman, Mike Anderson, Mike Axline, John Folk-Williams, Lucy Moore, and Bob Pelcyger gave huge amounts of their time working through difficult issues related to mining, grazing, Pacific salmon, timber, and water. Many others critiqued chapters or passages within their areas of expertise, corrected errors, and gave me valuable perspectives: Tom Kovalicky, Neal "Pete" Parsell, Ron Mitchell, John McDonough, Glenn Miller, John Hoak, Flavio Montecinos, Jim Peterson, Wayne Elmore, Charles Callison, Med Bennett, Bill deBuys, Kelley Green, Carl Bock, Greg Simonds, Rick Braun, Jim Butcher, John Butcher, Reed Benson, Rebecca Wodder, Ralph Johnson, Chuck Brendecke, Kai Lee, Jim Ruff, John Nichols, Bob Anderson, Jim Posewitz, Scott Reed, Phil Wallin, Tom Olson, Robert Grano, Larry Walkoviak, Fred Waltz, and Randy Kelly. I co-authored earlier articles with Mike Anderson and Dan Conner, on the national forests and Pacific salmon, respectively, and drew heavily upon those pieces here; I thank them once again for those lasting partnerships.

Karen Lewotsky, a lawyer-geographer-cartographer, did all of the maps. Her fine work helps bring life to many of the situations portrayed in the text. The painting on the cover, *Crooked River* by Chuck Forsman, is one of my favorite pieces by this leading western artist (and depicts a scene not far downstream from Camp Creek, described in chapter 3). My thanks for his permission to use it here.

Working with Island Press, which is so deeply committed to the West, has been an outstanding experience. Chuck Savitt, the president, has believed in this book all the way. My editor, Barbara Dean, has been a valued colleague—careful yet expansive, knife-sharp analytical yet rock-solid supportive. Beth Beisel was masterful with the production of this complex manuscript. Pat Harris did the copyediting with precision and good judgment.

Over the years, my research assistants have been able and creative young lawyers, colleagues in the full sense. Their diligence and ideas are spread throughout these pages. I thank Bob Coles, Will Barnes, Rick

Poulin, Scott Hardt, and Etta Walker. Jean Cunningham did valuable research for me in the Plumas County Museum in Quincy, California. Roger Flynn did superb work on various water issues, including an interviewing trip to New Mexico. The final work—the grueling job of updating facts and verifying the disparate sources relied on here—was done by Ellen Kohler, Brian Kuehl, and Val Russo. I owe them a special debt.

The same is true with the professional secretarial staff here at the law school. My heartfelt gratitude to Kay Wilkie, Marge Brunner, Anne Guthrie, Cynthia Shafer, and Kim Clay—organizers, typists, editors, and idea people *extraordinaire*.

The University of Colorado Law School has done everything possible to support this book. This includes not only the exceptional staff assistance just mentioned, but also the moral support of the faculty and deans. In 1987, nearly all of the faculty participated in a seminar in which we discussed the ideas in the first three chapters. Their views came during the formative time of the book and were of great assistance. Betsy Levin, dean during the early years of this project, and Gene Nichol, dean since 1987, have been wonderful. Cliff Calhoun and Mark Loewenstein were the associate deans, supportive in every possible way, during this time. Thank you.

I have received generous financial support for the writing of this book. Grants from the Ford Foundation and Ann Roberts allowed me to take leave from my teaching duties for a full semester in 1985, when I most needed to immerse myself in this project: I appreciate the efforts of Susan Sechler, Norm Collins, Jim Butcher, and Walt Coward, all of Ford, for their efforts; Ann Roberts, in addition to her financial support, regularly extended her much-appreciated encouragement. I also offer my sincere thanks to the American Indian Resources Institute and the Natural Resources Law Center.

Carl Brandt, my agent, has helped me in more ways than I can ever count. I thank him for his knowledge and advice, high standards, ready accessibility, love of the west, good humor, and loyalty. Other good friends have given me much over the years and I will take this chance to thank them: Yvonne Knight, John Cunningham, Terry Tempest Williams, Joe Sax, Deanna Martinez, Vernon and Lynn Peterson, Tom and John Fredericks, Marge Brown, Sam and Marie Knudsen, Mariana Roca Shulstad, Scott Little, Mimi Wesson, Eve and Don Sears, Stephanie Volkman, Mary Stegner, Gilbert White, Maggie and Rob Robertson, Carol Gillaspy, Bill Hornby, Barbara Sudler, George Frampton, Susan Kaslow, Tom Watkins, Christie Miklas, John and Cathy Echohawk, Larry Echohawk, Bob Golten, Don and Cindy Miller, and Dan Frank. When I needed getaway time, still other friends were kind enough to loan me places to write: I send out my appreciation to Jackie Volkman for the use of her cabin northwest of Pinedale, Wyoming, on the divide between the Colorado and Columbia River watersheds; and to Betty Lamont, for the use of her home in Quincy, California, in the Feather River country.

Last, I give my love to my family. Ann is my refuge. My boys, Ben, Dave, Phil, and Seth, have enriched this book more than I could ever say. I did this writing mostly at home, and for me *Crossing the Next Meridian* will always be a book of motion, excitement, and affection—the sounds and flashes of the four of them, over the course of eight years, racing through my office, cuddling in my lap as I wrote, blessing me with their company on several of my trips. Because of them, the future has grown ever more vivid and cherished during the long journey that is now this volume.

Boulder, Colorado
July, 1992

Index

374 *Index*

Pulaski, Edward, 133
Pumice, 63
Puter, Steven A., 121
Pyramid Lake, 9–13, 15, 21, 25–26,
    283, 304
Pyramid Lake Indian Reservation, 12,
    22, 84

Rahall, Nick, 69–70
Railroad patents, 60
Railroads, 18, 84, 88
Ranches, establishment of, 83–84
Randolph, Jennings, 144
Range rights, 86–87
Reagan, Ronald, 99–100, 146–47,
    280–81
Reallocation, 287
Reclamation, 243–46, 248–53, 281–
    82
Reclamation Act of 1902, 12, 241,
    244, 246–47, 277, 286
Reclamation Project Act of 1939, 249
Reclamation Reform Act of 1982,
    282
Reclamation Service, 248–49, 252–
    53. *See also* Bureau of
    Reclamation
Recreational mines, 57
Reisner, Marc, 253, 281
Resource development, 17, 25
Resources for the Future, 149
Rest-rotation grazing, 106
Revenue flows, evaluation of, 24
Rio Blanco, 265
Riparian zones, 78–79, 102–105, 108,
    112–13, 265
Roaring Fork River Valley, Colorado,
    92
Robertson, Dale, 151
Robinson, Glen, 130–31
Rodeo Creek, 31
Roosevelt Franklin, 93, 136, 195, 258
Roosevelt, Theodore, 51, 54–55, 89–
    91, 120, 125–27, 174, 191, 246,
    253
Rudman, Warren, 170
Russell, Israel, 76

Sacramento–San Joaquin Valley, 193
Sagebrush Rebellion of 1980s, 99
Salmon, 8–9, 21, 179–87, 294–95
    canneries, 188–90
    chinook, 8–9, 176, 180–81, 188,
    209, 215

government regulation of, 209–10
    habitat, 192–201
    hatcheries, 191
    species, 180
Salmon River, 8–9, 21, 140, 217
Salmon runs, 192, 201, 217–18
Salmon Summit, 215, 283
San Juan–Chama Project, 220–23,
    225, 227–31, 258, 260, 264–65,
    267–68, 280, 283, 287, 291, 296
San Juan River, 220
Sargent, Aaron, 43
Sargent, Len, 277, 299
Sargent, Sandy, 277
Saunders, Glenn, 262
Savory, Allan, 82, 104–109
Sawtooth National Recreation Area,
    Idaho, 73
Schurz, Carl, 122
Scientific Panel on Late-Successional
    Forest Ecosystems, 165, 172
Selenium, 14, 263
Settlement Act, 26
Seufert Brothers Company, 188–89
Severance Reservoir, 76, 81, 101, 262
Sheepherding, 76, 78, 85
Sher, Jeff, 115
Sherars Bridge, 179
Sherman, Moses, 253
Sherrill, F. G., 135
Sherwood, Don, 72
Shoshone Indians, 78
Shoshone National Forest, Wyoming,
    122
Shupe, Steven, 287
Sieberling, John, 170
Sierra Pacific Power Company, 26
Silko, Leslie Marmon, 153
Silver, 63, 82
Silver City, New Mexico, 61
Sioux, 37–38
Siuslaw River, 140
Skimmerhorn, John, 10
Sloan, William Glenn, 269
Smith, Emmett, 7–8, 114–15
Smith, Sylvester, 253
Smith, Zona, 7–8, 114–15
Smythe, William, 244
Snake River, 8, 197, 214–15, 217
Snow, Don, 269
Society of American Foresters, 149,
    165
Sohappy v. Smith, 205
Soil movement, 262–63

About the Author

Charles F. Wilkinson is the Moses Lasky Professor of Law at the University of Colorado. A graduate of Stanford Law School, he taught for many years at the University of Oregon. He is a former staff attorney for the Native American Rights Fund and currently serves on the governing council of the Wilderness Society. In 1990, he received the National Wildlife Federation's National Conservation Award in Education. The co-author of standard law texts on federal Indian law and public land law and the managing editor of *Felix S. Cohen's Handbook on Federal Indian Law*, he is the author of *Land and Resource Planning in the National Forests* (with Anderson); *American Indians, Time and the Law: Native American Societies in a Modern Constitutional Democracy*; and *The American West: A Narrative Bibliography and a Study in Regionalism*. Some of his essays on the West are collected in *The Eagle Bird: Mapping a New West*. He lives with his family in Boulder, Colorado.

Also Available from Island Press

Balancing on the Brink of Extinction: The Endangered Species Act and Lessons for the Future
Edited by Kathryn A. Kohm

Better Trout Habitat: A Guide to Stream Restoration and Management
By Christopher J. Hunter

Beyond 40 Percent: Record-Setting Recycling and Composting Programs
The Institute for Local Self-Reliance

Coastal Alert: Ecosystems, Energy, and Offshore Oil Drilling
By Dwight Holing

The Complete Guide to Environmental Careers
The CEIP Fund

Death in the Marsh
By Tom Harris

Farming in Nature's Image
By Judith Soule and Jon Piper

The Global Citizen
By Donella Meadows

Healthy Homes, Healthy Kids
By Joyce Schoemaker and Charity Vitale

Holistic Resource Management
By Allan Savory

Inside the Environmental Movement: Meeting the Leadership Challenge
By Donald Snow

Land and Resource Planning in the National Forests
By Charles F. Wilkinson and H. Michael Anderson

Last Animals at the Zoo: How Mass Extinction Can Be Stopped
By Colin Tudge

Learning to Listen to the Land
Edited by Bill Willers

Lessons from Nature: Learning to Live Sustainably on the Earth
By Daniel D. Chiras

The Living Ocean: Understanding and Protecting Marine Biodiversity
By Boyce Thorne-Miller and John G. Catena

Making Things Happen
By Joan Wolfe

Media and the Environment
Edited by Craig LaMay and Everette E. Dennis

Nature Tourism: Managing for the Environment
Edited by Tensie Whelan

The New York Environment Book
By Eric A. Goldstein and Mark A. Izeman

Our Country, The Planet: Forging a Partnership for Survival
By Shridath Ramphal

Overtapped Oasis: Reform or Revolution for Western Water
By Marc Reisner and Sarah Bates

Plastics: America's Packaging Dilemma
By Nancy Wolf and Ellen Feldman

Race to Save the Tropics: Ecology and Economics for a Sustainable Future
Edited by Robert Goodland

Rain Forest in Your Kitchen: The Hidden Connection Between Extinction and Your Supermarket
By Martin Teitel

The Rising Tide: Global Warming and World Sea Levels
By Lynne T. Edgerton

The Snake River: Window to the West
By Tim Palmer

Steady-State Economics: Second Edition with New Essays
By Herman E. Daly

Taking Out the Trash: A No-Nonsense Guide to Recycling
By Jennifer Carless

Trees, Why Do You Wait?
By Richard Critchfield

Turning the Tide: Saving the Chesapeake Bay
By Tom Horton and William M. Eichbaum

War on Waste: Can America Win Its Battle with Garbage?
By Louis Blumberg and Robert Gottlieb

Western Water Made Simple
From *High Country News*

For a complete catalog of Island Press publications, please write:
Island Press, Box 7, Covelo, CA 95428, or call: 1-800-828-1302